MILTON STUDIES

XXVII

MILTON STUDIES

XXVII

Edited by

James D. Simmonds

UNIVERSITY OF PITTSBURGH PRESS

MILTON STUDIES

is published annually by the University of Pittsburgh Press as a forum for Milton scholarship and criticism. Articles submitted for publication may be biographical; they may interpret some aspect of Milton's writings; or they may define literary, intellectual, or historical contexts—by studying the work of his contemporaries, the traditions which affected his thought and art, contemporary political and religious movements, his influence on other writers, or the history of critical response to his work.

Manuscripts should be upwards of 3,000 words in length and should conform to the old *MLA Style Sheet.* Manuscripts and editorial correspondence should be addressed to Albert C. Labriola, Department of English, Duquesne University, Pittsburgh, PA 15282-1703. Manuscripts should be accompanied by a self-addressed envelope and sufficient unattached postage.

Milton Studies does not review books.

Within the United States, *Milton Studies* may be ordered from the University of Pittsburgh Press, Pittsburgh, Pa. 15260.

Library of Congress Catalog Card Number 69-12335

ISBN 0-8229-3683-6

US ISSN 0076-8820

Published by the University of Pittsburgh Press, Pittsburgh, Pa. 15260

Eurospan, London

Manufactured in the United States of America

CONTENTS

MILTON STUDIES

XXVII

MILTON'S *THE PASSION*

R. Paul Yoder

THE CRITICAL PROBLEMS presented by John Milton's *The Passion* are evident in its long and peculiar history of being noted only to be dismissed. And it has been dismissed by some of the best, including Samuel Johnson, E.M.W. Tillyard, Cleanth Brooks, and Northrop Frye. All of these critics in fact are simply following the apparent lead of Milton himself who, when the poem was published in 1645, claimed to have been "nothing satisfied with what was begun."[1] I think these critics are wrong, and that in the poet's breaking off of the poem, *The Passion* succeeds in the only way that it could, given the subject and the poet's proposed approach to that subject. In the following discussion I shall first argue that in its fragmented form *The Passion* ends exactly where Milton knew that it must, and that this fragmented appearance is an important part of the relationship between the "uninspired" poem and the Passion of its title. This part of the discussion will build on the work of John Via and Philip Gallagher, the only two critics I have found who have anything positive to say about *The Passion.* In the second part of my discussion I shall argue that the history of critical response to the poem exactly matches the pattern in the poem of introducing a topic only to dismiss it, and that this pattern of critical response is in fact dictated by the poem.

I. The Grave

In chapter 3 of *Self-Consuming Artifacts,* Stanley Fish writes, "The displacement in his poetry of the object of praise by the act of praising is here recreated in the verse."[2] Fish writes here of George Herbert's "Jordan II," but his words could just as easily apply to the movement in Milton's *The Passion,* for in this poem, Milton's only published fragment, the poet confidently sets out to elegize Jesus on the anniversary of his Passion, but he ends desperately searching for an image worthy of his aspirations. Unlike the poet of "Jordan II," no friend interrupts the poet of *The Passion* with advice about how to "save expense." Instead, the speaker in Milton's poem interrupts himself, breaking off his poem with a dream of infectious potency that testifies both to the poet's ego and to that ego's impotence.

Negotiating a course through *The Passion* will be difficult, so I want to clarify now the basic components of my discussion: Milton distances himself from the aborted poem by creating a persona to act as poet, a poet who can easily be confused with Milton himself, but who can be seen nonetheless to be a distinct entity; Milton intends for the reader to witness the humiliation of this persona as he struggles to write his poem, and, in order to facilitate this humiliation, Milton presents him with an impossible task—that of elegizing the Savior. I read the fragmenting of the poem as equivalent to the death of the poem, and in this analogy the poet's surrender of his project parallels Christ's surrender of himself in death. Milton then presents a second persona, the critic who appends the explanatory note, a persona distinct from but easily confused with both Milton and the "poet" of the poem; this critical persona misunderstands the "failure" of the poem in a way that extends the sense of inadequacy beyond the limits of the poem and thereby undermines any too easy interpretation or dismissal of it. In this regress of doubt and humiliation, Milton succeeds in reflecting, however dimly, Christ's Passion in the reader's experience.

In the last twenty years, two critics have begun to see the possibilities in *The Passion* upon which I base my reading. In 1971, John Via argued that, in its lack of success, *The Passion* "illustrates the perfectly normal human rhythm of response which oscillates at different levels of intensity, but nevertheless maintains at its center the basis of the experience which elicits the varying intensity of response. . . . It shows the normal fluctuation which the regenerate man may anticipate as a real and significant part of his religious life."[3] Via contends further that the poem "is retained because it also shows a perfectly normal situation for the poet, who is not always inspired, but who, when lacking inspiration, is no less a poet." He concludes that "Milton's lack of success here makes possible his use of the entire poem as an ironic comment on religious and poetic experience" (36–37). Via's strategy here is to recognize as the subject of the poem the lack of inspiration noted by all previous critics, but he does not discuss the implications of his strategy for a reading of the poem's details. Further, while I think Via does well to place *The Passion* in the context of other Miltonic works concerned with his poetic vocation, I also think that his assertion about the poet's being a poet even when he does not write inspired poetry must be qualified; certainly a poet need not be writing poetry every minute of his or her life, but a poet who does not write an elegy can hardly be considered an elegiac poet.

Six years after Via, Philip Gallagher similarly recognizes that *The Passion* is a poem about a lack of poetic inspiration, but he goes further in turning the poem's faults into its strengths.[4] Gallagher argues first that, rather than being a fragment, *The Passion* is a completed proem to a poem that Milton realized he was not inspired to write. He then argues that the poetic persona who lacks the inspiration to write the poem about the Passion must be distinguished from Milton, who writes a successful poem about the failure of that poetic persona. He recognizes the poem's pervasive egocentricism as deliberate, contending, "The poet [Milton] is concerned to depict not the Passion, but the psychological state of a speaker who is attempting—without success—to become inspired about that event. Since, however, inspiration is . . . a free gift of God, any attempt to force it must by definition backfire" (45). Gallagher also sees Milton's "cold-blooded" use of the pathetic fallacy (shorn of its pejorative sense) as further evidence of Milton's deliberate "dramatizing [of] his speaker's inspired dilemma" (47). While I think Gallagher is correct in suggesting that the persona refuses to continue with the proposed poem, I do not believe that the eight stanzas of *The Passion* constitute a completed unit; rather, I contend that the abrupt break in the poem, the absence of conventional closure, leaves the reader suspended in a way that allows him to imagine the futility of the poet's elegiac endeavor. I agree with Gallagher's distinction between Milton and the poem's persona, and I suggest that Gallagher's distinction is analogous to Via's distinction between the constant "basis of the experience" and the oscillating response between the poet and his occasional lack of inspiration. What neither Via nor Gallagher consider, however, is why Milton chose the occasion of the Passion, the most heart-rending episode in the Christian story, to depict a lack of inspiration.

Most readings of *The Passion* assume simply that the occasion of the poem gives it its title: Milton tried to write a poem on the Passion just as he had written a poem on the Nativity, and even though he could not get inspired about the subject (an assumption I find difficult to accept), and wrote a poem with which he was "nothing satisfied," he nonetheless kept the occasional title regardless of the emotional contradiction between the title and the apparent lack of inspiration in the poem's execution. I have no intention of denying the occasion of the poem, but the emotional distance between title and poetic execution is too extreme, the irony too obvious, to be the result of occasional accident. Milton could easily have changed the title between 1630 and 1645; he certainly made more substantial changes between the first two editions of *Paradise Lost*. I contend that he retained the title in order to emphasize the distance between Christ and the poet and to suggest a parallel but opposing movement in Jesus' acceptance of his desperate situation and the persona's desperate attempt to elegize Jesus in that situation. That is, while Jesus becomes most heroic when he rejects his own self-interest by accepting death, the persona becomes more unheroic as he becomes increasingly self-interested and self-absorbed in his search for an image that will satisfy his own poetic aspirations. Despite this opposing movement, both figures end in a death that demonstrates their humanity.

The poetic persona's attempt to commemorate Christ's Passion aligns the poem with the meditative works of poets like Vaughan, Crashaw, and Herbert, all of whom wrote poems on the Passion. In many of these poems the poet tries to visualize various aspects of Christ's suffering. In his own poem called *The Passion,* Henry Vaughan examines the sweat, blood, and bruises of the Savior. Crashaw wrote a series of poems on the various aspects of the Passion, including the wounds of Christ. Herbert expresses his frustration and sense of relative insignificance in "The Reprisall," where he finds that "There is no dealing with thy mighty passion" (2).[5] Despite this claim, he devotes several poems early in *The Temple* to the Passion, visualizing it in "The Agonie" and "Sepulchre," and even presenting Christ's own viewpoint in "The Sacrifice." Similarly, in *The Passion,* Milton tries to visualize the scene, claiming, "Mine eye hath found that sad Sepulchral rock" (43). Louis Martz has suggested that these attempts to visualize Christ's suffering are intended to enhance religious meditation by inspiring a strong emotional response.[6] Nevertheless, for Milton's persona, this strategy fails.

In a move that ensures the frustration of the poet's project and emphasizes the ego that undertakes that project, Milton has him aspire to write an elegy for Christ—a poetic form superficially applicable, but finally impossible, given this particular subject. In the *Milton Encyclopedia,* E. Richard Gregory suggests that "we cannot guess" at the "envisioned form" of the uncompleted poem. I disagree with Gregory, but I also disagree with most of the guesses that have been made about the poem's "envisioned form." Martz, noting that the lute and viol of line 28 are "instruments for Herbert or Crashaw," suggests that Milton failed because he tried to write a "love-song," more akin to Catholic or Anglican than to Puritan meditation. E.M.W. Tillyard and J. B. Broadbent both note the description of Christ as "Most perfect Hero," and both see *The Passion* as part of Milton's preparation to write an epic. John G. Demaray, focusing on "the stage of Air and Earth" (2) and the line, "O what a Mask was there, what a disguise" (19), sees the poem as a failed masque in which Christ was to be the "featured figure."[7] I do not wish to deny the presence of these elements, but I contend that they signify the confused and desperate groping of the poet in his futile effort to elegize the Savior.

I have found only two commentaries whose authors recognize the elegiac intent of the poem. One is the discussion by Brooks and Hardy in which they mention in passing the "elegiac strain" and suggest that the poem's self-consciousness and the "problem of style" are somehow (they do not say how) related to the elegiac form. The second commentary is by Northrop Frye, who nevertheless has nothing good to say about *The Passion* (he calls it Milton's "one obvious failure").[8] In his essay on *Lycidas*, Frye, in rather callous terms, notes Milton's interest in elegy: "Milton was deeply interested in the structure and symbolism of funeral elegies, and had been practising since adolescence on every fresh corpse in sight, from the university beadle to the fair infant dying of a cough" (125). At Easter of 1630, Christ's was the freshest corpse around, and after the success of the Nativity ode it is not surprising that the poet would try his hand at a funeral elegy for Jesus. But there is an insurmountable problem with this endeavor, for Jesus is the one person who, given the elegiac tradition, cannot be elegized.

The Passion everywhere announces its elegiac intention. Joy is "swallow'd up in dark and long outliving night" (7), a conventional elegiac description of death. The poet must "set [his] Harp to notes of saddest woe" (9) because "the stroke of death [Jesus] must abide" before lying "meekly down fast by his Brethren's side" (20–21). The poet must use instruments "more apt for mournful things" (28); he speaks of his "woe" and his "sorrows . . . too dark for day to know" (32–33). Moreover, with its incorporation of the meditation strategy of visualizing the scene, the intended poem is a particular type of elegy, a forerunner of the graveyard school of the eighteenth century, for Milton does not simply commemorate Christ's death; he envisions the "sad Sepulchral rock / That was the Casket of Heav'n's richest store" (43–44) and imagines an entire "race of mourners." Milton had used the visualization strategy earlier in *On the Death of a Fair Infant*, in which he asserts his difficulty in accepting "that thy corse corrupts in earth's dark womb, / Or that thy beauties lie in wormy bed" (31–32). But in the *Fair Infant*, Milton is able to offer the consolation of comparing the child to Christ, seeing her welcomed into heaven, and even of denying her death, calling it a "false imagin'd loss" (72). It is just this type of elegiac consolation that is impossible for Christ.

An elegy is essentially a meditation on the death of a particular person; more generally, elegy is a meditation on the fact that death comes to all people regardless of worldly status. But the elegy also offers consolation in what Stephen F. Fogle calls "the contemplation of some permanent principle."[9] In Christian elegy, this permanent principle is the eternal life that humanity gains as a result of Christ's sacrifice, of his dying in order to overcome human death. The consolation based on this sacrifice generally involves either the denial of death or the substitution of Jesus's death for the deceased's—options that are finally the same. The elegiac denial of death is possible because Jesus has substituted himself for all the dead since Adam, overcoming humanity's death by dying himself. Christ's resurrection, with its implied promise of human resurrection and salvation, transforms the finality of death into the transitory state of sleep so that death becomes a long night after which the deceased will awaken at the last judgment. The elegists of the graveyard school, like Robert Blair or James Hervey, adopt the strategy of the religious meditation and dwell more extensively on the horrors of death, often depicting themselves in the graveyard (as Milton does in *The Passion*), perhaps looking into the sepulchre, envisioning the decay of the body (as in *Fair Infant*) or the legions of the dead. The point in these morbid imaginings is to emphasize the sacrifice and heroism of Christ in undergoing death so that the reader will achieve a sense of awe and a heightened appreciation of Christ's sacrifice. Indeed, these poems usually end with an image of Christ rescuing the dead from the horrors of the grave, a rescue that supposedly results in the reader's rededication of him or herself to a Christ-like life.

However, because elegiac consolation depends on the substitution of Christ for the deceased, Christ cannot be elegized. The requisite substitution is not possible for the Savior precisely because he is himself the Savior. If the poet denies the Savior's death, he denies the humanity of Jesus and thereby invalidates the covenant with God because Jesus must be both God and man in order for his sacrifice to redeem the descendants of Adam. Milton himself addresses this issue of substitution in *Christian Doctrine.* What I have been calling elegiac consolation Milton calls "the effect and design of the whole ministry of mediation," which he says "is, the satisfaction of divine justice on behalf of all men, and the conformation of the faithful to the image of Christ" (*CM* XIV, 315; *YP* VI, 443). He explicitly notes that Jesus functions as a "substitute," that he died "in our stead," not "merely for our advantage in the abstract, and as an example to mankind" (*CM* XIV, 317–19; *YP* VI, 444). This substitution is exactly the role that Christ plays in elegiac consolation, and it is exactly the role that he cannot play for himself, for as Milton in a different passage remarks, "it cannot be explained how any one can be a mediator to himself on his own behalf" (*CM* XIV, 207; *YP* VI, 218). Moreover, in his death, Christ cannot even take consolation in the fact that he is God and that he will rise in three days, for as Milton argues in his discussion of Christ's humiliation, even the divine aspect of Christ's being must die (*CM* XIV, 307–09; *YP* VI, 443).

Given these circumstances, the position of the poet who intends to elegize Christ is, like Christ's position in the Passion, hopeless. Christ must die with no substitution or consolation, and in this situation the only appropriate elegy is an elegy that itself dies, as Milton knew that it must. It must be an elegy that imitates Christ, an elegy that surrenders itself, written by a poet who surrenders himself and his ambitions because he recognizes that his efforts are completely useless. This poet who surrenders his ambitions (and not without a struggle) is the creation of Milton, who uses that persona's frustration to write a poem that celebrates Christ's victory-in-death even as the persona's poem appears to fail. The impending demise of both the Savior and the poem results in a reading in which practically every stanza can be seen to forecast the approaching death of the poem. The "long outliving night" that swallows up "headlong joy" refers to the death that follows the birth of the Savior, but it also refers to the eventual fate of this poem begun in ambitious confidence. Both the common end of Christ and poet, and the distance between those parallel ends, is evident in the next stanza's admission that Christ's "labors" are "too hard for human wight" (14). Stanza 3 is the only stanza in which the poet is not overtly present, the only stanza in which he actually considers the "object of praise," but that object is the humiliation of Christ, and both the poet's sense of comparative inadequacy and his resistance to that sense are evident in the anxiety that dominates the rest of the poem.

As the persona's anxiety increases, he places less emphasis on Christ's Passion and more emphasis on his own desperate attempt to write his poem. In stanza 4 the poet complains that his ambitions have been anticipated by "*Cremona's* trump" (26), but his complaint can be read as an anticipatory rationalization, "just in case" the poem does not work, even while it forecasts more mournful things to come. Confined as he is to the narrow scope of the grave, the poet turns next to "Night, best Patroness of grief" (29), and his prayer is an admission of his inability to find an image that would "work [his] flattered fancy to belief" (31). He then calls upon the vision of Ezekiel to transport him, but as Gallagher points out (p.46), the word "there" (41) betrays the fact that his fancy has not been turned to belief, for if he did believe, his "soul" would be "here," not "there." Stanza 7 finds the poet "here" at the "sad Sepulchral rock" (43), but in his quest for the right image he cannot maintain his focus on the image before his eyes. His dissatisfaction is evident in the conditional "would" that qualifies the scoring of his verse and the fit falling of his tears. As the poet becomes more anxious and more absorbed in his self-interested search for apt words, he moves on to another image, trying to create a mournful harmony between himself and the world, but again the conditional verbs betray his sense of failure, and his feeling of impotence is evident in the dream of potency that ends the poem, as he fantasizes that he "Had got a race of mourners on some pregnant cloud" (56). The poet's growing desperation is measured in the extremity of his images, and when his increasingly urgent search for an appropriate image suddenly breaks off, leaving the reader suspended ("Or should I . . ."), the implications of the fragmentary form are clear: the rest of the poem would be, could only be, an endless line of images that will immediately be judged as failures, of conceits becoming more desperate, less relevant, as the poet becomes more self-absorbed in his search for the words that will allow him to sing of the Savior "as lively as before." The poetic persona will never be satisfied. The poem, like its images, is begun only to be discarded.

The persona who enacts this self-destruction is defined by the success of the Nativity ode, a tactic that allows Milton to create the confident, young, doomed elegist, and to invite confusion between that persona and himself as the author. It is not surprising that a poem with as many first person pronouns as *The Passion* (twenty-five in fifty-six lines) would also have autobiographical references, but in *The Passion* the autobiographical references all refer to the Nativity ode, although that poem is never mentioned by name. Inasmuch as *The Passion* was originally published following the Nativity ode and Milton's paraphrase of Psalms 114 and 136 in the 1645 *Poems*,[10] the identification both of the song of "joyous news" (3) with the ode and of the persona with Milton is inevitable; this is especially true since all that the persona says about himself is that he once wrote a successful—at least in his own opinion—poem about Christ's birth. The characterization of the persona grows out of the establishment and use of the Nativity ode as the standard of comparison against which to measure the present work: the confidence, the egocentricism, the increasing desperation as he gropes for images all point back to that earlier success.

When the poet opens *The Passion* with reference to the Nativity ode he betrays his pride in that poem and his desire to claim credit for its success. He appropriates the voice of heaven for himself, confusing it with his own voice, when he changes the ode's "Heav'nly Muse" (15) to "my muse" (4), and his claim that he divided the earlier song with the angels (4), denying the claims of "harmony" in the ode, emphasizes his pride in his own role in the earlier work. The image of "headlong joy" (5) that is "ever on the wing" conflates the world's joy at the birth of Christ with the poet's joy at his success in singing of that birth. His complaint about the priority of the

Christiad recalls his ambition in the Nativity ode that the heavenly muse might "have . . . the honor first, thy Lord to greet" (26). The temporal indicators of the poem also imply a comparison with the Nativity ode: the poet notes that "now to sorrow must I tune my song" (8), as opposed to "then" when he sang of joy, and when he envisions the "sad Sepulchral rock" he wishes that he could write his verse "as lively as before" (43–47). Even in the one stanza in which the poet is not overtly present, he introduces the "Poor sovereign Priest" with a conceit based on the Nativity, the site of his earlier success. The success of the Nativity ode haunts the poet of *The Passion,* constantly holding up to him what he once was, a poet who sang joyously of the world's joy. The confidence inspired by that success even helps to explain the persona's apparent choice of elegy in *The Passion,* for the elegist's position as consoler puts him in a position superior to the deceased and to the other survivors. Perhaps the most damaging effect of the persona's confidence in his own ability is the relentless self-criticism that leads him to reject one image after another, just as he finally rejects the poem itself. As long as the poet maintains this superior position, as long as his attention is focused on his own trial, he will never find the words appropriate to honor Christ's trial.

The presence of Milton in *The Passion* is distinguishable primarily in the consistency with which the poem enacts its own demise, but it is also felt in the confusion and self-deceit into which Milton allows the persona to be led by his increasing self-absorption. Gallagher (46, 49) has noted the fact that the persona's implication that the Passion is not one of Christ's "Godlike acts" (24) is directly repudiated in *Paradise Lost* (XII, 427), and he also notes the "there/here" confusion in stanzas 6 and 7. However, the distance between Milton and his persona is most acutely felt in the reference to the *Christiad,* a reference that all critics note, but that no one seems to have explored. In stanza 4 Milton suggests that he is writing about the Passion because it is the only event in Christ's life still left unsung:

> His Godlike acts and his temptations fierce,
> And former sufferings other-where are found;
> Loud o'er the rest *Cremona's* trump doth sound. (24–26)

If the assumption about the occasional status of the poem is correct, then the poet's suggestion is clearly confused, for it is not literary predecessors but the religious calendar that dictates his topic. Moreover, Vida's six-book *Christiad* does in fact recount the Passion; the narrative present of the epic is Holy Week, and most of Book V is taken up with the account of Christ's suffering and death.[11] Even if the "latter scenes" (22) that confine the poet's verse refer specifically to Christ's funeral (suggested in the immediately preceding line's comment on Christ's lying "meekly down fast by his Brethren's side" [21]), Vida has again preempted the poet, for Book VI of the *Christiad* opens with the preparation of Christ's body and its placement in the sepulchre.

We have to assume that Milton is aware of the persona's error in this instance, but is the reader to assume that the persona is lying or simply confused? It is impossible to tell, but either way, the implications for the persona's ego are not pleasant. If he is lying, then in the center of the poem he has already sunk to deception in order to justify his own project; if he is confused, then his self-absorption has already advanced far enough to distort his understanding. There is perhaps a suggestion that it is grief that has beguiled the poet, but, as Gallagher points out (p. 48), his ability to note that "grief is easily beguiled" (54) argues that he has not been so beguiled, at least not by grief. I would add that this superiority over grief also compounds, in the poem's final lines, the reader's sense of the poet's egotistical self-absorption.

The reader who follows the poet's increasingly desperate attempts to justify himself and his poetic confidence sees a man digging his own grave. The more the poet gropes for an appropriate image for his poem, the farther he gets from the object of that poem. It is not that the images are not good enough to commemorate Christ, it is that the images are not good enough for the poet of the Nativity ode to commemorate Christ. His "flattered fancy" cannot turn to "belief" precisely because it is flattered by the poet himself. How then are we to read the breaking off of the poem? One option is to see it as the poet's final throwing up of his hands in frustration at his own inability to find just the right image; it is the final act of egotism in which the original intention to remember Jesus' Passion is completely forsaken in the poet's obsession with his own inadequacy and disappointment. But, inasmuch as the fragmentary form of the poem signifies the repudiation of the elegiac ego, Milton's dramatization of this final rejection of the self-interest that had inspired the poem is exactly the image for which the persona has been searching. In this repudiation of his self-interest the persona has finally, under Milton's direction, become like the Christ who underwent the humiliation of the Passion. The poem could end no other way, and therein lies Milton's success.

In Milton's depiction of a poet being drawn to attempt an elegy for Jesus, we see a pattern that might be considered a paradigm for much of Milton's poetry—the tension between an assigned task and the (im)possibility of the assigned agent's fulfilling that task. Often this pattern emerges as the anxiety resulting from premature endeavor, as in *At a*

Vacation Exercise, where the poet confesses to his apostrophized "native Language" that "my tongue but little Grace can do thee" (10), or in *Lycidas,* where the poet reluctantly plucks the laurel "with forc'd fingers rude" (4). This tension between task and ability is the subject of the invocations in *Paradise Lost,* and in *Paradise Regained* it informs the plight of Satan, who has the unenviable and impossible task of tempting the Savior. The poet who created the poet of *The Passion* is the same poet who depicts the Father's order to the angels to protect Adam and Eve, the same poet who asks if God exacts "day-labor, light denied." The breaking off of *The Passion* is equivalent to one of Milton's most triumphant concluding recognitions, that "They also serve who only stand and wait" (*Sonnet XIX,* 14), and the frustrated elegist of *The Passion* might well take a lesson from the sonneteer that "God doth not need / Either man's work or his own gifts" (9–10).[12]

The confusion that Milton invites between himself and the persona of *The Passion* makes it difficult to distinguish between Milton's success and the persona's failure; indeed, most critics up to now have not made this distinction. However, the critics are not entirely to blame for their misunderstanding, for they have been misled by the explanatory note appended to *The Passion.* One might expect that this note would clarify the inconclusiveness of the poem, but instead it only compounds the problem by introducing yet another persona, distinct from both the poetic persona and from Milton.

The "critic" of the note clearly tries to distance himself from the "poet" of the poem. The formal third person diction of the note starkly contrasts the first person complaining of the poem. The critic and poet may finally be the same "entity" (such as it is), but they are distanced from each other at least by enough time to allow for retrospection and abstraction. The critic can look back at the aborted effort and see that the poet's confidence was premature, that he was too young for the projected work. But in that assessment the reader can see the distance between the critic who appends the note and Milton who juxtaposed that critic and his note to the poet and his poem. The problem with the critical note is that the critic still thinks that the poet's ego could have been justified by his own efforts if only he had been older. In order to demonstrate Milton's awareness of the critic's error, and the relationship between the error and the poet's misguided efforts in his poem, I want to consider two correspondences between *The Passion* and its note and the antiprelatical tracts written three years before the poem appeared in the collected edition.

The first correspondence is between stanza 7 and the *Apology for Smectymnuus.* Since the stanza contains one of the poem's more clearly metaphysical images, it has attracted some attention from Tillyard, who compares it unfavorably with Crashaw's "Upon the Death of a Gentleman," and from Brooks and Hardy, who cite it as the point at which the poem collapses in a conceit that "serves finally no other purpose than that of an absurd decoration."[13] In fact Milton himself suggests a retroactive comment on the stanza in perhaps the most famous sentence of the *Apology;* this is the sentence that begins with Milton's admission that he is not "utterly untrained in those rules which the best rhetoricians have given" and concludes,

> yet true eloquence I find to be none, but the serious and hearty love of truth: and that whose mind soever is fully possessed with a fervent desire to know good things, and with the dearest charity to infuse the knowledge of them into others, when such a man would speak, his words, (by what I can express,) like so many nimble and airy servitors, trip about him at command, and in well-ordered files, as he would wish, fall aptly into their own places. (*CM* III, i, p. 362; *YP* I, p. 949)

These well-ordered files are exactly what the poet says he cannot achieve in *The Passion:*

> Yet on the soft'ned Quarry would I score
> My plaining verse as lively as before;
> For sure so well instructed are my tears,
> That they would fitly fall in order'd Characters. (46–49)

The persona's youthful reliance on the fact that his tears have been "so well instructed" stands in stark contrast to Milton's later qualified admission of his own instruction and his unqualified reliance on "serious and hearty love," "fervent desire," and "dearest charity" to guide his words. The "absurd decoration" in *The Passion* is, then, the result of the poet's reliance on formal instruction in his search for an appropriate image with which to elegize the Savior, a reliance on externally dictated forms like those Milton repudiates in his attacks on the empty forms of the prelacy. The poet's problem in *The Passion* was his reliance, not on the scenes of Christ's Passion, but on his own personal qualities, including his previous success and the poetic instruction he evidently believes engendered that success.

We cannot tell whether the poetic persona ever recognizes the success of his failure; all Milton shows us is the persona's frustration. However, we can conclude that the critic who appends the note does not yet understand that the poet failed because of his idolatrous regard for his previous poetic success. This conclusion is clear if we compare the note to the poem with a line from the preface to *The Reason of Church-Government.* In the note, the critic stipulates that the poet found the subject "to be above the years he had, when he wrote it," a stipulation of the sort that Milton directly addresses in *Church-Government:* "And if any man incline to thinke I undertake a taske too difficult for my yeares, I trust through the supreme inlightening assistance farre otherwise; for my yeares, be they few or many, what imports it?" (*CM* III, i, p. 183; *YP* I, p. 749). This passage from *Church-Government* presents the logic of a person who has experienced both success and frustration at a young age, a person who knows that the ability to sing the truth depends not upon one's age, but upon "the supreme inlightening assistance" of God; in this sense, the author of *Church-Government* and the poet of *The Passion* could be identical. However, the effect of the correspondence between the pamphlet and the critical note is to undermine the critic's suggestion that the poet's young age caused the poem's failure. In both the *Apology* and *Church-Government,* Milton contends that instruction, pride, and age are no substitutes for Christian devotion in granting an author the ability to express himself well, but the critic who appends the note does not understand this principle. In fact, except for the avowal that the poet left the poem unfinished, the critic seems to hold open the possibility that the poem could have been completed once the poet was old enough.

The multiplying of personae and critical perspectives results ironically from the egotistical self-satisfaction with which the poet opens *The Passion.* Because of his pride in the success of the Nativity ode, the poet becomes torn between his roles as poet commemorating Christ's Passion and as critic judging the present work by the previous success. The triumph of the critic is evident in the fragmentary form of the poem and in the fact that the critic apparently has the last word. But by distancing himself from that poet/critic, Milton gives himself the last word, and he turns *The Passion,* in fine graveyard fashion, into a sort of *memento mori.* He publishes the poem not once, but twice, because it has become a reminder, even a receptacle, of his vanity, of his urge to take personal pride in what God has allowed him to do. The elegist's position is like that of Hamlet in the graveyard scene, contemplating Yoric's skull, or like the woman in the painting by Georges de la Tour, the discussion of which opens Martz's *The Poetry of Meditation;*[14] it is in this tradition of the melancholy person contemplating the inevitability of death that *The Passion* should be read, and the difference between Yoric and Jesus makes the meditation that much more humbling. For Milton's persona in *The Passion,* only the absorbing silence of the grave awaits.

II. *The Passion* and the Critics

In Milton's self-fashioned myth of himself, *The Passion* acts as something of a stumbling block on the road toward *Samson Agonistes*. It has also acted as a stumbling block for readers of Milton. The poem is cursorily mentioned by nearly all the critics who consider Milton's lifelong poetic development, but no one writing before 1970 takes the time to look at it very closely. The critical justification for this neglect has always been that the poem pales in comparison to the Nativity ode and that the poet himself was "nothing satisfied" with it. In light of my foregoing discussion, it should be clear that this critical justification parallels the concerns of the poem itself and has even been dictated by the poem. Confronted with the confusion and self-absorption of the poem and its poet, critics have been too willing to accept the judgment of the misguided critic who appends the explanatory note.

The critical tradition regarding *The Passion* begins with Milton himself, or at least with the "critic" who appends the explanatory note to *The Passion*. After fifty-six lines the poem stops and the critic's statement appears: "This Subject the Author finding to be above the years he had, when he wrote it, and nothing satisfied with what was begun, left it unfinisht" (p. 63). As I have already suggested, insofar as this critique implies that the poet could have finished the poem had he been older, it testifies to the critic's lack of understanding about where the poet went astray in the first place: the problem with the poem is not the poet's age, but his replacing of Christian devotion with the idolatrous regard for his earlier poetic success. Nevertheless, because the poem does not conform to the norms of poetic closure, and because Milton was rather young when he wrote it, critics have felt justified in accepting the critic's statement without question (or at least without questions that might elicit a productive reading).

The critical history that follows from this blind acceptance is remarkably consistent. As one might expect, Samuel Johnson, citing the note, sees only too clearly the egotism of the poem and its publication: "For his early pieces [Milton] seems to have had a degree of fondness not very laudable: what he has once written he resolves to preserve, and gives to the public an unfinished poem . . . supposing his readers less nice than himself." David Masson strikes the major chords more clearly, remarking of the poem's note, "The judgement is correct. No one can read the fragment called 'The Passion' without feeling its inferiority to the 'Ode on the Nativity.' " A quick catalog can show the consensus: Tillyard says, "The failure is complete"; Woodhouse says, " 'The Passion' was a failure";

Hanford and Taaffe say, "[Milton's] lack of inspiration in 'The Passion' is evident"; Demaray says, "Milton fails poetically to realize these scenes [of Christ's Passion and death]"; Brooks and Hardy say that "Milton's own feeling of dissatisfaction should be a guide in our estimation of 'The Passion.' "[15] Rarely does one find such a monotony of critical agreement.

Despite this consensus, however, there is little agreement on what is wrong with the poem, although most comments focus on the last three stanzas, the parts of the poem in which I have suggested we see most clearly the poet's increasingly desperate attempts to satisfy his own poetic standards. Sharon Cumberland and Lynn Veach Sadler, who think the poem fails, nevertheless note the last line of stanza 6 ("In pensive trance, and anguish, and ecstatic fit") as the most nearly successful line in the poem;[16] John Via, one of the few who thinks the poem succeeds, argues that this same line is "entirely unconvincing" (35). Stanza 7 (the "quarry" conceit), which Brooks and Hardy see as the point of collapse in the poem, and concerning which Tillyard says "Milton's intelligence . . . seems confined to counting the feet and seeing that the grammar is right," Leishman sees as "so very much more ingenious and, as we should say, far-fetched that it differs almost in kind from the conceit in the seventh stanza of the Nativity Ode"; he further notes, however, that it is "the kind of conceit of which there are many examples in Donne's poem on Mrs. Herbert entitled 'The Autumnall' . . . and of which there are very many examples in the anthology of early seventeenth-century academic wit, *Parnassus Biceps.*"[17] Concerning the final stanza, Martz calls the end of the poem ("I . . . / Might think th'infection of my sorrows loud / Had got a race of mourners on some pregnant cloud"), "the worst line [Milton] ever wrote," while Leishman sees in the image "an ingenious allusion to the legend of Ixion," and Woodhouse, speaking of the whole stanza, says, "How beautiful the lines are—and how exquisitely inappropriate!" Generalizing about all three stanzas, Hanford says simply that Milton "abandons the poem in the midst of a series of forced conceits."[18]

All the critics who discuss the poem at all note its ungratifying comparison with the Nativity ode, but beyond that, the most common criticisms leveled at the poem are those suggested in these remarks on the final three stanzas. The egocentricism is inappropriate and counterproductive; the poet's lack of inspiration yields a diction and imagery that feel forced. The way to get beyond these criticisms is to make the move that Via and Gallagher make, a move that in recent criticism in other areas has become commonplace: that is, to recognize the "problems" of the poem as the subject of the poem. The critics before Via and Gallagher, whether or not they agree on a given passage, all focus on the important elements of the poem; but, because of its lack of conventional closure and the appended critical note, none of these critics has tried to consolidate their criticisms into a coherent reading of it. They look at the title, at the self-consciousness, at the references to the Nativity ode, at the iamges that are rejected even as they are introduced, at the fragmentary form, and at the final explanatory note, and then they acquiesce in that note's judgment.

One conclusion drawn from this judgment, voiced most clearly by Hanford, seems to me to be particularly unjustified. In *John Milton, Englishman*, generalizing from his reading of *The Passion*, Hanford says, "The sacrifices of Christ awakened no authentic response in his religious nature" (p. 43); he voices this conclusion more strenuously in his essay, "The Youth of Milton," writing, "The crucifixion, neither now nor later, had the slightest hold on his emotions."[19] In the *Milton Handbook*, Hanford and Taaffe offer an explanation for Milton's indifference, asserting, "Even this early he seems to have felt instinctively that man's salvation depends upon himself and he needs Christ as a guide and model perhaps more than as a redeemer" (p. 115).

I can see no justification for these conclusions. Milton does in fact return to the Passion in Book XII of *Paradise Lost*, and his concern for and recognition of the nature of Christ's sacrifice is evident in the almost obsessively repeated references to death, dying, and doom in a discussion that covers roughly the same number of lines (*PL* XII, 393–450) as *The Passion*. Here Michael refers to Christ's "suffering death" (398), to his "cursed death" (406), to "His death for Man" (425), and in the lines that explicitly recall the earlier poem, Michael says, "this God-like act / Annuls thy doom, the death thou shouldst have di'd" (427–28). Combine these sentiments with Milton's emphasis in *Christian Doctrine* on the role of Christ as "substitute" dying "in our stead," and the comparison with Hanford's views indicates how far astray critics have been led by the limited reading of *The Passion* that the critical note encourages.

My point in this discussion of the critical history of *The Passion* is that the experience of critics reading the poem yields the same sort of silence into which the poet himself disappears in the poem, an experience that itself parallels the silence of Jesus in accepting death for humanity's sake. Like the poet confronted with the overwhelming task of elegizing the Savior, generations of critics who have confronted *The Passion* have felt it best to comment briefly and then lapse into silence, leaving only fragments of a reading of a poem that Woodhouse nevertheless suggests "had for [Milton] some special significance since he preserved it and printed it with his collected poems" (p. 19). The problem of the critics is the same as the problem of the poetic persona—they keep comparing *The Passion* to Milton's "more successful" work instead of focusing their attention squarely on the object of discussion. Leishman summarizes this error nicely when he remarks that *The Passion* is the "least Miltonic of all Milton's serious poems" (p. 68).

A different kind of dissociation of Milton from *The Passion* has been the basis for my reading of the poem. Milton succeeds in commemorating Christ's accomplishment of a task "too hard for human wight" by depicting a poet confronted with a task similarly too hard, and then compounding the reader's sense of that poet's humiliation by opposing the poem's "failure" to the poet's initial confidence and ambition. Then, by appending a misguided critical comment, Milton extends the sense of humiliation beyond the limits of the poem by showing how the poem could be, and in fact would be, misread. At every level the poem and reaction to the poem reflect the same pattern of notation followed by rejection: the poet begins to sing of Christ's Passion only to discard that intention in his search for a way to fulfill it; in his search, he introduces images and references only to discard them as inadequate for his poem; he begins the poem only to reject it as too difficult; critics cite the poem only to dismiss it as hardly worth the attention. The only person who seems to have kept what was begun is Milton. I have suggested that he kept the poem because it served as a grim reminder of what could happen to him but for the grace of God, which is finally the point of Christ's Passion; I also suggest that he published the poem because, in the myth of himself that Milton was creating, it constitutes a distinctly humanizing moment, and that, of course, is also the point of Christ's Passion. My study is by no means the last word on *The Passion;* there is certainly room for extensions and qualifications of my argument. My point is that this sort of discussion is long overdue, and it is enough for me now if I have returned this neglected poem to the Miltonic fold.

Duke University

NOTES

1. John Milton, *Complete Poems and Major Prose*, ed. Merritt Y. Hughes (New York, 1957), p. 63. References to Milton's poetry are to this edition. References to Milton's prose are cross-referenced to *The Works of John Milton*, 18 vols., ed. Frank Allen Patterson et al. (New York, 1931–38), and *Complete Prose Works of John Milton*, 8 vols., ed. Don M. Wolfe et al. (New Haven, 1953–82), hereafter cited in the text as *CM* and *YP* respectively.

2. Stanley E. Fish, *Self-Consuming Artifacts: The Experience of Seventeenth-Century Literature* (Berkeley and Los Angeles, 1972), p. 197.

3. John A. Via, "Milton's 'The Passion': A Successful Failure," *MQ* V (May 1971), 6.

4. Philip J. Gallagher, "Milton's 'The Passion': Inspired Mediocrity," *MQ* XI (May 1977), 44–50.

5. *The Works of George Herbert*, ed. F. E. Hutchinson (Oxford, 1941).

6. Louis Martz, *The Poetry of Meditation: A Study in English Religious Literature of the Seventeenth Century* (New Haven, 1954), pp. 167–68.

7. E. Richard Gregory, "The Passion," in *A Milton Encyclopedia*, ed. William B. Hunter, Jr. (Lewisburg, Pa., 1979), p. 120; Martz, *Poetry of Meditation*, p. 167; E.M.W. Tillyard, *The Miltonic Setting, Past and Present* (London, 1957), p. 177; J. B. Broadbent, *Some Graver Subject: An Essay on "Paradise Lost"* (London, 1960), pp. 27–28; John G. Demaray, *Milton and the Masque Tradition: The Early Poems, "Arcades," and "Comus"* (Cambridge, Mass., 1968), pp. 41–42.

8. Cleanth Brooks and John Edward Hardy, "The Passion," in *Poems of Mr. John Milton: The 1645 Edition with Essays in Analysis* (New York, 1951), p. 109; Northrop Frye, *Fables of Identity: Studies in Poetic Mythology* (New York, 1983), p. 126.

9. Stephen F. Fogle, "Elegy," *Princeton Encyclopedia of Poetry and Poetics*, ed. Alex Preminger (Princeton, 1974), p. 215.

10. The sequence of poems is incorrectly reported in James Holly Hanford and James G. Taaffe's *A Milton Handbook*, 5th ed. (New York, 1967), where Hanford and Taaffe begin their brief discussion of the poem by writing, " 'The Passion' immediately follows 'On the Morning of Christ's Nativity' in the 1645 edition [of Milton's *Poems*]" (p. 114). The fact that by 1967 this error had apparently been repeated through five editions testifies further to the critical neglect the poem has suffered.

11. Marco Girolamo Vida, *The Christiad*, trans. and ed. Gertrude C. Drake and Clarence A. Forbes (Carbondale, Ill., 1978).

12. There are other interesting parallels between *The Passion* and *Sonnet XIX*. For example, the sonnet's statement in 1652 that God's "State / Is Kingly" (11–12) is certainly loaded with ambiguity after the regicide in 1649, and so the line recalls both the sense and the political irony of *The Passion*'s "Sovereign Priest, stooping his regal head" (15), a line written twelve years before but published three years after the antiprelatical tracts.

13. E.M.W. Tillyard, *Milton*, rev. ed. (New York, 1967), p. 39; Brooks and Hardy, *Poems*, p. 111.

14. Bridget Gellert, "The Iconography of Melancholy in the Graveyard Scene of *Hamlet*" *SP* LXVII (1970), 57–66, does not mention Milton or his work, but her discussion has intriguing implications concerning the relationship between *The Passion* and *Il Penseroso*. In a discussion that uses paintings much as Martz does in the opening pages of *Poetry of Meditation*, Gellert argues that the graveyard scene, and especially Hamlet's contemplation of Yoric's skull, "provides a kind of emblematic epitome for several important themes in the play" (58). This emblematic quality aligns Hamlet with an iconographic tradition of "the melancholy thinker, meditating on objects of death" (59). Given the poet's invocation of Night and view of the "Sepulchral rock" in *The Passion*, and the invocation of Melancholy and the nighttime setting in *Il Penseroso*, the two poems may be related via the tradition Gellert cites.

15. Samuel Johnson, *Selected Poetry and Prose*, ed. Frank Brady and W. K. Wimsatt (Berkeley and Los Angeles, 1977), p. 425; David Masson, *The Life of John Milton: Narrated in Connexion with the Political, Ecclesiastical, and Literary History of his Time*, rev. ed. (London, 1881), vol. I, pp. 230–31; Tillyard, *Milton*, pp. 38–39; A.S.P. Woodhouse, *The*

Heavenly Muse: A Preface to Milton (Toronto, 1972), p. 19; Hanford and Taaffe, *Handbook*, p. 115; Demaray, *Masque Tradition*, p. 41; Brooks and Hardy, *Poems*, p. 107.

16. Sharon Cumberland and Lynn Veach Sadler, "Phantasia: A Pattern in Milton's Early Poems," *MQ* VIII (May 1977), 53.

17. Tillyard, *Milton*, p. 39; J. B. Leishman, *Milton's Minor Poems* (London, 1969), pp. 69–70.

18. Martz, *Poetry of Meditation*, p. 168; Leishman, *Milton's Minor Poems*, p. 72; Woodhouse, *Heavenly Muse*, p. 40; James Holly Hanford, *John Milton, Englishman* (New York, 1949), p. 43.

19. James Holly Hanford, *John Milton, Poet and Humanist* (Cleveland, 1966), p. 39.

MILTON'S EURIPIDES MARGINALIA: THEIR SIGNIFICANCE FOR MILTON STUDIES

John K. Hale

ALTHOUGH HAROLD BLOOM exempted Milton from that "anxiety of influence" which he saw in many major writers,[1] there still were influences. Homer, Virgil and Ovid, Dante and Ariosto, Spenser and Shakespeare come to mind, together with that greatest influence of all, the Bible. Yet Deborah Milton named the reading in which her blind father took most delight as Homer, then (equal with Ovid) Euripides.[2]

Now his reading of Euripides, and its influence upon him, can be tracked in a unique, albeit specialized way, since by good fortune there survives his copiously annotated copy of the plays of Euripides in the edition of Paulus Stephanus of 1602.[3] These annotations have not received much study by Miltonists. They have not been published *in toto*, and the most accessible published selection contains mistaken attributions.[4] Yet they should not thus remain out of sight, in the "decent obscurity" of their Greek and Latin, for they reveal much about Milton's intellectual life during the 1630s and 1640s and about his intellectual standing in his own age, not to mention that they suggest fresh lines of search into his main writings. The present essay seeks to illustrate their significance to scholarship, Euripidean as well as Miltonic.

First, I consider the standing accorded to some of the marginalia by the textual branch of classical scholarship, which is one of its most arduous, and therefore most esteemed, branches. The chosen marginalia are viewed both *sub specie aeternitatis* and in the context of seventeenth-century Greek scholarship. Next, his proposals are connected to a debate now current within textual studies (not only classical), which they illustrate: the question whether *praestat difficilior lectio,* whether the more difficult reading should prevail. Then, to move in a different direction, I examine his methods and grounds of emending in order to assess how his mind went to work on Euripides, to see when and how far his imaginative sympathies were engaged. Lastly, and more briefly, the order of operations is reversed: starting from known allusions to Euripides in Milton's writings, I consider how far the marginalia can illuminate those allusions or suggest new directions of search for the Miltonist.

I

In *Bacchae*, lines 170–224, the two aged men, Tiresias and Cadmus, announce themselves as devotees of the new religion of Dionysus and appear garbed and ready for its ecstatic dances. At line 188 the received text had read until Milton, "Being old men, we have forgotten about glad things"; that is, "glad things" (*hedeon*) was governed directly by the verb, giving a remark suitable enough to old men resigned to decrepitude. But Milton, in his 1640s hand, writes alongside "perhaps *pleasurably* (*f*[*or tasse*] *hedeos*)," thus changing the sense to "We have glad*ly* forgotten *that* we are old men."[5] Instead of an elderly remark about the deprivations of old age, Cadmus says the new rites of Bacchus make them forget their old age.

Why did Milton make the change? Why has it been accepted by subsequent editors? What does it exemplity about his powers as a textual critic and about his relationship with the tradition of classical editing?

He made the change because although any old man might at any time say, "Oh dear, I do feel old," the paramount consideration in the surrounding exchanges is that *these* old men, thanks to Dionysus-worship, feel rejuvenated. And classical scholarship has accepted the change of the letter *n* to *s* because whereas the received reading was vapid, the proposed one draws attention to the amazing stage spectacle, the old made youthful, just as the preceding and following words do: "I shall not grow weary, neither by day nor by night" and "I too grow young" (187, 190). Milton is alert to context, and the received reading shows the drifting back into tame platitude on the part of a scribe who was less alert. (That is, whether or not Milton had asked himself the question concerning how error might have occurred, when one does ask it the answer is plain enough: his proposal satisfies this further requirement of philology.) Since it has been termed "palmary"—prize-winning—by one modern professional,[6] we could hardly ask for more from a seventeenth-century amateur!

But simple eulogy needs modifying in two respects. In the first place, this is Milton's best effort. He by no means rose to this height in all his annotations. Nonetheless, the presence of an amateur who is also a major poet has attracted honorific mention in the *apparatus criticus* of major editors of Euripides, and these both English and German. Of what other poet can this be said?

A second factor gives particular cause as to why they so honor Milton.

His copy of the Paulus Stephanus has not only the two states of his hand in the marginalia, but also the hands of another three people; and some of the latter seem connected with the seventeenth-century Euripides edition by Joshua Barnes (1694). This matters because Barnes's use of Milton fluctuates greatly. Sometimes he acknowledges that he has taken over a reading, sometimes that he repudiates one, as is of course his right. Sometimes he silently appropriates one, and this does not accord with the ethics of his profession. But in the case of *Bacchae,* line 188, he does something else: he appropriates Milton noisily. His note declares, "I think we should read *hedeos* for *hedeon,* and then the sense runs much better, 'We have sweetly forgotten that we are old men.' No one before has had any inkling of this blemish." Someone had had an inkling—Milton. So the tradition of scholarship—which was slow to detect Barnes's carelessness (or worse) regarding attribution—has sought since to give the honor where it is due.[7]

Milton has other successes, as can be gauged by the fact that some twelve of his proposals are accepted in a standard modern edition, the Oxford Classical Texts series.[8] If that does not seem a great number, out of nearly seven hundred attempts, we should reflect with Kelley and Atkins (p. 687) that the acceptance ratio of the immortal Richard Bentley in his Horace edition does not greatly differ. Whereas Dr. Johnson "found nothing remarkable" in Milton's marginalia, many others from 1700 until now pay them respectful attention.[9]

To see why, it is enough to cite, then transfer, comments of Shackleton Bailey concerning the prized quality of *divinatio*—the capacity for inspired correcting of false text. "It is of the nature of the critical genius [that is, of the textual critic] to function unevenly. . . . But rare and mysterious genius, not ubiquitous defect, claims emphasis." Bailey is speaking of Bentley, but in a more modest degree the same holds for Milton's best efforts. Again, "The critic . . . generally gets his clue from the context. He is faced with a pattern of thought, part of which has been broken up. He has to adjust his mind to that pattern, run it into the mould of the author's as represented in this particular passage. . . . The critic as he reads is all the time adapting his mind to the author's, and when he feels a jar he suspects that something from outside has come between."[10] Exactly this occurs in *Bacchae,* line 188, and elsewhere.

It is not a claim that Milton was in general at the cutting edge of classical scholarship in his time. This could not be so since he did not consult any manuscripts, let alone collate them, whereas the professionals then knew the value of both activities.[11] Nor, in his use of the commentary by the Dutch scholar Wilhelm Canter (1542–75), had he absorbed Canter's discovery of the importance of "responsion" to emendation in choric meters. Since antistrophe and strophe must match each other metrically because the dancers have to travel the identical distance within the orchestra in each direction, one or both of two nonmatching readings is wrong; and it follows that emendations must always restore or preserve the correspondence, the responsion. In fact, Milton emended so much because his printed text was so bad.[12] It had so increased error, even over what the manuscripts had held, that he was prone to emend the wrong word or expend effort where there was no need. Mere recourse to a better edition would have obviated it. Collectively, that is, the marginalia give an effect of hit-and-miss.[13]

There is no question that he read his author in his entirety, more than once, and pen-wieldingly. Perhaps, he wielded that pen to keep his mind alert and to purge irritation with a bad text, but certainly he did it with persistent attention to the philologist's overriding question: Is this what left the author's hand? No question, either, that his marginalia went via Barnes straight into the mainstream of English editing of Euripides. No question, finally, that, since the very exacting tradition of classical scholarship has for two centuries paid attention, sometimes honor, to his best efforts at emendation, the tradition of Milton scholarship must do the same. It often has, but not always. The point merits periodical confirming.

II

To confirm it in a different way, I now take some more of his best efforts as illustrations of a current debate within textual criticism. Writing on the text of Shakespeare, Gary Taylor has proposed that, rather than lumping distinct arguments under the old principle that *praestat difficilior lectio*, scholars ought to distinguish a reading which is to be preferred because it is more difficult than its rivals from one which is to be preferred because it has greater density than the rivals (*densior lectio*), and both from a reading which is to be preferred because it is more unusual (*insolitior lectio*).[14] In all three types of cases, the argument justifying the preference is from direction of error: in the course of scribal transmission it is more likely that a true reading would be adjusted into something simpler, or less complex, or more commonplace than that corruption would move in the opposite direction.

Yet disagreement continues within Greek studies, both on the underlying principle and on its application to particular cruxes. Sophisticated arguments can be heard from textually conservative voices to the effect that simple received readings may outweigh meritoriously difficult (or dense, or unusual) ones, and all the more so as between a received reading, on the one side, and an emendation on the other. For present purposes, I simply record a recent exchange on these questions as they arose from, and applied to, Milton's proposals.

How the more difficult reading, even from emendation, may outweigh a received reading has been shown by the *Bacchae* example. It is less probable that "sweet things" (*hedeon*) would be accidentally corrupted into "sweetly" (*hedeos*) than vice versa, for whereas the former is the more commonplace sense, the second is more difficult and unusual and dense. But other weighty considerations support the arguments from probability: the received reading weakens the stage situation and spoils the characterization. Perhaps most decisively, Milton's proposal makes the *thought* come right.[15]

A more uncertain case is *Heraclidae,* line 602. Manuscript L reads, "My limbs are *sunk* in grief," but Milton proposes, "My limbs are *loosed* in grief"—the change of one letter, from *duetai mele* to *luetai mele.* The first meaning is acceptable, if generalized. The proposed reading is both stronger and more in accordance with Greek idiom concerning the effects of grief or strong emotion: limbs are regularly "loosened" or "slackened" by pain, desire, death, and so on.[16] One might, therefore, maintain that *duetai* is the less usual and the more difficult, yet not denser, and so, on balance, retain the received reading (rather than accept the idiomatic emendation) for reasons of textual conservatism. But Milton lived in a time when textual conservatism was less than reliable, given the badly printed texts, the poor availability of manuscripts or collations, and the absence of stemmatics.[17] At any rate, his proposal has excited debate, is still largely favored by editors, and attests to his knowledge of Greek heroic idiom—of the affinity between Euripides's and Homer's diction.

Paradoxically, *Hecuba,* line 115, constitutes the reverse case, where Milton's proposal seeks to correct the received reading by one which is less difficult (and less dense). Polymestor is describing how he was blinded and his children killed by Hecuba and her women (1132–82). A crowd of the Trojan women encircled him and, on the pretext of admiring the weave of his garment, removed his weapons. The received text has it, "Many hands [*pollai de cheires*], some on my left and some on the other side of me," held the robe up to the light, and so forth. Milton proposes "*Pollai de cheiros*": "Many women, some on my left *hand.*" This links the hand (now in genitive singular) with *ex aristeras,* meaning "on the left." It avoids making the hands (nominative plural) the subject of the main verb phrase, "praised the workmanship."

But in Greek that expression would not have seemed awkward but more likely idiomatic. Moreover, the genitive *cheiros* is needless since Greek regularly understands the word with expressions meaning "on the left" and "on the right." The clinching considerations for the colleague with whom I discussed the passage were (1) textual conservatism and (2) the poetic distinctiveness supporting it.[18] As to (1), the received reading makes sense, hence no emending need be done, so let none be done. As to (2), the emphasis on *hands* tallies with an emphasis throughout the speech on hands and the atrocity of what they did: if a sinister surrounding by hands controls the whole narration of the blind Polymestor it is better served by *pollai* here. In fact, the simpler reading proves to be actually denser.

Nonetheless, many if not most editors approve the emendation. Thus, the particular case and the general principle alike remain a subject for debate and for exercise of individual judgment. To both of these Milton makes a continuing contribution.

III

Such being the significance of Milton's marginalia to Euripidean scholarship, what about their significance in the other direction? What do they suggest about his intellectual and imaginative life in the period from 1634, when he bought the book, until blindness stopped him from annotating it?

First, they show he read the Greek with his ears as well as his eyes since he regularly restores the scansion of the staple meter of the action (as distinct from that of the choric and lyric interludes), namely iambic trimeters (lines of twelve syllables with caesura after the fifth). This may happen where only his Stephanus had metrical error: so at *Helena*, line 1703, he observes that *ho* (with long *o*) for *he* (with long *e*) "is more consonant with the meter" ("*versui magis quadrat*"). But at *Ion*, line 408, he is correcting the whole received tradition when he changes singular to plural, *manteum'* to *manteumat'*, because "thus the meter demands" ("*sic versus flagitat*"). Indeed it does, and editions have followed his change. Even where he miscorrects the meter, selecting the wrong part of a line for attention, he shows scholarly concern for right rhythm.

That is not always so. Where the meter is not iambic but a more arcane choric meter, he does not seek to hear as the Greeks had done (or he would have heeded responsion). Like a later and greater scholar, Richard Porson, Milton could not fathom Greek lyric meters.

A second feature of the marginalia is their interest in dramatic values, the stage moment. By this I do not mean staging itself, but character in context. Like the *Bacchae* example above, *Supplices*, lines 754–71, illustrate this well. The manuscript tradition had assigned the lines alternately to Chorus and Messenger, the former questioning the latter in stichomythia. Milton comments, "These speeches seem rather between *Adrastus* and the Messenger, not the Chorus." He has perceived that although the episode began as an exchange between Chorus and Messenger the role of interlocutor is taken over at line 734 by King Adrastus, or so editors since have thought. His rightness in suspecting error gains general support from the play's recent editor: "Few things in medieval mss. are less authoritative than the division and attribution of speaking or singing parts."[19] True, the trouble had been diagnosed by Brubach back in 1558. Nonetheless, since Milton had not read Brubach, Collard credits Milton with independent diagnosis and solution.

What is more, the metrical knowledge and the sense of the stage moment are not separate but rather parts of an interconnected empathy. Milton's annotating of *Iphigenia in Tauris*, line 1119, brings out the empathy. His Stephanus text, and likewise the manuscripts and other editions, had read "En gar anankais ou kamneis suntrophos on" ("For if you are reared amid adversity you don't make heavy weather of it as an adult"). The verb is in the "ideal" second person, that is, second person with generic or gnomic force, the force of a *sententia*. But the more usual Greek way of handling gnomic utterances is in the third person singular and hence Milton's proposal, in his neat 1630s hand, "*kamnei malim,*" ("I should prefer *kamnei* [*one* suffers]"). Editors have accepted this proposal for several reasons: because *kamnei* is the more idiomatic gnomic, because the cause of scribal error would be the easy dittography of sigma (*kamneis suntrophos*), and finally because some manuscripts unknown to Milton actually support him. This emendation therefore meets the main criteria. He brings together his sense of Greek idiom and of the stage situation.

But also his sense of Euripides's mind, its penchant for *sententia*. This instance shows that Milton shared it. After he had penned the two-word note in his 1630s hand, he read the text again in the 1640s and was led to make further comment by the fact that the obfuscation was continued by the Latin version printed below the text in his Stephanus, "In necessitate enim non laboras" (too badly and uninformatively "For undergoing harsh necessity you don't suffer under it"). Milton nailed down the true meaning, "In angustiis enim non laborat qui iis innutritus est") ("A person who has been reared to hard times is not [as an adult] crushed by them"). And then, because the Latin version mistakes the next line—and so blurs the contrast upon which the whole sententious comment by the Chorus on poor Iphigenia's situation hinges—he corrects that too. Its "Mutatur tamen interdum infelicitas" ("However, misery [always] changes sooner or later") has no possible application to Iphigenia now. Milton scrubs out (angrily?) *tamen interdum* and supplies the right meaning: "Infelicitas est quae in peius mutat" ("Misery is a situation which changes for the worse"). He that is down need fear no fall.

Skills combine to make up this empathy: a grasp of idiom and of the stage moment; a concern for accuracy, fidelity; perhaps an irritation with the flatness of the received text, exacerbated by the Latin version; an affinity with Euripides's habit of mind, its continual and natural rising to gnomic utterance. He is restoring the Euripidean qualities to the Latin version: "Infelicitas est quae in peius mutat," where the key word comes last, as climax: misery is change, loss.

My last example of his annotating empathy is *Hippolytus*, line 998. Accused by his father Theseus of misconduct with his stepmother Phaedra, Hippolytus defends his whole way of life (splendid chance for more *gnomai!*). Among this, he says, "I have learnt, first, to reverence the gods, and to consort with friends who essay no wrong, but would think it shame to report evil to their companions or to requite them with services that are vile" (997–99). The point is that such decent people would not give their friendship to one who could commit the atrocity of which Theseus is accusing Hippolytus. The point is couched in a parallel series: god-fearing, right-doing, neither "reporting" evil nor requiting friendship with evil. But something flat, and puzzling, intrudes into the series. The argument is sidetracked into reporting evil things, and the triviality of what people talk about reduces Hippolytus's urgency. Actions, not words, are the theme.

Milton proposes *epaggellein* (to "send evil behests") for *apaggellein* (to "report" evil). The excellence of this is double. The emphasis on actions, blurred by the received reading, is restored. And the Greek idiom is sharper, for whereas *apaggellein* meant only vaguely "ill-talking," *epaggellein* has a precise military usage which fits "sending commands to do evil."[20]

He may have felt excited about the issue, too, since he adds a Latin translation of his reading in the margin, "*i.e. neque inhonesta petere*" ("i.e., not to send evil behests"), and does it again alongside the Latin version at the foot of the page—three notes, to ensure the point. Because it is a good one.

IV

Finally, reversing the direction of reasoning, it could be valuable to move from episodes in Milton's life and writings which exhibit influence from passages in Euripides to the annotations which Milton made to those passages. But two attempts that have been made induce caution. Kelley and Atkins (p.686*n27*) find "possible biographical significance" in the fact that misogynistic passages in two plays are marked in the Stephanus, but the marks are not certainly Milton's. Can one in general securely ascribe a marginal mark, as distinct from handwritten words, to Milton (and differentiate a 1630s mark from a 1640s)? A better instance is the investigation by Davies and Dowling of the marginal annotation to the passage of the *Supplices* which Milton quotes on the title page of *Areopagitica*, for it is quoted in the Stephanus text, mistakes and all. Even here, however, the annotation consists of a hooked inkmark alongside not quite the requisite lines (440–43, not 438–41).

In my view, therefore, the first necessity is some strict counting. Of the annotations which are certainly Milton's because they consist of words which are certainly in his writing (identified further as 1630s or 1640s), do any turn up as allusions in his own writings? And among passages of Euripides alluded to in Milton's writings, do any receive a marginal note in the Stephanus? This work remains to be done. I suspect very few such secure correspondences will emerge. I suspect, too, since we know he read the whole of Euripides, and closely, at least twice, that the passages he alludes to will come from anywhere, not especially from annotated passages. To put that the other way around, we need not suppose he was especially retentive of passages which his edition had botched, for to think so would be to seek an improbably mechanistic connection, from a negative influence (an error) to a positive influence (an allusion).

A further form of counting may be more useful, namely to establish which plays elicited the most marginalia. This weaker form of the hypothesis would still be open to the rebuke that corrections of error correlate better with the badness of the text than with the interests of the corrector. But still, not all marginalia were corrections, so that ones which betoken interest in the subject or situation should repay study individually; and collectively, a play which scored highest on all marginalia would repay first approach by the systematic investigator. I record for such an investigator my own impression that the *Supplices* and the *Ion* received more notes, of greater seriousness, than other plays.[21]

Counting, though the time is ripe for it, will not suffice to establish significant influence. But it can support the investigation of influences established or proposed for other reasons, which is why I single out the *Supplices* and *Ion*. The one is quoted at the head of *Areopagitica*, a major work written on the theme of the play, the right and wrong relations of governors to governed and of both to the laws of a state. The play's debate element systematizes the respective positions of Athens, Thebes, and Argos (democratic, tyrannic, and anarchic versions of kingship, respectively, all bearing on the arguments of 1644). As for the *Ion,* it is even more the concatenation of plausible influences that claims attention: the numerous interesting, interested marginalia; the clear, extended allusion in "Ad Rousium" to Bodley's Librarian as the devoted guardian of a nobler treasure than Ion at Delphi (lines 52–60); the likelihood of further allusion elsewhere in the ode; the use of Greek choric meters for the Latin ode, with the 1673 disclaimer of strict responsion.[22] Let the counting begin, let the search continue.

The influence of Euripides (to return to our own starting point) was major, both in special and in general ways, and never more so than in the tumultuous 1640s. His great themes were the relations of men with women, of siblings and parents, citizens and rulers, men and gods, in time of war, and every one of these issues concerned Milton in the 1640s. The special debts, seen in the marginalia and the allusions, now need to be more systematically correlated. Then, perhaps, we shall be better placed to perceive how great the influencing by the Greek was.

From the sonnet, "Captain or colonel" of 1642, we can surmise that it may be very great indeed, for that poem has as its hinge and climax the applying of Euripides to Milton's own situation.

Captain or colonel, or knight in arms,
Whose chance on these defenceless doors may seize,
If deed of honour did thee ever please,
Guard them, and him within protect from harms,
He can requite thee, for he knows the charms
That call fame on such gentle acts as these,
And he can spread thy name o'er lands and seas,
Whatever clime the sun's bright circle warms.
Lift not thy spear against the muses' bower,
The great Emathian conqueror bid spare
The house of Pindarus, when temple and tower
Went to the ground: *and the repeated air*
Of sad Electra's poet had the power
To save the Athenian walls from ruin bare.[23]

The applying of Euripides here is an act of multiple wit. Not simply Euripides's lyric but also its fame in its own time are invoked. Nor are they invoked simply to climax the poem, but to avert the impending disaster of 1642 ("When the assault was intended to the City"). Running through the whole allusion is the delighted emulation of Euripides, alike as poet and as citizen and human being, one who became in his life by this writing "a true poem."

University of Otago

NOTES

1. Harold Bloom, *The Anxiety of Influence: A Theory of Poetry* (New York, 1973), pp. 34, 50.

2. Milton was "most delighted with Homer, whom he could almost entirely repeat; and next, with Ovid's *Metamorphoses* and Euripides." See *Milton's Poems*, ed. Thomas Warton (London, 1791), I, p. 569.

3. Bodleian Library Don. d. 27 and 28. I am most grateful for the library's permission to work on these volumes.

4. There has been less discussion in this century than in the previous one, as is made clear in the outstanding modern essay, "Milton's Annotations of Euripides," by Maurice Kelley and Samuel D. Atkins, *JEGP* LX (1961), 680–87. They give a full bibliography of their predecessors on p. 680*n2;* to which add J. T. Christie, "John Milton's Copy of Euripides," *Greece and Rome* XI (1941), 35–37. See also David Davies and Paul Dowling, "'Shrewd books, with dangerous Frontispices': *Areopagitica's* Motto," *MQ* XX, no. 2 (May 1986), 33–37. Selected annotations are printed in the Columbia *The Works of John Milton*, ed. Frank Allen Patterson et al. (New York, 1931–38), vol. XVIII, pp. 304–20, with notes at pp. 566–68. Detailed evidence and argument for rejecting the ascription to Milton of twelve marginalia, and for querying seventeen more, comprise the first part of Kelley and Atkins, "Milton's Annotations of Euripides," 680–84; summary at p. 684.

5. Reasons for assigning the annotation to Milton are (1) his usual crosses appear, one in the text at the appropriate place, the other in the margin, and (2) he adds his usual *f*, which stands for *fortasse*, meaning "perhaps." My reason for assigning it to the 1640s is that the Greek script corresponds to that of clearer (because they are lengthier) instances elsewhere. In all my selected instances, I follow the conclusions of Kelley and Atkins about handwriting questions, having confirmed them for myself as far as I am able; that is, any marginalia where I doubted their findings are avoided in the present essay.

6. Kevin Lee, of Canterbury University, who has edited the *Troades* and is currently editing the *Ion;* in a letter to me, 11 March 1987.

7. Christopher Collard, "J. J. Scaliger's Euripidean Marginalia," *Classical Quarterly* XXIV (1974), 242, points out how Barnes was as "negligent and dishonest" in his reporting of conjectures in Milton's copy of the Stephanus as in his reporting of Scaliger's conjectures made in a copy of Canter's edition, both which Barnes came to own. Collard therefore corrects the record in his own collating of the *Supplices* (pp. 246–47), as well as in his edition (Groningen, 1975). A similar act of restitution is performed by Richard Kannicht for the *Helena*, 2 vols. (Heidelburg, 1969), vol. I, pp. 118–19. Presumably, such correction of attribution of conjectures, as between Scaliger and Barnes or Milton and Barnes, remains to be done for other Euripidean plays.

8. I have consulted the three volumes of Gilbert Murray's 1902–09 edn., and the two so far published of J. Diggle (vol. I, 1984; vol. II, 1981).

9. Johnson's comment, in the *Life of Milton*, is discussed by David Masson, *The Life of John Milton*, rev. ed., 6 vols., (London, 1881), vol. I, p. 568, and Kelley and Atkins, p. 687. Scholars who commend Milton's conjecturing include Richard Porson (see Kelley and Atkins, "Milton's Annotations of Euripides," 680*n*2), Kannicht, *Helen*, and Collard, "Scaliger's Euripidean Marginalia," and several editors in the Oxford Clarendon editions of individual plays, for example, E. R. Dodds, *Medea* (1944; rev. ed. New York, 1960), line 188; M. Platnauer, *Iphigenia in Tauris* (New York, 1939), p. 154; W. S. Barrett, *Hippolytus* (New York, 1964), p. 349.

10. D. R. Shackleton Bailey, *Profile of Horace* (London, 1982), app. 2, "Bentley and Horace," pp. 105, 108, 109.

11. See L. D. Reynolds and N. G. Wilson, *Scribes and Scholars: A Guide to the Transmission of Greek and Latin Literature*, 2nd ed. (Oxford, 1974), chap. 5. See especially p. 161 on Canter's use of responsion in emendation and his classifying of types of scribal error. See also p. 162 on Franz Modius (1556–97), who insisted that "conjecture alone is useless and even dangerous, [and] that there must be a proper balance between manuscript authority and emendation." One certainly does not find Milton seeking such a balance. Still less does he follow Modius into awareness that "recension [reconstructing from the evidence of surviving manuscripts the earliest recoverable form of the text which lies behind them] is an essential preliminary to editing."

12. E. J. Kenney, *The Classical Text: Aspects of Editing in the Age of the Printed Book* (Berkeley and Los Angeles, 1984), chap. 1 passim.

13. Thus Kannicht, *Helena*, discriminates between proposals in adjacent lines of the *Helena:* at line 621 Milton's replacement of the meaningless *ho posei* by *so posei* ("your husband") is approved, as indeed it is by most editions, yet at line 620 his conjecture "has for a long time hindered the correct reading" (p. 118).

14. Gary Taylor, " 'Praestat difficilior lectio': *All's Well that Ends Well* and *Richard III*," *Renaissance Studies* II, no. 1 (1988), 27–46. Reynolds and Wilson, (*Scribes and Scholars*, pp. 199–200), discuss the principle involved thus: "Given the tendency of scribes to corrupt texts . . . if one of the available readings is more difficult to understand, it is more likely to be the correct reading. . . . [Scribes] tended . . . to remove from the text the rare or archaic linguistic forms that were no longer understood, or to simplify a complex process of thought that they could not master." On the other hand, "Many references to the maxim *difficilior lectio* will be found in commentaries, and there is no doubt of its value. But it has probably been overworked, for there is a temptation to use it as a defence of anomalous syntax or usage; in such cases the more difficult reading may be more difficult because it is wrong." Nevertheless, the principle had not been overworked in Milton's time, since it did not receive explicit formulation as a criterion until 1697 (p. 248).

15. The only safe method is to follow the rule explicitly enunciated by Haupt and reiterated by Housman: "The prime requisite of a good emendation is that it should start from the thought; it is only afterwards that other considerations, such as those of metre, or possibilities, such as the interchange of letters, are taken into account" (Reynolds and Wilson, *Scribes and Scholars*, p. 211.

16. Especially apposite is Euripides's own phrase at *Supplices*, line 46, "*thanato lusimelei*," or "death the loosener of limbs."

17. Emendation is only part of the editor's task, a part which should come second (and be adapted) to the primary task of recension. Stemmatics is the constructing of a genealogical tree of these manuscripts. Though Erasmus and Scaliger had conceived of an "archetype" manuscript, the genealogical model was not developed until the 1730s. The stemmatic

theory of recension is a nineteenth-century development, systematized by Karl Lachmann but used by others before him. See Reynolds and Wilson, *Scribes and Scholars*, pp. 188–89.

18. Agathe Thornton, author of *People and Themes in Homer's "Odyssey"* (London, 1970), *The Living Universe: Gods and Men in Virgil's "Aeneid"* (Leiden, 1976), and *Homer's "Iliad": Its Composition and the Motif of Supplication* (Göttingen, 1984).

19. C. Collard, Euripides's *Supplices*, vol. I, p. 43.

20. *Hippolytus*, ed. Barrett, p. 349.

21. Some support for the view that *Supplices* was of special interest to Milton can be drawn from the figures for allusions in Jackson Campbell Boswell, *Milton's Library* (New York, 1975), pp. 94–97. For evidence supporting my similar view of the *Ion*, see next note.

22. Cited and summarized in *The Latin and Greek Poems*, vol. I of *A Variorum Commentary on the Poems of John Milton*, ed. Douglas Bush, (New York, 1970), p. 330.

23. *The Poems of Milton*, ed. John Carey and Alastair Fowler (London, 1968), p. 285.

MILTON'S ST. MICHAEL AND HOLY AMBIDEXTERITY

Caroline Moore

I

THE NOTORIOUS "two-handed engine" of *Lycidas* has long ago directed attention on to the "huge two-handed sway" with which St. Michael wields his avenging sword in Book VI of *Paradise Lost;* yet the significance of the linking adjective has received little attention. Indeed, many commentators on *Lycidas* slur over the word, expounding it as "two-edged," or merely suggestive of some sort of doubleness. It is possible, however, that there is some meaning attached to the manner in which St. Michael brandishes his sword, which may cast light upon why this adjective, in particular, is applied to that potently veiled poetic threat, the "two-handed engine at the door."

The dictionary definition of "two-hand" and "two-handed" is "wielded with both hands" or, simply, "huge"; and to call a broadsword "two-handed" is so common that these must indeed be the main senses in which Milton uses the word. But Milton's use of language is nothing if not multilayered, and the adjectives seem to have another possible sense, which has escaped the compilers of the OED. It is possible to find examples of the adjective "two-hand" used in a context which demands that it should mean not "wielded with both hands, together," but "wielded with either hand, ambidextrously." None of the senses given in the OED. adequately covers Thomas Nashe's use of the word in *The Unfortunate Traveller*, for example, where the supremely unfortunate rebel, Jack Leyden, wears "the Image or likenes of a peece of a rustie sword, like a lustie lad, by his side: now I remember mee, it was but a foyle neither, and he wore it to shewe that hee should haue the foyle of his Enemies, which might haue been an oracle for his two-hand Interpretation."[1] "Two-hand" needs all the old connotations of slippery double-dealing associated with ambidexterity (and most memorably embodied in the Ambidexter of *King Cambyses*) if it is to catch the profoundly equivocal distrust of all signs and images—including the words of the Bible—that underlies this passage. Jack straps on his visual pun after misinterpreting a biblical text and will shortly lead his followers to slaughter upon the misinterpretation of a rainbow as a sign from heaven: whether it is the oracles that are juggling fiends, or "poore Jacke" who is the equivocator, "two-hand" can in this context only mean "ambidextrous."

Aubrey provides another example. Sir Willam Fleetwood's Janus-faced compliment to the citizens of London, " 'When I consider your wealth I doe admire your wisdome, and when I consider your wisdome I doe admire your wealth,' " is described by Aubrey as "two-handed rhetorication"; fortunately, "the citizens tooke it in the best sense."[2] Once again, such doubleness demands connotations of ambidexterity.

Less obviously, Sylvester's use of "two-hand" in *Lacrymae Lacrymarum* is given more point if it suggests moral duplicity. Sylvester is portraying a world in which all degrees have been corrupted by commodity, from the clergy who "too-too-oft have stood / More for the Church-goods, then the Churche's good," to the citizens who "make our *god* our GAIN." In this context of universal corruption, "two-hand" makes most sense if it suggests that, like an ambidexter—in its sense of a judge or lawyer who receives bribes from both sides—each one of us is two-handedly accepting the double bribes of profit and of pleasure.

> All, all are *guilty* in a high Degree,
> Of this *High-Treason* and *Conspiracy;*
> More brute then *Brutus*, stabbing more then *Caesar*,
> With Two-hand SINS of *Profit* and of *Pleasure;*
> And (th' odious *Jngine*, which doth all include)
> Our many-pointed proud *Ingratitude*.[3]

Such sinful ambidexterity, of course, is utterly unsuitable for the archangel Michael, and Milton's engine of just vengeance is worlds apart from Sylvester's "Jngine" of corruption. Yet, if "ambidexterously wielded" is accepted as a possible reading of "two-handed," there is a whole network of alternative associations, both Christian and classical, to explain why Milton might wish to draw upon this meaning. It is possible, as Donne says, to be "in an holy sense, *Ambidextrum*";[4] and the holy senses of the word include symbolic connotations that are highly appropriate for Milton's military angel.

Some of these, indeed, are applicable to all angels. In *De Doctrina Christiana,* Milton lists their biblically proven attributes. Angels, he tells us, are "extremely strong" and were "created perfect in holiness and righteousness";[5] and ambidexterity is a sign of strength, perfection, holiness, and righteousness. Since these qualities shade from the physical to the metaphorical and moral, it is perhaps easiest to start with the physiological and let "body up to spirit work."[6]

Ambidexterity implies not only strength, but warlike strength. Sir Thomas Browne claims that is "happeneth only unto strong and Athleticall bodies," and glosses "Athleticall" as "Apt for contention." Thus, no women could be ambidextrous, according to Hippocrates, Galen, and Pliny.[7] Right- or left-handedness was seen as a weakness or defect, usually attributed to a deficiency in vital heat or spirits upon one side; opinion varied, however, as to whether this defect was natural or imposed by custom. Aristotle and Plato disagree on the point, ·though they join in asserting that it is possible—and desirable—for all men to become ambidexters.

Aristotle usually maintains that the right hand is naturally superior to the left, though by practice we may all become ambidextrous. A striking metaphorical application of his belief in the possibility of perfected ambidexterity is found in the section on political justice in the *Nicomachean Ethics,* in a context which may add to its appropriate associations for the "sway" of the angel of justice. Aristotle uses the natural superiority of the right hand over the left to illuminate the distinction between things which are just by nature and things which are only legally just, according to merely human conventions; "yet," he adds, "it is possible that all men should come to be ambidexters."[8]

Plato, however, holds that there is no difference in nature between the right hand and the left, and it is unnatural, "acquired habit" alone that distorts our "native endowments."[9] This seems to be widely accepted in the seventeenth century; Bishop Hall, for example, meditating "Vpon the Sight of a Left-handed Man," refers confidently to the "old and easie observation that however the senses are alike strong, and active on the right side, and on the left; yet that the limbes on the right side are stronger then those of the left; because they are more exercised then the other."[10] Plato's version is well-known enough for Florio to make it the basis of an elegant compliment to two patrons: "Lame are we in *Platoes* censure, if we bee not ambidexters, using both handes alike."[11] And it would probably be the most congenial to Milton, with his deep-rooted belief that habit and custom work to cramp and deform man's natural freedom.

It is Plato, moreover, who is the *Laws* maintains that men and women ought to train themselves to be ambidextrous as part of their military education, a dictum repeated by Aristotle in his *Politics.*[12] To Plato's theory can be added Galen's assertion that men are, in practice, frequently ambidextrous. By way of proof, he cites examples drawn from poets, a list which to readers not in awe of the authority of his name will appear distinctly scrappy. It includes the Homeric warrior Asteropaeus from Book XXI of the *Iliad*, a line from an otherwise lost work by Hipponax, "I am ambidextrous, and strike unerringly," and a "two-handed" sword from Euripides (*Hippolytus*, line 780). Scaliger adds, "Parthenopaeum, unum e ducibus Aetolis," claiming rather vaguely that "poets" sing of his ambidexterity; and Sir Thomas Browne translates and identifies this, inaccurately, as "Parthenopaeus, the Theban Captaine in Statius."[13] These classical and poetical precedents might well have encouraged a man with Milton's beliefs in the benefits of rigorous moral and physical training to represent his angelic champion as a Platonic ambidexter.

There is biblical as well as classical warrant for warlike ambidexterity, however. "Such would Plato have the Cittizens of his Common-wealth to be," writes George Hakewill, "and such I take those sevean hundred Beniamites to haue been, mentioned in the 20th of Iudges."[14] Hakewill has chosen a controversial example, since most Protestants hold that these Benjamites were left-handed; but the case for those who believed that it would be easier to muster seven hundred trained ambidexters than seven hundred natural *scaevae* from the smallest of the tribes is strengthened by the existence of another army of Benjamites, who are unequivocally ambidextrous. These Benjamites (the name means "sons of the right hand," which is held to be appropriate for those who are doubly right-handed), are described as "mighty men, helpers of the war," and "could use both the right hand and the left in hurling stones and shooting arrows out of a bow" (1 Chron. xii, 2). Not St. Michael's chosen weapons, of course, but the comments of exegetes upon these passages are nevertheless interesting, for they show the assumption, backed by quotations from Plato and Aristotle, that ambidexterity is the mark of the best, strongest, and most strenuously trained fighters.[15]

To be ambidextrous, then, is to be physically perfect, with an unfallen perfection, for "such some conceive our Father Adam to haue been, as being perfectly framed, and in a constitution admitting least defect."[16] From here, it is an easy step to seeing ambidexterity as an emblem of spiritual perfection, of holiness; and when Cornelius à Lapide writes that "vir sanctus est ambidexter" ("a holy man is an ambidexter"),[17] his comment is only part of a long tradition associating the two. It is a tradition that appears to be derived from two main sources, John Cassian and Origen.

Cassian's *Conferences* offers an influential metaphorical interpretation of the holy ambidexter, which is eminently suitable if we are to read Milton's battle in heaven as, on one level, a *psychomachia*. If a commentator like Tostatus can see the military training of the biblical ambidexters as one of the five Aristotelian "modi fortitudinis" (Tostatus, VIII, p. 209c: "ways of fortitude"), Cassian presents instead "the better fortitude / Of Patience" (*PL* IX, 31–32). For Cassian, the perfect spiritual ambidexter is Job; and Milton, of course, describes the book of Job as a "brief model" of the epic form (YPI, p. 183). Job offers the type of un-Homeric, Christian heroic virtue.

Cassian's version of holy ambidexterity depends upon the common notion that God sends prosperity with his right hand, adversity with his left, but both blessings and afflictions have to be taken right, and both can be temptations to sin. It is these "enemies on the right hand" and "enemies on the left hand," in Bishop Hall's phrase,[18] that must be resisted by the Christian soldier, fighting "by the armour of righteousness on the right hand and on the left." Passing, like St. Paul, "by honour and dishonour, by evil report and good report" (2 Cor. vi, 7), the true Christian ambidexter is neither elated by good fortune nor cast down by bad, obtaining "gloriosissimum constantiae triumphum" ("the most glorious triumph of steadfastness"). Job, who steadfastly underwent extremes of prosperity and adversity, is the pattern of those

> qui figuraliter in scripturis sanctis ἀμφοτεροδέξιοι, id est ambidextri nuncupantur . . . quam virtutem ita poterimus nos quoque intellectualiter possidere, si ea quae prospera sunt dextraque censentur et ea quae adversa sunt ac sinistra dicuntur bono rectoque usu ad partem fecerimus dexteram pertinere, ut quaecumque fuerint inlata fiant nobis secundum apostolum arma iustitiae. . . . Erimus igitur ambidextri quando nos quoque rerum praesentium copia vel inopia non mutavit et nec illa nos ad voluptates noxiae remissionis inpulerit nec ista ad desperationem adtraxerit et querellam, sed similiter deo grates in utroque referentes parem fructum de secundis adversis capiamus.[19]

> [who in the holy Scriptures are figuratively called ἀμφοτεροδέξιοι, that is, ambidextrous. . . . And this virtue we too can spiritually possess, if, by the good and right use both of those things which are fortunate, and which are thought to be on the right hand side, and of those things which are misfortunes, and are said to be on the left, we make them all belong to the right hand side; so that whatever befalls becomes for us, in the words of the apostle, the armor of righteousness. . . . We shall therefore be ambidexters when neither plenty nor want alters us, when the one does not prompt us to the indulgence of dangerous slackness, nor the other draw us to despair and complaint, but, thanking God alike for either, we derive equal reward from prosperity and adversity.]

St. Paul is then "verus ambidexter doctor" ("a true ambidextrous teacher") when he writes, "I know how to be abased, and how to abound: everywhere and in all things I am instructed both to be full and to be hungry, both to abound and suffer need" (Phil. iv, 11–13).

This is one of the most influential interpretations of holy ambidexterity. It is Cassian's version that Donne seems to be recalling, for example—though he confuses the issue by fusing it with St. Gregory's—when he remarks that "therefore did *Gregory Nyssen* call *S Basil* in a holy sense, *Ambidextrum*, because he took everything that came, by the right handle, and with the right hand, because he saw it to come from God. Even afflictions are welcome, when we see them to be his" (*Sermons* V, p. 284).

Job's Christian patience may seem difficult to fit with St. Michael's military aggression, just as the sixth book of *Paradise Lost* is hard to take as part of Milton's scheme to inculcate "the better fortitude." Yet it could be the steadfastness of the archangel's "sway" that is being suggested: Michael's virtue carries him unaltered through the fortunes of war, undaunted by every reversal.

A more active spiritual ambidexterity, however, is offered by Origen, whose ambidexter, in an often quoted definition, "nihil habet in se sinistrum, sed utramque manum dextram habet" ("he has nothing sinister about him, but uses either hand as his right hand"). The double right-handed man, in fact, can be readily transformed into an emblem of righteousness, for he has nothing to do with the left hand, with all its "sinister" connotations of damnation, perversity, ill-fortune, and the works of darkness:

> Dignus vero populi princeps, et Ecclesiae judex qui nihil agat sinistrum, cujus quid agat dextera nesciat sinistra sua, in utraque parte dexter est, in fide dexter est, in actibus dexter est, nihil habet de illis qui collocantur a sinistris, quibus dicitur "Discedite a me, operarii iniquitatis, nescio vos, ite in ignem aeternum quem preparavit Deus Zabulo et angelis ejus."[20]
>
> [He is a truly worthy leader of the people, and judge of the Church, who does nothing *sinister*, whose right hand does not know what his left hand is doing, who is right on both sides, is right in faith, is right in works, and has nothing to do with those who are placed on the left hand side, to whom it is said, "Depart from me, ye workers of iniquity; I know you not; go into the everlasting fire, which God has prepared for the devil and his angels."]

All holy men, then, are spiritual ambidexters, according to Origen:

> secundum spiritualem intelligentiam, et sancti omnes ambidextri dicantur: et econtrario Zabulus, et principes ejus, si dici potest, ambisinistri dicuntur. Totum

enim quod agunt, sinistrum est, totum perversum, totum igni aeterno, cum iis qui a sinistris sunt, deputatum (*PCC*[*G*], XII, col. 96).

[According to the spiritual interpretation, not only are all saints said to be ambidextrous, but, conversely, the Devil and his captains are, if one may say so, called ambisinistrous. For everything they do is on the left hand side, all perverse, all destined for the eternal fire, along with those who belong to the left hand side.]

All saints, then, are ambidextrous; but Origen's somewhat rambling homily upon ambidexterity comes closer still to Milton's death-dealing angel. In the Bible, according to Origen, ambidextrously righteous "salvatores, vel judices" ("saviours, or judges") are raised by God for a suffering nation in response to the prayers of those who cry unto the Lord, and in this one can say that "imaginem ferant aliquorum principum ex coelesti militia, et supernarum virtutum": they are made in the image of princes of the celestial army—Milton's Michael is "of Celestial Armies Prince" (*PL* VI, 44)—and supernal powers. And in the examples Origen cites to show that God will send "virtutem suam coelestem" ("his heavenly power or virtue") to those who turn to him, these heavenly powers are, or are compared to, angels, sent by God in times of national or spiritual crisis in answer to our prayers. "Beati Angeli," as one Renaissance paraphraser of Origen puts it, "ambidextre nos ex Heglonia eripere conantur seruitute" ("the blessed angels . . . ambidextrously endeavor to rescue us from servitude to the Devil").[21] Such angelic champions are morally ambidextrous, for they make everything "right" for us, keeping us from the left-hand path of damnation. But the angels chosen by Origen to illustrate this sort of ambidexterity are of a particular sort, not readily recognizable as images of heaven-sent virtue. They display, in fact, a thoroughly Miltonic aggressiveness. There is the angel of death who laid waste (*vastaret*) all the first born of Egypt, and then, "vastatis Aegyptiis et protratis" ("when the Egyptians had been laid waste and destroyed"), led the children of Israel to freedom. Then there is the angel sent to king Sennacherib, who in one night smote in the camp of the Assyrians a hundred and fourscore and five thousand: "caesis sub una nocte et prostratis centum octoginta quinque millibus hostium" (*PCC*[*G*], XII, col. 966C, Exod. xii, 2 Kings xix, 35). Such widespread devastation, emphasized by the repetition of the verbs *vastare* and *prosternere*, is indeed reminiscent of how

> the Sword of *Michael* smote, and fell'd
> Squadrons at once, with huge two-handed sway
> Brandisht aloft the horrid edge came down
> Wide wasting. (*PL* VI, 250–53)

II

Strength, perfection, holiness, and righteousness; Origen's "dignus vero populi princeps, et Ecclesiae judex," and the punishing "virtutem coelestem" sent by God in times of national or spiritual crisis to help his chosen people: all these connotations are also appropriate for the two-handed engine of *Lycidas.* Yet I want to suggest that the famous lines might be prompted by something more definite than this. Lurking in the background of this discussion of St. Michael's ambidexterity is the hero of Origen's homily on the literal level: the most famous ambidextrous champion of the Bible, the tyrant-slayer and liberator of his nation, Ehud, killer of Eglon in the book of Judges.

Such a suggestion is, I am aware, problematic; and the reason had better be stated at once. Ehud is ambidextrous only in the Septuagint and the Vulgate. All the Reformed versions of the bible, from Junius-Tremellius to the Authorized Version, describe Ehud as left-handed, or "hauing an impediment in hys ryght hand";[22] and this translation is followed almost without exception by Protestant commentators. It is, therefore, unlikely that Milton would hold to the old translation; and if he were writing a commentary upon the book of Judges he would probably make Ehud left-handed.[23] But he is writing poetry, and poetry is "subsequent, or rather precedent to logic" (YP II, p. 403); I want to suggest only that the old interpretations of Ehud were somewhere in the back of Milton's mind when he wrote *Lycidas.* I hope to make this convincing by showing the peculiar aptness with which Ehud, as expounded by the commentators, fits—I believe uniquely—with *every* phrase of the two-line crux. For this reading will offer a two-handed champion of an afflicted nation, whose weapon might justly be described as an "engine"; who smites, quite explicitly, "once and . . . no more"; who smites the tyrant within doors—doors that are the subject of learned debate and even allegorical interpretation; and, above all, whose action is commonly interpreted as the type of the good priest or teacher, purging the corrupted church of greed, idolatry, and false doctrine.

There can be little doubt that Milton, despite his fierce Protestantism, would be familiar with the pre-Reformation interpretations. Scholarly Protestants did not need the passionate urging of *Areopagitica* to "read any book what ever come into thy hands, for thou art sufficient to judge aright, and to examine each matter" (YP II, p. 511), as is easily shown by the range of authorities upon which they draw.[24] If I too range through pre-Reformation and Catholic as well as Protestant exegetes to expound the story of Ehud (upon every point except that of his ambidexterity), this is with the understanding that the difference between the pre-Reformation, Catholic and Protestant attitudes to metaphorical and typological interpretation is largely a change in emphasis—a "significant" change, as Lewalski insists, but not a complete rejection.[25] In abandoning the elaborate fourfold interpretations of unreformed commentators for a "literal" reading, Protestants were very far from rejecting possible figurative and spiritual senses. Typology and tropology still flourished in Reformed theology and literature, though fused more closely with the literal meaning, rather than elaborately extrapolated from it; and Protestant commentators will often offer in the name of plain sense interpretations that used to appear in a more elaborate guise.

Indeed, it is perhaps possible to recognize an elaborate tradition resurfacing in Milton's most radical use of Ehud the tyrant killer. The character of Ehud naturally received a new prominence when events made it necessary to prove "that it is Lawfull, and hath been held so through all Ages, for any, who have the Power, to call to account a Tyrant, or wicked King"; and in *The Tenure of Kings and Magistrates* a brutally literal reading of Judges is used to prove that Ehud, in slaying Eglon, "went on just principles, such as were then and ever held allowable, to deale so by a Tyrant" (YP III, p. 215). But in *Pro Populo Anglicano Defensio,* Ehud's action is defended in terms which echo old interpretations. Ehud's tyrannicide, Milton argues, was performed at God's command, and "ad honesta quaeque & laudabilia hortari solet Deus"—"It is God's nature to encourage deeds upright and praiseworthy" (YP IV, pp. 56, 401). "*Laudabilis,*" however, is the adjective constantly and traditionally applied to Ehud's morally dubious actions simply because the traditional translation of the name Ehud was "*laus,*" "praise" (a mistranslation, in fact; the Hebrew means "strength"). This is how Origen justifies Ehud: "Aioth, qui interpretatur *laus*" ("Ehud, who is expounded as *praise*") acts therefore with praiseworthy deceit, "laudabili usus deceptione" (*PCC*[*G*], XII, col. 967A). "Hoc auliculorum stylo laudabiliter usus est Aod" ("Ehud praiseworthily employed this manner of deceit") echoes Emmanuel de Naxera, just one voice in the Catholic chorus reiterating this theme and this adjective.[26]

This is the story of Ehud the tyrant killer, as told in chapter iii of Judges:

And the children of Israel did evil again in the sight of the Lord: and the Lord strengthened Eglon king of Moab against Israel, because they had done evil in the

> sight of the Lord. . . . But when the children of Israel cried unto the Lord, the Lord raised them up a deliverer, Ehud the son of Gera, a Benjamite, a man left-handed [ambidextrous]: and by him the children of Israel sent a present unto Eglon the king of Moab. But Ehud made him a dagger which had two edges, of a cubit length; and he did gird it under his raiment upon his right thigh. And he brought the present unto Eglon king of Moab: and Eglon was a very fat man. And when he had made an end to offer the present, he sent away the people that bare the present. But he himself turned again from the quarries that were by Gilgal, and said, I have a secret errand unto thee, O king: who said, Keep silence. And all that stood by him went out from him. And Ehud came unto him; and he was sitting in a summer parlour, which he had for himself alone. And Ehud said, I have a message from God unto thee. And he arose out of his seat. And Ehud put forth his left hand, and took the dagger from his right thigh, and thrust it into his belly: And the haft went in after the blade; and the fat closed upon the blade, so that he could not draw the dagger out of his belly; and the dirt came out. Then Ehud went forth through the porch, and shut the doors of the parlour upon him, and locked them. (Judg. iii, 12–23)

Escaping in this way, Ehud "blew a trumpet in the mountain of Ephraim" and roused the children of Israel to a bloody and successful national uprising against the Moabites.

Few of the early Fathers wrote detailed commentaries upon this superficially unedifying story, except, with Augustine, to discuss whether or not Ehud was guilty of a lie (a fault that draws more attention than mere murder!). Most of the figurative readings therefore tend to derive, directly or indirectly, from Origen's allegorization; but even the most fanciful of these are apt to be mere encrustations upon a simple moral pattern which is eminently acceptable to the Protestant mind: a tale of wickedness punished by tyranny and tyranny punished by God. The rule of the tyrant Eglon is a punishment inflicted upon the Israelites for abandoning true religion, one of the many "mutationes vel defectiones a vera religione" ("alterations or desertions from true religion") that Ludovicus Lavater finds in the book of Judges;[27] for Tostatus, the "evil" that the Israelites did in the sight of the Lord is specifically idolatry (Tostatus, V, p. 38a). Yet, if Eglon is the scourge of God to punish the Israelites, he will nevertheless be punished himself. Lavater sees the story as a warning that all "tyranni et persequutores ecclesiae" ("tyrants and persecutors of the church") will at length suffer punishment at the hands of a just judge, since it is God's habit to throw into the fire the rod which he used to scourge the wicked (*Liber Ivdicvm*, p. 19b). The death of Eglon then shows, as Joseph Hall gloats, that "it is the manner of God, to take fearfull reuenges of the professed enemies of his Church" (Hall, p. 973)—a highly Protestant moral and highly suitable for *Lycidas*.

Eglon, then, is a persecutor of the church and "fidelium oppressor," oppressor of the faithful;[28] but this particular tyrant is especially appropriate for the depiction of the "Church-tyranny" of prelates who are "fat and fleshy, swoln with high thoughts," in Milton's memorable phrase (YP X, pp. 823, 793). Eglon neatly combines tyranny, greed, and idolatry.

Eglon is grossly fat, a tyrant who "non nisi venter fuit & inutile telluris pondus" (*Liber Ivdicvm,* p. 20a), ("was nothing but a belly and useless burden upon the earth"), like the "blind mouths" of *Lycidas,* who climb into the fold "for their bellies sake." He is one of those described by Moses, who "waxed fat, and kicked," and, "covered with fatness . . . forsook God which made him."[29] For many commentators of the old school, he is simply greed or gluttony personified: read tropologically, Eglon is "*cupiditas*" or "*gula,*" to be purged by the sword of the word of God;[30] others, like Montanus, claim more literally that the story shows that Eglon was killed by gluttony because he had grown too fat to dodge Ehud's blow.[31]

More elaborate extrapolations are gathered from the traditional interpretations of Eglon's name. Some claim that it means "bull-calf," which is linked, inevitably, with the idolatrous worship of the golden calf, to which indulgence of the flesh invariably leads, and with the bulls of Bashan, "which oppress the poor and needy," demanding drink from the masters they should serve (Amos iv, 1), and of which David complained, "Many bulls have compassed me; strong bulls of Bashan have beset me round" (Ps. xxii, 12).[32] Others, including Origen, render the name more accurately as "circle" or "wheel," representing the inherent instability of the wanton or vicious who are "inconstantes, & rotae instar mutabiles sunt" ("fickle and changeable like a wheel"). Origen's translation of the names of Eglon and Ehud may perhaps be relevant to the watery imagery of *Lycidas.* Eglon is the king of the Moabites, which Origen translates as "*fluxus* vel *effusio*" ("flowing, dissolute," or "flood, excess"). Eglon then is "fluxae et dissolutae gentis princeps vel dux" ("the prince or leader of a loose and dissolute people")—to be understood, Origen tells us, as the philosophy of Epicurus (*PCC*[*G*], XII, col. 967B). This translation of the name is of reasonable accuracy when stripped of its puns, since "Moab" means "water of a father", and Origen's watery interpretation was followed by most subsequent commentators. Name games offer as much scope for misplaced ingenuity to literary critics as to biblical exegetes, but it is tempting to point out how neatly the conflict between Ehud and the Moabite, "laus" and "effusio," fame and the threatening and unstable flood, would fit with the thematic patterns of *Lycidas.*

If Eglon is greed, fleshliness, and Bashan-like oppression, he is also idolatry and false doctrine. Eglon, it is generally agreed, has been setting up idols in holy places, desecrating Gilgal. This is not immediately apparent from the Authorized Version, where Ehud "turned away from the quarries that were by Gilgal." The word translated here as "quarries," and in Junius-Tremellius as "lapicidinis," is, however, "pesilim" in Hebrew, which is translatable as "carved stones," and is read as "graven idols" by most Protestants as well as all Catholics. These idols, most agree, had been placed by Eglon in deliberate profanation of a sacred spot, "sicut Antiochus Epiphanes posuit idolum in templo domini" ("as Antiochus Epiphanes placed an idol in the temple of the Lord").[33]

> For Gilgal was among the Jewes counted a religious place. For the arke of the covenaunt remayned there a while, and we read that the Israelites after they were passed over Jordane rested first in that place, and celebrated a general circumcision there. Wherfore it might easlye come to passe y[t] Eglon in contempte of the Hebrewes had there placed images and idoles (Martyr, p. 82b).

Many scholars follow Nicolaus de Lyra, who poses the question of why Ehud turns back from Gilgal and provides the answer that the sight of this idolatrous profanation fires him with righteous zeal and anger, so that he turns back to kill Eglon, displaying "laudabilem impatientiam" (*Lyra* II, p. 35b: "praiseworthy impatience")—the usual adjective.

To idolatry, according to some, Eglon adds the vice of hypocrisy by rising from his seat to honor the name of the Lord, "hypocrito animo" (*Liber Ivdicvm*, p. 19b) ("in a spirit of hypocrisy")—a sin particularly attacked by the Protestants, with their distrust of mere ceremony.

> This man was an Idolator, a Tyrant: yet what outward respects doth he giue to the true God? Externall ceremonies of piety, and complements of deuotion, may well be found with falshood in Religion. They are a good shadow of truth where it is: but where it is not, they are the very body of hypocrisy. . . . God would haue liked well to haue had lesse of his courtesie, more of his obedience. (Hall, p. 972)

To free the people of Israel from this tyrant of greed, idolatry, and hypocrisy, the Lord "raised up" Ehud to be the deliverer of his nation. For most Protestant commentators, Ehud is exonerated from blame—and not to be imitated by the ordinary faithful—because he is "stirred by some extraordinarie motion of the spirit," vouchsafed an "extraordinarie vocation."[34] The Protestant reading of Ehud as left-handed is worked into this interpretation of the extraordinariness of Ehud's raising, for it shows that "God seeth not as man seeth" (Hall, p. 971). The most literal rendering of the Hebrew describes Ehud's right hand as "closed" or "contracted"; and Protestants often represent Ehud as maimed or disabled. He is "ad bellandum ineptus" ("unfit for warfare"),[35] hardly the natural choice for the leader of an armed rebellion. "What a strange choice doth God make of an Executioner," remarks Hall, "a man shut of his right hand; either he had but one hand, or vsed but one, and that the worse, and more unready" (Hall, p. 971). It is Ehud's natural weakness that is stressed by the Protestants (even the fact that he was born into the smallest tribe is pressed into service).[36] God, proclaims Lavater, was only following his usual practice in choosing one who was "ineptus & mancus" ("useless and maimed"); for God chooses the meek and humble of this world to throw down the mighty and great; he uses mere women, like Judith, as instruments of his vengeance and chooses lowly men as his apostles (*Liber Ivdicvm*, p. 18b). Hall echoes this theme: "It is the ordinary wont of the Almighty, to make choyce of the vnlikeliest meanes. The instruments of God must not be measured by their own power, or aptitude, but by the will of the Agent" (Hall, pp. 971–72). The weakness of the instrument reflects the greater glory on God, whose power is revealed when Ehud is supernally and extraordinarily infused with strength, courage, and agility beyond his natural capabilities to fulfill his divine mission (*Republica*, p. 84). "Though *Ehud* had no hands, he that imployed him, had enabled him to this slaughter" (Hall, p. 972).

In contrast, pre-Reformation and Catholic writers stress Ehud's strength and perfection, developed, if at all, only by his military training. There can be no doubt that, even if Milton's conscious Protestant mind might reject this, it would be peculiarly congenial to his imagination, which is consistently stirred by self-sufficiency and power. And it is interesting that in *The Tenure of Kings and Magistrates* Milton insists, albeit for specific political purposes, that there is no biblical proof that Ehud possessed any "special warrant" (YP III, p. 215). Far from representing this tyrannicide as an extraordinary raising above all ordinary rules, Milton, in Goodwin's words, "reconcileth [it] with rules for standing practice."[37]

As an ambidexter, Ehud displays, not inaptitude for war, but, rather, "magna eius dispositio ad bellum" (Tostátus, V, p. 40c). Commentators who hold to the ambidextrous reading point out that it is improbable that a man deprived of the use of his right hand would be made the leader of active soldiers; moreover, of course, Ehud is a Benjamite, one of the "sons of the right hand" who are known, from the evidence of Chronicles, to practice ambidexterity in war.[38] Naturally, following the readings of Origen and Cassian, Ehud is also described as perfect, holy, and righteous in his strength. He is the ambidextrous "vir sanctus" of whom St. Jerome remarked that "iustum non habere sinistram" ("the righteous man has no left hand").[39] His holy ambidexterity is a sign of his worthiness: "puto namque eligisse Deum hominem, cui nihil sinistrum, quique ex omni parte meretur e[u]logium" (*In Ivdices*, I, p. 222) ("God, I believe, chose a man who is in no way 'sinister,' who in every respect deserves the highest praise"). Ehud, in these un-Reformed readings, in fact, is chosen by the Israelites to carry their gifts, and by God to fulfill his holy mission, because of his superior strength, skill in arms, and moral virtue. If he comes from the smallest, least famous and noble of the tribes, Emmanuel de Naxera adds, this only makes the personal qualities for which he is chosen the more obvious (*In Ivdices* I, p. 267).

Inevitably, like almost every Old Testament figure of any virtue at all, Ehud is seen as a typological prefiguration of Christ. Nicolaus Serarius gives a characteristically long-winded and elaborate version of this. Ehud "significat Saluatorem nostrum IESUM . . . qui humana diuinaque sua natura, rursumque vita sanctissima, & morte innocentissima totus ambidexter . . . fuit" (*Commentarij*, p. 95) ("signifies our Saviour Jesus . . . who in his human and in his divine nature, and again, in his most holy life and his most innocent death was a perfect ambidexter"). If Ehud tells Eglon that he has a message to deliver in secret from God, Christ is God's secret Word. His two-edged sword ("gladius anceps") is then the two-edged sword of the spirit in Hebrews, piercing even to the dividing asunder of soul and spirit and of the joints and marrow. This typological reading is not by any means solely Catholic. Protestants, too, subscribe to the symbolic understanding of the Old Testament, secure in the examples given by Christ himself. Lavater puts it baldly, "Ehud typus est Christi" ("Ehud is a type of Christ"), but then adds a touch of Protestant elaboration: Ehud kills Eglon alone as Christ is said by Isaiah to "have trodden the wine-press alone" (*Liber Ivdicvm*, p. 19b)—a traditional explanation of why Ehud sent away the other messengers.

Most directly relevant to the themes of *Lycidas*, however, is the common allegorical reading of Ehud as the type of the good pastor, purging the body of the church with the sword of the Word of God—"euangelicus sermo & propheticus qui gladio comparatur" (*Lyra* II, p. 35a) ("the word of the evangelists and prophets, which is compared to a sword"). This, like most symbolic readings, derives ultimately from Origen; and Origen draws a contrast between this just two-handed judge of the church and corrupt and inefficient ecclesiastical leaders, which has evident parallels with *Lycidas*. For Ehud is contrasted with the sort of judge "sub quo famem et sitim populus patiatur, 'non famem panis, neque sitim aquae, sed famem audiendi verbum Domini' " (*PCC*[*G*] XII, col. 969A) ("under whose rule the people suffer hunger and thirst, 'not hunger for bread, nor thirst for water, but hunger to hear the word of the Lord' "):

the hungry sheep look up and are not fed. For Origen, and commentators like Rabanus Maurus, the word of the evangelists and prophets destroys the false doctrines of worldly self-indulgence represented by Eglon. The truth of the swordlike word is driven home—so that it is felt in the guts, as it were—by this two-handed debater:

Quem interficiat et perimat evangelicus sermo, qui gladio comparatur: et sermo propheticus ipse in ventre eorum, atque in imis praecordiis ambidextri doctoris disputationibus concludatur (*PCC*[*G*] XII, col. 967B–967C)

[The word of the evangelist, which is compared to a sword, slays and destroys him; and the mere word of the prophet, in the stomach and in the inmost heart, is used to finish off the debate by the arguments of this ambidextrous teacher.]

The stabbing of Eglon, then, is a symbolic purging of false worldly doctrines: Ehud "extinguat omnem pravi dogmatis et crassae intelligentiae sensum, qui se extollit, et erigit adversum spiritualem scientiam Christi" ("destroys every misconception of false doctrine and of the gross and fleshly understanding that exalts itself and rises up against the spiritual knowledge of Christ").

From this is derived the reading of Ehud as the type of a good priest, killing greed. "Aod praelatus, Eglon cupiditas, ferrum verbum Dei" ("Ehud is a leader of the Church, Eglon greed, the sword the Word of God").[40] For Serarius, following Origen, "Aodi sunt . . . boni *Pastores* ac *Doctores*" ("all good pastors and teachers are Ehuds"); their spiritual ambidexterity, in preaching and practice, faith and works, is that of the blameless bishops described in St. Paul's letter to Timothy. And the work of these blameless and perfect priests, according to Serarius, is to purge the church of the Eglons who oppress it, "pristinamque Catholicae fidei tandem aliquando libertatem, quietem & tranquillitatem restituant" (*Commentarij*, p. 95) ("and restore at long last the original liberty, peace and tranquillity of the Catholic faith"). Such a dream of restoring a pure and original Church is, of course, readily translated into Milton's Protestant ideology.

Other details of the story of Ehud fit neatly with *Lycidas*. Ehud's dagger or sword would be, even more than most instruments of warfare, aptly described as an "engine," for it is prepared with ingenuity. "*Ingenium*" is the Latin root of "engine"; and Ehud's sword is deliberately and ingeniously wrought for a specific purpose. All commentators stress the cunning of Ehud: he prepared a sword "industrié laboratum callidè" (*In Ivdices* I, p. 303) ("carefully and cunningly wrought"), and killed Eglon "by a politick stratagem."[41] Indeed, there is even a tradition that goes further than this which suggests that Ehud's sword was in some way unique in its design. Jerome's translation of "two-edged" gives rise to the notion that it might have consisted of two blades, with a handle in the middle; even more elaborately, Tostatus compares Ehud's dagger to Joab's sword, which, he argues, was made with some mechanical device to enable it to leap from the scabbard of its own accord (Tostatus, V, pp. 40d–40e). Even without these rather fanciful extrapolations, Ehud's "Poniard, made of purpose with a double edge,"[42] perhaps retains enough elements of deliberate and ingenious contrivance to allow it to qualify as an "engine." And this weapon, in the story of Ehud, does indeed "smite once, and smite no more." In Peter Martyr's rendering, "The stroken was so vehement, that not onely the sworde, but also the haft persed into the body of the kynge. Yea & the whole skayn was so closed in with fat or greace that he was not able to plucke it out. And the king was killed with the selfe same stroke" (Martyr, p. 83a).

Such immediacy is sometimes cited as proof that Ehud is performing God's work. "Certe ipsa rei conficiendi celeritas, & facilitas praesentissimum Dei auxilium testata est" ("That speed and ease of dispatch surely testifies to God's most prompt and powerful aid"), as Emmanuel de Naxera puts it (*In Ivdices* I, p. 222). According to others, Ehud's sword sticks in Eglon's guts as a sign that the Word of God, or the exhortations of the good priest, will stick in the mind, working to lasting effect (*Allegoriae*, p. 131), as Milton doubtless hopes his own inspired poetic warning will operate.

Finally, this act of vengeance takes place behind doors—"doors" which feature in the story and which have received an undue amount of critical attention ever since Augustine raised the question of how Ehud could lock them behind him without a key. Inevitably, one or two commentators look for extra symbolic nuances. Godefricus Tilmannus, for example, returns to the motif of fame to suggest that Ehud shuts the doors behind him as a sign that it is not earthly fame he seeks (*Allegoriae*, p. 131): his fame, in fact, is no plant that grows on earthly soil.

III

I have tried to show that the story of Ehud, the ambidextrous scourge of greed and idolatry and the symbolic purifier of the church, is peculiarly appropriate to *Lycidas*, fitting the particular phrasing as well as the general tenor of Milton's warning. Yet I want only to suggest that Ehud may, on some level, have prompted the strange adjective "two-handed." This is less a matter of backtracking and hedging bets than a belief in the way that even so superbly conscious a poet as Milton uses language. And for those readers who think that Milton's poetry is too "simple, sensuous and passionate" (YP II, p. 403) or too rigorously Protestant to allow the influence of such exegesis, the appropriate associations of holy ambidexterity are not necessarily confined to the figure of Ehud.

At its most general, "two-handed" need only point to angelic or even God-like power and freedom. God himself, after all, can be represented as ambidextrous in his workings, as in Herbert's poem, "Providence": "To show thou art not bound, as if thy lot / Were worse then ours, sometimes thou shiftest hands."[43] Milton may then be showing the Christian liberty of God's chosen instruments, who "are not bound" by laws (or the Law).

The doubleness of two-handed dexterity, however, could be seen as more particularly appropriate for a poem within which most critics have found some form of duality. J. E. Hardy, for example, points to the tension between pagan and Christian contained in the dual meanings of the word "pastor" and finds that this provides the poem's dialectic—resolved, finally, in the synthesis of the poet who is also a prophet and teacher.[44] In this context, holy two-handedness may be the ambidexterity of one who straddles both the secular and religious spheres of activity, one who is, in the medieval definition of *ambidexter* quoted by Du Cange, "Aptus ad gerendas res tam spirituales, quam temporales" ("able to perform not only spiritual but temporal duties"). If, as Milton believed, God is pouring out his grace upon England, his chosen instruments will combine the spiritual and temporal to establish his kingdom upon earth.

For those critics who see the poem as attempting to reconcile the conflicting claims of humanism and Christianity, there is Gregory of Nyssa's praise of his brother Basil's holy ambidexterity of learning. St. Basil,

> qui sicut Moyses, eruditus fuit omni sapientia atque scientia externarum disciplinarum, sacris vero literis ab infantia usque ad perfectionem et consummationem innutritus, una crevit, in adulta atque confirmata aetate una versatus est, unde docens omnem hominem in omni sapientia tam externa quam divina, veluti vir quidam fortis et strenuus bellator ambidexter, per utramque eruditionem in adversarios sese armans, per utramque disciplinam vincit reluctantes, utraque armatura praecedens et superans eos, qui per alterutram adversus veritatem aliquas vires habere se putabant, eos quidem qui de haereticorum sententia scripturas proferrent, scripturis evertens atque confutans: graecos autem ac gentiles per suam ipsorum irretiens atque illaqueans eruditionem. (*PCC*[*G*] XLVI, col. 790B–790C)

[like Moses, was deeply versed in all wisdom and in secular studies; brought up, indeed, on the holy scriptures from the cradle, until he was perfectly accomplished, he grew up in one school; in his assured maturity, he turned to the other, thence instructing all mankind in all wisdom, secular as much as divine. Like some strong and active ambidextrous fighter, arming himself against his adversaries with either type of scholarship, he conquered their resistance, using either sort of learning, and surpassing and possessing better weapons of either kind than those who, armed with one or the other, fancied they were strong enough to attack the truth. Indeed, those who cited the Scriptures to uphold heretical opinions, he would confound and confute by the Scriptures; yet he would entangle and ensnare the Greeks and gentiles too through his knowledge of their own literature.]

This is another well-known passage: so much so that praiseworthy learning sometimes creeps—by what is apt to look like scholarly free-association—even into the discussion of Ehud. And Nicolaus Serarius's blameless and perfect priests, who are to purge the church of greed, are linguistic and cultural ambidexters too:

sacrarum litterarum scientia, prophanarum peritia: linguarum variarum cognitio, dicendi scribendique facultas, ut ad summam Dei laudem, veritatis professionem, omnium vtilitatem ambidextri sint. (*Commentarij*, p. 95)

[their knowledge of sacred literature, and expertise in prophane; their familiarity with various languages, and their oratorical and literary skill make them ambidexters, working for the highest praise of God, witness of the truth, and benefit of all.]

This proliferation of possibilities, I am aware, rather muddies the stream; and it will seem anticlimactic to end with a flurry of additional extras rather than clinching on a neat identification. Yet Milton's poetry and his threat would be alike diminished by such neatness. What makes the "two-handed engine" so effective is precisely what has made it into a scholar's will-o'-the-wisp, "hovering and blazing with delusive Light" (*PL* IX, 639). Its hovering is the "hovering between images" Coleridge found so characteristic of Milton's imagination:[45] it has become a crux because it is both very definite—one feels one should know what *that* engine is—and tantalizingly undefined. This gives the lines precisely the brooding potentialities suitable for such a threat: they seem more than a mere "I could an if I would," because one feels the pressures of imminent meaning, like the imminent revelation of violent enactment, to be close at hand, "at the door"; yet it is all the more impressive and menacing, of course, by virtue of its obscurity. It is as one of those potentialities pressing for realization that I would offer the figure of Ehud, a figure itself hovering uneasily in the realm between the acceptably symbolic and the brutally literal. However, like all the most potent oracular utterances, such as the "ambidextrous" prophecy offered to the tyrant of Corinth,[46] Milton's threat is two-handedly offered and withdrawn. In the decorum of prophecies, Milton's warning will and must always remain superbly dark, riddling, and difficult of application.

Peterhouse, Cambridge

NOTES

1. *The Works of Thomas Nashe*, ed. Ronald B. McKerrow (Oxford, 1958), vol. II, p. 233. Elsewhere, Nashe explicitly uses ambidexterity to indicate untrustworthiness: "a flearing false brother," a "Iohn indifferent" puffin, lawyers, and the devil are all "Ambodexters" (III, pp. 105, 202; I, pp. 162, 286).

2. John Aubrey, *Brief Lives and Other Selected Writings*, ed. Anthony Powell (London 1949), p. 183.

3. *Lacrymae Lacrymarum*, vol. II of *The Complete Works of Joshua Sylvester*, ed. Alexander B. Grosart (Edinburgh, 1880), pp. 277–78, lines 76–112.

4. *The Sermons of John Donne*, ed. George R. Potter and Evelyn M. Simpson (Berkeley and Los Angeles, 1953–62), vol. V, p. 284; hereafter cited as *Sermons* in the text.

5. *De Doctrina Christiana*, I, vii, in *Complete Prose Works of John Milton*, ed. Don M. Wolfe et al. (New Haven, 1953–82), vol. VI, pp. 314–15; hereafter cited as YP in the text.

6. *Paradise Lost* V, 478, (London, 1674), 2nd ed.; hereafter cited as *PL* in the text.

7. Sir Thomas Browne, *Pseudodoxia Epidemica*, ed. Robin Robbins (Oxford, 1981), vol. I, p. 308; Hippocrates, *Aphorismi*, sec. vii, no. 43, in *Hippocrates*, ed. G. P. Goold (London, 1931), p. 202; Galen, *Galeni in Aphorismos Hippocratis Commentaria Septem* (Lugundi 1552), sec. vii, no. 43, pp. 483–84; Pliny, *C. Plinij Secundi Naturalis Historiae*, ed. C. Mayhoff (Stuttgart, 1967), VII, ch. 17.

8. Aristotle, *Magna Moralia*, I, 34 (1194^b, 34); *Problemata*, XXXI, 12 (958^b, 20); *Historia de Animalibus*, II, 1 (497^b, 31); *Nicomachean Ethics*, V, 7 (1134^b, 34).

9. Plato, *Laws*, VII, 794d-795.

10. Joseph Hall, *Occasionall Meditations*, Med. CIX (London, 1633: "The third edition with the Addition of 49. Meditations not heretofore published"), p. 277.

11. John Florio, *A worlde of Wordes* (London, 1598), dedication.

12. Plato, *Laws*, VII, 794d–795; Aristotle, *Politics*, II, 12 (1274^b, 13).

13. Galen, *Galeni in Hippocratis Aphorismos Commentaria Septem*, vii, 43; Julius-Caesar Scaliger, *Aristotelis Historia de Animalibus, Ivlio Caesare Scaligero interprete* (Tolosae, 1619), p. 151; Brown, *Pseudodoxia Epidemica*, vol. I, p. 308.

14. George Hakewill, *An apologie or declaration of the power and providence of God in the government of the world* (Oxford, 1630), p. 5.

15. See, for example, Alphonsus Tostatus on Judges xx, 16 in *Commentaria in Ivdices, et Ruth; Omnia Opera* (Coloniae Agrippinae, 1613), vol. V, part iii, p. 335d; hereafter cited as Tostatus in the text.

16. Brown, *Pseudodoxia Epidemica*, vol. I, p. 308.

17. Cornelius à Lapide, *In Josve, Ivdices, et Ruth Commentarii* (Parisiis, 1642), p. 104; hereafter cited as *In Josve* in the text.

18. Joseph Hall, *Heaven vpon Earth: Characters of Vertves and Vices; The Works of Joseph Hall*, (London, 1625), p. 87; hereafter cited as Hall in the text.

19. John Cassian, *Vigintiquatuor Conlationes*, collatio VI, chs. 9–10, in *Patrologiae Cursus Completus*, Latin Series, ed. J. P. Migne (Paris, 1844–64), vol. XLIX, col. 655c–660a.

20. Origen, *In Librum Judicum*, Homilia III, in *Patrologia Cursus Completus*, Greek series, ed. J. P. Migne (Paris, 1857–1917), vol. XII, col. 965d; hereafter cited as *PCC*[*G*] in the text.

21. Nicolaus Serarius, *Commentarij in sacros Bibliorum libros, Iosve, Ivdicum, Rvth, Tobiae, Ivdith, Esther, Machabaeorum* (Lvtetiae Parisiorum, 1611), p. 95; hereafter cited as *Commentarij* in the text.

22. Peter Martyr, *Most fruitfull and learned Comentaries of Doctor Peter Martirvermil Florentine* (London, 1564), p. 81b; hereafter cited as Martyr in the text.

23. Probably, but not indubitably: it is worth pointing out that, despite Protestant claims, the Catholic interpretation is not founded on a simple mistranslation, and one version might be accepted by an open-minded scholar. Indeed, some modern interpreters have put forward the reading first, I believe, propounded by Serarius (who was aware of Protestant objections, and offered a sort of compromise). The Hebrew "itter yad yamin" can be understood as "closed or bound of the right hand," and, according to this argument, could refer to some form of *voluntary* restraint—a part of the military training which went to the formation of the artificially left-handed or ambidextrous Benjamite warriors for which there is evidence in Chronicles (*Commentarij*, p. 84).

24. To take one example: John Canne, in *The Golden Rule, or Justice Advanced* (London, 1649), backs a radical Protestant position by citing (among many others) Aquinas and Jerome, Nicolaus de Lyra, Cornelius à Lapide, Estitius, Hugo Cardinal, Carthus Pierus and Toletus, Calvin, Beza, Pareus, Piscator, Tremellius, Junius, Osiander, Pellicanus, Borrhaus, and Willet.

25. Barbara Lewalski, *Protestant Poetics and the Seventeenth-Century Religious Lyric* (Princeton, 1979), p. 111.

26. Emmanuel de Naxera, *In Ivdices Commentarii Litterales, Moralesqve* (Lugduni, 1656), vol. I, cap. 3, XXXIV, p. 270; hereafter cited as *In Ivdices* in the text.

27. Ludovicus Lavater, *Liber Ivdicvm, Homilijs CVII. Ludouici Lauateri Tigurinae Ecclesiae Ministri opera atque labore expositus* (Tiguri, 1585), cap. III, hom. XVIII, p. 17b; hereafter cited as *Liber Ivdicvm* in the text.

28. Conradus Pellicanus, *In Libros Historicos, Pvta Iosve, Ivdicvm, Ruth, Samvelis, Regum, Paralipomenon, Ezdrae, Nehemiae & Hester* . . . (Tiguri, 1582), p. 31.

29. Deut. xxxii, 15; quoted by Martinus Borrhaus, *In Sacram Iosvae, Iudicum, Ruthae, Samuelis & Regum Historiam, mystica Messiae seruatoris mundi adumbratione refertam, Martini Borrhai commentarius* (Basileae, 1557), p. 141.

30. Derived from Jerome, *Tractatus in Psalmos*, 14, in *Patrologiae Cursus Completus*, Latin series, *Supplementum*, ed. Adalberto Hamman (Paris, 1960), vol. II, col. 211.

31. Benedictus Arias Montanus, *De Varia Republica, sive Commentaria in Librum Ivdicvm* (Antverpiae, 1592), chap. 3, p. 86; hereafter cited as *Republica* in the text. Compare Lapide, *In Josve*, p. 104.

32. See Lapide, *In Josve*, p. 104; *Commentarij*, p. 4; Borrhaus, *In Sacram Iosvae, Iudicum, Samuelis & Regum Historiam*, p. 141.

33. Nicolaus de Lyra, *Textus biblie cum Glosa ordinaria, Nicolai de lyra postilla, Moralitatibus eiusdem* . . . (Basle, 1505–08), pt. II, p. 35b; hereafter cited as *Lyra* in the text.

34. Andrew Willet, *An harmonie vpon the First booke of Samvel* (Cambridge, 1607), ch. 26, p. 294: Quest. "Whether it be not lawful to kill a tyrant, seeing Dauid spared Saul." Willet, like Martyr, makes the orthodox division between "priuate men," for whom it is "not lawful . . . to lay hands, no not vpon a Tyrant," and those in public office. Yet private men who are stirred, "as Ehud was against Eglon King of Moab" by "some extraordinarie motion of the spirit," are "to be excepted" when their deeds are performed for the good of the nation and not for private revenge; so that, "though they liued as priuate men before, yet in these extraordinarie acts, they were declared to be publike gouernours and deliuerers: as Ehud was one of their Iudges."

35. Johann Brenz, *In Librum Ivdicum & Ruth, commentarij* (Francofurti, 1562), p. 8.

36. For example, see *Republica*, pp. 82–83. Oppressive princes, explains Montanus, take care to remove strong men, whom they perceive as threats.

37. John Goodwin, Ὑβριστοδίκαι, *The Obstructours of Justice, or a Defence of the Honourable Sentence passed upon the late King, by the High Court of Justice* (London, 1649), p. 80.

38. Several commentators cite Judges XX, 16 as proof that Ehud cannot be maimed or left-handed, for the same Hebrew word is used to describe the Benjamites, and six hundred trained ambidexters strain credulity less than six hundred left-handers from the smallest tribe. See, for example, Eusebius Pamphili, *Evsebii Pamphili Caesareae Palestinae Episcopi de Locis Hebraicis; siue Onomasticon Vrbivm et Locorvm Sacrae Scripturae* (Parisiis, 1659), p. 233.

39. Jerome, *Tractatus in Psalmos*, 14, vol. II, col. 211.

40. Stephanus Cantuarensis, quoted in Godefridus Tilmannus, *Allegoriae simul et tropologiae in locos vtriusque Testamenti selectiores iudicio collectae ac propensiore studio depromptae* . . . (Parisiis, 1551), pp. 130–31; hereafter cited as *Allegoriae* in the text. Compare *In Ivdices* I, p. 289.

41. Junius Brutus, *Vindiciae contra Tyrannos: A Defence of Liberty against Tyrants* (London, 1689), p. 139.

42. [Walter Raleigh], *The History of the World* (London, 1614), p. 418.

43. George Herbert, "Providence," 137–38, in *The Works of George Herbert*, ed. F. E. Hutchinson (Oxford, 1941), p. 121.

44. J. E. Hardy, "Reconsiderations: I, *Lycidas*," *Kenyon Review* VII (1945), 99–113.

45. John Payne Collier, *Seven Lectures on Shakespeare and Milton by the Late S. T. Coleridge* (London, 1856), p. 64.

46. Herodotus (5. 92 1[e]): the tyrant Cypselus is given "ἀμφιδέξιον χρηστήριον" (literally, an ambidextrous oracle) by the Delphic oracle.

LYCIDAS AND THE ECPHRASIS OF POETRY

Richard Hooker

THE CRITICAL reception of *Lycidas* in this century has largely centered on the idea that Milton's elegy centrally concerns the nature and function of poetry. The elegy has been read as a relatively coherent narrative that describes a development or dramatic conflict in which the poet comes to terms with his art and vocation.[1] The "theme" is John Milton's crisis, precipitated by the death of Edward King, concerning the ability of poetry to both represent and influence actuality. The "narrative" embodying this theme involves some kind of development through contrast, a dramatic dialogue or struggle between the constituent sections of the poem with their contrasting generic assumptions or lyrical modes.

However, defining the poem as a narrative, or even as a drama or argument, introduces a host of difficulties, particularly as this narrative is often made into a limited autobiography.[2] Because Milton's elegy consists primarily of interruptions, false starts, and textual fragments, it simply presents no single narrative. A narrative may appear in the autobiographical process suggested by a change or growth of the elegy's speaker, even if this autobiography actually moves away from the autobiographical subject in the course of the poem; it may lie in the typological development of apparently disparate images and elements of the elegy. On a metapoetic level, a narrative may appear in an active, dramatic dialogue between the poet and the tradition in which he is writing or in a conflict between the various genres within the poem; or this narrative may consist of the poet's efforts to control the poem he is writing.[3] That any of these processes constitutes a coherent and cohering narrative has never been fully demonstrated: the narratives are never central to the structure of the poem, but only intrude along the margins or are shaded out by other narratives. We are faced, at best, with a work suggesting coherent narratives along several tangents, but resisting an overall and simple unity.

Without a central narrative, the way in which Milton interrogates both the nature of poetry and the office of the poet—if this, indeed, is what Milton is up to—equally resists description. This questioning might be found in the struggle between pastoral genres or lyrical modes, or in the development of the lyric's tone or subject matter. From another perspective, this questioning might drive an autobiographical narrative in which the speaker systematically revises his attitudes toward his project, or it could underlie the poet's effort to control the poetry he is composing.

In any case, the two central interpretive perspectives are indissolubly bound together. The narratives of *Lycidas* are invariably made to describe how the elegy discusses the nature and purpose of poetry; attempts to read the elegy as a discussion of poetry or poetics unfailingly end up identifying some narrative process in which this theme works itself out in a unified way. The pastoral tradition in which *Lycidas* is steeped certainly sanctions these approaches to Milton's elegy; the principal concern of classical pastoral from its formal inception has been the nature and value of poetry, and the pastoral elegy in the Middle Ages and the Renaissance is uniformly narrational and often (if sometimes only marginally) autobiographical.[4] At the outset, then, the critical challenge of *Lycidas* is the need to define the structure of the lyric and its purpose, while at the same time attempting to describe the generic models that might lie behind this structure.

The most prominent structural element in the poem, evidently, is the framing of the elegy at its conclusion. This closing frame forces us both to revise our consideration of the speaker's relation to his audience and to reinterpret our notion of the nature of the utterance being read. Although, as Stanley Fish argues, the end-frame may render the elegist's voice "impersonal" and "anonymous"[5] (even though it may not be true that it renders the elegy itself impersonal or anonymous), more than anything else the end-frame sets the elegy off as a crafted and recited object primarily to be evaluated aesthetically, rather than as a spontaneous or dramatic utterance. In addition, the structure of *Lycidas* as a whole, characterized by sudden shifts in tense, by abrupt transitions between poetic styles and points of view, and by radical disjunctures and interruptions, does not so much push the narrator or the elegy into impersonality or anonymity as it draws attention to the nature of the constituent parts of the elegy as reproduced and replaceable objects. Gradually, this self-disruptive style does away with the fiction of spontaneous utterance and ultimately draws attention to the entire work as an object, a self-contained literary creation unmoored from occasion and temporality.

This relentless insistence on its own aesthetic independence reflects the elegy's ties to the classical pastoral tradition suffusing practically every other element of the poem. From its roots in Theocritus, the classical pastoral elegy is framed in such a way as to define the lyric as a self-contained, self-referential work of deliberate craft, and one that is to be evaluated on its own narrow, formal terms without reference to or bearing on the world of the frame. The framed poetry recitals in classical pastoral are ecphrases of poetry, that is, a setting off and highlighting of the lyric as a well-wrought object. As ecphrases, such recitals are comparable to Thomas Rosenmeyer's description of landscape in Theocritean pastoral:

> extended descriptions of landscapes in ancient literature occur in the form of enclaves, sealed capsules set aside from the larger action, to be enjoyed for their own sake. The effect usually comes close to that of *ecphrasis*, whereby an object described is made to look like a pictorial imitation of that object. The popularity of *ecphrasis* . . . is indicative of the Greek reluctance to describe organic entities that fit into larger entities. An object whose contours are not easily definable is refashioned into a painting or a work of sculpture, and suspended, fixed and independent, within the larger whole. This gets around the difficulty, especially acute in the case of landscapes, of doing justice to the subtle ties between the natural scene and the social action beyond it.[6]

Like ecphrasis, the setting off of a lyric as an object removes it from any relation to the world outside. The framed pastoral lyrics of Theocritus and Virgil are always absolutely dissociated, sometimes problematically, from the world of the frame. These lyrics demand to be evaluated on their own formal terms as works of design and skill. It is in this tradition that Milton both structures the narrative of *Lycidas* and foregrounds the nature of poetic discourse and its relation to actuality. If there is such a thing as a basic narrative in *Lycidas,* this narrative lies in Milton's framing, or ecphrasis, of the speaker's monody. Milton's sources, Theocritus's first Idyll and Virgil's fifth eclogue, mark off the recited lyric ecphrastically as a well-wrought object and establish the response such a poetic object ought to elicit; at the same time, these lyrics render problematic the relation of the poem, as an object, to the ethical demands implied in the frame.

I

Theocritus's first Idyll in its structure and in the framed response to Thyrsis's lyric, emphasizes the artificiality and artistry of the work of poetry to the exclusion of all other considerations. Structurally, Thyrsis's elegy appears in a complementary and contrastive relation to the ecphrasis of the ivy bowl (*kyssibion*) in the frame. The Idyll equates the song of Thyrsis and the *kyssibion* in several ways: the bowl is offered in exchange for the song; both the poem and the bowl are works of high art and craftsmanship at odds with the low value of the material and the setting; and, above all, the ecphrasis of the *kyssibion* usurps the place of the rival song in the singing contest.[7] The relation between the *kyssibion* and the elegy, then, is principally an aesthetic relation between objects of essentially equal artistic and barter value. In the frame, the *kyssibion* evokes wonder for no other reason than the sheer virtuosity of the craftsmanship: "αἰπολικὸν θάημα; τέρας κέ τυ θυμὸν ἀτύξαι" ("A wondrous thing it is to a goatherd's eyes, a marvel that will strike thy heart with amaze") (56).[8] Similarly, Thyrsis's elegy also appears as a crafted object, clearly not a spontaneous utterance but a deliberately composed lyric that has been recited on other occasions and is specifically asked for by the goatherd:

> ἀλλὰ τὺ γὰρ δή, Θύρσι, τὰ Δάφνιδος ἄλγε' ἀείδες
> καὶ τᾶς βουκολικᾶς ἐπὶ τὸ πλέον ἵκεο μοίσας,
> δεῦρ' ὑπὸ τὰν πτελέαν ἑσδώμεθα
> . . . . . .
> αἰ δέ κ' ἀείσῃς
> ὡς ὅκα τὸν Λιβύαθε ποτὶ Χρόμιν ᾆσας ἐρίσδων,
> αἶγά τέ τοι δωσῶ. (19–21, 23–25)

[But thou, Thyrsis, are wont to sing the woes of Daphnis, and art come to mastery in pastoral song. Come hither, then, and let us sit beneath the elm. . . . If you sing as once you sangest in thy match with Chromis from Libya, then I will let thee.]

The evocation of the singing contest with Chromis—the previous occasion of Thyrsis's performance of his Daphnis lyric—points to the absence of the rival song; we get neither the singing contest nor the rival song, but a variation on it by the addition of the ecphrasis of the *kyssibion* (29–56).

Since the ecphrasis replaces the rival song, the Idyll essentially draws attention to the ecphrastic nature of the framed song itself: in other words, a similarity exists between the procedure of ecphrasis and the procedure of the framed poem or song. They are both crafted works that are removed (with definite boundaries) from the living praxis in which they are set. Above all, the works demand a reaction dissimilar to the reactions that temporal, history-bound experience requires: the response is not to cross the boundaries of the aesthetic or the formal.[9] The ecphrasis of the *kyssibion* overwhelmingly emphasizes the artistry of the carving; although the designs suggest potential narratives, attention is concentrated on the quality of design and the skill with which seemingly inconsequential details are depicted, such as the circles beneath the lovers' eyes or the sinews of the fisherman's neck. The work is no more than an "object to make a goatherd marvel, / and strike your heart with amazement, too." The reaction to Thyrsis's lament is equally detached and aesthetic:

> πλῆρές τοι μέλιτος τὸ καλὸν στόμα, Θύρσι, γένοιτο,
> πλῆρες δὲ σχαδόνων, καὶ ἀπ' Αἰγίλω ἰσχάδα τρώγοις
> ἁδεῖαν, τέττιγος ἐπεὶ τύγα φέρτερον ᾄδεις. (146–48)

[Filled may thy fair mouth be with honey, Thyrsis, and with the honeycomb; and mayest thou eat the sweet figs of Aegilus, for thy singing outdoes the cicada.][10]

The performance of the dirge elicits not sadness, but pleasure on account of the craftsmanship: there is an absolute "disjunction between the experience represented in the poem and the aesthetic pleasure enjoyed at hearing the poem" (Halperin, *Before Pastoral*, p. 166).

In an even more fundamental way, Theocritus radically dissociates the representation of experience from experience itself, as the lament is detached from a larger narrative—the story of Daphnis—of which it forms but one moment. The lyric constitutes an arrested moment or fragment in a larger absent narrative; hence, the need felt by Renaissance commentators (and all subsequent commentators) to provide some background story in order to make the lyric intelligible.[11] The absence of the background story points to a final characteristic which the lyric shares with the scenes on the *kyssibion:* all are embedded in absent narratives and represent *kairotic* instants of arrested motion in which story and temporality are displaced outside the boundary of the work in favor of static and fixed design.

Virgil draws on Theocritus's framed lyrics as the central structural principle of his own *Eclogues*, the first and fourth ecologues being the only exceptions. The framed lyrics in the *Eclogues*, as in the *Idylls*, are set off as crafted works, recited to an audience and eliciting exclusively aesthetic responses.[12] There is in Virgil the same disjunction between the poem as crafted object and the actuality of the frame, as well as between the lyric as arrested moment and the absent narrative from which it is extracted.

The fifth eclogue has much in common with Theocritus's "ecphrastic" framing of the lyric in *Idyll* I. Mopsus clearly refers to his song as a crafted work: "Immo haec, in viridi nuper quae cortice fagi, / carmina discripsi et modulans alterna notavi, experiens" ("Nay, I will try these verses, which the other day I carved on the green beech-bark, and set to music, marking words and tune in turn") (13–15).[13] Menalcas's lyric also is set off as a crafted work that has been recited on previous occasions: "et ista / iam pridem Stimichon laudavit carmina nobis" ("but long ago Stimichon praised to me those strains of yours") (54–55). As in Theocritus's first Idyll, the status of the two lyrics as objects becomes apparent in their barter value in terms of other objects, the reed and the crook, at the conclusion of the eclogue. The concluding exchange also makes apparent the disjunction between the frame and the recited lyrics, since the objects that are of comparable value to the lyrics are the "fragili . . . cicuta" ("frail reed") (85) and the "pedum . . . formosum paribus nodis atque aere" ("crook with even knots and ring of bronze" (88,90), neither of which approaches the artistic value of Theocritus's *kyssibion*.

As in Theocritus's Idyll, the response to the lyrics in the frame, even though one is a dirge and the other a contrasting apotheosis, is solely an aesthetic one. The responses stress the value of the lyrics as crafted objects, not their experiential content:

> Tale tuum carmen nobis, divine poeta,
> quale sopor fessis in gramine, quale per aestum
> dulcis aquae saliente sitim restinguere rivo. (45–47)

[Your lay, heavenly bard, is to me even as sleep on the grass to the weary, as in summer's heat the slaking of thirst in a dancing rill of sweet water.]

As with the goatherd's response to Thyrsis's lyric, Menalcas ignores the affective content of the dirge. In turn, Mopsus's reaction to Menalcas's lyric duplicates the latter's earlier response:

> nam neque me tantum venientis sibilus Austri
> nec percussa iuvant fluctu tam litora, nec quae
> saxosas inter decurrunt flumina valle. (82–84)

[For no such charm for me has the rustle of the rising South, nor the beach lashed by surge, nor streams tumbling down amid rocky glens.]

Although these lines embed a fairly sophisticated theory of lyric poetry, we need only understand that the frame and in particular the responses to the Daphnis lyrics in the frame set the lyrics apart, affectively, cognitively, and temporally, from the world of the frame. The responses focus on the delight (*dulcis* [46]; *iuvant* [83]) the works provide as well-crafted objects,[14] and in this way ecphrastically displace, or bound, these lyrics from the world in which they are fixed.

In his bucolic project, however, Virgil introduces tensions not present in the Theocritean pastorals. Commentators rapidly seized the first and the ninth eclogues as essentially political poems[15] and recognized several eclogues as introducing an ethical contrast between the harshness of the exile and dispossession intruding on the pastoral landscape and the essentially disengaged and disinterested practice of poetry (Patterson, *Pastoral*, pp. 4–6). In particular, the ninth eclogue, which greatly influenced late medieval and Renaissance pastoral,[16] centers on the ethical disjunction between the political actuality of the frame and the writing of poetry: "sed carmina tantum / nostra valent, Lycida, tela inter Martia, quantum / Chaonias dicunt aquila veniente columbas" ("But amid the weapons of war, Lycidas, our songs avail as much as, they say, the doves of Chaonia when the eagle comes") (11–13).

The political pressures intruding on the world of the frame produce an inability to compose or remember poetry; the framed lyrics of the ninth eclogue remain, perpetually, in an inchoate or unremembered state: "immo haec, quae Varo necdum perfecta canebat" ("Nay, these lines, not yet finished, which he sang to Varus") (26).

> Omnia fert aetas, animum quoque; saepe ego longos
> cantando puerum memini me condere soles:
> nunc oblita mihi tot carmina: vox quoque Moerim
> iam fugit ipsa: lupi Moerim videre priores. (53–54)

[Time robs us of all, even of memory; oft as a boy I recall that with song I would lay the long summer days to rest. Now I have forgotten all my songs. Even voice itself fails Moeris; wolves have seen Moeris first.]

The eclogue consists of textual fragments of often uncertain provenance whose purpose and direction are cut short by the disjunctures created by incompletion or uncertain memory. The stress on incomplete composition and on memory draws attention to these lyrics as objects, things to be completed or remembered, as distinct from the spontaneous, historically determined utterances framing the incomplete lyrics. In contrast to the historical moment of the frame, these textual fragments speak from a past time of fullness, their message and trajectory dissolved by the course of time and transmission. Reified and static, the lyrics as objects are nevertheless deeply implicated in temporality; the "real" world of the frame, the world of history and the contingent, threatens the very existence of the lyrics and renders them ineffective and obsolete distractions.

By presenting the framing of the recited lyric in the classical eclogue as essentially ecphrastic, I am suggesting the following: first, that the lyrics are presented primarily as crafted objects, separated in a clearly bounded way from the "real" world of the frame, deriving their value and meaning not from their story, narrative, or argument, but from the quality and skill of the design. Second, the lyrics do not elicit sympathy in regard to their content but pleasure in the elaborate craft. Third, they do not refer beyond themselves to the world of the frame or a larger narrative, but are utterly self-contained. However, in the Middle Ages and the early Renaissance, as both the commentary tradition and the writing of pastoral show, the discontinuity in classical pastoral between the lyric as crafted object and the world of the frame—that is, the ecphrastic nature of the framed lyric—was not the principal way in which these works were read.

Perhaps the most obvious modification of the genre appears in the Carolingian transformation of the singing contest into a debate, a transformation ultimately sanctioned by Virgil's third eclogue. This modification, along with Servius's and Donatus's allegorical privileging of the frame, ultimately leads to the spilling over of the mood and content of the framed lyric into the frame itself in late medieval pastoral poetry. The framed elegy comes to be placed in a larger context of grief, and so loses the clear boundedness and specifically performative status as an object. The recited, composed lyric is no longer discontinuous with the frame, but develops into an integral part of the experience represented in the frame, and often arises directly from that experience. The proper response to the framed lyrics is no longer aesthetic appreciation of design but, rather, sympathetic grief. These qualities characterize the framed pastoral elegies of Petrarch, Boccaccio, and others and significantly affect Renaissance English pastoral.[17] In addition, Renaissance commentaries on both Theocritus and Virgil do not draw attention to the status of the framed lyrics as crafted objects, although they generally recognize the discontinuity between the lyrics and the frame in both the first and ninth eclogues of Virgil.

The very language of pastoral, however, with its stress on stasis and shade, not only implies that an ethical space removed from the active life is requisite for the composition and enjoyment of poetry, but also suggests a stylistic decorum in which detail and craftsmanship are of primary importance. The setting of the production and recitation of the framed lyrics of classical pastoral—the refuge from the noon sun under a shade tree—evokes stylistic expectations of refinement and detail in the lyrical object to be produced. As a result of its removal from larger ethical concerns, and its concomitant association with a refined and detailed style, the pastoral genre was seen, in the theoretical works of the Renaissance, as a poetical mode primarily concerned with craft and design and aesthetically removed from praxis. In such a context, Milton, reading his classical models against their transformation, could seize the essentially ecphrastic nature of the classical framed elegy and transform it in such a way as to problematize the very process of setting off a work of poetry "ecphrastically."

II

It is precisely an ecphrasis of poetry that informs the structure of *Lycidas* and focuses the elegy's concern with the nature and function of poetry. Milton found in Theocritus and Virgil a tradition in which the poetic work is set apart from the concerns of the frame as a deliberately and carefully crafted object eliciting an exclusively aesthetic response. This framing introduces discontinuities between the framed poem and the actuality which frames it; Milton, however, introduces a radical difference in the device. Since the frame appears only at the conclusion, the elegy is distinguished as an artifact only retroactively, that is, in time. Each major disjunction in the poem, including the final "frame," sets off all that precedes it as an artifact and draws attention to the lyric's status as a fixed object, but, nevertheless, an object deeply involved in temporality. This retroactive framing is not only the basic structural principle of the lyric, but also the locus of Milton's questioning of the status of poetry: the disjunctures problematize the fixed, independent, and disengaged status of the work of poetry in a world of change and contingency.

This retrospective framing is not entirely without precedent; one need look no further afield than Virgil's fifth eclogue. When Mopsus and Menalcas exchange gifts at the end of the eclogue, Menalcas offers a reed on which he has performed previously: "haec nos 'formosum Corydon ardebat Alexim' / haec eadem docuit 'cuium pecus? an Meliboiei?' "("This taught me 'Corydon was aflame for the fair Alexis'; this too: 'Who owns the flock? Is it Meliboeus?' " (86–87), referring, respectively, to the first lines of the second and third eclogues. This is a surprising turn of events: nothing in these two previous eclogues indicated that they were written or recited by anyone other than Virgil. Both eclogues are, like the fifth eclogue, framed poetry recitals: the former is framed by an anonymous narrator, presumably Virgil, and the latter by a dramatic dialogue. No poet or speaker outside the frame is indicated either within the poem or without. In particular, the third eclogue, drawing on Theocritus's fifth Idyll for the tone and structure of its frame, is dramatic, colloquial, and immediate, a chance meeting between two shepherds. Menalcas's remark, however, dramatically alters the status of these eclogues; they retrospectively become poems crafted and recited, not by Virgil, but by a shepherd named Menalcas; the frame of *Eclogue* V not only envelops the Daphnis lyrics but reaches back retroactively to encompass preceding eclogues. Virgil's device here poses several interpretive problems, not the least of which is the question of authorship and origination, but this question is intimately bound up with the poem's status as an object. Virgil's retroactive framing of *Eclogues* II and III does more than foreground the problem of authorship—that is, the status of the proper name (Virgil or Menalcas) that lends the work authority and unity. It removes the two eclogues, and, by extension, the other eclogues in the collection, from the necessity of authorial claim and provides a "context" (the pastoral world) and a "likeness" (the Daphnis lyrics) which govern the consideration of the works as independent, crafted objects. That is, Virgil sets off the two preceding lyrics ecphrastically; by doing so, the poet installs wider claims to the dissociation of the lyric from the "outside" world which the uncontested voice of the "author," because he is rooted in experience, originally could not claim for the lyric.

The critical response to Milton's retroactive framing in *Lycidas* and, in particular, the concluding frame, has focused entirely on what Paul de Man, in another context, calls the "readability of [the subject's] proper name"[18] rather than on the ecphrastic nature of this framing. In one camp, the end frame illustrates a clarification or growth of identity through the process of poetic creation, so that the poem progresses toward the constitution of a "proper name" (the swain). This proper name provides a subjective unity which makes the text intelligible in biographical and teleological terms.[19] In another camp, the frame draws the poem away from the proper name into anonymity or impersonality, or constitutes that proper name as "fiction."[20] This recession of the (presumably integral and authoritative) voice of the lyric into anonymity or fiction reconstitutes the preceding lyric as independent of the subjective, autobiographical proper name assumed at the start of the lyric. Although these approaches are poles apart, they nevertheless share the same focus on the subjective voice of the elegy, either as it creates itself or self-destructs in the process of poetic composition. However, the question of subject and authorship, the biographical question, appears to be the least important question in Milton's framing of the elegy. Instead, Milton claims for his elegy a status not so much as a record of subjective experience, but as an artifact which, because it is an artifact, bears a troubled relation to actuality.

The ecphrastic framing of the elegy begins before the concluding frame: the disjunctures that punctuate the elegy function in much the same way as the concluding frame, by rendering all that precedes as texts or fragments of texts composed or performed at a previous, unknown time. The first radical disjunction, as has been well noted, occurs at line 76, when the seamless flow of a seemingly spontaneous utterance is interrupted and, by the intrusion of the past tense, thrust out of the present into an indeterminate past. The first seventy-five lines of the poem are transformed from a monologic, immediate, occasion-bound utterance into a recitation. Nothing in the first seventy-five lines, however, indicates that the utterance is anything but a spontaneous composition. To be sure, the poem does have an introduction structurally similar to an opening frame (lines 1–14), which provides a specific occasion for the original composition of the lyric. These lines in turn lead to an invocation of the Muses to begin the lyric proper (line 15), which echoes the traditional opening refrain of the classical framed pastoral lyric.[21]

We are, however, misled in reading this invocation as an opening refrain. Instead of beginning the lyric, the refrain develops into another paragraph of the introduction, effectively blurring any line between the introductory "frame" which lays out the occasion for the elegy and the elegy proper. This blurring gives the first section of the lyric its spontaneous quality. In the tradition Milton inherits a clear distinction always exists between the introduction and the elegy proper—even in medieval and Renaissance pastoral, in which the framed elegy shares the same immediacy and contemporaneity of the frame. In *Lycidas*, the opening frame of the elegy is indistinguishable from the lyric the lines propose to introduce; so this opening gives to the lyric, the precise "beginning" of which is indistinct, the feeling of spontaneity, of composition nearly contemporaneous with the occasion and reading of the lyric.

When Phoebus interrupts the lyric at line 76, he does so in order to revise it: "but not the praise, / *Phoebus* repli'ed, and touch'd my trembling ears" (76–77). This interruption deliberately echoes similar interruptions in Ovid (*Amores* I, 1–4) and Virgil (*Eclogues* VI, 3–5), in which Phoebus tweaks the poet's ear with the specific intention of revising the poetic project, not just the utterance, of the speaker.[22] Above all, Phoebus's interruption in *Lycidas* alters the status of the speaker's utterance; the lyric contained in the first lines of the pastoral retrospectively assumes a performative, recitative character. The speaker, we now find, has been *reproducing* a present-tense speech of uncertain temporal provenance, a speech which, as implied by the opening lines and the literary echoes of the interruption, is a poetic project and a deliberately composed lyric rather than mere quotation. This lyric, however, is subject to revision and replacement, and so subject to alternate readings. Phoebus introduces a rereading by revising the text, correcting the poet's assertion that no "fair Guerdon" can be expected in "the homely slighted Shepherds trade."

Phoebus's interruption suggests that the text is unstable, in much the same way Terence Cave characterizes the writing of Rabelais: "the economy of shift and substitution, and the construction of a narrative *dispositio* that disperses or dissociates just when one might expect continuity and integration, constantly outwit the reader's desire for stability and certainty."[23] In this formulation, the instability and uncertainty of the fragmented text is located solely in the reading process; the instability of the text does not metonymically indicate the author's lack of control. In *Lycidas*, the interruption reveals that the first reading has no inherent stability; the instruction to revise the content of the utterance marks the preceding text as something provisional and temporary that does not claim "to represent the speaker in ways either final or safe," as Barbara Harmon says in a different context.[24] Unlike the identical, revisionary interruption of the lyric voice in Herbert's "The Collar," which both retroactively frames a present-tense lyric voice by thrusting it into the past and silences that voice to close the lyric, Phoebus's interruption is itself contained within a larger recital. The speaker simply reproduces the interruption as he redirects his poetic project along a revised trajectory.

The interruption as a frame begins an ecphrastic demarcation of the lyric. Through Phoebus's interruption, the "sad occasion dear" recedes into an unknown and unknowable past; the lyric becomes a performance, a recitation, a *reproduction*. As an object, the lyric is bounded by its own built-in obsolescence and revisability, which paradoxically establishes the lyric as fixed and immobile against the notion that writing and poetry can be reworked. Instead of revising or reworking the lyric, the speaker simply reproduces the lyric while dutifully reporting the external revision; the revision is not made to the original lyric but intrudes on it. The lyric becomes, as Rosenmeyer defines ecphrasis, "suspended, fixed and independent, within the larger whole." In the end, Phoebus's utterance does not so much revise as replace the preceding lyric; this process of replacement, which continues throughout the rest of the poem, gives the elegy its apparent dialogic or agonistic character. Yet the interruption is neither dialogic nor agonistic—there is no response by the poet; it above all determines the previous lyric as fixed and with a built-in obsolescence of the kind Plato ascribes to writing (*Phaedrus* 275D).

The frame in classical pastoral largely demarcates a conceptual space in which the framed lyric can be evaluated as an aesthetic object without reference to other concerns. The retroactive framing introduced by Phoebus's interruption, however, defines no such conceptual space for the preceding lyric. Phoebus's response, unlike the responses in classical pastoral (or, indeed, the lines in Ovid and Virgil which the interruption echoes) ignores any aesthetic concern; the poetic utterance framed by this interruption is not marked out as a work of design or craft, but simply as a fixed composition in need of revision.

The process of revision, or more specifically replacement, continues as the poet, immediately following Phoebus's speech, moves on to other matters rather than following the trajectory initiated in Phoebus's speech:

O Fountain *Arethuse*, and thou honour'd floud,
Smooth-sliding *Mincius*, crown'd with vocall reeds,
That strain I heard was of a higher mood:
But now my Oat proceeds,
And listens to the Herald of the Sea (85–89)

This unexplained and sudden abandonment of Phoebus's revision leads Stanley Fish to consider the reintroduction of the poet's voice as digressive;[25] however, neither Phoebus's interruption or the poet's new start on his lyric are digressions. The poet simply replaces Phoebus's "higher mood" and the narrative trajectory it introduces with another (separate) lyric, and this jarring replacement lends the new lyric its interpolative character. In addition, the poet's resumption of his lyric in turn ecphrastically frames Phoebus's speech by defining it as a poetic creation ("That strain I heard was of a higher mood"), and by dissociating it absolutely, in the manner of the frame in classical pastoral, from that which frames it—the following lyric. The effect, as in Phoebus's interruption, is to constitute Phoebus's speech as something fixed, an object to be reproduced but ultimately replaced.

By this point in the course of the lyric, it becomes obvious that the text, initially conceived as integral, has been breached in serious ways; moreover, the structural prominence of these breaches becomes a focal point in reading the text. The disjunctures in *Lycidas* created by Milton's poetics of replacement create a text which structurally and temporally has less in common with the syntagmatic integrity of traditional pastoral elegy and more in common with the sonnet sequence, in which narrative is left unsaid in "the blank spaces separating lyric 'fragments' . . . from each other."[26] Because the sonnet sequence simply compiles lyric "instants," it has no temporality or narrative,[27] but, most often, is characterized by a nonhierarchical, nonteleological structure of replacement. Unlike the sonnet sequence, which does not necessarily demand sequential reading, *Lycidas* promises a structural integrity and temporal continuity in the very generic contract implied from the beginning: we are to assume we are reading a *single* poem, not several, that in the end will purposefully lead to something. However, the ecphrasis of poetry at this point in *Lycidas* has established individual sections as fixed, independent, and autonomous, and severely threatens the poem's closure, undermining expectations that the lyric might "lead" somewhere.

But do the poetics of replacement in *Lycidas* create conflict or contrast, as well as fragmentation, between the ecphrastically autonomous sections of the elegy? Could not Phoebus's interruption and the poet's new start be primarily reversals rather than replacements? The search in *Lycidas* criticism for an essentially dramatic unity (implied in the terms "conflict" and "reversal") is primarily an effort to save the generic unity expected of the elegy. While Phoebus's interruption may revise the initial lyric, it does so by abruptly and permanently cutting off the trajectory of that lyric. The poet's new lyric immediately following Phoebus's interruption also permanently abandons the content introduced by the interruption. Neither break reverses or conflicts in a dramatic sense with what has gone on before; the breaks simply constitute the preceding sections as objects of recitation or reproduction, replaced with what the next break will in turn constitute as an object of recitation or reproduction. Rather than establishing a different teleological progress (one contained in a larger dramatic process of conflict or reversal), the breaks subvert the notion that such a teleological progress is possible.

The next disjuncture follows St. Peter's speech in lines 113–31, a speech which seems to be an interruption or digression. In fact, St. Peter's speech develops coherently out of a narrative and lyrical sequence—it does not interrupt but simply follows in the procession of mourners. The poet's voice in line 132 marks off the speech (and the whole of the procession itself) as something separate from the lyric to follow. We must also keep in mind that the poet does not interrupt St. Peter; rather, he is interrupting his own past-tense narrative, his own recitation. The entire procession becomes simply a narrative dead end: it is fixed and issueless in the sense that the procession, as a recited lyric, becomes dissociated absolutely from the lyric to follow. There is no conflict or reversal; the new lyric simply replaces the procession and effectively halts the elegy's development or progress up to that point.

The instruction to "Weep no more" in line 165 abruptly interrupts the entire elegy. Such sudden interruptions of a lament by a command to cease mourning are ubiquitous in medieval and Renaissance pastoral elegy. These interruptions, however, occur in dramatic situations in which one speaker, aware of the mourned one's imparadisement, interrupts the lament of another speaker in order to close the work with a *consolatio.* The dramatic *consolatio* in medieval and Renaissance pastoral elegy is principally dialogic and responsive; the speaker does not so much interrupt the lament as respond to it with the specific goal of providing an alternative perspective, an ordering logos that puts an end to the discourse. In *Lycidas,* however, the speaker is putting an end not to someone else's lament, but, presumably, to his own. This interruption does not develop out of the narrative sequence preceding it and has no dialogic or specifically dramatic justification. The *consolatio* does no more than abruptly replace the lament; it represents no growth or development in the speaker, nor, in fact, any progress in the lament. The trajectory of the lament is simply cut short, framed by the interruption as a composition from out of the past, fixed, autonomous, and ultimately abandoned.

The concluding frame explicitly sets off the entire elegy as a recitation, and in the process pushes the recitation out of the (seemingly) present into an unknown past ("Thus sang the uncouth swain," 186). The lyric loses any overheard quality it may have had and becomes a performance; all temporality and contingency are removed from the lyric as it enters a symbolic time of fixed reproduction. The elegy, which has throughout been broken apart by the disjunctures into recited or reproduced fragments, strung together like the lyrical instants of a sonnet sequence, is marked off by the concluding frame as a performance of a fixed text, as in classical pastoral elegy. The question of authorship or subjectivity—of the originary "proper name" that makes the lyric univocally comprehensible—is secondary to the objective status of the lyric. As in the retrospective framing in Virgil's fifth eclogue, the "new" speaker established by the frame brings into relief the objective, reproducible quality of the lyric. The lyric, fixed by its ecphrasis, is endlessly reproducible; the poem as artifact is disengaged from time, occasion, and authorship.

Ultimately this autonomous, objective, reproducible quality the elegy gains in its ecphrasis results in the final replacement in the poem. We have seen that the poem progresses not on any principle of development or dramatic contrast, but by simple replacement of one lyric fragment by another. The obsolescence of the written, crafted work does not allow for revision or development, but only for the alternation of one fixed, independent utterance after another. The final replacement is, basically, a walking away from the poem, a walking away that has implied for some readers Milton's abandonment of small genres for larger poetic projects, or possibly Milton's abandonment of the poetic vocation for a more politically engaged career. At the most fundamental level, however, the frame neither sanctions nor implies any biographical reading; it indicates merely that the composition or recitation of the lyric has reached a dead end. The elegy becomes immediately obsolete following its production or reproduction. Through its autonomy and fixity, it loses any dialogic or interactive relation to the constantly changing world of actuality, the world of "Tomorrow" and "Pastures new," and so loses any (temporary) claim it may have had on the swain's—and the reader's—attention. This closure through ecphrastic fixity and autonomy is primarily responsible for the troubled relation the lyric gains to actuality. The price for this type of closure—and it is possible that all poetry is a kind of ecphrasis—is fencing out the uncharted territory lying outside the lyric, the "fresh Woods, and Pastures new" (193). Although fixed and "timeless," the lyric is still deeply embedded in a world of temporality and change.

This final replacement (or abandonment) seems to devalue the poetic project, but, in fact, does no more than foreground the immediate obsolescence of the fixed, crafted, and written work. The structure of the poem throughout draws attention to the nondialogic nature of the fixed work of art in the same way the ecphrasis of poetry in classical pastoral draws attention to the separation of the crafted work from the actuality marked off from it. Milton simply strings together lyric fragments, each one cutting off or abandoning the lyrical or narrative trajectory of the preceding fragment. This structure draws attention to the fixed quality of each lyric fragment but still allows for some kind of revision—in the case of static, autonomous compositions, however, the only revision possible is replacement. The elegy concludes finally with an ecphrastic fixing of the lyric which purchases closure at the expense of the work's continuing interaction with temporality and change; the elegy goes no further than the impassable boundary of its closure. The work, timeless but obsolete at its conclusion, is abandoned, walked away from, and ultimately replaced in the ongoing process of experience.

Stanford University

NOTES

1. The range of possible narratives is as wide as the range of interpretations of the poem. For the poem as a "development," see Clay Hunt, *"Lycidas" and the Italian Critics* (New Haven, 1979), p. 126; as a "struggle" or "conflict," see Donald Friedman, "*Lycidas:* The Swain's Paideia," in *Milton Studies* III, ed. James D. Simmonds (Pittsburgh, 1971), p. 5; as "drama," J. Martin Evans, *The Road from Horton: Looking Backwards in "Lycidas,"* (Victoria, B.C., 1983), p. 67; as "dialectic," Jon S. Lawry, " 'Eager Thought': Dialectic in *Lycidas,*" *PMLA* LXXVII (1962), 27; as argument, Eric Smith, *By Mourning Tongues: Studies in English Elegy* (Ipswich, Eng., 1977), p. 37; as a "ritual" of gradually readjusted focus, Stewart Baker, "Milton's Uncouth Swain," in *Milton Studies* III, ed. James D. Simmonds (Pittsburgh, 1971), p. 38. F. T. Prince discerns vague "movements of thought and emotion": *The Italian Element in Milton's Verse* (Oxford, 1954), p. 170.

2. For Friedman, "The Swain's Paideia," p. 19, the poem documents Milton's conversion and subsequent dedication to the Christian faith; Evans, *Road to Horton,* pp. 22, 70, discovers a process of disengagement from the poetic project analogous to conversion. For Isabel MacCaffrey, the poem does not explicitly refer to Milton, but recounts the autobiographical journey of "the speaker" from innocence to experience ("*Lycidas:* The Poet in a Landscape," in *The Lyric and Dramatic Milton: Selected Papers from the English Institute,*

ed. Joseph H. Summers [New York, 1965], pp. 71, 76–78). Autobiography in these works is, of course, only marginal to the fictional world of the pastoral; generically, autobiography seems to depend "on actual and potentially verifiable events in a less ambivalent way than fiction does," and to belong to "a simpler mode of referentiality, of representation, and of diegesis . . . rooted in a single subject whose identity is defined by the uncontested readability of his proper name" (Paul de Man, "Autobiography as De-Facement," in *The Rhetoric of Romanticism* [New York, 1984], p. 68). The marginality of the autobiographical referent in Milton's elegy is most evident in the move away from the autobiographical subject at the end of the work. This lies behind critical caveats, such as David Shelley Berkeley, *Inwrought with Figures Dim: A Reading of Milton's "Lycidas"* (Paris, 1974), p. 12, not to confuse the persona (the swain) with the author.

3. Autobiographical readings are cited above, note 2. For the typological reading in its most complete form, see Berkeley, *Inwrought with Figures Dim;* also Caroline W. Mayerson, "The Orpheus Image in *Lycidas*," *PMLA* LXIV (1949), 189–207, and Rosemond Tuve, "Theme, Pattern and Imagery in *Lycidas*," in *Images and Themes in Five Poems of Milton* (Cambridge, Mass., 1962), pp. 73–111. For the dialogue between the poet and his tradition, see Berkeley, *Inwrought with Figures Dim,* pp. 205–06. For a dialogue or agon between genres or lyrical modes, see Friedman, "The Swain's Paideia"; also MacCaffrey, "The Poet in a Landscape," pp. 71, 75, 78; Baker, "Milton's Uncouth Swain," pp. 39–43; and Edward W. Tayler, "*Lycidas* in Christian Time," in *Milton's Poetry: Its Development in Time* (Pittsburgh, 1979), ch. 2. For the speaker's efforts to assert his own voice over the "anonymous" conventions of tradition, that is, to "retain control" of the poem, see Friedman, "The Swain's Paideia," pp. 14–16; Baker, "Milton's Uncouth Swain," p. 50; and Stanley Fish, "*Lycidas:* A Poem Finally Anonymous," in *Glyph: Johns Hopkins Textual Studies*, vol. 8 (Baltimore, 1981), pp. 1–18.

4. On the origins of pastoral and its early concern with the nature and status of poetry, see David Halperin, *Before Pastoral: Theocritus and the Ancient Tradition of Bucolic Poetry* (New Haven, 1983), pp. 118–31, 161–89, 244–57. For an overview of the pastoral eclogue in the Middle Ages and the Renaissance, see Helen Cooper, *Pastoral: Medieval Into Renaissance* (Ipswich, Australia, 1977), pp. 8–46, 100–26.

5. Fish, "A Poem Finally Anonymous," p. 12. Evans, *The Road to Horton*, p. 69, for whom the poem is "one long act of disengagement," has an essentially similar view.

6. Thomas G. Rosenmeyer, *The Green Cabinet: Theocritus and the European Pastoral Lyric* (Berkeley and Los Angeles, 1969), p. 192.

7. See Salvatore Nicosia, *Teocrito e l'arte figurata* (Palermo, 1968), p. 36; A.S.F. Gow, *Theocritus*, 2 vols. (Cambridge, 1952) vol. II, p. 14; Halperin, *Before Pastoral*, p. 162; Gilbert Lawall, *Theocritus' Coan Pastorals: A Poetry Book* (Cambridge, Mass., 1967), p. 27; Ulrich Ott, *Die Kunst des Gegensatzes in Theokrits Hirtengedichten* (Hildesheim, 1969), p. 85. With the exceptions of Idylls II and IV, the first eleven idylls represent some form of the framed lyric and suggest that the "primary mode" from the genre's outset was the country singing match most typically presented in *Idyll* VIII: Anna Rist, *The Poems of Theocritus*, (Chapel Hill, N.C., 1978), pp. 224–25.

8. All quotations and translations from Theocritus are from Gow, *Theocritus*.

9. See Rosenmeyer, *The Green Cabinet*, p. 119, and B. Effe, "Die Destruktion der Tradition Theokrits mythologische Gedichte," *Rheinische Museum für Philologie* CXXI (1978), 50–53, for the importance of aesthetic distance in Theocritus.

10. This echoes the earlier comment spoken by the goatherd in the opening frame: ἅδιον, ὦ ποιμήν, τὸ τεὸν μέλος ἢ τὸ καταχὲς / τῆν' ἀπὸ τᾶς πέτρας καταλείβεται ὑψόθεν ὕδωρ ("Sweeter, shepherd, falls thy song than yonder stream that tumbles plashing from the

rocks" (7–8). For sweetness as a characteristic of bucolic poetry and how this "sweetness" specifically refers to a pleasure which is detached from considerations of utility in both Theocritus and Virgil, see E. A. Schmidt, *Poetische Reflexion: Vergils Bukolik* (Munich, 1972), pp. 27–32.

11. Annabel Patterson, *Pastoral and Ideology: Virgil to Valéry* (Berkeley and Los Angeles, 1987), pp. 33–34, 89–90.

12. Halperin, *Before Pastoral*, p. 164; for Virgil, see Rosenmeyer, *The Green Cabinet*, pp. 120–22, and Schmidt, *Poetische Reflexion*, pp. 200–01.

13. All quotations and translations of Virgil taken from *Virgil: Eclogues, Georgics, Aeneid I–VI*, ed. and trans. H. Rushton Fairclough, rev. ed. (Cambridge, Mass., 1965).

14. For the necessary connection between detail and well-craftedness and the aesthetic response of delight in Roman poetics and rhetoric, see Wesley Trimpi, "Horace's 'Ut pictura poesis': The Argument for Stylistic Decorum," *Traditio* XXXIV (1978), 33–43.

15. Servius Grammaticus, *In Vergilii Bucolica et Georgica Commentarii*, ed. George Thilo (Lipsius, 1887), pp. 4–5, 108–09. See also Juan Luis Vives's specifically political response (particularly in relation to the sack of Rome) to the first and ninth eclogues in his *In Bucolici Vergilii interpretatio, potissimum allegorica* (Basel, 1537). On Vives, see Patterson, *Pastoral*, pp. 85–92.

16. Patterson, *Pastoral*, pp. 134, 188–89; Evans, *The Road to Horton*, p. 33.

17. For example, Petrarch's "Galatea" eclogue, Boccaccio's "Olympia" eclogue, Alamanni's first eclogue. English examples include Gager's *Daphnis* and Spenser's November *Æglogue*. The latter adds a double perspective: not only does the lament evoke grief, it also produces a curiously contrary pleasure at the quality of the lyric.

18. Paul de Man, "Autobiography," p. 68.

19. MacCaffrey, "The Poet in a Landscape," pp. 77–78; Friedman, "The Swain's Paideia," pp. 11, 20.

20. Fish, "A Poem Finally Anonymous," pp. 16–17; Evans, *The Road to Horton*, p. 68.

21. "Begin then, Sisters of the Sacred Well" (*Lycidas*, 15); "Ἄρχετε βουκολικᾶς, Μοῖσαι φίλαι, ἄρχετ' ἀοιδᾶς" ("Begin, dear Muses, begin the pastoral song.") (Theocritus, *Idyll* I, 64); "incipe Maenalios mecum, mea tibia, versus" (Virgil, *Eclogue* VIII, 21).

22. Virgil:

Cynthius aurem
vellit et admonuit: "pastorem, Tityre, pinguis
pascere oportet ovis, deductum dicere carmen.

[The Cynthian plucked my ear and warned me: "A shepherd, Tityrus, should feed sheep that are fat, but sing a lay fine-spun."]

Ovid:

Arma gravi numero violentaque bella parabam
edere, materia conveniente modis.
par erat inferior versus; risisse Cupido
dicitur atque unum surripuisse pedem.

[Arms, and the violent deeds of war, I was making ready to sound forth—in weighty measures, with matter suited to the measure. The second verse was equal to the first—but Cupid, they say, with a laugh stole away one foot.]

(Text and translation from *Ovid: "Heroides" and "Amores"*, ed. and trans. Grant Showerman [Cambridge, Mass., 1971])

23. Terence Cave, "Reading Rabelais: Variations on the Rock of Virtue," in *Literary Theory/Renaissance Texts*, ed. Patricia Parker and David Quint (Baltimore, 1986), p. 85.

24. Barbara Leah Harmon, "The Fiction of Coherence: George Herbert's 'The Collar'," *PMLA* XCIII (1978), 872.

25. Fish, "A Poem Finally Anonymous," p. 12.

26. John Freccero, "The Fig Tree and the Laurel: Petrarch's Poetics," *Diacritics* V (1975), 20.

27. Ibid., p. 21.

LYCIDAS: ETERNITY AS ARTIFICE

Thomas H. Blackburn

THOUGH READERS from Samuel Johnson to John Crowe Ransom have questioned the aesthetic, emotional, and intellectual coherence of *Lycidas*, the most prominent current readings of the elegy see it as achieving in a unity of form and content the status of eternal artifact, an image or mimesis of transcended change which confers the benefits of that transcendence on reader and speaker/poet alike. Two brief quotations from Edward W. Tayler's essay on the poem may represent the conclusions of this sort of reading at its best:[1]

Both *Lycidas* and Lycidas sink in order to mount. By what may be thought of as an almost muscular effort of the verse itself—the successive movements of the three sections—Milton readies us to acknowledge yet once more the truth of the Christian truism, for this pastoral monody owes a large part of its artistic success to its having been constructed in imitation of itself. *Lycidas* endures, triumphantly, as a work of art that *is* what it *says*.

. . . .

The natural cycle that had been interrupted within nature and time before the season due has been perfected in the eternal realm. Three times, following the efforts of the pastoral singer, we have sought the greatest vision, each time mounting higher than the time before, until at last we see the analogy of the sun made good by the Son—no fond dream, no false surmise. It is the "season due." (Patrides, p. 314)

While I do find that many aspects of form, image, and statement in the elegy support this notion of the work as an effective *mimesis* invoking the real presence of a "paradise within," my aim is to suggest the simultaneous presence of a counterreading that comprehends and reveals eternity *as* artifice.[2] My focus is on the gaps in the development of a transcendent reading, the moments when the poem seems undecidable, silent, or contradictory—as in the recourse to pastoral images for a vision which purports to transcend the limits of pastoral—and on the way in which the elegy at once suggests and violates the sort of formal unity which may represent the changeless stability of art free from nature's vicissitudes. It is toward this final point that my analysis will move, but I first need to admit my understanding of what the poem is about.

M. H. Abrams, writing in 1957, identified "five types" of *Lycidas,* adding what he called his "doggedly literal" sixth, necessarily superior, reading (Patrides, p. 225). In the succeeding four decades I am sure at least half a dozen more *Lycidas*'s could easily be identified, including dialectical, pedagogical, and oedipal versions, several of which Abrams alludes to in the 1983 postscript to the revised edition of the Patrides anthology, which first printed the 1957 article (Patrides, pp. 341–45). I am much less concerned than Abrams with confining the poem's possibilities to a single subject or purpose, and much less certain of the possibility of a "literal" reading, though I willingly agree with him that how one interprets depends largely on the perspective one brings to the work. I read the elegy as at least "about" Edward King, Milton, the pastoral tradition, poetry and poets, death, and the central mystery of Christian faith. Though the issue of the speaker, or speakers, in the poem is even more complex than most readers assume, I see *Lycidas* as a dramatic search for a satisfying answer to large questions which the poem treats as urgently occasioned by the death of one with whom the speaker has multiple affinities. The questions can be summed up in the query which Adam in *Paradise Lost,* having in vision witnessed the murder of Abel by Cain, addresses to Michael: "Is Piety thus and pure Devotion paid?" (XI, 452).[3] Like the repeated questions in *Lycidas* about the value of chaste poetry and religious vocation, Adam's query incorporates an expectation, or at least a wish, that virtue should receive some reward other than untimely and apparently undeserved death; it makes problematic, at least for a moment, the distributive aspect of divine justice from the perspective of one who is seeking to discover how to live "in this world of evil, in the midst whereof God hath placed us unavoidably" (*Areopagitica,* p. 733).

The formal configuration of the last eight lines of *Lycidas* for many readers seems to affirm and embody the achievement of an answer to fearful doubts about the destiny of one who virtuously pursues the "faithful Herdman's art" in poetry and priesthood. Fully rhymed in an *ottava rima* and syntactically a complete unit, the stanza appears to confirm the resolution of the uncertainties which drive earlier movements in the elegy. As the end to a procession of verse paragraphs so varied in length and irregular in rhyme scheme as almost to deserve John Crow Ransom's epithets, "willful and illegal," the fully formed stanza also contrasts specifically with two earlier imperfect intimations of form (Patrides, p. 75). The first of these is the opening fourteen-line paragraph of the elegy, which to many readers has seemed a shadowy sonnet. The hint of a form not perfected suggests a formal analogy to the speaker's announced emotional and artistic unreadiness to deal with the poetic task at hand. The integrity of the closing *ottava rima*, in contrast, would thus express dramatic arrival at confident artistic control and emotional resolution. Louis Martz suggests a second contrast based on the evocation of sonnet form rather than its imperfection. The shadowy sonnet, he argues, calls appropriately at the opening of the elegy on the form's "tradition of intimate personal utterance," while the *ottava rima* stanza, associated with the narrative objectivity assumed by epic poets, signals at the end of the poem the speaker's success in dealing with the work of mourning.[4]

The second trace of stanza form is in the *ottava rima* scheme of the rhymes in St. Peter's speech (124–31). One might see these rhymes, using Martz's insight, as fitting for a speech which promises an eventual objectivity of justice. This eventuality, however, is not realized within the poem and the lines do not really form a stanza since line 124 is part of a separate syntactical unit. These lines, moreover, conclude with the notorious crux of the "two-handed engine" (130). Set against these two evocative but incomplete forms the coda might well be read as a final turn from intimate anguish to objectivity in the calm of regular form. So interpreted, the coda becomes an important part of those readings which see the poem—albeit by a bewildering variety of pathways—arriving through a complex yet finally unified movement at an unequivocal emotional, theological, and aesthetic conclusion.

The coda, however, is not placed in the poem only by its contrasts with preceding irregularities. Though in that aspect it may seem to epitomize closure, from another perspective it works to reveal closure itself as a "false surmise," through the elegy's most radical departure from the conventions of form which it evokes. In placement and content the coda recalls the closing half of the narrative framing devices conventional in pastoral poems generally, in dream-vision poems, and in funeral elegies such as Milton's own Latin Elegy II. But *Lycidas* has no opening "frame." Ellen Z. Lambert is among those critics who note this anomaly: "Milton is, to my knowledge, the only pastoral elegist to dispense with the opening frame while retaining the closing one." She goes on, however, to treat the coda as nonetheless expressing closure as the culmination of the elegist's gradual discovery of "those assurances of order traditionally conferred by the frame."[5] Though this analysis recognizes the way in which the coda evokes an idea of order, it ignores the even greater impact of the unexpected emergence of the half-frame. The coda at once evokes the framing convention and calls attention to its violation.

The half-frame also introduces as speaker an equally unexpected new voice. This new voice further surprises us by calling the speaker of the preceding verses an "*uncouth* swain" (my emphasis). Many readers, rightly impressed by the erudition and complex art of those verses, simply ignore the negative connotations of this naming. Among those who do pause at the appellation, some turn only to the sense of "uncouth" as "unknown," suggesting a relationship between the swain and the Milton of *Sonnet VII* or *Ad Patrem,* acutely conscious of the fact that he had not yet made his mark in the world. Brooks and Hardy do note the surprise of the coda and the derogatory connotations of the adjective as it links crudity and ignorance to being unknown in civil society. They limit this criticism, however, to the "Doric" strain in the swain's utterances, to the limitations of that low pastoral which the elegy finally functions to subsume in "the truth of Christian revelation" (Patrides, p. 156). Tayler recognizes the unavoidable force of "uncouth" as "ignorant and rude," and as perhaps "afford[ing] the poet some mild amusement" (Patrides, pp. 314–15), and reminds us that the swain initially presents himself as "uncouth" in that sense in his plucking unripe poetic leaves with "forced fingers rude" (4).

By the coda, however, rudeness and ignorance are supposed to have been replaced by transcendent vision, by an apotheosis not only of Lycidas, but also of the art of song which completes the work of mourning and the voice that sings it—or so most readers of the elegy would have us conclude. Tayler integrates further connotations of "uncouth" into his exemplary reading noted earlier: "the song has moved from the personal to the impersonal, from the vision bounded by time to the vision of eternity. The swain, no longer merely unknown and rustic, may now bear as well the other meanings of *uncouth* that were current at the time: marvelous, uncommon, strange, wonderful—as in the 'uncouth revelations' of St. Bridgit (1648; cited OED) (Patrides, p. 317).

The release of these positive connotations linking the swain, as Tayler puts it, to "Lycidas and the sun and the Son and (hopefully) the reader," depends on the reader's assent to a prior metamorphosis in the pastoral vision, though it is also treated as evidence for that assent. Caught up in this process, the continuing presence of the negative meanings seems to fade away. I shall later question the quality of that prior metamorphosis in the vision of Lycidas among the saints, as well as the coda's utility as evidence for it. For the moment, I want only to note that the multiple possibilities of meaning for "uncouth," and the difficulty of deciding which shade of meaning should prevail in context, present in small an image of the difficulty of reading *Lycidas.* I hope to show that interpretations which subsume the unruly possibilities in pursuit of a unified vision of art and belief are reductive. They fail to do justice to *Lycidas* in particular, and in general to Milton's own lifelong resistance to simple closure, as the equivalent in art and life of "cloistered virtue."

I have thus far argued that the absence of an introductory framing narrative counters and subverts the closural implications of the coda's *ottava rima* form. I do not intend, however, to argue that this subversion negates closure absolutely—that too would be reductive. I propose a mode of representation in *Lycidas* which, to put it fashionably, resists reading—if by reading we mean fixing on a single univocal signified for each signifier—at the same time as it expresses the necessity of reading, of making the choices which enable act and song. Before exploring further the ways in which the swain's "uncouthness" points to this mode of representation, I want to look at several other instances in which the language of the coda invites a negative reading of its apparent affirmations.

In one of the few attempts at a reading of *Lycidas* from a postmodern critical perspective, Herman Rapaport suggests that the coda is one in a series with the swain's earlier repetitions of return to a pastoral landscape after successive assays at resolution fell short of closure. That he is headed for "fresh *woods*" and "*pastures* new" (my emphasis), Rapaport suggests, indicates "that he has not been able to overcome or exit from the problematic of loss."[6] Many other readers have found that "fresh" and "new" qualify the rural scene to signify that the swain departs for "woods" and "pastures" essentially different from the fragile lawns and woods of the shattered idyll once shared with Lycidas.[7] Such readings of the coda's landscape again presume that the elegy pits a pastoral with naturalistic and pagan mythological referents against a second whose context is the "Good Shepherd" of the Christian supernatural. When this second set of referents is evoked through the "dear might of him who walk't the waves" (173), the "false surmise" of images and figures traditional in pagan versions of immortality is said to become privileged as "true surmise": a set of "shadowy types," as it were, in which the promise of Christian eternity may be perceived.

We may question, however, the extent to which "fresh" and "new" can effectively confer privilege when we look at close verbal contexts in the poem rather than depending on assumptions of a prior metamorphosis in vision. The word *fresh* appears twice before in the poem: first in the "fresh dews of night" which satisfied the thirst of the flocks in the recollected Cambridge idyll (29), and again in the penultimate effort to seek pastoral consolation in those flowers of the spring on whose "fresh lap" the "swart star sparely looks" (139). These pleasant associations, however, will not by themselves suffice to free *fresh* from the network of difference which is its context in the poem and thus to signify a transformed value. Just as *new* depends on *old,* so is the very idea of freshness defined by the always threatening alternative of staleness or rot (e.g., by "Canker" or "Frost" or "rank mists" [45–47]). "Fresh dews" are fully subject to "heavy change" as the loss of Lycidas affects all objects of evanescence and innocence. Though the dogstar may cast its withering look only sparingly on the freshness of spring flowers, it reminds us again of the transcience of these natural beauties and their inadequacy as literal consolations for human mortality. *New* and *fresh* cannot so easily escape their contexts to create immutable landscapes. The final scene of the elegy remains no less susceptible to the ruthless shears of the furies, or the mysterious "curses dark / That sunk so low that sacred head" of Lycidas (102). That pastures and woods appear renewed and refreshed for the swain does nonetheless point to a changed vision, but not one which finds the swain impossibly freed from the risks of time by incorporation into a literal vision of eternity.

Another detail in the coda may involve a return as much as a new beginning. The "blue" of the swain's mantle has come to be read primarily as an emblem of hope, again signifying the mourner's transformation.[8] Blue, however, is also the hue of Cambridge University. Camus, the river god who represents the university in mourning for its "dearest pledge," is dressed in academic robes adapted to pastoral allegory as "mantle hairy" and "bonnet sedge" (104). The "mantle blue," then, as adapted academic gown, hints at a return to the university where Lycidas and the surviving singer practiced their poetry to the delight of "old Damoetas," and pursued their learning for that other pastoral trade, the ministry. In the context of the coda, to wrap oneself in such a garment is, on the one hand, to reclaim the practice of those "trades," the temporal value of which the unresolved fate of Lycidas had called into question. In the tradition of the pastoral elegy we may also recognize that the swain's mantle affirms his status as inheritor of Lycidas's pastoral role. On the other hand, we know that neither all the powers of song nor all the pastoral virtues nurtured at the university could keep Lycidas literally alive in the swain's world. Any assumption that merit as poet or priest will guarantee long life or mortal renown belongs to the same world of "false surmise" as the illusion of immortal flowers decking the "Laureate hearse where *Lycid* lies" (151).

On a more literal level, the swain's "twitch[ing]" of the mantle seems to image the settling of a blanketlike garment closer about the shoulders, perhaps as the setting sun takes warmth from the air. The need for such a mantle reminds us that the "mount[ing] high" of "him who walk'd the waves" has not repealed the cycle of light and dark for men "in this world of evil." Though sunrise may figure Christ's resurrection, the swain must continue to live in a world where sunset also figures a daily repetition of the lapsarian "eclipse" in which was rigged the ship of Lycidas's untimely fate.

I have been suggesting ways in which the coda, in its structural relation to the elegy as a whole, and in some aspects of its content, opens the possibility of a counter reading, one which questions the completeness of a supposed transfiguration of time and landscape. The shift to a third person speaker in the coda may also lead us in a negative direction. Donald Friedman, like Tayler, finds ironic humor in his speaker's insistence on the rustic artlessness of the highly wrought verses which have gone before, but though self-deprecating humor is attractive, that is not all there is in the shift (Patrides, p. 299). Labeling the preceding singer an "uncouth swain," and his song a "Doric lay," distances us from him. He becomes the object of the discourse of a superior speaker rather than the speaking subject of his own song. Looking back at the song from this distance, we may wish to ask whether there is some context other than the rustic associations of the poem's conventions which defines the entire preceding utterance as "uncouth" or "swainish."

The fundamental paradox of the pastoral convention makes "swainish" discourse the vehicle for complex views of life and art, views which we take to be those of the "couth" city poet who creates the country voice. The coda of *Lycidas*, though it maintains the pastoral scene, reveals that superior "city" voice. This superiority suggests in part a self-referential knowledge of the conventionality of the pastoral genre itself. It also implies recognition of the conventionality—the artifice—of the immortality mythos. Immortality, like the bygone days of pastoral innocence in the childhood of man and his world, can be known only as a fiction by fallen mortals, who are all by definition "uncouth" when it comes to actual experience of life after death or to the larger issue of knowing God as he "really is." The swain is uncouth because he cannot "know" God in any way beyond his own "pin-fold" perspective, in any unmediated way which can literally perceive or express radical otherness. In this aspect, the swain may represent the irremediable mortal ignorance of all humankind—the poet's recognition that nothing in the poem, nothing in the conventions of human art or human language, can represent God without an accommodation to human capacities.

In making this argument I am inevitably arguing as well that Milton, creator and manipulator of all the voices in the poem, is in some way conscious of the limits of expression defined above. In a more extensive study, I believe a case could be made for a progressive decline in Milton's naive confidence that the "deep transported mind may soar / Above the wheeling poles, and at Heav'n's door / Look in, and see each blissful deity," (*Vacation Exercise*, 33–35), even while the effort to "know God aright" remains the center of his agenda as man and poet.[9] The notion of accommodation developed in *Paradise Lost* and *Christian Doctrine* is usually read to affirm the possibility of conveying to mortals knowledge of God and his plan for man. Accommodation, however, as this passage from *Christian Doctrine* makes clear, is necessary precisely because it is impossible to know God "as he really is":

> When we speak of knowing God, it must be understood with reference to the imperfect comprehension of man; for to know God as he really is, far transcends the powers of man's thoughts, much more of his perception. . . . Our safest way is to form in our minds such a conception of God, as shall correspond with his own delineation and representation of himself in the sacred writings. For granting that both in the literal and figurative descriptions of God, he is not exhibited as he really is, but in such a manner as may be within the scope of our comprehensions, yet we ought to entertain such a conception of him, as he, in condescending to accommodate himself to our capacities has shown that he desires we should conceive. (Hughes, p. 905)

By no intellectual or sensible effort can one reach the transcendent other, the signified which would fix the meaning of all signs.[10]

Raphael (most prominently) in *Paradise Lost*, like Milton in the passage above, urges the reader of the available signs to suspend awareness of their limits, as he wonders how he may

> unfold
> The secrets of another world, perhaps
> Not lawful to reveal? yet for thy good
> This is dispens't, and what surmounts the reach
> Of human sense, I shall delineate so,
> By lik'ning spiritual to corporal forms,
> As may express them best, though what if Earth
> Be but the shadow of Heav'n, and things therein
> Each to other like, more than on Earth is thought? (V, 568–76)

Raphael's speech suggests that one should not question too far the degree to which accommodated expression really does bring one to "Heaven's door," but it never itself gets beyond terms such as "shadow" and "like," which always point at least as much to difference as to identity. To say, as Milton does in *Christian Doctrine* and through Raphael, that it is impossible, and perhaps even dangerous, to know God as he really is, but that we can know he wishes us to accept accommodated revelation as a sufficient sign of his reality, clearly begs the question: a priori knowledge obtained from some source other than the accommodated signs to be validated is necessary. The language of scripture and of the poet who seeks to share the offices of scripture can be known as true expressions of divine reality only when interpreted with faith as a premise. Without that extrinsic source of privilege one faces only an array of signs endlessly deferred, "images that fresh images beget," without ever reaching the source of all images. The rereading of the "low" pastoral images as true signs of the "good shepherd," and the reading of the vision of apotheosis as a scene truly other than the "cursed" lawns and rills of life, require privileging by faith. Moving from formal irregularity to regularity, from "rural ditties" to sacred song, from questions to what seems to be an answer, *Lycidas* has seemed for many readers to go beyond deferred signification to reveal that absent term which confers privilege, that is, to reach somehow beyond its language to enact faith. The counterreading I am exploring recognizes the force of this supposed penetration, but finds in its climactic moments only another layer of artifice and a continuing absence—not eternal reality fixed forever, but, again, "fresh images."

Any argument for this particular variety of double reading must rest not only on interpretation of the coda, but also on a rereading, which the coda encourages, of the ostensibly transcendent movement that immediately precedes it, that "prior metamorphosis of vision" to which I earlier alluded. I have characterized the coda as a "return" to the mutable "lower" pastoral landscape of pagan myths and symbolic flora which the elegy, in the vision of heavenly groves and streams, is presumed to have transcended. A significant "return," however, takes place before the more obvious shift in the coda. James Holly Hanford notes this earlier reversion, and is puzzled by it, but, as a solution to his unease with the invocation of Lycidas as "Genius of the shore," offers only Milton's obeisance to tradition (Patrides, p. 44). Renato Poggioli simply conflates pagan and Christian terms to see Lycidas made "sacred patron" and "holy protector" of the shore and seafarers.[11]

After convincing us of the pagan genealogy of the genius in Milton's earlier poems, William Oram nonetheless asserts its function here as an image of Christ and an "abiding example of the dedicated Christian."[12] But such claims cannot disassociate the "Genius of the shore" from the kind of pastoral that in preceding repetitions signified the failure of "higher mood" to bring closure. Lycidas does not here become Christ, or even an uneasily Roman Catholic intercessory saint, but joins the company of the nymphs, of Calliope herself, the local druidic deities, Phoebus Apollo, St. Peter, and even St. Michael (as near an approach to a Christian "Genius of the shore" as the elegy affords).[13] None of these "holy protectors" could insure long life or just reward for Lycidas, nor can the "Genius" he becomes truly protect the surviving swain. Reversion here to the "low" pastoral norm of local deities reveals parallels in structure with the preceding major movements of the elegy, in which each attempt to reach closure ends in continuing deferral and reveals the failure of a "higher mood" to reach beyond itself. That the final movement does lead to the end of the poem can be read as defining a crucial difference within the parallelism, but the parallel also places the purportedly transcendent vision itself as yet another reentry into the maze of repetitions which characterize mortal life and language.

Simply to assert that the landscape which Lycidas now enjoys is of "*other* groves and streams" (174, emphasis added) cannot decisively differentiate them from the fragile pastoral of lawns and forsaken primroses, nor from the uncertainties of the "woods" and "pastures" the "uncouth" singer will enter at the end of the elegy. Driven by the swain's declaration that Lycidas is not dead, we may at first want to assume that the analogy between his "mounting high" and that of the sun somehow voids the sequel of sunset, but again that assumption requires a leap past language which language cannot make. The scene "out of nature" must still bear nature's form if it is to be intelligible. The moment one aspires to give the absolute otherness which defines divinity a "local habitation and a name," a fall into language takes place and accommodation cannot be avoided—heaven will have groves and streams and Lycidas will return in the mundane fiction of "Genius of the shore."

I realize that this denial of the transforming power of the swain's vision goes against the testimony of many very skillful and sensitive readers of the poem. It presses against the emotional power which I feel in the cadences of the saints "That sing, and singing in their glory move, / And wipe the tears for ever from his eyes" (180–81), and the vision does lead to the end of the swain's mourning and of his song. I nevertheless understand this vision in the perspective of the declaration which both precedes it and purports to follow from it, and of the descent to "genius" and the coda which come after. The space between the exhortation to the poet-loving dolphins and the command that the shepherds "Weep no more" is one of profound silence (164–65). I know of no explanation—psychological, imagistic, or structural—which satisfactorily bridges the gap between the new command and the last appeals to "false surmise" in the hope that St. Michael or a dolphin might "waft" Lycidas back unscathed to the shores from which he departed. How one reads that silence will determine, or rather overdetermine, a reading of the vision. Only the assumption that the silence expresses the influx of divine inspiration will lead to the further assumption that the vision is "real" in a presence beyond the language in which it must be expressed. The privileging of this assumption depends, as I suggested earlier, on an a priori commitment to that reality as the basis of interpretation, or at least on a critical commitment to upholding the seamless artistic unity of the elegy, the "prophetic strain" of its author, or all of these. To deconstruct that privileging does not necessarily make a reader "of the Devil's party." I would contend that understanding a "double" reading of *Lycidas* allies one with Milton's party, and humanity's.

In *Lycidas* the superior voice of the speaker in the coda has revealed the limitations which the necessity of accommodation places on the song and the understanding of the shepherd elegist. As the restorative effect on the swain seems to affirm the reality of transcendent referents for his pastoral fictions, this speaker makes us nonetheless aware that it is still artifice which results, and insists on the literal inexpressibility of that reality. The pastoral vision in which Lycidas is immortally justified remains at the same distance from any transcendent truth as the "trifling fictions" of the "lower" strain. Entry into any reality "invisible to mortal sight" (*PL* III, 55) remains deferred throughout the elegy, not only at the end of the Phoebus and St. Peter sections. This deferral is inherent in the language of the "higher" strain itself, and is recognized in the series of returns and new beginnings which make up the movements of the poem, including the descent to "Genius of the shore" and the "Tomorrow" of the coda's objectified swain.

The deferral of unaccommodated reunion with Lycidas does not for me, as it might for Dr. Johnson, require a negative reading of the elegy as a whole. Deferral is essential for the life of the swain and the song of the elegist. The process of mourning originates in the mourner's identification with the departed, but can only end if the necessity of separation is accepted. The swain's (and "Milton's") likenesses to Lycidas give rise to anxieties about his own future, and then to the possibility of finding consolation and assurance in the vision of Lycidas among the saints. At this point, however, complete identification must also be resisted. Genuine closure of the gap between mortal and immortal sight requires and is synonymous with death, or at least with an ecstatic inspiration which escapes the human condition at the cost of a paralysis of action and speech.[14] I sense in the return to the visible landscape in the coda a relief much like that when Milton as narrator in Book VII of *Paradise Lost* asserts, "More safe I Sing with mortal voice" (24), as the epic scene becomes "narrower bound / Within the visible Diurnal Sphere" (21–22). In Book III the attempt to express God directly, as the narrator wonders whether he may do so "unblam'd," brings the poet to the brink of silence in "Bright effluence of bright essence increate" (6) and "Dark with excessive bright" (380), both formulations at some distance from "common intelligible sound." In *Lycidas* the silence which is supposedly overcome in the accommodated landscape of the visionary apotheosis is acknowledged for a moment in the "*unexpressive* nupital Song" (176, emphasis added). Though Milton affirms his desire for the revelations of those moments when it seems possible to hear celestial harmonies and see heavenly sights, he is always aware that were he actually to do so sight and sound would be shrouded in the dark silence of death or ecstasy. To claim to speak God literally is to aspire to know as he knows, and, as we know from *Paradise Lost*, in life that is not only impossible but also blasphemous and hubristic.

The question for swain and poet in *Lycidas* may be restated as how one is to live a life in which act and choice have meaning in a world which kills Lycidas and rolls on "To good malignant, to bad men benign" (*PL* XII, 538). On the one hand, the swain's vision must be distanced, recognized as a fiction, if a return to a life of song and action is to be possible. To live, on the other hand, also requires some comforting garment in which one can wrap oneself against mortal despair. This garment, however, can only be structured visibly in language, and the languages of faith and fiction are shown in the artifice of *Lycidas* to be the same. Eternal life for the "faithful Herdman" becomes what we might call a "necessary fiction." Two other readers have seemed willing to accept the vision of Lycidas at the marriage feast of the Lamb as such a fiction. Both, however, go on to turn that fiction into an effective signifier of a transcendent reality, and thus not in my sense a fiction at all. Isabel MacCaffrey, for instance, speaks of the elegy's final paragraphs as recording "a development in the speaker's treatment of his metaphor, from the naive assumption that it represents actuality, to the recognition of it as one of man's great symbols for ultimate reality, securely rooted in the imaginative life" (Patrides, p. 265). Donald M. Friedman comes even closer to a notion of the irremediable absence of that "ultimate reality" but still finds it made present through the fictions of pastoral: "This fiction has opened the way to a truth that can be expressed only in fiction; yet the discovery of that truth renders us, and the swain, forever unable to mistake fiction for what it is supposed to represent" (Patrides, pp. 299–300). The essence of fiction, I would argue, is just that mistake: a "truth" which can be expressed only through a fiction is inescapably itself a fiction.

We have, in a sense, come full circle back to Dr. Johnson's complaint about the danger of "trifling fictions." The way in which the poet's "fictions" make problematic the reality of the faith they purport to represent is given a more modern cast by Peter Sacks. In a psychological reading of the way in which *Lycidas* completes the work of mourning by moving "from submissive gestures of compulsion and loss to an internalizing counter-usurpation of totemic power," Sacks discovers complications in the elegy similar to those I have been exploring:

> We find it hard to avoid the recognition that it is, after all, the poet who has Christ raise Lycidas. The frame of fictionality encompasses even that supreme action, which brings us to the disquieting region of conjecture, so important to Milton, of whether Christianity may be no more than a superior product (superior to classical mythology, for example) of man's imagination. What we have already seen to be the poem's repeated questioning of its own fictions cannot entirely be escaped (. . . how is he who walked the waves so different from Palaemon? Is he more real, or is he simply more powerful?).[15]

"Truth" or "ultimate reality" superior to imagination can be found in the fictions of language only if one believes it is already there, a priori. The label *truth* is only the privileging of one way of reading (or misreading) the fictive medium.

The important matter, I believe, for Milton's speaker is the difference between a good fiction and a bad one. A good fiction provides a paradigm for life which enables "wayfaring" and "warfaring," the poet's song and the politician's actions. The adequacy of the fiction which in *Lycidas* promises to supplant the "false surmise" of pagan and naturalistic pastoral is defined by the existence of the poem itself, and within it by the completion of the swain's song and his observed willingness to arise and reimmerse himself in the world of choice where the outcome of choice cannot be guaranteed. The superior voice in the coda may approve of and share that readiness, but reveals its dependence on an always deferred closure, on a gap which mortal sight cannot bridge nor mortal voice close. The "artifice of eternity" into which Lycidas is gathered is accepted as a necessary construction, but both poet and reader remain aware of the equally necessary resistance of life and language to the silence that true closure brings with it.

Swarthmore College

NOTES

1. My debt to the legions of scholars and critics who have written on *Lycidas* is immense and implicit throughout this paper. An early version of this essay was read in the

Milton General Session at the 1985 MLA Convention in Chicago. Though I frequently cite his work as a focus for my disagreement with current readings, I owe Edward W. Tayler, chair of that session, a special debt for helping me to more clearly shape my ideas. The many references to essays in the late C. A. Patrides's anthology, *Milton's "Lycidas": The Tradition and the Poem,* new and rev. ed. (Columbia, 1983), are cited parenthetically in my text.

2. Here and in my title I am obviously playing with that "artifice of eternity" yearned for by the aging speaker in W. B. Yeats's "Sailing to Byzantium." In seeking a timeless existence in art "out of nature," he fixes ironically on the natural form of a golden bird. In "Byzantium" this artifact from the "Golden smithies of the Emperor" reappears among images of art which in gold and marble seem to transcend all "complexities" of "blood-begotten spirits," but are seen to "crack" and are revealed again as "images that fresh images beget, / That dolphin-torn, that gong-tormented sea." The "eternity" cannot be realized through "artifice," as only images which endlessly defer access to an imagined transcendence can be the poet's material; "eternity," then, *is* "artifice." Quotations are from *The Variorum Edition of the Poems of W. B. Yeats,* ed. Peter Allt and Russell K. Alspach (New York, 1957), pp. 408, 498.

3. All of my citations of Milton's poems and prose, unless noted otherwise, are from *John Milton: Complete Poems and Major Prose,* ed. Merritt Y. Hughes (New York, 1957).

4. Louis Martz, *Poet of Exile* (New Haven, 1980), p. 74. Tayler points out that the rhyme scheme of the coda might also be identified with the Tuscan stanza called *strambotta.* See *Milton's Poetry: Its Development in Time* (Pittsburgh, 1979). The associations of this stanza are with peasant singers rather than with the writers of narrative. See Ernest H. Wilkins, *A History of Italian Literature* (Cambridge, Mass., 1954), p. 10. This identification would make the stanza of the coda itself "swainish," and could support the ironies of deferred closure which I examine later in this essay.

5. Ellen Z. Lambert, *Placing Sorrow: A Study of the Pastoral Elegy Convention from Theocritus to Milton* (Chapel Hill, N.C., 1976), p. 176. Among others noting the missing frame are Cleanth Brooks and John Edward Hardy (in Patrides, p. 155), Tayler (in Patrides, p. 136), and Emory Elliot, "Milton's 'Uncouth Swain'," in *Milton Reconsidered* (Salzburg, 1976), p. 9.

6. Herman Rapaport, *Milton and the Postmodern* (Lincoln, Neb., 1983), p. 127.

7. See especially MacCaffrey, in Patrides, p. 264.

8. See, for example, Robert C. Fox, "Milton's *Lycidas,* 192–3," *Expositor* IX (1951), 54. Tayler relates the swain's "mantle blue" to the blue skies accompanying the rising sun in a general paradigm of resurrection (Patrides, p. 318).

9. The phrase is from *Of Education,* in Hughes, *Complete Poems,* p. 631.

10. My assertions here about accommodation deserve explanation at a length not possible on this occasion. Let me note only that in the theory of signs which incorporates accommodation, at least from Augustine to Milton, the signified is always prior to the signifier, and the validity of the signifier is dependent on knowledge by faith of the signified. See, for instance, Marcia L. Colish, *The Mirror of Language: A Study in the Medieval Theory of Knowledge* (New Haven, 1968), p. 34: "Signs never produce knowledge in the first instance. The subjective function of the signs in helping to communicate knowledge depends on the knower's previous relationship to the object. If he is already a believer, he can recognize the sign as a sign of God and can judge how Godlike it is; the sign in turn can deepen his awareness of God."

11. Renato Poggioli, *The Oaten Flute* (Cambridge, Mass., 1975), p. 98.

12. William Oram, "Nature, Poetry and Milton's Genii," in *Milton and the Art of Sacred Song,* ed. J. Max Patrick and Roger H. Sundell (Madison, Wis., 1979), pp. 47–64.

13. For a useful analysis of the conception of the archangel Michael in lines 159–64, see Jason P. Rosenblatt, "The Angel and the Shepherd in *Lycidas*," *PQ* LXII (1983), 252–58.

14. For Milton, if his later announced mortalism may be assumed here, the closure of this gap may even await the final trump when God becomes all in all and the distinction between heaven and earth, creator and created, is ended eternally. Barbara Johnson, "Fiction and Grief: The Pastoral Idiom of Milton's *Lycidas*," *MQ* XVIII, no. 3 (1984), 69–76, recognizes this complication, but resolves it by assuming that the speaker takes consolation in a notion that the angelic choirs will sing for Lycidas "at the end of time."

15. Peter Sacks, *The English Elegy* (Baltimore, 1985), p. 116. In an essay which finally arrives at a point quite different from mine, Lawrence W. Hyman, "Belief and Disbelief in *Lycidas*," *CE* XXXIII (1972), 532–42, also raises the issue of the fictionality of the poem's vision. He asserts that the coda cannot be brought "into the perspective of the rest of the poem. For Milton is quite obviously focusing our attention on the imaginary nature of his vision, just as a novelist [or a dream-vision poet] might tell us at the end of his story that the actions occurred in a dream" (p. 539).

THE POLITICS OF MARITAL REFORM AND THE RATIONALIZATION OF ROMANCE IN *THE DOCTRINE AND DISCIPLINE OF DIVORCE*

Charles Hatten

IN 1643, as the armies of Charles I and the Long Parliament were beginning the long civil war that historians call the English Revolution, Milton published a tract entitled *The Doctrine and Discipline of Divorce.* This work is of considerable interest both in its own right and as Milton's first extended treatment of the subject at the center of *Paradise Lost*—marital relations. That the tract represents a significant moment in Milton's political evolution, as he moved toward the Independent position of *Areopagitica,* and that its exegetical approach to Scriptures is singularly radical, have long been recognized. But the tract's significance lies not merely in what it reveals about Milton's intellectual development, but in what it tells us about the tensions and conflicts surrounding the construction of gender and private life in this historical moment. The tract expresses the pervasive anxiety about the maintenance of gender hierarchy that accompanied the emergence of a rationalized and postfeudal concept of marriage in the early modern period. In a larger perspective, the tract's complex dynamics are most fully understandable if we see it as a manifestation of the societal process of rationalization, or reification, a centuries-long process that occurs along a number of dimensions—political, economic, and social. Such an understanding, allowing the integration of long-range historical change and immediate polemical context, requires the knowledge of three aspects of societal rationalization which manifest themselves in the text. *Doctrine and Discipline* articulates a rationalization of the marital bond with acute, because polemical, clarity; it does so polemically because it participates in the rationalization of political life that occurred in England in the seventeenth century; such a rationalized vision of marital relations generates a correspondingly deidealized, or realistic, rationalized model for romance narratives. The chief value, I would suggest, of the term *rationalization,* which refers to the organization of social institutions on the basis of rational self-seeking by individuals, is that it draws our attention to the affiliations between the text's proposed reform of the marital relation and the more general rationalization of economic and political relations, of which this proposed reform was a part.

My alternative term of *reification,* understood as detaching a relationship from a network of social relations and communal practices which previously sustained and structured it, suggests the necessarily conflictual nature of this rationalization of marriage.[1] This conflict is, most obviously, with the traditional, organic, and somewhat mystical vision of marriage as a sacrament that heretofore was dominant, but it involves an effort to disrupt and dominate both aristocratic and plebeian marital practices as well as political, theological, and domestic ideologies. This conflictual nature of the text's reification of the marital relation is particularly visible because it occurs in a field of contestation with, and responds to, a number of alternative responses to England's political crisis; indeed, the text is implicated in a historical process of rationalizing English politics in the direction of greater responsiveness to public opinion and pressure. This rationalization is visible both in the structure of the text's theological position and in its effort to co-opt popular sentiment on the issue at hand, the marital relation, on behalf of an elite-led revolution against a traditional feudal state. The term *displacement* will be useful in discussing this process as a shorthand for the mechanism by which, for instance, popular sentiments against unruly wives can be directed against the institutions of the Anglican Church and its canon law—a process that involves transfering energies from the realm of the private and psychic to the realm of the political and national and, correlatively, involves the figuration of the political in the intimate language of the marital.

I. *The Doctrine and Discipline* and Domestic Handbooks

A striking paradox to the modern reader of *Doctrine and Discipline* is that, while it proposes the progressive reform of easing the restrictions on divorce, its rhetoric employs a sexism of a remarkably archaic and stringent type. The central anxiety that the text expresses is that a man will be indissolubly bound to an unfit wife; the tract's accounts of the unfit wife seem to provide support for charges that Milton was a bitter misogynist. But to see the text's anxiety about the influence of wives as merely a sign of Milton's personal idiosyncrasies is to read the text ahistorically. The early seventeenth century was a period in which societal anxiety about insubordination, including the insubordination of women, was pervasive and intense, a fact reflected in court records, in the deployment of social rituals against women who violated gender norms (the charivari and the cucking stool), in the persecution of witches, and in literary evidence, both elite and popular. At a time of increasing class polarization and of social tensions generated by the spread of market relations that were disrupting the communal traditions of English life, it is highly probable that a preoccupation with gender insubordination expressed an anxiety about broader social tensions that was displaced onto the sphere of gender relations.[2] In any case, the tract's preoccupation with affirming proper gender hierarchies must be seen as typical of the Puritan "middling sort" 's class discourse, that is to say a discourse that expressed in large measure the aspirations and interests of an elite social group concerned with a larger project of social reform embodied in Puritan criticisms of waste, revelry, and laxity in moral life. Viewed thus, the tract's obsession with affirming gender hierarchies can be seen as, on the one hand, an effort to reassert moral boundaries and values in a time of social instability. On the other hand, and more centrally, the Puritan current of thought, to the extent it represented the interests of the middling sort, can also be said to have attempted a cultural revolution in values in the direction of a more rationalized social order based on the increasing potency of market forces.

Thus, far from being idiosyncratic in his obsessive preoccupation with the proper role of the wife, Milton is merely elaborating and overtly politicizing, as part of this cultural revolution, a tradition of prescriptive discourse on marriage for laymen that had its roots in a sixteenth-century genre, that of the domestic handbook.[3] The domestic handbook, a genre particularly associated with the Puritans, can be seen as abetting the Puritan project of cultural revolution, of "reforming" the English countryside, albeit in a far less divisive way than some other Puritan reforms. The most obvious break with more conservative Christian positions on marriage in these works, in fact, was rather generally Protestant than distinctively Puritan, namely the tendency to view marriage as a contract rather than as a sacrament. Milton simply follows earlier Protestant thinkers and certain radical Protestant sects in arguing from this contractual conception to the permissibility of divorce.

Already by creating a privatized space, mediated only by the impersonal marketplace in which such books were bought, and in which the individual read advice on marital and familial concerns, this genre begins to reify, or detach from a network of social relations and communal practices that often impinged on personal life, the area of marital life. Written for lay people, rather than clergy, it isolates the prospective family member from hierarchical structures such as that of the church. By stressing personal compatibility, domestic handbooks isolate the individual marital unit and its formation from larger networks of kinship and community, which often mediated both aristocratic and plebian marital practices. Some of the advice in these books, such as on the advisability of wives being younger than husbands (to preserve the gender hierarchy in marriage), which would have been only easily attained by wealthier readers, would have actually increased class differences by establishing norms inaccessible to poorer readers. Thus the books' popularity, and their conception of marriage as contractual, begins a process of rationalization and reification that *Doctrine and Discipline* attempts to complete.

Not merely the conception of marriage as contractual, but the violent juxtaposition of it with, and dismissal of, the traditional Anglican notion of marriage as indissoluble sacrament, reveal the culturally revolutionary nature of Milton's project. In proposing that divorce be allowed to dissolve a marital union *on the basis* of its contractual character, he places a rational model of marriage as a quasi-commercial venture, undertaken by individualist and rational actors, at the heart of his conception of marriage. This rationalizing and reifying reconception of marriage, which implicitly denies the prerogative of church or state authorities to suppress or prohibit certain personal and marital choices, on the basis of the right to make contracts, was clearly radical and innovative. Paradoxically, the evidence for its novel and disturbing character is in part the very multiplicity of images and metaphors for marriage that the tract deploys, as it seeks to secure the cooperation of a number of traditional metaphors for family in this radical revision of marital conceptions.

The rationalization of marital relations proposed, like other rationalizations of social life, is not imaginable without conflict and tension, and the text reflects this. It does so in part because the domestic handbook tradition itself was not univocal, but contained within itself a diversity of emphases concerning the nature of the marital bond. The reconceptualization of marital life as preeminently contractual, with its implicit emphasis upon personal consent and autonomy, had an obvious potential to undermine social hierarchies and their reliance on obedience and deference. Thus we find the domestic handbooks proposing more reassuring conceptions of the marital relation. A common image of the family saw it as a miniature church, with the husband presiding over religious instruction and observance. But, in a period of divisive religious conflict, this image raised the possibility of schisms and sects, or at least of backsliding, entering into the marital relation itself. And indeed Milton briefly mentions the possibility that the basis for divorce might be spousal heresy; little attention is given to this argument, however, presumably since it could so easily be turned against a radical Protestant stance, which could be seen, in its individualism, as encouraging religious tension within the family.

Similarly double-edged was the conception of the family as a miniature state with the husband as sovereign. Here too there was a possibility for the family to be seen as a microcosm of the conflicts that disordered the larger social arena. In fact, the commonplace that the family was a miniature commonwealth would become somewhat embarrassing to parliamentary apologists, who were forced to explain away the traditional analogy between the husband and the king to justify the Parliament's revolt. But Milton's strong commitment to a rationalization of political and marital life encourages him to defend his radically contractual conception of marriage by aligning it with an implicitly contractual defense of the Parliament's rebellion:

> He who marries, intends as little to conspire his own ruine, as he that swears Allegiance: and as a whole people is in proportion to an ill Government, so is one man to an ill marriage. If they against any authority, Covnant, or Statute, may by the soveraign edict of charity, save not only their lives, but honest liberties from unworthy bondage, as well may he against any private Covnant, which hee never enter'd to his mischief, redeem himself from unsupportable disturbances to honest peace, and just contentment.[4]

Both people and husbands can defend themselves against bonds, of marriage or allegiance, traditionally thought of as sacred and indissoluble, by a rational appeal to the right of the individual to make and unmake contracts. Thus does the rationalizing and marketplace-oriented Puritan conception of the world mentally dissolve an older feudal conception of society and replace it with rationalized social structures.

Yet Milton's formulation here resolves the contradiction between the traditional conception of the family as a source of social stability and hierarchy and his implicit conception of it as a privileged site of freedom (comparable to the "whole people" embodied in parliament) by ignoring the traditional power relationship embodied in the family. If the people were in rebellion against the government, they were most obviously analogous to a woman rebelling against her husband, not to a man ("he") rebelling against a "Covnant." Indeed, conservative critics of Milton's position were quick to point out that many of his arguments for divorce seemed equally applicable to both sexes, an argument contemporaries considered highly damning. Thus when Milton writes: "For no effect of tyranny can sit more heavy on the Common-wealth, then this household unhappines on the family," he necessarily avoids any reference to the identity of the domestic tyrant that corresponds to the political one (YP II, p. 229). In fact, the overwhelming tendency of his argument is to suggest that it is the wife, though the logical analogy would be between the head of the state and the head of the household, between tyrant and husband. This slippery elision of the tyrannic husband and indictment of the tyrannic wife is not accidental, but arises from the incompatibility between the tract's rationalizing conception of social life and its commitment to gender hierarchy. The elision of the husband and displacement of tyranny toward the wife also mirrors the general social phenomenon by which social and political tensions and conflicts were displaced in this period onto a language of gender: the political and class threat of "tyranny" is displaced onto the tyranny of the unfit wife. Such a displacement allows the political program of a rationalizing elite to be identified, at a time when an earlier feudal conception of masculinity founded on the mastery of physical violence was in crisis, with the creation of a new image of masculinity which is associated with the mastery of the feminine (both the "feminine" aspects of the self and of the wife in marriage). This displacement of anxieties about "tyranny" onto the wife also functions to minimize the tension between the tract's radically contractual conception of marriage, with its implicitly rationalist ethos, which is potentially disruptive to social hierarchy, including gender hierarchy, and the tract's typically Puritan obsession with social discipline and control. This tension, I will suggest, between the subversion of social hierarchy and a desire to contain threats to social order, is central to the tract's dynamics; the displacement of anxiety about loss of individual freedom onto women, in the figure of the unfit wife, is similarly a pervasive strategy.

If the application of the contractual conception of marriage to society was potentially explosive, this is hardly surprising, for the domestic conduct handbooks themselves suggest that this conception is potentially the locus of conflict within the marital bond itself. Marriage, as a contract, was often thought of as a sort of business relationship, but there were tensions between opposing interpretations of the nature of this business relationship. Thus Alexander Niccholes, writing in 1615, was clearly trying to emphasize the value of marriage to men: "In thy marriage thou not only unitest unto thy self a friend, and comfort for society, but also a companion for pleasure, and in some sort a servant for profite."[5] But, in stressing the value of a wife, Niccholes touches upon an important ambiguity: if the wife is "in some sort" a servant, she clearly had a higher status than servants generally. She was more often understood as a kind of junior partner, the husband's "assistant . . . in all his travel [labor] and in his troubles,"[6] who shared with him the labor of supervising the servants and instructing the children, often shared in the work of production in the home, and had responsibility for a great deal of domestic labor. The image of the junior partner and of the servant are both images of economic efficiency and presumably appealed to the middle strata for whom the home was often a crucial site of the exploitation of labor. Despite such encomia to the economic virtues of wives in general, the dominant point of the handbooks was that the wife was not a mere servant but had duties and deserved a respect from her husband of another order; beating one's wife, as opposed to one's servants, for instance, was generally condemned.

Much of the text's, and the society's, anxiety about wives resided in this problem; if wives needed to be distinguished from servants, it was because their positions were somewhat analogous. Legally, women, children, and servants were nearly equivalent. Thus wives, by virtue of their ambiguous status, had to be particularly guarded for signs of rebellion; yet degrading the wife to a servant's level was paradoxically a sure way to engender the domestic rebellion above all to be avoided. Not only could the wife's insubordination threaten the efficiency and happiness of the household, but such rebellion disabled the household as an agent of socialization into the hierarchical relations of the wider society.[7]

In implicit tension with the conception of the wife as a servant, her position contingent on her marketplace value, the domestic handbooks emphasize the idea of her as a partner, indeed one who exceeded a mere business relation, through companionship and friendship inspired ideally by love. This emphasis certainly strikes us as humane; however, it is also functional for a rationalizing elite in four ways. It mystifies the contractual basis of marriage to avoid the wife seeming either servant or business partner, either degradingly servile or potentially equal; it strengthens the ties between spouses as communal pressures and forces regulating marital bonds were being weakened; it places stress in the marital relation upon the internalization of values rather than upon external coercion, in accordance with larger religious and social trends that encouraged internalization of elite values by the subordinate; and, finally, it provided a flexible marker of class status to displace the eroding prestige of lineage and office. Thus the domestic handbooks' emphasis on the element of friendship in marriage is designed to support rather than to undermine the gender hierarchy in marriage by elevating the wife above the temptation to rebellion of a servant and by keeping her loyal to her spouse. This is why such texts also tend to subordinate sexuality and passion; potentially, they undermine the gender hierarchy. To William Perkins, an important Puritan theologian and authority on domestic life, the concept of "spiritual adultery" included excessive passion for one's wife, which was tantamount to adultery. And William Gouge was sufficiently fearful of overdoting spouses to warn:

> Remember the fearful issue that had like to have fallen out by reason of such compellations given by Sarah and Rebekah to their husbands. Not unlike to those are such as these, Sweet, Sweeting, Heart, Sweet-Heart, Love, Joy, Dear, &c. and such as these, Duck, Chick, Pigsnie, &c. husband's Christian names, as John, Thomas, William, Henry, &c. which they be contracted (as many are use to contract them thus, Jack, Tom, Will, Hall) they are much more unseemly; servants are usually so called. But what may we say of those titles given to an husband by his wife, not seldom in passion, but usually in ordinary speech, which are not fit to be given to the basest men that be, as Grub, Rogue, and the like, which I am even ashamed to name.[8]

The rigid circumspection of affection that Gouge proposes here is clearly linked to anxiety about social status or class; the authority of the husband over the wife must be maintained by her manner of addressing him, which in turn signifies his class status; if she were to call him "Jack" or "Dear," he would be indistinguishable from a servant. The wife's position of inferiority in the home makes her proper subordination, hence, a mark of masculine class status. The threat of a too affectionate or too sexually charged bond is also a threat of the dissolution of hierarchical categories, including class boundaries. Milton's vehement stress upon the priority of companionship over procreation in marriage must be seen in this class-structured context: "he who affirms adultery to be the highest breach, affirms the bed to be the highest [end] of mariage, which is in truth a grosse and borish opinion, how common soever; as farre from the light of all clean philosophy, or civill nature" (YP II, p. 269). Milton's stigmatization of the physical in marriage, and his linking of it with the lower classes ("grosse and borish"), clearly reflects the anxiety that Puritans felt concerning sexuality in marriage and their affiliated anxieties about the blurring of social hierarchies.

The companionate marriage was from the outset an elite discourse. It has long been noted that the Puritan stress upon "election" was an intensely elitist discourse that underwrote a stratified social world. For the domestic handbooks, the marital relation can be assimilated to this elitist theological current; thus Thomas Gataker, a handbook writer, comments: "Children are the gift of God, but the Wife is a more speciall gift of God; shee commeth in the first place, they in the second."[9] Gataker places mutual society above procreation, as against earlier writers' stress on the latter, and derives from the beginning of marriage (in Genesis) that its end is the removal of loneliness; in both regards he anticipates Milton's arguments. Moreover, the implication that a properly companionate marriage is a sign of God's favor ("special gift") suggests that it is a sign of election. Since signs of election tended to operate as markers of class status, the vast majority being understood as damned, we can see how this religious discourse makes the properly affectionate character of marital bonds a sign of social standing. Similarly Milton, in discussing the importance of a properly companionate marriage, links the marital bond with the Puritan individual's efforts to feel himself spiritually elect—a man with a bad wife, he writes, feels a pain "like Reprobates feel" (YP II, p. 246). Such a preoccupation with the husband's spiritual status in marriage emphasizes the elite character of Milton's discourse, for such a preoccupation is undoubtedly more consistent with a privileged status than with the poverty of many of his contemporaries. While such discourses are elitist, they are also antiaristocratic: the individualist conception of marital affection and the strong disapproval of child marriages in the handbooks and Milton's tract are marks of their hostility to a waning aristocratic practice of arranged marriages.

In short, *Doctrine and Discipline* responds to social anxieties of its moment by an emphatically radical reassertion of the rationalizing and reifying tendencies of earlier elite discourses on marriage. In so doing it evinces a subterranean anxiety about the individualist character of its conception of marriage, at times reproducing versions of anxieties and tensions about marital life that had long characterized such discourses. The light that brings these tensions to our attention in Milton's tract, of course, is the larger political and ideological crisis to which it responds.

II. *Doctrine and Discipline* and the Separatist Challenge

If Milton's tract elaborates on the language of the domestic conduct handbooks, with their hints of fissures in the social order, it responds as well to the chasm of social crisis opened by the emergence of lower-class religious and political activism. In doing so, most clearly in the tract's theological argument, it suggests its implication in another dimension of societal rationalization, a far-reaching rationalization of political life.

Separatist religious groups first became widely visible in 1641, when many groups sprang up in London and its suburbs; besides the threat to the discipline of an elite-dominated state church such congregations represented, their relative egalitarianism—in theology, organization of congregations, and, to some extent, between the sexes—embodied an ideological and political threat to the social order.[10] Milton's reaction to this challenge to the established order was complex. Though like his contemporaries in associating lower-class and feminine insubordination and feeling uneasy about both, in *An Apology Against a Pamphlet* he initially defended the entry of both groups into the political sphere:

> the meanest artisans, also women, assembling with their complaints, and that sometimes in a less humble guise than for petitioners, have gone with confidence, that neither their meannes would be rejected, nor yet their urgency distasted wither by the dignity, wisdom, or moderation of that supreme Senate; nor did they depart unsatisfied. (YP I, p. 926)

The reference here is to petitions to Parliament of lower-class Londoners and women in early 1642. The fierce demonstrations and rioting against the bishops are euphemistically passed over ("less humble guise"), though their mention suggests the anxiety which Milton's class felt about lower-class political action; yet the moral he draws is of the supreme wisdom of the Parliament in responding to popular pressure. In a process that unfolded as an opportunistic response to a short-term crisis, but which anticipates and begins a long-term change in political structure, the defense of the proper ordering of society, including the subordination of the lower classes, occurs not through coercion but through a controlling responsiveness to popular demands. The crisis of the parliamentary struggle with the crown encouraged an acceleration of this long and slow process of a rationalization of the political sphere. This happened because the outbreak of civil war and the rise of religious separatism made the problem of how to respond to lower-class sentiment an urgent problem; the issue of whether to co-opt lower-class political sentiment, and hence to tolerate the separatists, became a central division among the political elite. *Doctrine and Discipline*, with its radical conception of marriage, suggests how far Milton was willing to go in his political strategy in conceding to the lower classes and their separatist ideologues. The very substance of his argument here is concerned with an effort to respond to as well as to co-opt their concerns.

The separatists challenged the very fabric of elite ideological hegemony, a threat evident in their articulation of an alternative theology. Thus Milton, even while concurring with the separatist position on certain points and co-opting their views in *Doctrine and Discipline*, must simultaneously respond to the ideological threat inherent in their dissident theology. The Puritans' Calvinist theology had an obvious elitism, and the ethical duality between good and evil, elect and damned, legitimated the inegalitarian structure of class relations; but the radical sects often undermined this by stressing the wide availability of God's grace. The sects' stress on grace legitimated their more egalitarian church structure and subverted the hegemonic values of the ruling elite. The experience of God's grace empowered some of the separatists to oppose their social betters, just as Calvinism encouraged resistance to the orthodox church. But to the radical Protestants, the Calvinist God seemed at best too indifferent to his people's suffering to be truly God and seemed at worst a false conception propagated by the Antichrist to ensnare the faithful into servility and despair.

This is the threat, ideological and implicitly political, to which Milton responds at the opening of *Doctrine and Discipline*, when he writes, in a passage which establishes the central logical and moral problem that his text will address:

> Many men, whether it be their fate, or fond opinion, easily perswade themselves, if GOD would but be pleas'd a while to withdraw his just punishments from us, and to restraine what power either the devill, or any earthly enemy hath to worke us woe, that then mans nature would find immediate rest and releasement from all evils. But verily they who think so, if they be such as have a minde large anough to take into their thoughts a generall survey of humane things, would soone prove themselves in that opinion farre deceiv'd. For though it were granted us by divine indulgence to be exempt from all that can be harmfull to us from without, yet the perversenesse of our folly is so bent, that we should never lin hammering out of our owne hearts, as it were out of a flint, the seeds and sparkles of new miseries to our selves, till all were in a blaze againe. And no marvell if out of our own hearts, for they are evill; but ev'n out of those things which God meant us, either for a principall good, or a pure contentment, we are still hatching and contriving upon our selves matter of continuall sorrow and perplexitie. (YP II, pp. 234–35)

Radical theology, by stressing man's potential for receiving grace, either locates God as the source of evil or at least sees the Calvinist conception of a God who rarely grants grace as a sort of image of evil. Setting up such a radical position as one that "many men" hold, though not men with "large mind[s]" who have taken a "generall survey" of the "humane," Milton rhetorically associates such a position with ignorance, which was traditionally associated with the lower class; thus he begins to disrupt and control the lower-class discourse of the radical sects.

But the tract's effort to control the radical theological position is part of a larger aim: to construct a unified and coherent ideological opposition to the royalist aristocracy and their allies in the Anglican church by coopting radical and lower-class concerns. Milton overtly and insistently targets the Anglican canon courts, which are harshly criticized and identified with Catholicism throughout the tract, and covertly targets the radical sects. Against what the text sees as the Anglicans' corrupt values it promotes the values and ideals of the Puritans. The most obvious and pervasive form of this promotion is the massive and aggressive celebration of a rationalized ideal of the family which the text enacts. The entry of the conceptions and ideals of the domestic handbooks into the arena of political debate is an emphatic assertion of the values of the "middling sort" and the Puritan gentry. Just as the political initiative of Parliament represents an assertion of the commercial gentry and their allies against the feudal state, so, homologously, Milton's text proposes that the feudal structure of canon law be judged by the ethical norms of the commercial gentry and the middling elites as these were articulated in Puritan domestic handbooks. But this elite-promoted reform of social life involves the cooptation and defeat of the more radical reforms embodied in the separatists' theology and practice.

Milton himself implies the necessity of containing radical theology for the success of the Puritan project of "Reformation" when he links such a containment with the defeat of Catholicism, the great Satan of the Puritans, in a passage he added to the second edition of *Doctrine and Discipline:* "The Jesuits, and that sect among us which is nam'd of Arminius, are wont to charge us of making God the author of sinne" (YP II, p. 293). The Arminian position, often associated with the radical sects, was that believers could exercise free will in sinning or not.[11] This sect rejected the Calvinist concept that God predestines some to damnation, which, as Milton points out, they saw as making God "author of sinne." This passage thus restates a version of the moral problem with which he originally framed his argument: the tension between his Calvinist stress on human responsibility for evil and the radical tendency to protest the harshness of the Calvinist God. Significantly, he here associates rebellion against the Calvinist emphasis upon God's active intervention with the Puritan *bête noire,* Catholics, and radical Protestants. Milton's God, like the Puritan individual, was preeminently an active being, and Milton stresses here the importance of not denying God's omnipotent activity even if it appears to make God evil.

The view that God (or the devil) was ultimately responsible for evil, which Milton stigmatizes at the outset of his tract, is a theological position that could justify passivity before divine omnipotence or quasi-magical efforts to control it; both of these attitudes, which were associated with Catholicism, were anathema to Puritans and to Milton's activist Puritanism in particular.[12] By stressing God's activity, but minimizing his ultimate responsibility for evil, Milton encourages active human effort to suppress evil such as is embodied in his proposed marital reform. He thereby avoids at once the passivity before evil he associated with the Catholic conception of God, and, simultaneously, eschews the democratizing tendencies of radical Arminianism which would minimize human responsibility for evil. Moreover, in both cited passages, first implicitly and here openly, his association of Arminianism with Catholicism, like his characteristic association of Anglicanism with Catholicism, functions to rhetorically discredit his Protestant target. Such an association implicitly identifies the radical Protestant position as an enemy of a true Reformation.

As the tract's main overt polemical target is the Anglican orthodoxy and its canon law, it may seem a paradox to observe that its moral and political problematic is framed by the threat posed by the radical Protestant sects. But, in fact, the paradox is merely apparent, for by 1643 the rise of lower-class radicalism helped to generate the split in the parliamentarian ranks between Presbyterians and Independents; the leaders of both factions were gentry, but they were divided largely on their relation to lower-class political and religious expression and to spontaneous lower-class military action against the Royalists. Brian Manning has pointed out how the emergence of the separatists placed pressure on the Puritans to adopt more radical stances in order to keep control of popular sentiment.[13] Similarly, it was necessary for the Independents to champion religious toleration if they were to employ radical sectarians to fight against the king. Relapsing into traditional repression of the radical sects would only ensure the victory of the Royalists. The Independents had to make sufficient concessions to the radicals to ensure their support in an alliance with the parliamentary gentry against the king, while co-opting them into an alliance which the gentry would lead in order both to protect the Independents' own elite class interests and to avoid scaring the Presbyterians into rallying to the Royalist side out of fear of an aroused populace.

That Milton had just such a project of co-optation of radical sentiment in mind in *Doctrine and Discipline* is indicated by a later passage in which he argues that radical religious views arise from men "by nature addicted to a zeal of Religion, of life also not debausht," who feel they suffer under "the restraint of some lawfull liberty, which ought to be given men, and is deny'd them" (YP II, p. 279). In short, Milton suggests tolerating and allowing the radicals' marital practice to co-opt and control their subversive theology. Of course, the Independents' (and Milton's) strategy would ultimately fail, and gentry alarm in the face of popular political action would make the Restoration inevitable. At this political moment, however, a class alliance between the gentry and the radicals, led by the former, seemed the only way of ensuring the victory of the Parliament and of Reformation—hence Milton's anxiety to co-opt and control the ideological currents of radicalism.

Though the tract's overt polemics center on theological issues, the text's historical specificity must be located in the political dynamics of its theological stance. The important point is that discussions of lower-class theological positions *represent* such positions rather than merely stigmatizing them. Spenser provides a useful point of contrast. In his Levelling Giant (*FQ* V, ii, 30–54), he caricatures and rhetorically exorcises radical religious discourse of his period but does not seriously argue against it nor attempt to recuperate some of its elements. Milton, crucially, does attempt to recuperate elements of the radical Arminian position for his own purposes. He argues, in effect, that its critique of Calvinist elitism and indifference to human suffering can only be defended against by the promotion of actual reforms, including a reform of divorce which validates the practice of some of the radical groups themselves. What is a rhetorical exorcism of the lower class in Spenser becomes an effort at co-optation in Milton. Of course, Milton's proposals are directed primarily to his peers among the ruling elite (hence the phrase "charge us"), and his desire to avoid alarming the more conservative members of his class precludes his openly defending the radicals' position in his opening paragraphs. He does, as we have seen, explicitly mention the radicals, but not merely to stigmatize them; indeed, he implicitly defends them against upper-class prejudice, saying that those who object to predestination do so "perhaps out of a vigilant and wary conscience" (YP II, p. 296).

Milton's use of general and abstract terms in establishing the framework of his argument is comparable to the tradition of allegory in which a figure represents a moral failing, such as Spenser's Despaire. But again there is an important difference. Rather than representing an abstract moral failing, Milton's figures ("Many men") hold a quite specific theological position held by significant actors in the contemporary political arena. The text's effort to resolve a political contradiction by representing a lower-class ideological position marks it as engaging in a specifically bourgeois form of political discourse because it allows the representation of that which had previously been thought too low or mundane to be represented. Milton's discourse represents the lower-class position in order to control it, rather than, as feudal texts characteristically do, merely stigmatizing women and the lower classes and legitimizing their coercion. Milton's willingness to verbally represent lower-class positions in a politically charged theological debate is precisely analogous to the Puritan elite's willingness to deploy anti-Catholic and anti-court rhetoric to mobilize the lower classes as voters, demonstrators, petitioners, and finally as an armed force against the power of the feudal state.[14]

III. The Political Function of Deidealized Romance

Doctrine and Discipline's political tension, born of its response to a political crisis, between its radical impulse and its desire to maintain social and class hierarchies, structures the text's arguments and helps explain what has long embarrassed Milton scholars and led them to speculate about Milton's personal marital experience: the tract's persistent, even obsessive, invocation of narratives about unfit wives. The real importance of these narratives, however, is that they are readable as symptomatic of yet another rationalization, a rationalization on a literary level of the institution of romance narrative: a deidealization of romance as a narrative paradigm. Though part of a larger process of deidealizing romance (the plays of Middleton and *Don Quixote* participate in an analogous realism), the process of deidealizing romance here derives energy from its political context, where it serves a definite purpose.

We have seen how, given the widespread anxiety about social stability in the seventeenth century, and the universal stress on social hierarchy, an argument from the contractual nature of marriage had disturbingly atomizing overtones. The text's reification of marriage as a contractual tie raises the specter of social atomization by making the individual the basic unit of society and by destabilizing the Puritan conception of the family as a commonwealth or church that subordinated women and the lower class through paternalistic bonds. In this context, the tract's rhetorical strategy is to stress that a refusal to acknowledge marriage's contractual nature leads to its own socially disruptive consequences; simultaneously, the tract stresses the importance of a model of marriage in which proper gender hierarchies are preserved. The tract's central argument figures social stability as embodied in an ideal marriage, seeing marriage as "a happy conversation" structured by male dominance. To express forcefully how the contractual conception of marriage is necessary to the operation of this ideal, Milton deploys narratives in which, typically, the domestic ideal, embodied in a "godly" male seeking "morall conversation" through marriage, is disrupted by the unfit wife, whose "flat & melancholious" mind is "unable to performe the best duty of mariage in a cheerfull and agreable conversation," and who then must be subordinated to the male spiritual quest, which requires the retrieval of marriage's contractual nature through divorce, lest the godly husband "dispair in vertue, and mutin against divine providence" (YP II, pp. 246–50).

As obstacle to a masculine spiritual quest, the unfit wife tends to be associated in such narratives with both poles of opposition to the Puritan process of Reformation. A domestic tyrant, her oppressive presence corresponds on the domestic level to the oppressive Anglican church courts that sanctioned her presence by refusing divorce, and, more generally, to the tyrannic force of the feudal state; an "image of earth and fleam" (p. 254), her earthy and insubordinate character associates her also with the tumultuous lower class that the text evinces such anxiety to contain. But these obsessive narratives of unfit wives perform a more general function: they naturalize and rhetorically bind together the tension in the text between hierarchical and contractual ideals of marriage and society; they resolve the anxieties engendered by the text's own reifying movement. Narratively embodying the tension between the potential egalitarianism of the contractual conception of marriage expressed in the domestic handbooks and such texts' stress on female subordination, these narratives imaginatively overcome the anxiety about the atomizing and subversive implications of the contractual conception of marriage by generating it as narratively "caused" by the "godliness" of the male and his superordination. Divorce, the actualization of marriage's contractual basis, becomes an absolute sine qua non for masculine transcendence, even for masculine spiritual salvation.

Viewed generically, these politically functional narratives are extremely interesting as early instances of a characteristic Miltonic revision of traditional romance narratives.[15] As in romance narratives, the individual seeks an erotic goal through various trials; as often in romance, the erotic goal is more than merely sexual and is associated with the reestablishment of crucial social values. The text revises traditional romance in that, in contrast to the model of romance provided by the masques popular at court, the central actors are not more than human in their attributes. This revises the feudal tradition of romance, and is closely related to a second revision, namely that the characters are explicitly imagined as being of a wide range of social types. Given the political project that we have seen the text is committed to, this opening of the marital narrative paradigm to various social types is essential. This opening of social positions, even as the marriage is treated as psychically, religiously, even politically momentous, sharply distinguishes this sort of romance narrative from the romance of the masque or traditional romance narrative in general. Lastly, and because of the breadth of social actors that the text admits into the role of hero of romance, the narrative itself has an almost parodic relation to more elaborately articulated romance narratives, both because the narrative is intensely simplified and because, rather than rising quasi-magically above the difficulties and dangers he faces, the protagonist of the narrative is overwhelmed by them.

And the difficulties and dangers the protagonist encounters in turn are not mythic in stature, but merely mundane and quotidian versions of romance figures of evil. The wife is less an ontologically evil being such as Duessa than a mundane woman whose function in the narrative is to disrupt the male protagonist's search for transcendence. If romance is characteristically a genre that enacts transcendence, the wife becomes the embodiment precisely of the parodic disruptions of the mundane which subvert the male individual's effort to form a romance narrative. So the tract's romancelike narratives, in which the protagonist's quest is an internal as well as external effort to actualize an ideal of marriage, suggest a tension between the ideal of marriage and its actuality. This dynamic tension is a profound revision of romance, presenting an unstable and dynamic relationship between the ideal and the actual in place of the comparatively stable juxtaposition and confrontation of good and evil forces which is typical of feudal romance.[16]

Thus the revision of romance narrative in the direction of including broader social strata complicates the confrontation between good and evil which characterizes romance. The more-than-human characteristics of typical romance figures express the rigidities of the feudal class system; the more fluid boundaries and less overtly coercive social relations of a bourgeois order generate a version of romance that possesses broader social horizons and is more deeply imbedded in the particularities of social life. While the more-than-human traits and magical resolutions of feudal romance inspire values of awe and identification which support feudal social relations based on deference, in Milton's new romance these mythic attributes of the traditional protagonist cede their central role to the male quest itself. At once erotic and social, this questing impulse becomes the new protagonist of romance; while figuring broader social aspirations, it continues to instill values of deference, now localized in the deference that women feel toward men and men feel toward moral ideals. The resultant complicated and deidealized version of romance, always standing implicitly in tension with mundane realities that may puncture it, as the postlapsarian quarrel in *Paradise Lost* disrupts the Edenic love the couple expresses earlier, becomes the basis both of Milton's version of romance in his marital epic and, through the influence of that work, of the novel. Recalling the roots of this complex and rationalized version of romance in the political innovations of a revolutionary period suggests the political dimensions even of narratives centered on the most personal of life's concerns.

Bellarmine College

NOTES

1. My use of *reification* and *rationalization* in these senses derives from Fredric Jameson, *The Political Unconscious* (Ithaca, N.Y., 1981), who derives it from Lukacs and Weber; the latter's interpretation of Protestantism and the spirit of capitalism initiates the general line of interpretation of Puritanism I follow. Christopher Kendrick, *Milton: A Study in Ideology and Form* (New York, 1986), uses a different sense of reification in a reading of Milton that complements mine.

2. For discussions of societal tensions and their gender components in this period see David Underdown, *Revel, Riot and Rebellion: Popular Politics and Culture in England, 1603–1660* (Oxford, 1985), pp. 9–43, and David Underdown, "The Taming of the Scold: The Enforcement of Patriarchal Authority in Early Modern England," in *Order and Disorder in Early Modern England*, ed. Anthony Fletcher and John Stevenson (Cambridge, 1985), ch. 4; for efforts to place Milton in his historical context, see Christopher Hill, *Milton and the English Revolution* (Harmondsworth, 1977); Andrew Milner, *John Milton and the English Revolution* (London, 1981); Michael Wilding, *Dragon's Teeth: Literature in the English Revolution* (Oxford, 1987); Kendrick, *Ideology and Form*.

3. Chilton L. Powell, *English Domestic Relations* (New York, 1917), Kathleen Davies, "Continuity and Change in Literary Advice on Marriage," in *Marriage and Society*, ed. R. B. Outhwaite (London, 1981), pp. 58–80, and Margaret Todd, "Humanists, Puritans and the Spiritualized Household," *Church History XLIX* (1980), 18–34, are useful discussions of the genre. Laurence Stone, *The Family, Sex and Marriage in England: 1500–1800* (New York, 1977), which stresses the subordination of the wife in Puritan families, remains the single best source of information on the family history of the period. William Haller, *Liberty and Reformation in the Puritan Revolution* (New York, 1955), pp. 78–99, valuably relates Milton's divorce writings to contemporary political debates, as does Hill, *Milton*, pp. 117–39; Haller points out the continuities between Milton's views of marriage and those of the domestic handbooks. The most complex analyses of the domestic handbooks and Milton's relation to them are found in James T. Johnson, "English Puritan Thought on the Ends of Marriage," *Church History XXXVI* (1969), 429–36, James T. Johnson, "The Covenant Idea and the Puritan View of Marriage," *JHI XXXII* (1971), 107–18, and James T. Johnson, *A Society Ordained by God* (New York, 1970).

4. John Milton, *Complete Prose Works of John Milton*, 8 vols., ed. Don Wolfe et al. (New Haven, 1953–82), vol. II, p. 229, hereafter cited as YP. The problem parliamentary apologists had with marital analogies is discussed in Mary Lyndon Shanley, "Marriage Contract and Social Contract in Seventeenth-Century English Political Thought," *Western Political Quarterly LXXIX* (1979), 79–91.

5. Alexander Niccholes, *Discourse at Marriage and Wiving* (London, 1615), quoted in Johnson, "The Covenant Idea," p. 110.

6. Thomas Gataker, *A Wife in Deed* (London, 1623), quoted in Johnson, "The Covenant Idea," p. 110.

7. Even the well-known anxiety of Elizabethan and Jacobean men about cuckoldry, evident in Shakespeare, seems to have had, partially, a class basis. Since women were often married by older men, many women were left as attractively prosperous widows by their spouses' death; given the restrictions placed on women's sociability, and the small social distance between mistresses and servants, particularly head servants, the latter were obvious choices as second husbands, and such marriages appear to have been common; this probably exacerbated fears of adultery in middle-class males and encouraged an association

of women with rebellious servants. See Geoffrey Robert Quaife, *Wayward Wives and Wanton Wenches* (New Brunswick, N.J., 1979), pp. 132–133, 145, 246.

8. William Gouge, *Of Domestical Duties* (London, 1622), quoted in Louis B. Wright, *Middle-Class Culture in Elizabethan England* (Chapel Hill, N.C., 1935), p. 222; on Perkins, see Robert V. Schnucker, "La Position Puritaine a l'égard de l'adultère," *Annales: économie, sociétés, civilisations XXII* (1972), 1379–88.

9. Thomas Gataker, *A Good Wife God's Gift* (London, 1623), quoted in Johnson, *Society Ordained by God*, p. 95.

10. See Brian Manning, *The English People and the English Revolution* (London, 1976); on the English Revolution generally I draw on Christopher Hill, *Puritanism and Revolution* (London, 1958) and Christopher Hill, *The World Turned Upside Down: Radical Ideas During the English Revolution* (London, 1972), Lawrence Stone, *The Causes of the English Revolution: 1529–1642* (London, 1972); and William Hunt, *The Puritan Moment* (Cambridge, Mass., 1983).

11. See Hill, *Milton*, pp. 268–78, for the radical associations of Arminianism; the Puritans, of course, also accused the Laudians of a conservative form of Arminianism. Milton himself would later, in the private *Of Christian Doctrine*, adopt a radical Arminian position.

12. On Puritan hostility toward magic and superstition, see Keith Thomas, *Religion and the Decline of Magic* (New York, 1971).

13. Manning, *The English People*, pp. 43–45, 69–70.

14. See Derek Hirst, *The Representatives of the People?* (Cambridge, 1975).

15. My general conception of romance derives from Northrop Frye, *The Secular Scripture* (Cambrdge, Mass., 1976) and *Anatomy of Criticism* (Princeton, N.J., 1971). The narratives I describe are also indebted to Puritan conversion narratives, which are themselves versions, as Frye remarks about saints' lives, of romance narrative paradigms.

16. For a similar contrast between the masque tradition and Milton's *Comus*, see Maryann Cale McGuire, *Milton's Puritan Masque* (Athens, Ga., University of Georgia Press, 1983).

MILTON'S "DIVORSIVE" INTERPRETATION AND THE GENDERED READER

Olga Lucía Valbuena

> O Why did God,
> Creator wise, that peopled highest heav'n
> With Spirits masculine, create at last
> This novelty on earth, this fair defect
> Of nature, and not fill the world at once
> With men as angels without feminine,
> Or find some other way to generate
> Mankind?[1]

I

WHEN IN *Paradise Lost* Eve doomed herself by tasting of the forbidden fruit, Adam had a critical choice to make. He could have refused her society and, divorced from her, returned to his solitary life in Eden. To choose Eve necessarily meant to identify with her humanity, her difference from God. "Against his better knowledge, not deceived, / But fondly overcome with female charm," Adam obeyed "the bond of nature" and, against the law of the patriarch, cleaved to his "other self," his wife.[2] Writing on the thorny subject of divorce beginning in 1643, Milton implicitly reverses Adam's choice.

Milton's project in the *Doctrine and Discipline of Divorce*, as in *Tetrachordon* and, to some extent, in *Christian Doctrine*, is to recover the primacy of what he calls "all the divorsive engines in heaven or earth."[3] He applies what he takes to be three complementary strategies to this end. Rhetorically, Milton invests divorce with origins and sublimity by calling it "the first and last of all [God's] visible works" (*DDD*, p. 273). Raising divorce to the level of a divine mandate, he speaks of God's "divorcing command" (p. 273), the "unchangeable command" (p. 264), and "this divorsive Law" (pp. 244–45), all the while insisting that marriage "is neither a law nor a commandment" (*CD*, p. 355). But to win the reader's heart and mind Milton must awaken a longing for divorce from whatever may be associated with the feminine. To this end he attempts to stir in his readers a political horror of physical or teleological identification with the feminine, with sexuality, and with marriage, the latter two being entailments of the first. For the purposes of his argument, marriage—as it now stands—is of all conditions the most threatening to masculine liberty.

The definitive step in Milton's argument for divorce, the question to which I will return in the latter part of this essay, is his privileging of the Hebraic tradition over the Christian with respect to divorce law and exegetical method. Stressing the Hebraic biblical dialect as the "*Metropolitan* language" against which the gospel must be read, he patterns his method of biblical interpretation on that of Midrash, the ancient exegetical system of the Jews (*Tetra.*, p. 671). In that connection, he also asserts that the word *fornication* in Matthew, Chapter xix, verses 8–9, can and should be harmonized with the more "enlightened" rabbinical interpretations of the term *some uncleanness* in Deuteronomy, chapter xxiv, verses 1–2.[4] Midrash itself, as will be shown below, operates on a principle of divorce, and thus provides symbolic if not actual validation of his efforts.

Milton, then, attempts to convince his audience, so certain of the interrelatedness of the public and private spheres, that although marriage might be the "fountaine and seminary of all other sorts and kinds of life, in the Commonwealth and in the Church," no external authority should legislate an Englishman's private, conjugal life.[5] He makes this claim on the basis that the more ancient law of Moses "left [divorce] to a mans own arbitrement to be determin'd between God and his own conscience" (*DDD*, p. 318).

Milton would seem, like his contemporaries, to accept the relation between family life and the life of the Commonwealth. But he does not share the belief that every marriage and household contributes to the overall integrity of the polity. Having raised the precept of "mutual solace" and not simply the state of marriage to an absolute standard, Milton views divorce as one important antidote to the current social anomie:

> For no effect of tyranny can sit more heavy on the Common-wealth, then this houshold unhappines on the family. And farewell all hope of true Reformation in the state, while such an evill as this lies undiscern'd or unregarded in the house. On the redresse wherof depends, not only the spiritfull and orderly life of our grown men, but the willing, and carefull education of our children. (*DDD*, pp. 229–30)

At its most fundamental level, this passage affirms Milton's unshakeable belief in the idea of "separate spheres" for the sexes. Marital unhappiness can lead to nonfulfillment of a woman's domestic responsibilities, "the willing, and careful education of our children." The spiritual demoralization of men thwarts "true Reformation in the state" and, in *Tetrachordon*, "degenerates and disorders the best spirits, leavs them . . . unactive to all public service, dead to the Common-wealth" (*Tetra.*, p. 632). Domestic tyranny, "against the good of *man* both soul and body," effects a deadening or virtual depletion of masculine vigor: it turns a man into the "thrall" of "an inferiour sexe" (*DDD*, p. 276; *Tetra.*, p. 589; my emphasis).

Milton asserts, "both in the Scriptures, and in the gravest Poets and Philosophers I finde the properties and excellencies of a wife set out *only from domestic vertues*" (*Tetra.*, p. 613, my emphasis). By equating the wife with domesticity, Milton confines each to the other and radically separates the masculine from both. Here Milton seems to make an implicit distinction between the terms *wife* and *woman*. But, in fact, he negates the possibility of an individual feminine subjectivity and civic presence. He steadfastly maintains that woman was "instituted" by God for the sole purpose of accommodating man in the domestic sphere precisely so that he may assume his productive role in civil society. If a man should find he is mistaken in his choice of partner, he can be certain that the woman in question is no wife, which means she is nothing: "Such an associate he who puts away, divorces not a wife, but disjoyns a nullity which God never joyn'd, if she be neither willing, not to her proper and requisite duties sufficient, as the words of God institute her" (*Tetra.*, p. 670).

Milton repeatedly urges men to recognize in their gender the absolute superiority to, and liberty from, external restrictions in matters of conscience. This much granted, he encourages them to view current divorce law as an "encroachment" on the very essence of their masculinity. Since under the "Canon bit" marriage is indissoluble except for adultery, the institution of matrimony itself threatens to effeminate the individual man, not only before the "inferiour sexe" whose "thrall" he may well become, but also politically and religiously, before the "Scholasticks and Canonists" whose "crabbed" interpretations "inslave the dignity of man" (*DDD*, pp. 230, 228). Then, of course, there is the irresistible analogy between the bad wife and the bad ruler. As if reminding the parliamentarians of their oath to defend the Commonwealth, he suggests that all men become thralls if one is "unreasonably yoakt" (*DDD*, p. 249): "He who marries, intends as little to conspire his own ruine, as he that swears Allegiance: and as a whole people is in proportion to an ill Government, so is one man to an ill mariage" (*DDD*, p. 229).

He further reminds them that the institution of marriage, like woman herself, was created for the solace of man. Milton might pay lip service to the Puritans by speaking of companionship and mutual solace in marriage, but he always returns to "the occasionall end of [woman's] creation" as man's helpmate, not as an individual in the same sense as man. Thus in *Tetrachordon,* Milton asserts:

seeing woman was purposely made for man, and he her head, it cannot stand before the breath of this divine utterance, that man the portraiture of God, *joyning to himself for his intended good and solace an inferiour sexe,* should so becom her thrall, whose wilfulnes or inability to be a wife frustrates the occasionall end of her creation, but that he may acquitt himself to freedom by his naturall birthright, and that indeleble character of priority which God crown'd him with. (*Tetra.*, pp. 589–90, my emphasis)[6]

Milton hoped, in effect, to do something impossible: he wanted to deracinate from the cultural imagination the idea that marriage is the dominant metaphor for political order. Marriage, says Milton, is a thing indifferent and therefore not susceptible to legal or religious tampering. But divorce is another matter; for him it is no less than the primordial agency of creation and progress, the principle through which, if the Parliament is listening, men can justify "putting away" whomever obstructs their liberty, their masculine sovereignty:

or if they meet through mischance, by all consequence to dis-joyn them, as God and nature signifies and lectures to us not onely by those recited decrees [the law of Moses], but ev'n by the first and last of all his visible works; when by his divorcing command the world first rose out of Chaos, nor can be renew'd again out of confusion but by the separating of unmeet consorts. (*DDD*, p. 273)

Writing *Doctrine and Discipline of Divorce,* Milton knows that he faces a formidable army of traditionalist interpreters of the Bible who would "envie and cry-down the industry of free reasoning, under the terms of humor, and innovation" (*DDD*, p. 224). To conjoin in his readers' minds terms that they must have perceived as antithetical, namely interpretive conservatism and sexual license, Milton claims that "he who affirms adultery to be the highest breach, affirms the bed to be the highest of mariage, which is in truth a grosse and borish opinion" (*DDD*, p. 269).

In his prefatory address to *Doctrine and Discipline of Divorce,* Milton parodies the canonical indissolubility of marriage in a Spenserian vision of "Custome" and "error," a grotesque marriage that lacks a "head," in both the sexual and political senses. So as to impart to his audience a horror of the loveless marriage, Milton represents dissatisfied men as mere drones before the "slavish errands of the body," or, put another way, as servants to canonical law (*Tetra.*, p. 599). There is no gender-neutral language in Milton's English. Error finds "what he wants" when "by secret inclination" he is seduced by the feminine "Custome": "Custome being but a meer face, as Eccho is a meere voice, rests not in *her* unaccomplishment, untill by secret inclination, shee accorporat her selfe with error, who being a blind and Serpentine body without a head, willingly accepts what *he* wants, and supplies what her incompleatnesse went seeking" (*DDD*, p. 223, my emphasis).

"Custome," the "meer face" of propriety, and error, "a blind and Serpentine body without a head," entering into a mock union, graft their deformed parts in a conspiracy to close up "the womb of teeming Truth" (*DDD*, p. 223). This dark conceit of bestial sexuality is meant to prefigure its human equivalent, "to grind in the mill of an undelighted and servil copulation," an unhappy marriage (*DDD*, p. 258). Both kinds of debasement result from the contagion of a whole group of Christian men (with "Custome") or an individual (in "servil copulation") with a malign agency, for Milton the gender of Discord and Sin itself, the feminine.[7]

I do not intend to ferret out misogyny in Milton. On the contrary, I believe that the feminine is crucial for Milton inasmuch as he depends on it to supply qualities that can improve men's lives. These might include having an unchallenging companion, an undemanding domestic life, in short, the leisure to do one's work in the world. Indeed, Milton idealizes the strictly ancillary role he envisions for women in his culture. Speaking of men in civil society, he observes:

> We cannot therefore alwayes be contemplative, or pragmaticall abroad, but have need of som delightfull intermissions, wherein the enlarg'd soul may leav off a while her severe schooling; and like a glad youth in wandring vacancy may keep her hollidaies to joy and harmles pastime: which as she cannot well doe without company so in no company so well as where the different sexe in most resembling unlikenes, and most unlike resemblance cannot but please best and be pleas'd in the aptitude of that variety. (*Tetra.*, p. 597)

This passage fully anticipates the eighteenth-century sentimentalization of "feminine" feeling, of sympathy and beauty that is supposed to pleasantly distract a thinking and productive male citizen.[8] Yet Milton also associates the feminine with properties that he envisions as specifically nonmasculine or especially deleterious to masculine nature. Among those I will point to are "Custome," Sin, and hell, all given feminine gender markers or decisive association with the feminine. In addition, seemingly less harmful terms are consistently aligned with the feminine: charm, sensuality, guile, changeability, and marriage. They may be found wherever one works with Milton and the question of gender, but this essay is restricted to a discussion of Milton's major writing on divorce, with *Paradise Lost* as additional "prooftext."[9]

The terms below should be taken, like Adam and Eve, as belonging to matched pairs rather than as antitheses. While a few entailments of the feminine are treated as worthy though dependent counterparts of the masculine, the total effect of Milton's project is to gather by accretion a list of constraints to masculine liberty that he identifies with the feminine and, put somewhat polemically, its contagion. He must, in short, discourage men from allowing themselves to be absorbed and disnatured by that which can be called "palpably uxorious" (*DDD*, p. 324):

"Custome"	individual reason
Beguilement (charm)	"Error"
Sin	Law
hell	heaven
subject dependence	individual liberty
charity	conscience
companionship—Eve	solitude—Adam
domestic life	civil life
external beauty	sublimity
sensuality	contemplation
"indefinite likenesse of womanhood"	"portraiture of God"
changeability	self-identity, oneness
marriage	divorce[10]

These matched pairs, let alone the entire list, do not usually occur together in his writing. Yet Milton intends their cumulative force to result in contempt of the feminine, by which I do not mean "a Turkish contempt of females." When Milton speaks of a disgruntled husband as one "train'd by a deceitful bait into a snare of misery," he taps into the dread of feminine consumption already fixed in the cultural imagination. Milton explores as well the corollary threat of becoming indistinguishable from the feminine by becoming one body with woman through sexual contact, itself a type of contamination. At the level of social discourse, this debasement occurs in the suggestion that the two sexes are equal before God: "It might be doubted why he saith, *In the Image of God created he him,* not them, as well as *male and female* them; especially since that Image might be common to them both, but *male and female* could not, however the Jewes fable, and please themselvs with the accidentall concurrence of *Plato's* wit, as if man at first had bin created *Hermaphrodite*" (*Tetra.*, p. 589).

In seeking to recover the original power of divorce, Milton would like to awaken in a select group, in men "of eminent spirit and breeding," his nostalgia for a golden age prior to woman, before all that which Milton associates with the feminine entered the world. But this being an unrealistic goal, he lobbies instead for the reinstatement of the Hebraic law of divorce and its supporting method as he sees it—the rabbinical system of biblical exegesis. Milton's desire for internal consistency will find him arguing for the restitution of Mosaic divorce law and, somewhat implausibly, also for the polygamy and concubinage practiced in ancient times. Not even the most radical Puritan reformers of Milton's day were prepared for such innovations.

When Milton argues for the husband's absolute rule as "the master of family," he simply enlarges upon the husband-as-king analogy already available in marriage treatises of the seventeenth century (*DDD*, p. 318). The fundamental difference between him and his Puritan predecessors is that Milton treats divorce as a private matter, a "power which Christ never took from the master of family, but rectify'd only to a right and wary use at home" (*DDD*, p. 318). Indeed, Milton invests the prosperity of the nation with the patriarch's absolute right when he states "how hurtfull and distractive it is to the house, the Church and Common-wealth" that the husband's will to divorce be usurped by the "undiscerning Canonist" and made a matter for the courts (*DDD*, p. 318). Clearly, Milton perceives in this denial of power more than a merely symbolic threat to masculine liberty, to the freedom to make independent determinations on private matters with a man's conscience and the scriptures as his only guide.

While Puritan thinkers emphasize the ideal of the companionate marriage, one in which the spouses have distinct moral and social duties—but are both accountable for its success—Milton lays the burden of proof squarely on the wife.[11] Unlike the Puritan theologians that preceded him, Milton assigns no distinct responsibilities to the husband beyond naming him the "master of family." It is Milton's opinion that God created the male as an autonomous being, one who nonetheless felt a "rationall burning" for another with whom to share all of creation (*DDD*, p. 251). Woman, on the other hand, was not made an autonomous creature but was intended as a "meet or like help" meant to fulfill man's need for companionship. Though Milton never says precisely what makes "a meet help," he does equate a good wife with a good marriage. Under Milton's system there would be no scrutiny of the man; he would decide whether his wife, and, by extension, his marriage is acceptable or flawed. Milton further argues that if man must never divorce, then God must fulfill "that sacred and not vain promise of [his] to remedy mans lonelines by *making him a meet help for him*, though not now in perfection, as at first, yet still in proportion as things now are" (*DDD*, p. 309).

Milton's conception of marriage not only necessitates and justifies divorce in the fallen world, but it also conditions his notion of the feminine and women's role in civilization. As soon as the man feels that his wife no longer fulfills the purpose for which she was created, the marriage cannot be said to conform to God's promise. Then the element that for Milton makes the marriage worthy of continuation, that which defines it as a marriage, is the conformity of the woman to her husband's potentially changeable expectations. The man's right to judge his wife's meetness is implicit in Milton's belief in individual freedom of interpretation and is supported by his belief that the government of the family should be left to the husband.

The following passage demonstrates that for Milton the test of a marriage's authenticity falls on the woman. His main assumption is that the home provides the base of support for a man's "publick enterprizes" and that his satisfaction in marriage is the very measure of the "household estate." Further, because he accepts in principle the "little commonwealth" model of the household and family, Milton imagines a husband's marital dissatisfaction as "unprofitable and dangerous" to the political community as a whole. Nowhere does the woman's stake in the "household estate" or "publick enterprizes" enter into his calculation: for Milton the husband's complacence in marriage constitutes the wife's validity. If Milton's convoluted prose in the following passage was reduced to its barest expression, it would read: "if the wife fails to fulfill the goal of her creation as promised by God, then such a woman can be no wife and the marriage can be no marriage":

> if the woman be naturally so of disposition, as will not help to remove, but help to encrease that same God-forbidd'n lonelines which will in time draw on with it a generall discomfort and dejection of minde, not beseeming either Christian profession or morall conversation, unprofitable and dangerous to the Common-wealth, when the houshold estate, out of which must flourish forth the vigor and spirit of all publick enterprizes, is so ill contented and procur'd at home, and cannot be supported; *such a mariage can be no mariage* whereto the most honest end is wanting. (*DDD*, p. 247; my emphasis)

Further ahead in this pamphlet, Milton states that "shee who naturally & perpetually is no meet help, can be no wife; which cleerly takes away the difficulty of dismissing such a one" (*DDD*, p. 309). When Milton speaks of "solace and satisfaction of the minde" as the most important values in marriage, he speaks primarily, if not exclusively, of the man's needs. That observation might seem to conflict with Milton's repeated insistence on the necessity of mutual compatibility in marriage. However, it is important to bear in mind that Milton consistently refers the aims of marriage to male prerogatives, while he measures a good marriage solely on the husband's subjective valuation of the wife's fitness. He concludes that in the case of an "ill mariage," understood as a man wed to an unmeet wife, divorce does not constitute the severance of a covenant with God. For if that "help" should prove no solace, then God cannot have joined the man and woman in wedlock, for that would involve God in a contradiction:

> So when it shall be found by their apparent unfitnes, that their continuing to be man and wife is against the glory of God and their mutuall happines, it may assure them that God never joyn'd them; who hath reveal'd his gratious will not to set the ordinance above the man for whom it was ordain'd: not to canonize mariage either as a tyrannesse or a goddesse over the enfranchiz'd life and soul of man. (*DDD*, p. 277)

An examination of this passage reveals a great deal about the status of the feminine in Milton. He opens by emphasizing the centrality of "mutuall happines," but soon asserts that God created "the ordinance" of marriage for "the man." He then represents an unsatisfactory marriage as a female, a "tyrannesse or a goddesse" that frustrates the purpose for which "she" (marriage and, by extension, the woman), was created. Regarding the question of whether divorce law was instituted for the protection of the woman, Milton writes: "God . . . counsels the man rather to divorce then to live with such a collegue [who would usurp "house-rule" from the man], and yet on the other side expresses nothing of the wives suffering with a bad husband; is it not most likely that God in his Law had more pitty towards man thus wedlockt, then towards the woman that was created for another" (*DDD*, p. 325).

Moreover, to enforce marriage beyond the point where it is "found unfit" contradicts the purpose of matrimony as God instituted it. He suggests that to persist in such a marriage violates the first commandment, the prohibition against keeping false gods: "to injoyn the indissoluble keeping of a mariage found unfit against the good of man both soul and body, as hath been evidenc't, is to make an Idol of mariage" (*DDD*, p. 276). The telling feature of this statement is Milton's exclusion of the wife where one would expect her "good" to be mentioned too, namely, after "against the good of man." Instead, he inserts the word "Idol" in close proximity to his attack on those who would "canonize mariage either as a tyrannesse or a goddesse" (*DDD*, p. 277).

Always suspicious of any literalist reading of Scripture, Milton opposes what he sees as a legal-exegetical narrowmindedness which attempts to "set straiter limits to obedience, then God had set" (*DDD*, p. 228). Thus, he repeatedly argues for the "dignity of man" and his freedom not to entrap himself in an idolatrous relation to the very institution that should serve, not oppress him. Here Milton implicitly condemns the Puritans along with other Protestants and Catholics who maintain the indissolubility of marriage: "I make no wonder, but rest confident that who so preferrs either Matrimony, or other Ordinance before the good of man and the plaine exigence of Charity, let him professe Papist, or Protestant, or what he will, he is no better then a Pharise, and understands not the Gospel" (*DDD*, p. 233).

Much of Milton's diatribe against "our Canon Courts in *England*" centers on the sacramental status of marriage (*DDD*, p. 237). He contends that declaring marriage a sacrament, "another act of papal encroachment it was, to pluck the power & arbitrement of divorce from the master of family, into whose hands God & the law of all Nations had put it" (*DDD*, p. 343). What should be left to the conscience of the individual man, according to God's law, has been turned into a matter of papal superstition and judicial arbitration, neither of which should interfere in a man's domestic affairs. Clearly, what Milton most objects to is the loss of "Christian liberty" suffered by the husband under a literal interpretation, or "alphabetical servility" to the New Testament, which he denies has repealed Moses' divorce law.

In his opening epistle to the readers of *Christian Doctrine*, Milton states that long before he decided to embark upon his "systematic exposition of Christian teaching," even as a boy he began "an earnest study of the Old and New Testaments in their original languages," gradually moving to commentaries and larger theological systems predicated on the Bible (*CD*, pp. 120, 119). Gradually, as the deficiencies of earlier scriptural interpretation became apparent to him, he says, "I pursued my studies, and so far satisfied myself that eventually I had no doubt about my ability to distinguish correctly in religion between matters of faith and matters of opinion" (*CD*, pp. 120–21).

II

Critics have long recognized that Milton makes ample use of the Hebrew Bible both in his poetry and in his prose. It has also been noted since at least the nineteenth century that his prose writings show midrashic influences in both allusions and exegetical practice. Still, there is great critical disagreement regarding Milton's understanding of the midrashic tradition and its correct application in the interpretation of Scripture.[12]

While it is true that Milton was not a trained Hebraist, he did read Midrashim both in the original and in at least one reliable translation.[13] A linguistically demanding and tradition-bound form of biblical exegesis, Midrash appealed to Milton in part because its methods allow for a divorcing of text from context, an "opening up of the text" to individual, though methodologically informed, interpretation. He preferred Midrash's decontextualization and rearrangement of Scripture to what he deemed the ossified interpretations of the Bible prevalent in his day. The availability of vastly different Midrashim for a single verse also appealed to him; if one rabbinical school rejected divorce except for adultery, another interpreted "uncleannes" as "whatever was unalterably distastful, whether in body or mind" (*Tetra.*, p. 620). In addition to his intellectual preference, Milton also relished the opportunity to participate in the Hebraic textual dialogue that lent authority and meaning to his own work as a politico-religious lobbyist. That he absorbed the *spirit* of midrashic interpretation even if he lacked the tradition and extensive training of the rabbis is evident from his exegetical method.

Just as Scripture for the Jews "became the guide of the nation after the exile," Milton, among other Protestant reformers, also believes that answers to his nation's problems can be found in a right interpretation of the Bible.[14] For Milton, one of the most urgent problems to be addressed was divorce. After having written four tracts in its favor between 1643 and 1645, Milton returns to this topic in his last prose work, "my dearest and best possession," the *Christian Doctrine.*

Certainly, Milton's reliance on the Hebrew Bible as his main prooftext is conditioned by the spirit of the Protestant Reformation, whose leaders looked to the Pentateuch for inspiration as this was God's earliest pronouncement on the ordering of civil society. As Golda Werman notes, "theologians of the Reformation leaned heavily on Jewish exegesis to fill the gap left by the Protestants' rejection of Catholic authority. . . . Furthermore, it was important for the Protestants to demonstrate that Jewish exegesis, some of which was, according to tradition, as ancient as Scripture itself, sided with them rather than with the Catholics" (Werman, p. 36)

But there are other reasons for Milton's favoring the Hebrew over the Christian Bible. The first reason, which should not be overlooked, is quite simply that the Hebrew Bible appears to support his case. Another reason Milton chooses the Hebrew Bible lies in his ultimate preference for the authority of God's Word over that of Christ, God being the originary lawgiver. Milton does not believe in the divinity or authority of

Christ independent of the Father and, moreover, he will be tenacious about keeping power centralized in one being. Milton, then, cites the Hebrew Bible in his defense of divorce and polygamy because coming from God it establishes a law which precedes Christ's seeming qualification of the law in Matthew, chapter xix, verses 8–9. Milton defends his position by arguing that God allowed, and even commanded, divorce under Hebrew Law, and that Christ cannot be seen as "condemning, altering, or abolishing this precept of divorce, which is plainly moral, for that were against his truth, his promise, and his prophetick office" (*DDD*, p. 326).

From the standpoint of hermeneutics, the most intriguing way in which Milton adopts Hebrew biblical practice is in his use of Midrash. As Renée Bloch points out, Midrash developed among the Jews out of a felt need to codify community and individual behavior in the face of a precarious postexilic existence.[15] Milton views himself and other nonconformist Christians as existing in an analogous spiritual exile, from both the Catholic Church and the Anglican Church of England, the latter by Puritan standards retaining too much of the dogma and superstitious practices of the former.

Bloch argues that Midrash promotes the successive "actualization" of Scripture for "men of all times." That is, midrashic exegesis is predicated upon the idea that the Bible should "open indefinitely to all new understandings of the message" (Bloch, p. 33). While the ground or "message" will remain constant and temporally embedded within the narrative that carries it, adherence to the precise details of the laws (halakah) and interpretation of the anecdotes (haggadah) will vary according to the demands of changing historical conditions.

Now Milton takes certain details of the Bible literally; at least in regard to the marriage code, Milton has a tremendous will to turn back time, to replicate the ancient Hebrew world where men could practice polygamy, keep concubines, and divorce at will (*CD*, pp. 355–56). Such a regress would certainly radicalize Golda Werman's merely formal supposition that the Puritans of Milton's day "believed in the possibility and virtue of reestablishing a contemporary religious order and political system based on Scriptures."[16] However, Milton so desires to reform the nation according to the Hebraic model that he obscures the distinction between regarding the Bible as the living word of God and recognizing that the historical circumstances which conditioned laws and practices during the biblical era do not obtain in seventeenth-century England.

Numerous recent expositions of Midrash have become available, due in part to the influence of poststructuralism and the interest it has generated in etymology and the discussion of textual authority and agency. Critics have become conscious of the similarity between the midrashic project and poststructuralism, the "questioning" of texts and consciousness of the inter- and intra-text. Although explications of Midrash vary according to a writer's interest in demonstrating its significance for ancient exegesis or for modern criticism, one finds a degree of continuity in the understanding of its basic tenets.[17] With its attention to historical development and delineation of subgenres, Bloch's essay, "Midrash," offers a representative definition:

> In rabbinic literature midrash has the general sense of "search," with the double nuance of *study* . . . and explanation. . . . As opposed to the literal explanation, called *pešat*, the term midrash designates an exegesis which *moves beyond the simple and literal sense in order to penetrate into the spirit of Scripture;* to scrutinize the text more deeply and draw from it interpretations which are not always immediately obvious. (p. 31, my emphasis)

Coming to an understanding of the "not always immediately obvious" lies at the heart of Midrash, at its inception. The method involves explaining discrete verses of the Bible which have proven difficult by juxtaposing them to others. As Michael Fishbane explains ("Inner Biblical Exegesis," p. 21), scriptural interpretation begins around the first millenium BCE with the subsumption of the ancient oral culture by a nascent textual culture. The earliest evidence of exegesis is found as the scribe "patiently copied out a text and reacted to its ambiguities and oddities," commenting on them, but generally not altering or otherwise reducing the problematic verse or passage (Fishbane, p. 21). Certainly, with the advent of a relatively stable written text, individual reason becomes an increasingly important factor in the midrashic process of biblical interpretation—but a good deal of received tradition always informs the Midrash on a particular verse.[18] In his practice, Milton will proceed in the spirit of this interpretive method but will disregard both the historical contexts and accepted readings of Scripture when submitting the text to his individual reason, to "the reasonable Soul of man" (*DDD*, p. 227).

The fundamental strategies of Midrash, the juxtaposition of verses from different contexts for mutual clarification, and the move beyond the simple or literal meaning to "penetrate into the spirit of Scripture," all operate in Milton's hermeneutical practice. Like the rabbis, Milton believes that "places of Scripture wherein just reason of doubt arises from the letter, are to be expounded by considering upon what occasion every thing is set down: and by comparing other Texts" (*DDD*, p. 282).

In contrast to the midrashist's attempt to clarify God's laws, Milton also evaluates their usefulness: he concludes that God, in his benevolence, could not have logically imposed any law to the detriment of man, for to do so would amount to contradicting himself as well as the "law of nature." Now the law of nature has a long tradition dating back to at least the fourth century BCE. The Stoics conceived of it as "a ray of . . . celestial fire" or "seminal reason" related to man's intellectual and moral position within the "divine order of the universe." As appropriated by the church fathers, it is a "remnant of the authoritative pattern written in man's heart at creation . . . which is available to the reason of fallen man, variously aided by the enlightenment of grace."[19] Although the orthodox Christian mind has been careful to shape the obligatory piousness into this concept, it nevertheless lends itself to individual interpretation. And any time Milton refers to reason or the law of nature, he invokes individual reason, guided by charity, as the touchstone of all law.

This last point introduces a significant inversion of the traditional Christian understanding of the law of nature: the reasonableness God had originally imprinted on man at creation now becomes a mandate for God's actions toward men. Nor is a man bound to any law—even a divine law—which frustrates the benign end to which it was directed. This position is made explicit in *Doctrine and Discipline of Divorce* when Milton argues that "this is a solid rule that every command giv'n with a reason, binds our obedience no otherwise then that reason holds" (*DDD*, p. 308). Once the Creator has endowed man with reason, God and man have implicitly entered into a covenant wherein God, because of his necessary univocality, cannot contradict Himself and still be God.[20]

In *The Doctrine and Discipline of Divorce*, Milton states that Christ, Moses, and the Law would be involved in an intolerable contradiction were Christ to abrogate God's earlier commands concerning divorce (*DDD*, pp. 283–84). In *Christian Doctrine*, Milton reminds his audience that "the most holy patriarchs and pillars of our faith" had practiced both polygamy and divorce under Hebrew Law, the "gift" of God the Father (*CD*, p. 356). According to Milton, God and his agents must act consistently, that is, they must not promulgate a law or custom that would implicitly repudiate that of the "patriarchs" and by implication Moses or even God. That would undercut Christ's promise of "not condemning, altering, or abolishing this precept of divorce, which is plainly moral," for that would be "against his truth, his promise, and his prophetick office" (*DDD*, p. 326).

One of Milton's professed goals in writing *Doctrine and Discipline* is to demonstrate that the Bible is not full of "cranks and contradictions, and pit falling dispenses," as the "crabbed textuists" and "extrem literalists" have made it seem (*DDD*, p. 230, 233). Indeed, it is his opinion that, by employing the charitable method of harmonizing discrete passages in Scripture, the gospel can be shown to agree with the Hebrew Bible in allowing divorce. Furthermore, Milton believes that Christ would not impose a stricter law—to the contradiction of the Father—than that which already existed under Mosaic law: "if therfore [Christ] touch the law of *Moses* at all, he touches the moral part therof; which is absurd to imagine that the covnant of grace should reform the exact and perfect law of works, eternal and immutable; or if he touch not the Law at all, then is not the allowance therof disallow'd to us" (*DDD*, p. 318).

Milton attempts to resolve contradictions between the Hebrew Bible and the New Testament by taking the former as the clearer or axiomatic prooftext, contending that Christ purposely obscured his sayings in the New Testament to baffle the Pharisees more.[21] In that sense he actually gives the text or the law of the Hebrew Bible preeminence over that of the New Testament. But having said this it is necessary to make one important qualification. While Milton does not see Christ as having abrogated the law, he believes that Christ intended "to vindicate from abusive traditions," to lift "the licencious Glosse which traduc't the Law" that the Pharisees had used without charity (*DDD*, p. 317). That is, Christ opposes not the practice or the law of divorce, but its frivolous misuse by uncharitable men. Milton will not abide that the received Word of God should contain inconsistencies. When the Bible fails to disclose a univocal and "reasonable" response to a difficult issue, Milton approaches the problem with a view to save God from a contradiction. But given Milton's political objectives as he prepares for the leap from divorce to regicide, this will by no means be a disinterested defense.

When Milton speaks of divorce, he uses the word in a very general way; he does not explain the different contexts in which the Bible represents types of separation, but rather disconnects or *divorces* scriptural verses from the historical or otherwise special conditions that give rise to the pronouncement. As James L. Kugel explains (p. 93), this practice of verse decontextualization forms part of the midrashic practice: "each verse of the Bible is in principle as connected to its most distant fellow as to the one next door." To support his position that Moses' law constitutes "an unchangeable command," Milton disregards the restricted contexts in which separation of men and women could not properly be called divorce, but is merely the severance of a formal, often economic, not a spousal relation.

Milton's suppression of the historical context of verses from Exodus and Deuteronomy introduces ethical problems that also permeate his main project, namely, how to divorce the feminine, how to dislodge this historically constituted subject from its biblical context. Milton's disregard of the economic and social concerns that in the Bible place limitations on divorce corresponds to his indifference to questions of family economics in seventeenth-century England. Milton never considers the social dislocation of wife and children that would necessarily follow the deregulation of divorce. So Milton argues: "God in his most holy, just and pure law has not only allowed divorce on various grounds, but has even, on some occasions, sanctioned it and on others very firmly insisted upon it: Exodus xxi. 4, 10, 11; Deut.xxi. 14 and xxiv.1; Ezra x.3; Neh.xiii.23, 30" (*CD*, YP VI, p. 372).

We may first consider the main prooftext Milton cites on the admissibility of divorce and its relation to two major verses he offers as evidence of God's "divorsive Law." There are, of course, various rabbinical schools, and their interpretations of ambiguously phrased verses are often diametrically opposed. On the question of divorce, the most important verse is Deuteronomy, xxiv, 1, and the Shammai and Hillel schools present its strongest readings. As David Amram explains, the rabbinical school of the Shammai has a much stricter reading of this verse than does the Hillel school.[22] We might first consider Milton's standard citation of Deuteronomy, xxiv, 1: "*When a man hath taken a wife, and married her, and it come to pass that she find no favour in his eyes, because he hath found som uncleannes in her, then let him write her a bill of divorcement, and give it in her hand, and send her out of his house*" (*Tetra.*, p. 614).

The Shammai school understood this "uncleanness" as referring to sexual immorality only, whereas the Hillel school interpreted this word more liberally so that the husband "may, for instance, if he please, divorce his wife for spoiling his food" (Amram, p. 33). In this connection Milton defends "Expositers" who widen the meaning of "uncleanness" in the spirit of the Hillel school:

> When Expositers began to understand the Hebrew Text, which they had not done of many ages before, they translated word for word not *uncleannes*, but the *nakednes of any thing;* and considering that nakednes is usually referr'd in Scripture to the minde as well as to the body, they constantly expound it any defect, annoyance, or ill quality in nature, which to bee joyn'd with, makes life tedious, and such company wors than solitude. (*Tetra.*, p. 620)

This reading of Deuteronomy, xxiv, 1, grants the husband the liberty that Milton claims God intended the "master of family" to enjoy. But as Amram shows, this particular class of divorce law was actually instituted by Moses himself as a qualification to the tradition that the oldest male ascendant's "rule over his wives, children and slaves was supreme":

> At the very beginning, or at least, as far back as the history of this institution can be traced, the husband's right to divorce was absolutely untrammelled, and it was only with the gradual breaking up of the patriarchal system, and the substitution of an individualistic for a socialistic state, that the woman acquired, at first merely negative rights, such as protection against her husband's acts, and, finally, positive rights, under which she could proceed against him. (Amram, pp. 22, 24).

Certainly the early protections for women in general can properly be called "negative rights" only. They in no sense allow a woman to proceed against her husband in the way of initiating a divorce, but they do check his formerly "untrammelled" power to dismiss her without further explanation. Exodus, chapter xxi, though Milton's citation does not acknowledge this, corresponds exactly to the spirit of this reform. The law here does not "very firmly insist" upon divorce so much as stipulate conditions for carrying it out.

To begin with, Exodus, Chapter xxi, deals with the separation of indentured servants and does not deal with divorce, properly speaking. Rather, it addresses the breaking of the economic relation between the master and his male and female servants after their period of indenture. Verse 4 addresses the male servant and states that "If his master have given him a wife, and she have born him sons or daughters; the wife and her children shall be her master's, and he shall go out by himself." This case does not constitute divorce as Milton defines it, for no spiritual falling-out in marriage is herein implied. That the male servant must leave his wife behind with the master is due to the master's ownership of her; for if the bondsman brings a wife with him at the inception of his service, as verse 3 clearly states, "then his wife shall go out with him." Verse 4 does not command a "divorce," but rather a separation that, while it may seem heartless to modern sensibilities, is rooted in the need to protect the master's household economy from sudden liquidation.

Verses 10 and 11 address the rights of the female bondswoman who has been given as a wife to the master's son: "If he take him another wife; her food, her raiment, and her duty of marriage, shall he not diminish." And verse 11: "And if he do not these three unto her, then shall she go out free without money." That is, the neglected wife is given the right to leave without being ransomed from the husband who has failed to provide *her* needs. While this separation constitutes a type of divorce, it occurs precisely under circumstances which contradict the thrust of Milton's argument: it is not a recommendation to divorce, but rather a measure for restricting egregious abuses on the part of the husband.

Upon examination of these verses, one finds that they do not indicate separation for reasons of emotional incompatibility with "things base, wretched, ill-omened and disastrous" (*DDD*, pp. 371–72). Instead, they demonstrate the Hebraic culture's introduction of political and economic restrictions to various abuses of patriarchal power. Milton is correct in stating that divorce was previously sanctioned and even insisted upon, but he does not account for the historical and economic contexts to which his prooftexts corresponded. Milton's argument is weakened by his failure to consider the specificity of those conditions and their incongruity with the England of his day.

As for his citation of Deuteronomy, xxiv, 14, this verse also has a restricted application and again checks the unlimited power of the husband. Verses 10 through 14 deal with the right of the captive maiden acquired as a spoil of war. The verses preceding the one Milton cites give the prescribed conditions for her treatment. Among the symbols of her reduced status in the community, she is to have her head shaved and her nails pared. However, she must be allowed, untouched, the space of one month to bewail her parents: "and after that thou shalt go in unto her, and be her husband, and she shall be thy wife (13). Verse 14 continues, "And it shall be, if thou have no delight in her, then thou shalt let her go whither she will; but thou shalt not sell her at all for money, thou shalt not make merchandise of her, because thou hast humbled her." As Calum M. Carmichael argues, this verse specifies the treatment of a woman who is "*prima facie* a slave" and could lawfully have been sold had her captor not married her: "By virtue of the marriage, however, the Hebrew master must accord her special treatment. . . . Since in D [Deuteronomy] she is married to him, he may divorce her but he must not sell her for money, thereby treating her as an article of trade, because he has humiliated her."[23]

The bonds of matrimony, then, make it impossible for a man to retain his relation of master to the captive maiden he takes as wife. In the Hebrew Bible, the sex act normally implies the will to marry or marriage itself, and there exist elaborate measures by which to redress fornication. Most significant here is that being joined in marriage protects the former captive or servant from being sold or otherwise disposed of by her husband: this especially during and after Moses' time, when the particular laws to which Milton erroneously appeals were instituted. Clearly, the purpose of these laws lies precisely in curtailing the putting away of wives for spurious reasons. While these acts do not constitute an abrogation of the earlier divorce law, they do limit its power, and were, as Amram notes, disliked by the men of Moses' day who preferred "their ancient privilege of sending away their wives to his restrictive measures, though the latter were neither many nor unreasonable" (Amram, pp. 27–28).

Perhaps the strongest check on divorce at will occurs in Deuteronomy, xx, 13–19. These verses deal with bringing accusations of premarital incontinency against a woman whose father promises her virginity intact at the time of marriage. If it can be proven by the stained garments, "the tokens of the damsel's virginity," that she has been slandered by the man who takes her as a wife, and "go[es] in unto her, and hate[s] her," then that man must pay the bride's father a hundred shekels of silver (verses 13, 17, 19). And as for the bride's relation to the husband, "she shall be his wife; he may not put her away all his days." Not surprisingly, Milton does not address this passage of Scripture, since it directly contradicts his notion that marriage is "not indissoluble or indivisible" (*CD*, p. 371). Clearly, there exist circumstances in which a man cannot, under Mosaic law, divorce a wife; another instance of its proscription involves the man's seduction or rape of a virgin of Israel (Deut. xxii, 28–29).

But these laws to restrict divorce are in no way meant to serve the woman's individual interests first. Certainly, she may well benefit from entering the community by way of marriage. But the primary issue here is not that a young woman has been slandered by an ungrateful man. It is the father of the bride who surfaces here as the injured party; it is he who must approach the elders of the city and demonstrate "by tokens" his daughter's innocence. Moreover, the father, not the daughter, will collect the one hundred shekels in restitution. Whether or not the bride wishes to live with the man she might reasonably disdain does not surface in this nexus of considerations. The point is that, for the sake of establishing legitimate heirs, a woman must neither be incontinent nor subject to being cast out of her husband's home on false charges. This law, diminishing the husband's freedom to dispose of an innocent wife, centers on the necessity to effect honorable exchanges of women, in this instance, between men.

The foregoing discussion points back to one of the questions I have explored in this essay. Protestants maintain that the only authoritative interpretations of Scripture are those illuminated by the Spirit in the individual. The relation of freedom from "receav'd opinion" to the specific historical context of biblical verses is interesting and problematic in Milton.

As is widely recognized, Milton certainly proves adept in making use of different systems of interpretation and even of theology. We have his own word that he has read the testaments "in their original languages . . .

[and] the shorter systems of theologians" (*CD*, p. 119). But above and beyond these authorities and even the text of the Bible itself, when we try to understand the significance of his interpretations, we are finally confronted with the radical humanism of Milton's "inner illumination." Despite Milton's protestations that the Bible is his final authority, there exists the ultimately competing notion of "the authority of the Spirit."

Despite his disclaimer at the outset of *Christian Doctrine*, "I . . . have striven to cram my pages even to overflowing, with quotations drawn from all parts of the Bible and to leave as little space as possible for my own words" (*CD*, p. 122), one must nevertheless question his results. It is precisely because Milton embeds his "own words" in a plethora of authority that we must examine the "divorsive engines" of his method.

It will be fruitful once again to cite Milton's advocacy of individual reason for scriptural interpretation, a matter which, as it is tied to individual salvation, is of no small concern to a Protestant. In *Christian Doctrine*, Milton abruptly inverts the deference to God that he has observed all along and states that: "Nowadays the external authority for our faith, in other words, the scriptures, is of very considerable importance and, generally speaking, it is the authority of which we have first experience. The pre-eminent and supreme authority, however, is the authority of the Spirit, which is internal, and the *individual possession* of each man" (*CD*, p. 587, my emphasis).

This statement has two important ramifications. Milton's "individual possession" of the "Spirit" shows how far the economic apologetics of his day were compatible and interchangeable with the Protestant rhetoric of individual scriptural interpretation. As for the status of the received, the canonical text in Milton, it is clear that Milton's intentions always lay in departing from the orthodox theologies that he had received, read, and rejected.

Divorce for Milton is a process of coming to masculine consciousness. It involves radical separation and realignment, in this case from embracing the feminine to absolutely repudiating it. Divorce means freedom from the tyranny of enslavement to any woman, monarch, or way of thought that would constrict masculine self-determination. For Milton, the process of divorcing "things unmeet" constitutes for man the highest possible approximation to God. For the individual, to "let the statutes of God be turn'd over, be scann'd a new, and consider'd" (*DDD*, p. 230) amounts to participation in the re-membering of reason, a return to God's original "divorcing command" that the world should rise out of chaos.

University of North Carolina

NOTES

1. John Milton, *Paradise Lost*, X, 888–95. Quotations are from *Paradise Lost*, ed. Scott Elledge (New York, 1975), hereafter cited as *PL*.

2. *PL* IX, 998–99, 956; VIII, 450. On the question of Adam's choice, see Catherine Belsey, *John Milton: Language, Gender, Power* (Oxford, 1988), pp. 73–74.

3. *Doctrine and Discipline of Divorce*, p. 264. All quotations of Milton's prose are from *Complete Prose Works of John Milton*, 8 vols., ed. Don M. Wolfe et al. (New Haven, 1953–82). Further references to *Doctrine and Discipline of Divorce* (vol. II) will be cited in the text as *DDD; Tetrachordon* (vol. II) will be cited as *Tetra.; Christian Doctrine* (vol. VI) will be cited as *CD*.

4. On Milton's "harmonizing" of apparently incompatible verses in Scripture, see Jason P. Rosenblatt, "Milton's Chief Rabbi," in *Milton Studies* XXIV, ed. James D. Simmonds (Pittsburgh, 1988), pp. 43–71. Rosenblatt identifies "as exclusively rabbinic the central argument in all of Milton's discussions of divorce, that Christ's pronouncement on divorce can be accommodated to the Deuteronomic permission" (p. 60). See also Mary Nyquist, "The Genesis of Gendered Subjectivity in the Divorce Tracts and in *Paradise Lost*," in *Re-membering Milton: Essays on the Texts and Traditions*, ed. Mary Nyquist and Margaret W. Ferguson (New York, 1988), pp. 99–127. Nyquist observes that "the most taxing exegetical feat Milton has to perform is the reconciliation of Matthew 19:3–11 . . . and Deuteronomy 24:1–2" (p. 105).

5. *Christian Oeconomie, Or a Short Survey of the Right Manner of Erecting and Ordering a Family, According to the Scripture*, trans. Thomas Pickering (London, 1618), p. 671.

6. For further evidence of Milton's valuation of masculine over feminine, see *PL* IV, 288–301 and note 7, below. For a thoroughgoing investigation of Milton's exegetical method in this connection, see Mary Nyquist, "Gynesis, Genesis, Exegesis, and the Formation of Milton's Eve," in *Cannibals, Witches and Divorce: Estranging the Renaissance*, ed. Marjorie Garber (Baltimore, 1987), pp. 147–208, and her essay, "Gendered Subjectivity," in *Re-membering Milton*, cited above, n. 4.

7. See *DDD*, p. 223n9, in which it is noted that Milton's allegory of "Custome" and "error" resembles Spenser's representation of Error in *Faerie Queene*, I, i, 13–24. In *Paradise Lost* Milton follows the mythologic tradition of feminizing Discord: "but Discord first / Daughter of Sin, among th' irrational" (*PL* X, 707–08). For the feminization of Sin as a debased version of the myth surrounding the birth of Athena from Zeus' head, see *PL* II, 758–96 and *Tetra.*, p. 657: "When sin revels and gossips within the arcenal of law, plaies, and dandles the artillery of justice that should be bent against *her*, this is a faire limitation indeede" (my emphasis).

8. See Mary Nyquist, "The Genesis of Gendered Subjectivity": a wife provides respite from serious masculine work "only if woman is constituted as less grave, more attractive, more lightsome and more amiable than her male counterpart; and if both she and marriage itself are associated with a world apart" (p. 112). Richard Corum, "In White Ink: *Paradise Lost* and Milton's Ideas of Women," in *Milton and the Idea of Woman*, ed. Julia M. Walker (Chicago, 1988), pp. 120–47, notes that "woman is a colonial territory, earth. At this distance from the imperial center [the sun], woman becomes valuable when she is transformed into an ideal space for the imperial male, whether a procreative vessel to nurture his seeds, a serviceable nursery environment to care for, support, and satisfy him throughout his life, or a political and economic space for him to rule and profit from as father, monarch, or deity" (p. 123).

9. On similarities between Eve and the serpent in *Paradise Lost*, see King-Kok Cheung, "Beauty and the Beast: A Sinuous Reflection of Milton's Eve," in *Milton Studies* XXIII, ed. James D. Simonds (Pittsburgh, 1987), pp. 197–214: "both Eve and the serpent in *Paradise Lost* are remarkable for their physical charm and potential danger" (p. 199).

10. For the contexts in which Milton specifically engenders his terms, refer to the following pages from Milton's prose: "Custome," error (*DDD*, p. 223); Begu*ile*ment (*DDD*, p. 310); "false bait" (*DDD*, p. 272); "deceitfull bait," "enticing sorcery" (*DDD*, p. 260); marriage as "a perilous hazard and snare" (*DDD*, p. 355); "bashfull mutenes of a virgin" (*DDD*, p. 249); Sin—see note 6 above; "domestic" as feminine, see *Tetra.*, p. 613; "the different sexe in most resembling unlikenes" (*Tetra.*, p. 597); "indefinite likenesse of womanhood" (*DDD*, p. 273); charity as feminine (*DDD*, pp. 228–29); charity cannot act on its own, but depends upon the individual conscience for its realization; "the portraiture of God" (*Tetra.*, p. 589).

11. Like other Puritans, Milton asserts that "in matrimony there must be first a mutuall help to piety, next to civill fellowship of love and amity, then to generation, so to houshold affairs, lastly the remedy of incontinence" (*Tetra.*, YP II, p. 599), but that is where the similarity between him and mainstream puritanism ends. See also James Turner Johnson, *A Society Ordained by God: English Puritan Marriage Doctrine in the First Half of the Seventeenth Century* (Nashville, Tenn., 1970), p. 22.

12. See Golda Werman, "Milton's Use of Rabbinic Material," in *Milton Studies* XXI, ed. James D. Simmonds (Pittsburgh, 1985), pp. 35–47, esp. 35 and 45n1; Jason P. Rosenblatt, "Milton's Chief Rabbi," in *Milton Studies* XXIV, ed. James D. Simmonds (Pittsburgh, 1988), pp. 67n8, 67n10.

13. In "Milton's Chief Rabbi," Rosenblatt argues that "John Selden (1584–1654), the most learned person in England in the seventeenth century and author of a half dozen immense rabbinical works, is the principal source of Milton's Jewish learning" (p. 46). Though critics are quick to take sides on the question of Milton's rabbinical *learning*, no one that I know of has examined Milton's use of the midrashic *method.*

14. Renée Bloch, "Midrash," in *Approaches to Ancient Judaism: Theory and Practice*, ed. William Scott Green (Missoula, Mont., 1978), p. 36.

15. "At every stage in their progressive formation, and especially in the post-exilic community. . . . the people constantly inquired of them to find responses—divine responses—to the many problems which life posed. . . . [The Midrashim were] constantly conditioned not only by the ideas and religious doctrines of the period and the milieu, but more especially by the practical goal to which they responded" ("Midrash," 37).

16. Werman, "Rabbinic Material," p. 36. Harris Fletcher, *Milton's Rabbinical Readings* (Urbana, Ill., 1929), p. 18, argues that interest in biblical exegesis "was itself an outgrowth of the attempts of Protestant scholars to maintain the Protestant position wholly on the basis of Scripture."

17. See, for example, James L. Kugel, "Two Introductions to Midrash," and Michael Fishbane, "Inner Biblical Exegesis: Types and Strategies of Interpretation in Ancient Israel," in *Midrash and Literature*, ed. Geoffrey H. Hartman and Sanford Budick (New Haven, Conn., 1986); also Hermann L. Strack, *Introduction to the Talmud and Midrash* (Philadelphia, 1931), p. 6, ch. 11, and pt. 2.

18. James L. Kugel, "Two Introductions to Midrash," p. 83: "In such a world of texts . . . God's human intermediaries become by necessity students of old scrolls, manipulators of documents, *soferim*, bookmen and copyists. And it would not be long before reading was no longer simply reading. For the words of God, whose simplicity and straightforward-

ness were once so obvious . . . now were felt to require careful study and inspection in order to be understood."

19. Ernest Sirluck's General Introduction, YP II, p. 24.

20. "Herein he appears to us as it were in human shape, enters into cov'nant with us, swears to keep it, binds himself like a just lawgiver to his own prescriptions, gives himself to be understood by men, judges and is judg'd, measures and is commensurat to right reason" (*DDD*, p. 292). See also *DDD*, pp. 264, 310, 321; *Tetrachordon*, p. 633.

21. Theodore L. Huguelet, "The Rule of Charity in Milton's Divorce Tracts," in *Milton Studies*, VI, ed. James D. Simmonds (Pittsburg, 1974), pp. 199–214, esp. 207.

22. David W. Amram, *The Jewish Law of Divorce* (New York, 1968), 2nd ed., pp. 32–33. See also Rosenblatt, "Milton's Chief Rabbi," pp. 59–62.

23. Calum M. Carmichael, *The Laws of Deuteronomy* (Ithaca, N.Y., 1974), p. 59.

MILTONIC VOICES IN HAYDN'S *CREATION*

Noam Flinker

HAYDN'S *CREATION* is a work for voices and orchestration in more than the usual sense. The libretto introduces echoes of its many texts in ways that complicate and enrich the work as a whole. The first published edition of *The Creation* presents the German words along with an English version that is syllabically equivalent so that the work can be sung in either language. More so than the German, the English version echoes many phrases from Milton's *Paradise Lost* as well as passages from the King James Version of the Bible. Although some of these echoes merely provide a fairly straightforward narrative context for the dramatic situation in the oratorio, others deepen the significance of the libretto by inscribing ironic gaps between Haydn's work and its Miltonic inspiration. This means that the voices of Satan and Milton's narrator are participants in Haydn's *Creation* along with Adam, Eve, Raphael, Uriel, and Gabriel. The discrepancies between Milton's characters and those of Haydn, and between the language of the libretto and the English of the King James Bible and Milton, should be taken as a distinctive aspect of the work as a whole. Not unlike T. S. Eliot's *The Wasteland,* Haydn's oratorio ties together a vast number of intertextual fragments from earlier works. Many of the voices appear in a register that is somewhat plain or at least nondistinguished. The context of the entire work charges these elements with their artistic power. This results in a complex texture which contains numerous ambiguities and discrepancies, especially as the work reaches its conclusion in part 3. The final effect of these various fragments is to present creation in all its volatile irregularity. One's initial impression that the oratorio is primarily about a movement from the disorder of chaos to the harmony and regularity of creation is thus complicated by the tendency of Haydn's work to provide a parody of God's creation rather than a mimetic imitation. In some sense, then, Haydn's work comprises a human misrepresentation of creation.

Central to the ambiguity of the oratorio is the issue of the fall. The libretto that Gottfried van Swieten adapted and translated from an English text supposedly given to Haydn in England in 1795 is divided into three parts.[1] The first two of these treat the six days of creation, while the third is devoted to Adam and Eve. Despite the clear Miltonic inspiration of this text, the libretto concludes before Adam and Eve have been tempted. The penultimate vocal passage in *The Creation*, a recitative by Uriel, warns: "O happy pair! and always happy yet, if not misled by false conceit, ye strive at more as granted is, and more to know, as know ye should."[2] The final chorus merely sings praise to God and makes no further reference to the fall, which the libretto thus seems to ignore in its portrayal of creation.

A close examination of some of the Miltonic voices in *The Creation* is useful in interpreting the significance of the fall in the oratorio and in understanding Haydn's treatment of allusive echoes in the work. Despite the fact that the libretto was supposedly "compiled . . . largely from *Milton's* Paradise Lost,"[3] its relationship to Milton is somewhat complex. Edward Olleson has discussed certain aspects of the Miltonic texture of the libretto and demonstrated that the German text is clearly derived from the English originally published along with it. He points to a number of passages that are close paraphrases of scattered lines from Milton's epic, but there are many more.[4] Fifteen of the thirty-four passages of the oratorio contain fairly clear parallels to *Paradise Lost*, while thirteen others are based on biblical quotations that Milton explicitly echoes. There are thus only six passages in the oratorio that have no direct parallels in Milton's poem.

Nonetheless, the presence of Miltonic parallels has not saved the English in the libretto from the barbs of countless critics. Phrases such as "miserable broken English" and "arrant nonsense" were typical of critical views until fairly recently (Landon, p. 343). Contemporary scholarship, however, has tended to temper such complaints with a greater respect for Haydn's interest in what Nicholas Temperley has shown to be "the original English."[5] Nevertheless, despite Temperley's demonstration that Haydn composed his music with serious attention to the English text of the libretto, the literary quality of the text is quite poor. In most cases the English librettist kept a few of Milton's key words but filled out the lines with clichés that considerably reduced the original poetic intensity. This, however, is not unlike the musical passages that Siegmund Levarie has described as containing "commonplace conventionality of . . . musical substance."[6] Levarie analyzes a pattern of parody in which man's activity is compared to God's creation and explicates the importance of this pattern for the conclusion of the oratorio. It is noteworthy that a similar parodic technique has long been recognized as basic to *Paradise Lost*.[7] The most obvious example is the way in which Satan, Sin, and Death establish themselves as an infernal trinity (Book II) even before the appearance of the Father, Son, and Holy Spirit in Book III of the epic. To have hell parody heaven was thus quite standard after Milton. Haydn's musical adaptation of this procedure extends the thematic parody to the use of literary materials that parodically reduce Milton's language to cliché. Throughout *The Creation*, Haydn made use of conventional materials, few of which have much artistic integrity if taken outside the context of his oratorio. Haydn shaped these conventional materials so as to make them fit together as fragments in his human representation of God's creation. The English libretto suits Haydn's style in reducing the poetic intensity of Milton's lines while retaining echoes of the original power, dignity, and seriousness of the epic. In addition, the libretto introduces various echoes from Milton that function ironically in the oratorio. This irony adds depth and complexity to Haydn's work. Although some examples demand a close knowledge of Milton's poem, others are easily available even to listeners with only a secondhand familiarity with the English epic.

Most of the participants in the oratorio are superficially similar to characters with the same names in *Paradise Lost*. Raphael, Uriel, Gabriel, Adam, and Eve all have important parts in the epic. Beyond the similarity of the names, however, Haydn's angels have little in common with those of Milton. Uriel and Gabriel are less important in Milton's poem than Raphael. Uriel acts as God's "Eyes / That run through all the Heav'ns" (III, 650–51),[8] but does not function as a narrator of the events of the epic as Raphael does (books V–VIII). The libretto gives the three angels more or less equal roles as parallels to Milton's epic narrator. Thus, their voices echo the narrator of *Paradise Lost* as he describes events in hell at the outset of the poem. At the beginning of Raphael's air (6) the angel sings of the sea "Rolling in foaming billows" (p. 25). Early in *Paradise Lost*, the epic narrator describes how Satan first rose out of the "burning Lake." As he rises, "the flames / Drivn backward slope thir pointing spires, and rowl'd / In billows, leave i' th' midst a horrid Vale" (I, 210, 222–24). Haydn's librettist has taken Milton's description of hell and applied it to the sea at the dawn of the third day of creation. On another level, however, Raphael's words echo Milton's narrator and ascribe something hellish to the roaring, "boisterous sea." In Haydn's music, this reaches a climax in the description of the emerging mountains and rocks ascending among the clouds. Landon observes that here (bars 42–44, pp. 26–27), "the musical line has to do with the text. . . . the top of the mountain coincides with the top of the bass line" (p. 417). The violence of the music sustains the Miltonic echoes from the burning lake, in effect darkening the particular moment of creation and lending it more power. When the tone suddenly changes to present rivers flowing "in serpent error" and "thro' silent vales the limpid brook" (pp. 27–28), the contrast between the earlier force and the ensuing delicate pastoral landscape helps to present a statement about the extremes of creation which are all relevant to the theme, even when the voices seem to contradict each other. The contrasts that are combined in this air and exaggerated by the distant echoes of Milton's hell remain fragments of a larger, incomplete whole which is part of the work's rendition of God's creation.

There are also other Miltonic echoes here that are closer to the specific theme under discussion. Olleson has pointed out in passing (157) that the description of the third day in Book VII of *Paradise Lost* is relevant to the passage under consideration. Raphael is telling Adam and Eve how rivers and brooks were created:

> the watrie throng,
> Wave rowling after Wave, where way they found,
> If steep, with torrent rapture, if through Plain,
> Soft-ebbing; nor withstood them Rock or Hill,
> But they, or under ground, or circuit wide
> With Serpent errour wandring, found thir way,
> And on the washie Oose deep Channels wore;
> Easie, e're God had bid the ground be drie,
> All but within those banks, where Rivers now
> Stream, and perpetual draw their humid train. (VII, 297–306)

There are, however, no billows here, so that despite the similarities, the passage from Book I contributes its own voice. Likewise, the clear echo of "serpent errour" carries with it another suggestion of Satan and hell. For Milton this line seems fully innocent since there is nothing evil about the serpent at this point in his prelapsarian world. The clashing voices in Haydn are not so clearly distinguished. They echo the fury of Milton's epic conflicts, yet they make no explicit reference to the presence of evil.

The Miltonic tone of the oratorio can also be heard in Uriel's first air although here the echo depends to some extent upon different versions of the libretto. The English originally published by Haydn (and maintained in most dual language scores published since) renders "Now vanish before the holy beams the gloomy dismal shades of dark" (p. 8). These lines were changed slightly by Vincent Novello in his English edition of the score, first published in the midnineteenth century. Novello's version of the air reads: "Now vanish before the holy beams / The gloomy shades of ancient night; / The first of days appears."[9] In *Paradise Lost* Satan journeys from hell to the newly created world in the role of a Dantean Ulysses figure. At one point he turns to the powers of night and asks for assistance:

> Ye Powers
> And Spirits of this nethermost Abyss,
> Chaos and ancient Night, I come no Spy,
> With purpose to explore or to disturb
> The secrets of your Realm, but by constraint
> Wandring this darksome Desart, as my way
> Lies through your spacious Empire up to light,
> Alone, and without guide, half lost, I seek
> What readiest path leads where your gloomie bounds
> Confine with Heav'n. (II, 968–77)

The "gloomy . . . shades" of Uriel's air provide a slight echo of Satan's speech, especially when the context of Chaos is considered. Novello's rendition of "gloomy shades of ancient night" recalls Satan's speech even more directly, as it provides Miltonic references to the realm of Chaos as called up by the orchestra prior to the first vocal passage of the oratorio. As an amateur Shakespearean actor and a friend of Keats and Shelley, Novello may have been aware of the Miltonic echo his version added to the text. On the other hand, Novello made other adjustments to the libretto that often eliminated Miltonic echoes. Thus he changed the original "Outrageous storms now dreadful arose" (p. 16) to "Now furious storms tempestuous rage" (p. iii), even though Raphael describes how the angels view the "vast immeasurable Abyss / Outrageous as a Sea, dark, wasteful, wild" (VII, 211–12). That is, the librettist may have had this passage in mind when he wrote of "Outrageous storms." It seems likely that Novello took it upon himself to correct and adjust the English of the libretto, even though he appreciated and understood the Miltonic echoes of the original. He seems to have added some extra echoes while eliminating others, such as "Outrageous storms," perhaps because of awkwardness.[10]

In any case, the librettist has simplified this passage by making the light/gloom imagery much more obvious than in Milton's poem. Uriel refers to "hell's spirits black" which "sink in . . . endless night" (pp. 10–11). As this follows almost immediately after the first creation of light, which Haydn presents in what Landon terms "a burst of choral and orchestral splendour" (p. 415), the attention to light imagery is thematically supported by the music. Uriel has also eliminated all of the epic drama in which Satan is reduced to asking for help from Chaos and ancient night. The satanic echoes of Uriel's air here are faint but audible. They help to establish a sense of mythic mystery with regard to what existed before creation. The forces of evil depart in a "despairing, cursing rage" (p. 11), not unlike the "furious rage" (VIII, 244) Raphael reports issuing from behind "The dismal Gates" of hell (VIII, 241). Uriel's attitude toward Chaos and ancient night is clearly negative, yet, by echoing Satan's attempt to cajole these powers, he is in a sense alluding to a more complex relationship between chaos and creation than his words seem to articulate. Milton's Satan promises to try to return much of creation to primeval Chaos, who therefore agrees to help the fallen angel on his journey. Milton's mythic machinery places evil and chaos together as forces that are anticreative; God the Father forces Satan to be the unwilling agent of his creative plan. Thus, even an alliance with Chaos leads ultimately to the triumph of creation in *Paradise Lost.* Haydn achieves a similar triumph in his marshaling of orchestral and vocal sounds that transcend the individual tensions and conflicts of particular elements.[11]

Novello's version of Uriel's air has the angel report a clear dichotomy between chaos and creation in words that are to some extent based upon Satan's intimation that the creative process is reversible. This is also the case in the music, where the motif of creation is constantly juxtaposed against the description of the rage and despair of the fallen angels. Uriel first sings of the "holy beams," then of "the gloomy . . . shades" (p. 8), and then again of the light: "the first of days appears" (p. 9). Soon thereafter, the Chorus joins in with a fugue that storms and rages about rapid fall (pp. 11–12). Almost immediately thereafter they sing softly and melodically of "a new created world" (p. 12). The interplay between these two motifs continues until the end of the section. It is of note that a recent account of Haydn's Chaos concludes that it consists of "the joining of two different styles of the *ricercar,* other 'distempering' juxtapositions, and the bringing together of appropriate musical figures."[12] This makes it not unlike the juxtaposition of the two styles in Uriel's air. That is, the words claim to establish a clear-cut victory of creation over chaos, while the Miltonic echoes add intensity to the negativity and chaos already surging in the music.

Haydn's Gabriel confronts and extends her Miltonic parallel on a number of different levels. Most obvious is the sexual identity of the soprano voice. Milton's Gabriel is a "winged Warriour" who is "chief of th' Angelic Guards" (IV, 576, 550). His masculinity, however, is primarily an illusion since Raphael clarifies that the angels have no sexual identity in response to Adam's question about angelic lovemaking (VIII, 612–43). In a moment of comic madness Adam later assumes that the angels are men:

O why did God,
Creator wise, that peopl'd highest Heav'n
With Spirits Masculine, create at last
This noveltie on Earth, this fair defect
Of Nature, and not fill the World at once
With Men as Angels without Feminine,
Or find some other way to generate
Mankind? (X, 888–95)

This speech, however, is filled with irony since Adam exaggerates his complaints and sounds quite ridiculous.

By making Gabriel feminine, Haydn resisted the sexist forms of biblical interpretation that might have read Adam's lines literally. On another level, Gabriel's voice is modeled on that of Raphael in Book VII. Her air has two Miltonic phrases in the English version which serve to echo Raphael's description of the creation of vegetation in Book VII of *Paradise Lost*. The first of these, "verdure clad," functions differently in both syntax and poetry. In *Paradise Lost* it is the verdure of "the tender Grass" which clothes the "Universal Face" of Earth "with pleasant green" (VII, 315–16), while in the libretto of *The Creation* the fields appear "With verdure clad" (p. 31). This passive rereading of Milton's active voice is another indication of the way in which the pastoral scene of Gabriel's air echoes Raphael's rather different voice in Milton's poem.

The most striking difference between Milton's poem and Haydn's oratorio concerns the conclusion. Here, the librettist cuts off the action before Adam and Eve confront the forbidden fruit. The implications of this presentation of the biblical myth are potentially far-reaching. *Paradise Lost* attempts to "justifie the wayes of God to men" (I, 26) in the wake of the fall of Adam and Eve. Without their sin, Pauline Christianity loses most of its force. This was clear to radical sects in England such as the Ranters, contemporaries of Milton who developed an entire millenarian doctrine which denied the very existence of sin for the spiritually enlightened. As the Ranters celebrated God's commandment to "Be fruitful and multiply" (Genesis i, 28), they closely resembled Milton's Adam and Eve.[13] Of course, one need not suggest that Haydn was a latterday Ranter merely because he portrayed Adam and Eve before their fall. Nonetheless, his oratorio does emphasize an unbounded horizon for humanity. By presenting Milton's characters with only echoes of the possibilities of evil, Haydn was treading on ground that was politically and theologically threatening. This may have been partially responsible for the objection to the oratorio that Landon reports coming from the Roman Catholic Church (p.

346).[14] In any case, anyone with minimal familiarity with Milton's poem would have to be aware of this clear difference between Haydn's work and its Miltonic inspiration.

Less obvious, perhaps, but surely no less central to understanding both works, is the nature of the love relationship between Adam and Eve. For Milton their love is a major motif throughout the epic. In some sense the poet presents the climax of his poem in terms of a conflict in values for Adam between holy and sexual love. At a crucial point he decides to eat the fruit of the tree of knowledge because he refuses to be separated from his wife. Milton's poem develops this theme with considerable complexity. Adam and Eve in Haydn's oratorio are apparently more naive in their love. Their idyllic lovers' world seems to recognize no thorns or problems. One effect of the echoes from *Paradise Lost* is thus to allude to complications and complexities that the libretto has no opportunity to introduce. This usually involves either the presence of Satan or his language. For example, when Adam asks Eve to follow him in his recitative with Eve he offers to be her "guide" (p. 132). Milton's use of this word traces the development of many of the thematic issues of the epic. The homonymic similarity between "guide" and "God" underlies most of the passages in which the word appears. For Satan on his journey through Chaos, "Alone, and without guide" (II, 975), there is a deliberate parallel between his spiritually degenerate condition and his being lost. In heaven, God the Father speaks of conscience, which he will "place within . . . as a guide" (III, 194). Eve recognizes Adam as her guide (IV, 442), but confuses him and Satan in her dream (V, 91), just as she accepts first the serpent (IX, 646) and then the tree of knowledge and the experience it provides (IX, 808) as her "guide." To what extent Adam and Eve will accept the correct "guide" is thus a major issue in *Paradise Lost,* and it is ironic that Eve takes Satan as her true guide both in her dream and in his guise as serpent. In Milton's poem this means that Eve is on the brink of disaster as she allows Satan to confuse her about the true nature of the guide she has accepted. In *The Creation,* Adam's apparently innocent offer to guide Eve echoes Eve's confusions about guidance in Milton. The oratorio is thus charged with irony in that the innocent love relationship of the libretto is significantly darkened by Miltonic echoes. Eve's Miltonic self was to make mortal mistakes as to the identity of the guide that Haydn's Adam presents.

In a similar vein, the coolness of the evening is a motif that is associated in *Paradise Lost* with Satan's song of seduction in Eve's dream. Eve recalls her dream the next morning and reports to Adam how

methought
Close at mine ear one call'd me forth to walk
With gentle voice, I thought it thine; it said,
Why sleepst thou *Eve?* now is the pleasant time,
The cool, the silent, save where silence yields
To the night-warbling Bird. (V, 35–40)

She has assumed that her lover is Adam, whereas it is, of course, Satan's voice that tempts her with the cool of the evening. Thus when, in her duet with Adam, Eve sings "The coolness of ev'n, o how she all restores" (p. 137), she is using a motif that Satan developed in order to seduce her in *Paradise Lost.* The libretto seems to present the listener with a simple song of perfect love, but the sound of Satan's voice infiltrates Eve's response to Adam and adds an ironic twist to the straightforward observation about the restorative nature of the cool of the evening. Eve is apparently telling Adam how much she loves him, but the text is also intimating that she will betray him to Satan and destroy the Edenic perfection of their song. These faint echoes of the satanic voice from Milton's epic thus add complexity and depth to the libretto.

Haydn's concluding music can likewise be interpreted ambiguously with regard to the issue of the fall. For H. C. Robbins Landon, there is no question about the fallen nature of Adam and Eve: "The fall from grace is spectacularly illustrated in Haydn's choice of keys for Part Three. The basic key of *The Creation* is C, as we shall observe in section (5)(p. 400). But the Oratorio ends in B flat: literally a fall from grace, preceded by a still further fall, the E flat Duet between Adam and Eve. Naturally, the language of the first couple cannot be the same as that of the Divine Spirit" (p. 397). He cites the essay by Siegmund Levarie: "If Haydn's deliberate deflection from the perfection of the world needed extra-musical support, the last and rather unexpectedly threatening recitative (No. 33) spells it out. Uriel here begins in the dominant of the real tonic as a reminder of his origin but quickly descends into flats as he foretells man's fall from grace. The parody, as we have called it, appropriately remains in a lower key than the ideal" (p. 320). For both Landon and Levarie, Haydn's music clarifies that which van Swieten's libretto leaves unresolved: the fall of Adam and Eve and its place in the created universe. On other levels, however, both of these musical critics point to ambiguities in the music which can be applied to a more openended view of the musical texture of sections 32 and 33. Levarie speaks of "the open end of *Die Schöpfung*" (p. 321), while Landon reminds us of its "many different and strongly contrasting sections" (p. 353), including "the actual conclusion [which] is almost abrupt" (p. 426). These qualities of ambiguity and strong contrast should be applied to an understanding of the fall in the oratorio so as to take account of what Landon terms Haydn's "fascination with combining voices and instruments" (p. 409).

The attempts of scholars such as Levarie and Landon to claim that the music reflects a fall which the libretto never makes explicit implies a conflict between Haydn and van Swieten on this issue. Landon has shown that van Swieten's explicit advice to Haydn on how to treat the music for the various sections is generally "in good taste, sensible and to the point." He suggests that "Haydn followed it gratefully but not, of course, slavishly" (p. 350). One of the most significant discrepancies between what van Swieten recommended and what Haydn actually wrote occurs in the sections with Adam and Eve. Whereas the librettist suggested that "there could be a more solid rhythm for Adam than for Eve, and the difference in emotion caused by the difference in their sex could be suggested by alternating major and minor keys . . . Haydn took great pains in this particular case not to follow the Baron's advice: the lovers are treated as one entity and their song interspersed and woven into the Chorus of the Angels." The biographer concludes that "Haydn obviously treated the whole section in a different way" (p. 352).

It is thus possible that the differences between composer and librettist with regard to the treatment of Adam and Eve extended to the entire issue of the fall. Such an assumption would, however, require more biographical research than is provided by Landon's recent five-volume biographical opus. It would also predetermine the ways in which the oratorio can be heard. Instead, we could assume that divergent approaches to the music and/or the libretto need not be resolved, and that the conflicting voices are part of the overall design of the work. The recurring loose ends and fragments can be heard as attempts to represent the ongoing nature of human creation in its ultimately futile struggle to present the world God created. Levarie's notion of parody can be extended in this way to encompass the one aspect of the essence of the oratorio. The human music parodies creation rather than imitates it.

Haydn's oratorio makes its fullest use of Milton's poem in the concluding appearance of Adam and Eve. The treatment of their love is textually simple but musically complex, especially because of the "introduction of the tavern into the proceedings," which Landon claims "must come as a shock" (p. 426). Haydn's biographer hears what he calls the "oom-pah-pah-oom rhythm" of the accompaniment at the end of the duet and concludes that "Adam and Eve have become Papageno and Papagena" (p. 426) from Mozart's *Magic Flute.* His assumption is that the mixture of heaven and earth, represented by the chorus of angels singing along with Adam and Eve, is problematic. These and other unresolved complications are, however, precisely the point of the parodic structure of the oratorio. The obvious gaps between humanity and God reflect the only kind of creation that Haydn, like Milton, was willing or able to offer. There is a definite parallel between these gaps on the one hand and the parody on the other. Haydn chose to fashion his *Creation* in ways that echo the divine creation by parodying it. This adds a theoretical justification to the "word pictures" or "Thonmahlerey" that Haydn critics have recognized throughout the oratorio.[15] The ways in which the music imitates the roaring of lions or the creeping of the worm (sec. 20) need not be taken as proof that "composers . . . went on with their *Thonmahlerey* despite critical objections" (Landon, p. 404). In *The Creation* this technique adds a certain indecorousness that contributes to the parody that is established on other levels of the work as well. By presenting a musical parody of creation Haydn was in some sense insisting upon the impossibility of representing God's creation literally or mimetically.

The Miltonic echoes in the presentation of Adam and Eve contribute to a parodic breakdown in the continuities between the oratorio and the epic. Adam and Eve sing in language that clearly resembles that of *Paradise Lost*, but the echoes generally reduce Milton's language to parodic cliché. At the same time, the Miltonic echoes increase the complexities in the relationship between the two and add darker elements to their voices. Neither the parody nor the darkening complexity contributes to the apparent light spirit of the libretto, so that these echoes add significantly to the fragmentation in the oratorio.

Early in part 3, Uriel introduces Adam and Eve in a recitative that opens with a description of the morning: "In rosy mantle appears, by tunes sweet awak'd, the morning young and fair" (p. 109). The connection between the dawn and the tunes is not established in the libretto, but it is based upon Satan's more sinister rhetorical ploy in his song of seduction in Eve's dream. Satan refers to the song of "the night-warbling Bird, that now awake / Tunes sweetest his love-labor'd song" (V, 40–41). Satan's language thus ascribes sweetness to the natural song of the nightingale and captures the effort of singing in the activity of tuning. The way in which song, nature, and sweetness are combined in praising the night looks forward to the fall of Eve in Book IX, when all her senses will contribute to her tasting of the forbidden fruit. The language of the libretto reduces the verbal sense of "tunes" to a trite noun whose sweetness is left unexplained. This reduction of Satan's seduction at night to praise of the morning is thus a parody in which the libretto makes nonsense of the epic. At the same time, the satanic ominousness of Milton's text echoes faintly yet clearly in a manner that darkens the optimism of Uriel's "morning young and fair." This technique is apparent throughout the following passages in which Adam and Eve sing to each other.

The motif of clasped hands operates in a similar fashion. In Milton's poem, holding hands is an action that suggests both innocent lovemaking before the fall and the bittersweet conclusion in which Adam and Eve are exiled from the garden of Eden. At best, it conveys a yearning for divine perfection even while it is woefully inadequate as an imitation of that condition. Echoes of both these situations resound in Uriel's description of the two at the outset of part 3: "Behold this blissful pair, where hand in hand they go! / Their flaming looks express what feels the grateful heart" (pp. 109–110). This is exactly the way in which holding hands proceeds in *Paradise Lost.* In a crucial passage near the end of Book IV, Adam and Eve proceed to their bedroom: "Thus talking hand in hand alone they pass'd / On to thir blissful Bower" (IV, 689–90). There they prayed thankfully to God and then "into thir inmost bowr / Handed they went" (738–39). At this point Milton's narrator goes out of his way to point to sexual experience as integral to prelapsarian Eden. He concludes his digression on the sexuality of "wedded Love" with the address to Adam and Eve that Uriel adopts in his penultimate recitative: "Sleep on / Blest pair; and O yet happiest if ye seek / No happier state, and know to know no more" (IV, 773–75).

The Miltonic context thus echoes through the conclusion of the oratorio, stressing the centrality of human love. Milton has his couple's "blissful Bower" allude to Spenser's Bower of Bliss (*Faerie Queene* II, 12), without the evil the Elizabethan poet had ascribed to the world of sexual temptation. His lovers are doomed to confuse holy and sexual love later on in the epic, but at this point their wedded love is praised as blameless and wholly proper. Haydn's couple behaves in a similar manner and, in so doing, suggests a basic affinity with the sexual ideology of *Paradise Lost.* Yet the libretto deletes the problematic connections between holy and sexual love that are at the center of Milton's epic. Uriel's recitative has their holding hands lead to "flaming looks" and thence to "louder praise of God" (pp. 109–10). There is here an attempt to gloss over the way in which Milton's poem accounts for Adam's fall in terms of a confusion between his love for Eve and for God. The Miltonic voices provide the requisite echoes, however, and add to the fragmentation of Haydn's oratorio. The musical juxtaposition of heaven and "the tavern," along with the "almost abrupt" conclusion of the final chorus, provides additional evidence of the manner in which the oratorio binds together voices of various kinds to produce an effect that is often fragmented and imperfect. This, of course, is part of the human parody of divine creation.

Milton and Haydn both confronted a serious religious and aesthetic problem when they set out to represent God's creation. Haydn's libretto took on some of Milton's rhetorical technique by using as much biblical language as possible, so that the same kinds of accommodation of God's truth to human language that Christian scholarship read in the Bible could be applied to human texts that quote the Bible. The echoes of Miltonic voices in the libretto of *The Creation* provide a similar means of building on Milton's epic to imitate a reality that neither poet nor composer could ever fully express. Haydn's oratorio combines voices taken from a medley of sources to approximate the complexity and confusion of the world of humanity. The fragmentary texture of so many of the seams that tie the work together is part of the composer's way of representing a heavenly opus in human terms. The echoes of *Paradise Lost* through conventionalized paraphrases of Milton's texts provide Haydn's oratorio with additional voices that represent divine creation through a process of ongoing misrepresentation.

University of Haifa

APPENDIX

In the following juxtaposition of passages from *The Creation* and *Paradise Lost*, the text quoted for Haydn is either from Heuberger (H), Stern (S), or Novello (N). I have put Novello's texts in brackets to indicate that there are slight differences in his numbering of the sections. The Miltonic citations are all from Shawcross's edition. See my notes 2 and 8 for bibliographical detail.

ERSTER THEIL

The Creation	*Paradise Lost*
1. RECITATIV. RAPHAEL	
In the beginning God created the heav'n and the earth; and the earth was without form and void; and darkness was upon the face of the deep. (H6)	Thus God the Heav'n created, thus the Earth, Matter unform'd and void: Darkness profound Cover'd th' Abyss. (VII, 232–34)
And the spirit of God moved upon the face of the waters; (H7)	but on the watrie calm His brooding wings the Spirit of God outspred. (VII, 234–35)

And God said: Let there be Light, and there was Light. (H7)

Let ther be Light, said God, and forthwith Light
Ethereal, first of things. (VII, 243–44)

And God saw the Light, that it was good; and God divided the Light from the darkness. (H7)

God saw the Light was good;
And light from darkness by the Hemisphere
Divided. (VII, 249–51)

2. ARIE. URIEL

Now vanish before the holy beams the gloomy dismal shades of dark. (H8)

[3. AIR

Now vanish before the holy beams
The gloomy shades of ancient night. (Niii)]

Ye Powers
And Spirits of this nethermost Abyss,
Chaos and ancient *Night*, I come no Spy,
. . . .
Alone, and without guide, half lost, I seek
What readiest path leads where your gloomie bounds
Confine with Heav'n. (II, 968–70, 75–77)

3. RECITATIV. RAPHAEL

Outrageous storms now dreadful arose. (S16)

They view'd the vast immeasurable Abyss
Outrageous as a Sea, dark, wasteful, wild. (VII, 211–12)

[4. RECITATIVE. RAPHAEL

Now furious storms tempestuous rage. (N iii)]

4. SOLO UND CHOR. GABRIEL

The marv'lous work beholds amaz'd the glorious hierarchy of heav'n, and to th'ethereal vaults resound the praise of God. (H18–19)

All these with ceasless praise his works behold
Both day and night (IV, 679–80)

5. RECITATIV. RAPHAEL (GEN. i, 9–10)

Let the waters under the heaven be gathered together unto one place, and let the dry land appear, and it was so. And God called the dry land: Earth, and the gathering of waters called he Seas, and God saw that it was good. (S24)

Be gather'd now ye Waters under Heav'n
Into one place, and let dry Land appeer. (VII, 283–84)

6. ARIE. RAPHAEL

Rolling in foaming billows uplifted, roars the boist'rous sea. (H25)

Forthwith upright he rears from off the Pool
His mighty Stature . . . and rowl'd
In billows, leave i' th' midst a horrid Vale. (I, 221–24)

Mountains and rocks now emerge, their tops into the clouds ascend. (H26)
Thro' th'open plains outstretching wide in

so the watrie throng,
Wave rowling after Wave, where way they found,

serpent error rivers flow. (H27)
Softly purling glides on, thro' silent vales the limpid brook. (H28)

If steep, with torrent rapture, if through Plain,
Soft-ebbing; nor withstood them Rock or Hill,
But they, or under ground, or circuit wide
With serpent errour wandring, found thir way,
And on the washie Oose deep Channels wore;
Easie, e're God had bid the ground be drie,
All but within those banks, where Rivers now
Stream, and perpetual draw thir humid train. (VII, 297–306)

7. RECITATIV. GABRIEL (GEN. i, 11)
And God said: Let the earth bring forth grass, the herb yielding seed and the fruit tree yielding fruit after his kind, whose seed is in itself upon the earth; and it was so. (H30)

Let th' Earth
Put forth the verdant Grass, Herb yeilding Seed,
And Fruit Tree yeilding Fruit after her kind. (VII, 309–11)

8. ARIE. GABRIEL
With verdure clad the fields appear delightful to the ravish'd sense, by flowers sweet and gay enhanced is the charming sight. Here vent their fumes the fragrant herbs, here shoots the healing plant. By load of fruits th' expanded boughs are press'd; to shady vaults are bent the tufty groves; the mountain's brow is crown'd with closed wood. (H31–33)

He scarce had said, when the bare Earth, till then
Desert and bare, unsightly, unadorn'd,
Brought forth the tender Grass, whose verdure clad
Her Universal Face with pleasant green,
Then Herbs of every leaf, that sudden flowr'd
Op'ning thir various colours, and made gay
Her bosom smelling sweet: and these scarce blown,
Forth flourish't thick the clustring Vine, forth crept
The smelling Gourd, up stood the cornie Reed
Embattell'd in her field: and the humble Shrub,
And Bush with frizl'd hair implicit: last
Rose as in Dance the stately Trees, and spred
Thir branches hung with copious Fruit. (VII, 313–25)

[9. AIR
With verdure clad the fields appear
Delightful to the ravish'd sense;

By flowers sweet and gay
Enhancèd is the charming sight.
Here the fragrant herbs their odours shed;
Here shoots the healing plant.
With copious fruit th' expanded groves are hung;
In leafy arches twine the shady groves;
O'er lofty hills majestic forests wave.
(Niii–iv)]

9. RECITATIV. URIEL

And the heavenly host proclaimed the third day, praising God and saying: (H35)

No significant Miltonic parallels

10. CHOR

Awake the harp, the lyre awake! In shout and joy your voices raise! In triumph sing the mighty Lord!
For he the heavens and earth has clothed in stately dress. (H35–36)

[Raphael's account of war in heaven]
ours joy fill'd, and shout,
Presage of Victorie. (VI, 200–01)
[Angels' praise of creation]
with joy and shout
The hollow Universal Orb they fill'd,
And touch't thir Golden Harps, and hymning prais'd
God and his works. (VII, 256–59)

[11. CHORUS

Awake the harp, the lyre awake,
And let your joyful song resound.
Rejoice in the Lord, the mighty God;
For He both heaven and earth
Has clothèd in stately dress. (Niv)]

11. RECITATIV. URIEL (GEN. i, 14, 16)

And God said: Let there be lights in the firmament of heaven, to divide the day from the night, and to give light upon the earth, and let them be for signs and for seasons and for days and for years. He made the stars also. (H41)

Again th' Almightie spake: Let there be Lights
High in th' expanse of Heaven to divide
The Day from Night; and let them be for Signes,
For Seasons, and for Dayes, and circling Years
. . . .
and made the Starrs.
(VII, 339–42, 348)

12. RECITATIV. URIEL

In splendour bright is rising now the sun and darts his rays: an am'rous, joyful, happy spouse, a giant, proud and glad, to run his measur'd course. With softer beams and milder light steps on the silver moon thro' silent night. The space immense of th'

[based on Ps. xix, 5, the sun is]
jocond to run
His Longitude through Heav'ns high rode.
(VII, 372–73)

[Eve to Adam]

azur sky in num'rous host of radiant orbs adorns, and the sons of God announced the fourth day in song divine proclaiming thus his power: (H42–43)

and sweet the coming on
Of grateful Eevning mild, then silent Night
With this her solemn Bird and this fair Moon,
And these the Gemms of Heav'n, her starrie train. (IV, 646–49)

[13. RECITATIVE. URIEL

In splendour bright is rising now the sun,
And darts his days: a joyful, happy spouse,
A giant, proud and glad
To run his measur'd course.
With softer beams, and milder light,
Steps on the silver moon through silent night;
The space immense of th'azure sky
A countless host of radiant orbs adorns.
And the sons of God announcèd the fourth day
In song divine, proclaiming thus His power: (Niv)]

13. CHOR MIT SOLI

Chor

The heavens are telling the glory of God. The wonder of His works displays the firmament. (H44)

[Passage modeled on Ps. xix, 1]
No significant Miltonic parallels

Gabriel. Uriel. Raphael

To day that is coming speaks it the day: The night that is gone to following night. In all the lands resounds the word, never unperceived, ever understood. (H45, 47)

[Cf. Ps. xix, 2–4]
No significant Miltonic parallels

Zweiter Theil

14. RECITATIV. GABRIEL (GEN. i, 20)

And God said: Let the waters bring forth abundantly the moving creature, that has life, and fowl, that may fly above the earth, in the open firmament of heaven. (H56)

And God said, let the Waters generate
Reptil with Spawn abundant, living Soul:
And let Fowl flie above the Earth, with wings
Displayd on th' op'n Firmament of Heav'n. (VII, 387–90)

15. ARIE. GABRIEL

On mighty pens uplifted soars the eagle aloft, and cleaves the sky in swiftest flight, to the blazing sun. His welcome bids to morn the merry lark, and cooing calls the tender dove his mate. From ev'ry bush and grove resound the nightingale's delightful

Mean while the tepid Caves, and Fens and shoares
Thir Brood as numerous hatch, from th' Egg that soon
Bursting with kindly rupture forth disclos'd
Thir callow young, but featherd soon and

notes. No grief affected yet her breast, nor to a mournful tale were tun'd her soft enchanting lays. (H57–62)

fledge
They summ'd thir Penns, and soaring th' air sublime
With clang despis'd the ground, under a cloud
In prospect; there the Eagle and the Stork
On Cliffs and Cedar tops thir Eyries build:

. . . .

From Branch to Branch the smaller Birds with song
Solac'd the Woods, and spred thir painted wings
Till Ev'n, nor then the solemn Nightingale
Ceas'd warbling, but all night tun'd her soft layes. (VII, 417–24, 433–36)

16. RECITATIV. RAPHAEL (GEN. i, 21–22)

And God created great whales, and ev'ry living creature, that moveth, and God blessed them, saying: Be fruitful all, and multiply, ye winged tribes, be multiply'd, and sing on ev'ry tree. Multiply, ye finny tribes, and fill each wat'ry deep! Be fruitful, grow and multiply! And in your God and Lord rejoice! (H64–65)

And God created the great Whales, and each
Soul living, each that crept, which plenteously
The waters generated by thir kinds,

. . . .

Be fruitful, multiply, and in the Seas
And Lakes and running Streams the waters fill. (VII, 391–93, 396–97)

17. RECITATIV. RAPHAEL

And the angels struck their immortal harps, and the wonders of the fifth day sung. (H66)

No significant Miltonic parallels

18. TERZETT.

Gabriel

Most beautiful appear, with verdure young adorn'd, the gently sloping hills. Their narrow sinuous veins distil in cristal drops the fountain fresh and bright. (H67)

No significant Miltonic parallels

Uriel

In lofty circles plays, and hovers thro the sky the cheerful host of birds. And in the flying whirl the glitt'ring plumes are dy'd as rainbows by the sun. (H68)

No significant Miltonic parallels

Raphael

See flashing thro' the wet in thronged swarms the fry in thousand ways around. Upheaved from the deep th'immense Leviathan sports on the foaming wave. (H69)

each Creek and Bay
With Frie innumerable swarm. (VII, 399–400)

Haydn	Milton
Gabriel. Uriel. Raphael How many are thy works, o God! Who may their numbers tell? (H70)	
19. TERZETT UND CHOR	
Gabriel. Uriel. Raphael The Lord is great, and great his might, his glory lasts for ever, and forever more. (H72–73)	No significant Miltonic parallels
20. RECITATIV. RAPHAEL (GEN. I, 24) And God said: Let the earth bring forth the living creature after his kind; cattle and creeping thing, and beasts of the earth after their kind. (H79)	Let th' Earth bring forth Soul living in her kind, Cattel and Creeping things, and Beast of th' Earth, Each in their kind. (VII, 451–53)
21. RECITATIV. RAPHAEL Straight opening her fertile womb, the earth obey'd the word, and teem'd creatures numberless, in perfect forms, and fully grown. Cheerful roaring stands the tawny lion. In sudden leaps the flexible tyger appears. The nimble stag bears up his branching head. With flying mane and fiery look impatient neighs the sprightly steed. The cattle in herds already seeks his good on fields and meadows green. And o'er the ground, as plants, are spread the fleecy, meek and bleating flock. Unnumbered as the sands, in whirl arose the host of insects. In long dimensions creeps with sinuous trace the worm. (H80–82)	The Earth obey'd, and strait Op'ning her fertil Woomb teem'd at a Birth Innumerous living Creatures, perfet formes, Limb'd and full grown. (VII, 453–56) The grassie Clods now Calv'd, now half appeer'd The Tawnie Lion, pawing to get free His hinder parts, then springs as broke from Bonds, And Rampant shakes his Brinded main; the Ounce, The Libbard, and the Tyger, as the Moal Rising, the crumbl'd Earth above them threw In Hillocks; the swift Stag from under ground Bore up his branching head. (VII, 463–70) Fleec't the Flocks and bleating rose, As Plants. (VII, 472–73) At once came forth whatever creeps the ground, Insect or Worm (VII, 475–76) These as a line thir dimension drew, Streaking the ground with sinuous trace. (VII, 480–81)
22. ARIE. RAPHAEL Now heav'n in fullest glory shone; earth smiles in all her rich attire. The room of air with fowl is fill'd, the water swell'd by shoals of fish; by heavy beasts the ground is	Earth in her rich attire Consummate lovely smil'd; Air, Water, Earth, By Fowl, Fish, Beast, was flown, was

trod. But all the work was not complete: There wanted yet that wond'rous being, that grateful, should God's pow'r admire, with heart and voice his goodness praise. (H82–85)

swum, was walkt
Frequent; and of the Sixt day yet remain'd;
There wanted yet the Master work, the end
Of all yet don.

. . . .

But grateful to acknowledge whence his good
Descends, thither with heart and voice and eyes
Directed in Devotion, to adore
And worship God Supream.
(VII, 501–06, 512–15)

23. RECITATIV. URIEL (GEN. I, 27; II, 7B)

And God created man in his own image, in the image of God created he him. Male and female created he him. He breathed into his nostrils the breath of life, and man became a living soul. (H86)

Let us make now Man in our image

. . . .

and in thy nostrils breath'd
The breath of Life; in his own Image hee
Created thee, in the Image of God
Express, and thou becam'st a living Soul.
Male he created thee, but thy consort
Female for Race. (VII, 519, 525–30)

24. ARIE. URIEL

In native worth and honour clad, with beauty, courage, strength adorn'd, to heav'n erect and tall he stands a man, the Lord and King of nature all. The large and arched front sublime of wisdom deep declares the seat, and in his eyes with brightness shines the soul, the breath and image of his God. (H87–88)

Two of far nobler shape erect and tall,
Godlike erect, with native Honour clad
In naked Majestie seemd Lords of all.
(IV, 288–90)

With fondness leans upon his breast, the partner for him form'd, a woman fair and graceful spouse. Her softly smiling virgin looks, of flow'ry spring the mirror, bespeak him love, and joy and bliss. (H89–90)

but endu'd
With Sanctitie of Reason, might erect
His Stature, and upright with Front serene
Govern the rest, self-knowing, and from thence
Magnanimous to correspond with Heav'n.
(VII, 507–11)

25. RECITATIV. RAPHAEL (GEN. I, 31)

And God saw ev'ry thing, that he had made; and behold it was very good; and the heavenly choir in song divine, thus closed the sixth day. (H91)

Here finish'd hee, and all that he had made
View'd, and behold all was entirely good;
So Ev'n and Morn accomplish'd the Sixt day. (VII, 548–50)

26. CHOR

Achieved is the glorious work, the Lord beholds it and is pleas'd. In lofty strains let us rejoice! Our song let be the praise of God! (H91–93)

No significant Miltonic parallels

27. TERZETT

Gabriel and Uriel

On Thee each living soul awaits, from thee, o Lord, they beg their meat. Thou openest thy hand, and sated all they are. (H95–96)

Raphael

But as to them thy face is hid: with sudden terror they are struck. Thou tak'st their breath away: they vanish into dust. (H96–97)

Gabriel. Uriel. Raphael.

Thou let'st thy breath go forth again, and life with vigour fresh returns. Revived earth unfolds new force and new delights. (H97–98)

for the mind and spirit remains
Invincible, and vigour soon returns.
(I, 139–40)

28. CHOR

Achieved is the glorious work. Our song let be the praise of God! Glory to his name for ever; he sole on high exalted reigns, alleluja. (H100–01)

No significant Miltonic parallels

DRITTER THEIL

29. RECITATIV. URIEL

In rosy mantle appears by tunes sweet awak'd, the morning young and fair. From the celestial vaults pure harmony descends on ravished earth. Behold this blissful pair, where hand in hand they go! Their flaming looks express what feels the grateful heart. A louder praise of God their lips shall utter soon. Then let our voices ring united with their song. (H109–10)

[Satan to Eve]
Tunes sweetest his love-labour'd song.
(V, 41)
Thus talking hand in hand alone they
pass'd. (IV, 689)

30. DUETT UND CHOR

Adam. Eva

By thee with bliss, o bounteous Lord, the heav'n and earth are stor'd. This world, so great, so wonderful, thy mighty hand has fram'd. (H110–11)

Chor

For ever blessed be his pow'r. His name be ever magnify'd! (H112–13)

Adam

Of stars the fairest, o how sweet thy smile at dawning morn! How brighten'st thou, o

Fairest of Starrs, last in the train of Night,
If better thou belong not to the dawn,

sun, the day, thou eye and soul of all! (H115–16)

[Adam
Of stars the fairest, pledge of day, That crown'st the smiling morn; And thou, bright sun, that cheer'st the world, Thou eye and soul of all: (N vi)]

Sure pledge of day, that crownst the
smiling Morn. (V, 166–68)

Thou Sun, of this great World both Eye
and Soul. (V, 171)

Chor
Proclaim, in your extended course, th' almighty pow'r and praise of God!

Eva
And thou that rul'st the silent night, and all ye starry host, spread wide and ev'rywhere spread wide his praise in choral songs about!

and sweet the coming on
Of grateful Eevning mild, then silent Night
With this her solemn Bird and this fair
Moon,
And these the Gemms of Heav'n, her
starrie train. (IV, 646–49)

Adam
Ye strong and cumbrous, strong elements, who ceas'less changes make, ye dusky mists, and dewy steams who raise and fall thro' th'air. (H118–19)

[ye Elements] let your ceasless change
Varie to our great Maker still new praise.
Ye Mists and Exhaltations that now rise
From Hill or steaming Lake, duskie or
grey.

. . . .

Rising or falling still advance his praise.
(V, 183–86, 191)

Adam. Eva. Chor
Resound the praise of God our Lord! Great his name, and great his might. (H119–20)

resound
His praise, who out of Darkness call'd up
Light. (V, 178–79)

Eva
Ye purling fountains, tune his praise, and wave your tops, ye pines! Ye plants exhale, ye flowers breathe at him your balmy scent. (H121)

and wave your tops, ye Pines,
With every Plant, in sign of Worship wave.
Fountains and yee, that warble, as ye flow,
Melodious murmurs, warbling tune his
praise. (V, 193–96)

Adam
Ye, that on mountains stately tread, and ye that lowly creep; ye birds, that sing at heaven's gate, and ye, that swim the stream (H121–22)

Joyn voices all ye living Souls, ye Birds,
That singing up to Heaven Gate ascend,
Bear on your wings and in your notes his
praise;
Yee that in Waters glide, and yee that walk
The Earth, and stately tread, or lowly
creep. (V, 197–201)

Adam. Eva. Chor.
Ye living souls, extol the Lord! Him

celebrate, him magnify! (H122–23)
[Let all who breathe praise Him! (Nvi)]

Adam. Eva

Ye valleys, hills, and shady woods, our raptur'd notes ye heard;
[Made vocal by our song, (Nvi)]
from morn till eve you shall repeat our grateful hymns of praise. (H124)

Witness if I be silent, Morn or Eev'n,
To Hill, or Valley, Fountain, or fresh shade
Made vocal by my Song, and taught his praise. (V, 202–04)

Chor

Hail, bounteous Lord! almighty, hail! Thy word call'd forth this wond'rous frame. Thy power adore the heav'n and earth. We praise thee now and ever more. (H125–27)

Hail universal Lord, be bounteous still
To give us onely good; and if the night
Have gather'd aught of evil or conceald,
Disperse it, as now light dispels the dark. (V, 205–08)

31. RECITATIV.

Adam

Our duty we performed now, in off'ring up to God our thanks. Now follow me, dear partner of my life! Thy guide I'll be, and ev'ry step pours new delights into our breast, shews wonders ev'rywhere. Then may'st thou feel and know the high degree of bliss, the Lord allotted us, and with devoted heart his bounty celebrate. Come, follow me! thy guide I'll be. (H132–33)

My Guide was gon. (V, 91)
yet God hath here
Varied his bounty so with new delights,
As may compare with Heaven. (V, 430–32)

Eva

O Thou, for whom I am! My help, my shield, my all! Thy will is law to me. So God, our Lord ordains, and from obedience grows my pride and happiness. (H133)

[Son to God]
That from thy just obedience could revolt,
Whom to obey is happiness entire. (VI, 740–41)

[Eve to Adam]
My Author and Disposer, what thou bidst
Unargu'd I obey; so God ordains,
God is thy Law, thou mine. (IV, 635–37)

32. DUETT

Adam

Graceful consort! At thy side softly fly the golden hours. Ev'ry moment brings new rapture; ev'ry care is put to rest. (H133–34)

When *Adam* thus to *Eve:* Fair Consort, th'hour
Of night, and all things now retir'd to rest
Mind us of like repose. (IV, 610–12)

Eva

Spouse adored! At thy side purest joys o'erflow the heart, Life and all I am is thine; my reward thy love shall be. (H134–35)

to give thee being I lent
Out of my side to thee, neerest my heart
Substantial Life, to have thee by my side
Henceforth an individual solace dear. (IV, 483–86)

Adam

The dew-dropping morn, o how she quickens all! (H136–37)

Sweet is the breath of morn. (IV, 641)

Eva

The coolness of ev'n, o how she all restores! (H137)

fragrant the fertil earth
After soft showers; and sweet the coming on
Of grateful Eevning mild. (IV, 645–47)

Adam

How grateful is of fruits the savour sweet!

Eve

How pleasing is of fragrant bloom the smell!

[Satan to Eve]
Why sleepest thou *Eve?* now is the pleasant time,
The cool, the silent, save where silence yields
To the night-warbling Bird. (V, 38–40)

Adam. Eva

But without thee, what is to me the morning dew, the breath of even, the sav'ry fruit, the fragrant bloom. With thee is ev'ry joy enhanced, with thee delight is ever new; with thee is life incessant bliss; thine, thine it whole shall be. (H137–39)

But neither breath of Morn when she ascends
. . . .
nor herb, fruit, flowr,
Glistring with dew, nor fragrance after showers,
Nor grateful Eevning mild.
. . . .
without thee is sweet.
(IV, 650, 652–54, 656)
which for thee
Chiefly I sought, without thee can despise.
(IX, 877–78)

33. RECITATIV. URIEL

O happy pair! and always happy yet, if not misled by false conceit, ye strive at more, as granted is and more to know, as know ye should! (H144)

Sleep on
Blest pair; and O yet happiest if ye seek
No happier state, and know to know no more. (IV, 773–75)

34. SCHLUSS-CHOR MIT SOLI

Sing the Lord ye voices all! Utter thanks ye all his works. Celebrate his pow'r and glory, let his name resound on high! The Lord is great, his praise shall last for aye. Amen. (H144–45)

Unfained *Halleluiahs* to thee sing,
Hymns of high praise. (VI, 744–45)

[Jehovah's praise for ever shall endure. Amen. (Nvi)]

[of David as type of Christ]
that his Regal Throne
For ever shall endure. (XII, 323–24)

NOTES

1. Compare accounts in H. C. Robbins Landon, *Haydn: The Years of "The Creation" 1796–1800*, vol. 4 of *Haydn: Chronicle and Works*, 5 vols. (London, 1977–80), pp. 116–17.

2. Unless otherwise noted, citations of the libretto refer to *Joseph Haydn, Die Schöpfung*, piano score by Richard Heuberger, (Vienna, n.d.). Except where indicated, Heuberger's version of the English text is exactly the same as that provided in Julius Stern's piano score, *Die Schöpfung* (Leipzig, n.d.). Generally the pagination in Heuberger is the same as that of Stern. In this particular passage, Heuberger's edition follows Haydn's original published version. The libretto published by Johann Peter Salomon, *The Creation: A Sacred Oratorio, Composed by Dr. Haydn, as performed at The Concert Room, King's Theatre, Hay-market, under the direction of Mr. Salomon* (London, 1800), provides a slightly different version of this passage. All information about the libretto text follows the careful documentation of Nicholas Temperley, "New Light on the Libretto of *The Creation*," in *Music in Eighteenth-Century England: Essays in memory of Charles Cudworth*, ed. Christopher Hogwood and Richard Luckett (Cambridge, 1983), pp. 189–211. Temperley reproduces p. 15 of the Salomon libretto (200). I regret that I had no access to the following versions of the text of *The Creation* when preparing this essay: *The Creation and the Seasons: The Complete Authentic Sources for the Word-Books*, forward by H. C. Robbins Landon (Cardiff, 1985) and *The Creation: An Oratorio for Solo Voices, Chorus and Orchestra, English Version*, Urtext ed., Nicholas Temperley (London, 1988).

3. From letter by Gottfried van Swieten, cited in Landon, *Haydn*, p. 116.

4. Edward Olleson, "The Origin and Libretto of Haydn's *Creation*," *Haydn Yearbook* IV (1966), 148–66. In an article which I did not see until after completing this essay, "From the State of Innocence to the Fall of Man: The Fortunes of *Paradise Lost* as Opera and Oratorio," in *Milton's Legacy in the Arts*, ed. Albert C. Labriola and Edward Sichi, Jr. (University Park, Pa., 1988), pp. 93–134, Stella P. Revard devotes considerable attention to Haydn's *Creation* (pp. 104–110). Her essay provides an overview of various musical treatments of Milton's poem since the seventeenth century. It does not, however, attempt a close analysis of the implications of specific Miltonic passages in Haydn's work. Instead, Revard provides more general comparisons of the ways in which Milton and Haydn each treated themes such as chaos (p. 105), the creation of light (p. 105), angelic singing (p. 106), adaptation of the narrative solo (pp. 106–07), comic effects (p. 107), and Adam and Eve (pp. 107–10).

5. Temperley, "New Light on the Libretto of *The Creation*," p. 208.

6. Siegmund Levarie, "The Closing Numbers of *Die Schöpfung*," in *Studies in Eighteenth-Century Music: A Tribute to Karl Geiringer on his Seventieth Birthday*, ed. H. C. Robbins Landon with Roger E. Chapman (London, 1970), p. 319.

7. See, for example, B. Rajan, *"Paradise Lost" and the Seventeenth-Century Reader* (1947; rpt. London, 1966), pp. 46–52; J. B. Broadbent, *Some Graver Subject: An Essay on "Paradise Lost"* (1960; rpt. New York, 1967), pp. 103, 111, 129; Joseph H. Summers, *The Muse's Method: An Introduction to "Paradise Lost"* (London, 1962), pp. 40, 48–53; Northrop Frye, *Five Essays on Milton's Epics* (1965; rpt. London, 1966), 18, 52–55, 77.

8. All citations from *Paradise Lost* refer to *The Complete Poetry of John Milton*, rev. ed., ed. John T. Shawcross (Garden City, N.Y., 1971).

9. Joseph Haydn, *The Creation: An Oratorio*, Vocal Score with a Separate Accompaniment for the Organ or Piano, arranged by Vincent Novello (New York, n.d.), p. iii. According to the *National Union Catalog, Pre-1956 Imprints*, Novello's original octavo edition was published in London sometime during the nineteenth century. Another London

edition is dated 185–?. Novello himself was an arranger and publisher of sacred music who was well known in musical and literary circles of nineteenth-century London. According to the *Dictionary of National Biography*, he "was a constant reader of Shakespeare" and entertained such luminaries as Charles and Mary Lamb, Leigh Hunt, Keats, Shelley, and Hazlitt at his home.

10. The Miltonic echo here escaped Olleson, "Origin and Libretto of Haydn's *Creation*," p. 161, who wondered, "But were Haydn's 'outrageous storms,' his hail and snow, added by van Swieten?:—or was it the original English librettist who saw that an oratorio would benefit more from contrast than uninterrupted Paradise could offer?" Other changes by Novello that add Miltonic echoes to Haydn's *Creation* are as follows. In no. 15 Novello substituted "air" (p. iv) for the original "sky" in Gabriel's "On mighty pens uplifted soars the eagle aloft, and cleaves the sky [air] in swiftest flight" (pp. 57–58). Thus he increased the echo of Milton's description of birds such as eagles: "They summ'd thir Penns, and soaring th' air sublime" (VII, 421). In Adam and Eve's duet no. 30, Novello made changes that increased the Miltonic echo significantly. One of Adam's original lines opens: "Of stars the fairest, o how sweet thy smile at dawning morn!" Novello changed this slightly to read: "Of stars the fairest, pledge of day, / That crown'st the smiling morn" (p. vi). In *Paradise Lost*, Adam and Eve address the morning star as part of their morning prayer: "Fairest of Starrs . . . / Sure pledge of day, that crownst the smiling Morn" (V, 166–68). Novello thus added the echo of the prayer to language that was otherwise without Miltonic force. Later in the same duet no. 30, Adam and Eve sing of their connection to the environment: "Ye valleys, hills, and shady woods, our raptur'd notes ye heard" (p. 124). Novello complicated the imagery by deleting the personification that had the valleys, hills, and woods merely hear. He substituted a phrase that turns nature into song: "Ye valleys, hills, and shady woods, / Made vocal by our song" (p. vi). This is a clear echo of the conclusion of Adam and Eve's morning prayer: "Witness if I be silent, Morn or Eev'n, / To Hill, or Valley, Fountain, or fresh shade / Made vocal by my song" (V, 202–04). Finally, at the conclusion to the entire oratorio, the chorus speaks of God's praise which "shall last for aye" (p. 151). Novello changed this slightly to "for ever shall endure" (p. vi), so that it echoes Michael's final narration to Adam (XII, 324).

11. For a recent discussion of Milton's Chaos, compare Regina M. Schwartz, " 'And the Sea Was No More': Chaos vs. Creation," in *Remembering and Repeating: Biblical Creation in "Paradise Lost"* (Cambridge, 1989), pp. 8–39.

12. A. Peter Brown, "Haydn's Chaos: Genesis and Genre," *The Musical Quarterly* LXXIII (1989), 59.

13. Compare my "Milton and the Ranters on Canticles," in *A Fine Tuning: Studies of the Religious Poetry of Herbert and Milton*, ed. Mary A. Maleski, (Binghamton, N.Y., 1989), pp. 273–90.

14. Nonetheless, Joachim Hurwitz, "Haydn and the Freemasons," *Haydn Yearbook* XVI (1985), 73, reports that, "according to P. A. Autexier it is not true that *Die Schöpfung* was forbidden in the churches: it was played in some at least (personal communication)".

15. Compare Landon, *Haydn*, p. 403, for a summary of some of the relevant scholarship.

ANDREW MARVELL DISPUTANT AS READER OF *PARADISE LOST*

Robert L. King

IN HIS DEDICATORY poem to the second edition of *Paradise Lost* (1674), Andrew Marvell announces one of the assumptions with which he approached Milton's epic; he questions whether his friend could decorously subordinate the personal "Argument" to the eternal "sacred Truths":

> When I beheld the Poet blind, yet bold,
> In slender Book his vast Design unfold,
> *Messiah* Crown'd, *Gods* Reconcil'd Decree,
> Rebelling *Angels*, the Forbidden Tree,
> Heav'n, Hell, Earth, Chaos, All; the Argument
> Held me a while misdoubting his Intent,
> That he would ruine (for I saw him strong)
> The sacred Truths to Fable and Old Song,
> (So *Sampson* groap'd the Temple Posts in spight)
> The World o'rewhelming to revenge his Sight.[1]

Seventeen lines later, Marvell says that his doubts were removed: "Thou hast not miss'd one thought that could be fit, / And all that was improper dost omit." Because of Marvell's reputation as a poet and because of his friendship with Milton, "*On Mr.* Milton's *Paradise Lost*" has prompted many provocative studies,[2] yet in our admiration for the voice of the metaphysical poet we have not attended to another Andrew Marvell, the rhetorician who speaks clearly about decorum in his dedication. That Andrew Marvell—the disputant, controversialist, satirist—was the one known to his contemporaries; he is truly the fit reader of *Paradise Lost.* His rhetorical training and practice take his reading of Milton's poem close to the "intent" that he did "a while misdoubt"—closer to parts of it than critics with a less traditional view of rhetoric have come.

Both Milton and Marvell were trained in the techniques of the disputation at Cambridge and practiced it in print. Marvell responded to several books by Samuel Parker in *The Rehearsal Transpros'd*, the first part of which was published in 1672 between the first two editions of *Paradise Lost.* Milton's *Animadversions* and *Eikonoklastes* are akin to Marvell's as examples of the respondent's role in a dispute. Both men follow long-established procedures as readers and respondents, procedures that would doubtless condition Marvell's reading in general. Students were trained first to abstract an opponent's argument; Marvell endorses this practice in his summary of a John Owens reply to Parker: "he hath been obedient and abstracted the Argument sufficiently; and if he hath been any where severe upon him [Parker], he hath done it more cleanly and much more like a Gentleman, and it hath been only in showing the necessary interferences that must follow upon the Authors Maximes, and unsound Principles."[3] Besides abstracting Parker's arguments, Marvell attempts to force him "into admitting the exact opposite of his thesis";[4] he distinguishes the meanings of Parker's central terms, and he replies to arguments with ones of the same kind. In *Eikonoklastes,* Milton's parenthetical commentaries on his procedure are casual enough to argue for its general acceptance: "(I use his own Argument)" and "(for his own words condemn him)."[5] Both men are self-conscious and comfortable in this role and assume that simply identifying an opponent's strategy is one way of countering it: "For in the disputes of the Schools there is nothing more usual, than *Hoc est Verum. Hoc est falsum*" (*1RT,* p. 90); "There is no more home-thrust in disputation than the *Argumentum ad hominem*" (*1RT,* p. 96). In the debate in hell, both Mammon and Beelzebub properly include summaries of the preceding speeches in the introductions of their own; they also draw out inferences:

> [Mammon] Suppose he should relent
> And publish Grace to all, on promise made
> Of new Subjectation; with what eyes could we
> Stand in his presence humble, and receive
> Strict Laws impos'd
>
> . . . .
>
> [Beelzebub] so the popular vote
> Inclines, here to continue, and build up here
> A growing Empire; doubtless; while we dream,
> And know not that the King of Heav'n hath doom'd
> This place our dungeon.[6]

Milton's argument for Book IX summarizes the dialogue between Adam and Eve in disputant's terms: "Eve *proposes* . . . Adam *consents not, alleging danger* . . . Eve . . . *urges;* Adam . . . *yields*" (Hughes, p. 378). In his reply to Eve's argument, Adam distinguishes one of its terms, "not to irksome toil, but to delight / He made us" (IX, 242–43), before he distinguishes the question itself: "But other doubt possesses me" (IX,

251). Eve responds in kind: "But that thou shouldst my firmness therefore doubt / To God or thee, because we have a foe / May tempt it, I expected not to hear" (IX, 279–81). Adam's final inference presents an Eve whose strength is in her moral character—her *ethos*—alone: "Go in thy native innocence, rely / On what thou hast of virtue, summon all, / For God towards thee hath done his part, do thine" (IX, 373–75).

In hundreds of pages of controversial prose, Marvell displays a talent for identifying the issue, exploring the logical consequences of its language and relating usage to the character of the speaker—rhetorical ethos. This moral concern is directly related to a more pervasive one, for Marvell's talents in controversy are, as Thomas Sloane has demonstrated of Milton, in service to the "sacred Truths."[7] That is, some matters are simply beyond debate. Controversy between mortal men (and men, not daughters of Eve, they all were) was inevitable; from Marvell's point of view it was often unfortunate because the faithful Christian should not controvert or argue the other side of questions governed by divine justice or mercy. The potential circularity of this thinking apparently did not trouble Marvell; rather, any danger lay in the presumption and futility of raising questions about "sacred Truths." At least through the filter of his public personae Marvell makes it clear that the nature of God and his ways are mysterious givens and that, hence, questioning them is impertinent. To John Trott, who had just lost his second son and remaining heir to smallpox, Marvell writes in a letter of consolation: "But upon a private loss, and sweetned with so many circumstances as yours, to be impatient, to be uncomfortable, would be to dispute with God and beg the question" (Margoliouth, II, p. 298). Marvell would hear a sympathetic voice in Abdiel's challenge to Satan:

> Shalt thou give Law to God, shalt thou dispute
> With him the points of liberty, who made
> Thee what thou art, and form'd the Pow'rs of Heav'n
> Such as he pleas'd, and circumscrib'd their being? (V, 822–25)

In friendly tones, Raphael makes the same point for Adam's benefit:

> To ask or search I blame thee not, for Heav'n
> Is as the book of God before thee set,
> Wherein to read his wond'rous Works, . . .
> . . . .
> the rest
> From Man or Angel the great Architect
> Did wisely to conceal. (VIII, 66–68, 71–73)

Pursuing knowledge beyond their grasp will earn the "disputes" of men God's "laughter" (VIII, 77, 78). Later in the same speech, Raphael's ambiguous use of the superlative stresses the absolute supremacy of both God's knowledge and his ethos: "The rest / Ordain'd for uses to his Lord best known" (VIII, 105–06). I maintain that to Andrew Marvell or a likeminded contemporary a proper reading of *Paradise Lost* is similarly circumscribed by the conventions of disputation and by an overriding moral commitment that gives priority in discourse to the ethical proof.

For disputants, arguments were initially generated out of single words; to determine how Parker "hath behaved himself, and how come off in this Dispute" (*1RT*, p. 94), Marvell traces the meaning of *sacrament* and distinguishes its use in Parker and Owen. In *A Short Historical Essay, Concerning General Councils, Creeds, and Impositions, in Matters of Religion* (1676), he warns the "Christian of honour" not only to "weigh every word, every syllable," but also, given the gravity of the Arian heresy, to examine the least unit of meaning, because "the great business of this Council of Nice was but one single letter of the alphabet, about the inserting or omitting of an iota."[8] His practice illustrates William Costello's point that "by far the commonest . . . reply was to distinguish the meaning of any of the terms,"[9] and he knows that the technique can be a dodge: "A terrible Disputant he [Parker] is, when he has set up an hard word to be his Opponent; 'Tis a very wholesome thing he knows, and prolongs life: for all the while he can keep up this ball, he may decline the Question" (*1RT*, p. 96). Such a reader is not likely to be lulled by rhetorical patterns of deception, for examining single words in a proposition precedes any other kind of response. Under this procedure, meaning tends to be narrowed rather than expanded; distinguishing, while a challenging and sometimes ingenious intellectual exercise, takes place within the boundaries of the term being distinguished and leads—like reflecting upon "sacred Truths"—back to something already known. Milton's famous summary of the virtuous life in part parallels the respondent"s role: "He that can *apprehend* and *consider* vice with all her baits and seeming pleasures, and yet abstain, and yet *distinguish*, and yet prefer that which is truly better, he is the true warfaring Christian" (YP II, pp. 514–15). The field of battle is clearly drawn; one fights within the lines.

Besides distinguishing meaning in terms central to a proposition, both Milton and Marvell readily pounce on lesser usages as a means of responding. In playing this elaborate game, they sometimes seem petty, but a serious point is invariably at stake, for the person who questions meaning, whether in sober or satiric tone, exercises control over discourse. In the first part of *The Rehearsal Transpros'd,* Marvell deliberately breaks off a quotation from Parker at "*For my part, I know none,*" so that he can play with unintended meanings for more than a page before supplying the crucial qualification from the rest of his opponent's sentence. "I crave you mercy," Marvell ironically adds, "I took you a little short" (*1RT,* pp. 119, 121). In *Mr. Smirke; Or, the Divine in Mode,* Marvell interrupts at the conventional "I confess" to interject parenthetically "do so then, and make no more words" (p. 28). Besides repossessing meaning through his parentheses, Marvell can break the rhythm of Parker's Latin and so disrupt its rhetorical flow: "But your last Collect is something strange, praying for him; *ut sero tandem in Triumphatis Ecclesiae Gloriam & dignatatem* (that *dignitatem* comes off at last very poorly) *cooptetur*" (*2RT,* p. 262). Similarly, Milton's voice in *Eikonoklastes* breaks in on Charles's to introduce a jarring note in the King's narration: "*That I went,* saith he of his going to the House of Commons, *attended with some Gentlemen;* Gentlemen indeed; the ragged Infantrie of Stewes and Brothels; the spawn and shiprack of Taverns and Dicing Houses; and then he pleads *it was no unwonted thing for the Majesty and safety of a King to be so attended, especially in discontented times*" (YP III, pp. 80–81).

Such glosses from Milton and Marvell invite a disputant to interrupt the serpent when he tells Eve that he had "apprehended nothing high" (IX, 574); had Eve heard the secondary meaning, all the satanic claims to superior knowledge that follow would have depended on "nothing" and rung false. At this same fundamental level, Milton draws on stasis theory to penetrate one rhetorical form in Charles I's immensely popular *Eikon Basilike:* "But the matter heer considerable, is not whether the King, or his Household *Rhetorician* have made a pithy declamation against Tumults, but first whether these were Tumults or not, next if they were, whether the King himself did not cause them."[10] Milton's *first* reveals a method of reading that is skeptical of both oratorical form ("declamation") and usage ("Tumults"); following the model of Quintilian, Milton questions the factual basis of the claims made rhetorically. He is like Marvell as a respondent, skilled and poised in his ability to hold in suspension distinct, sometimes conflicting meanings, the better to judge and control them. Modern, less rigorous training in debate is designed to foster such skills: to identify the true issue behind the one declared in attractive language, to seize on a revealing term and turn it back upon an opponent, to anticipate arguments before their full development lest a weak link in a chain go undetected. One need not have the genius of a metaphysical poet to acquire some of the disputant's talents; even the dreariest seventeenth-century animadversions make some strong points in rebuttal. Surely, then, Stanley Fish oversimplifies the makeup of Milton's audience and excludes a Marvell when he outlines the process of reception:

> It is not enough to analyse, as Lewis and others have, the speciousness of Satan's rhetoric. It is the nature of sophistry to lull the reasoning process; logic is a safeguard against a rhetorical effect only after the effect has been noted. The deep distrust, even fear, of verbal manipulation in the seventeenth century is a recognition of the fact that there is no adequate defence against eloquence at the moment of impact.[11]

Marvell was trained, successfully, to resist "eloquence at the moment of impact"; further, where Fish sharply distinguishes between logic and rhetorical effect, Marvell fuses thought and emotion with a self-awareness that credits his reader's ability to see their relative values: "I speak with some emotion, but not without good reason," and later, "I shall conclude this reasonable transport" (*Smirke,* pp. 81, 82). Fish defines a sequence with clear demarcations: first rhetorical effect, then logical analysis. Marvell, however, assumes that the reader understands his rhetorical priorities and structures, that he is indeed suspicious of "emotion" and "transport" even as they are experienced. Marvell's self-consciousness pays tribute to the reader's ability to resist rhetorical effects "at the moment of impact," surely because of the critical attitudes created by schooling in the disputation. Fish endorses Sister Miriam Joseph's claim that practice in linguistic analysis led schoolboys to "habits of subconscious observation and appreciation" of tropes and figures;[12] similarly, university training made disputants habitually critical of false eloquence.

Marvell occasionally addresses his audience as if it knows the rules of the disputation, but he also silently acknowledges another audience, one which needs him as a guide. Still others are so incapable of sorting out questions that they should not be exposed to controversial writing at all. Milton is much more explicit in his distrust of the "mindes of weaker men" (YP III, p. 338), but both men recognize an unschooled audience, like Fish's, easily swayed. Indeed, the disputation in the manner of its staging had a double audience: the participants themselves and their fellow students. As a result, much like the creative writer operating within established literary conventions, the clever disputant would try to be original while observing the constraints of the form and its attendant conventions. In *The Rehearsal Transpros'd,* for example, Marvell often follows the rules of formal debate as he disputes with Parker the questions of liberty of conscience and the right to dissent, but he also writes passages of polished satire. He will frequently identify techniques of disputation, logic, and rhetoric by their names, but he never says that he is writing rhetorically designed satire. Milton's censures of rhetoric as he writes rhetorically display a kindred complexity of tone, inconsistent perhaps to a twentieth-century reader but not, I believe, to his contemporaries. That part of the audience with rhetorical training would read warnings and labels in at least two ways—as possible guides to proper interpretation and as indications of the intelligence of the speaker. The narrator's or speaker's comments are, on a higher level, part of his ethical proof; the ability to analyze is a sign of personal worth, and the speaker's superior intelligence lends him credibility.

Marvell sees his intellectual superiority as a kind of moral trust; knowledge and values are yoked:

> there is a great part of oratory consists in the choice of the person that is to perswade men. And a great skill of whatsoever orator is, to perswade the auditory first that he himself is an honest and fair man. And then he is like to make the more impression on them too, if he be so prudent as to chuse an acceptible subject to speak on, and manage it decently, with fit arguments and good language. (*Smirke*, pp. 79–80)

Marvell's use of "first" and "then" argues for the priority of ethos over other modes of rhetorical proof, while his emphasis on persuasion of moral worth and the "impression" a speaker creates allows for those values to reside in a persona distinct from the actual speaker. Nonetheless, this insistence on ethos creates real constraints, for persona Marvell is obliged to stay in moral character or lose creditability and to honor the ethical priorities that his rhetorical vision projects. In his satiric portrait of Samuel Parker, he reverses these priorities so that technique triumphs over truth:

> He . . . was sent early to the *University:* and there studied hard, and in a short time became a competent Rhetorician, and no ill Disputant. He had learnt how to erect a *Thesis*, and to defend it *Pro* or *Con* with a serviceable distinction: while the Truth (as his Mr. *Bayes* hath it on another occasion).
>
> *Before a full pot of Ale you can swallow,*
> *Was here with a Whoop and gone with a Hollow.* (*1RT*, p. 29)

The truth is so "sacred" that only in an ideal version of the disputation "there may be no danger, by controverting the truth, to unsettle the minds of the youth ever after, and innure them to a disputable notion about the most weighty points of our religion" (*Smirke*, p. 39).

For a more mature audience, one capable of following the "good [i.e., effective] disputant" Arius, Marvell will not summarize the entire debate: "which I studiously avoid the relation of, that in all these things I may not give occasion for men's understandings to work by their memories, and propagate the same errors by the same means they were first occasioned" (*Historical Essay,* p. 115). There is, then, a clear danger in a presentation which, like Arius's, drives his adversary "from one to a second, from a second to a third, seeming absurdity" (p. 115), but the danger comes from an unethical person who would confuse the unpracticed or unskilled audience with a rush of argument that sacrifices "sacred Truths" to victory. In the Arian disputation before Alexander, "the arguments flew so thick that they darkned the air, and no man could yet judge which side should have the victory" (p. 116). Marvell's summary of the debate questions its fitness because the truth was known all along; his allusion to Horace affirms a tradition, living and valid, where nothing is new under the theological sun:

> These great bishops, although they only had the decisive voices, yet thought fit to bring along with them certain men that were cunning at an argument, to be auxiliary to them, when it came to hard and tough disputation . . . you may imagine that *hypostasis, persona, substantia, subsistentia, essentia, coessentialis, consubstantialis, ante saecula coaeternus, &c.* were by so many disputants pick'd to the very bones, and those broken afterwards, to come to the very marrow of divinity. . . . Thus this first great General Council of Nice, with which the world had gone big so long, and which look'd so big upon all Christendom, at last was brought to bed, and after a very hard labour deliver'd of *homoousios.* (*Historical Essay,* pp. 118–19)

As the bone imagery suggests, all the talk led inward because the subject was divine truth; "marrow of divinity" parodoxically enforces Marvell's point about the absurdity of such discourse, talk that "affect[s] the academic glory of justifying a paradox" (*Smirke,* p. 40). Arius, Samuel Parker, and Milton's Satan are like these bishops because they dispute—as Marvell feared Milton would—about "sacred Truths"; they also fail to meet Marvell's fundamental standard for rhetorical ethos because they aim for victory instead of truth. So, while Marvell writes for and about the audience that Fish imagines, he also exemplifies another audience and urges his reader to join him in resisting eloquence at the moment of impact. The similarities between his portrayal of Parker and Milton's of Satan argue that his standards and Milton's were alike and that Marvell read *Paradise Lost* without being surprised by sin.

Marvell's Parker, created between the first two editions of *Paradise Lost,* parallels Milton's Satan in several ways. Parker, too, is like a serpent: He "creep[s] into the Church" and is "a creature most noxious" (*1RT,* p. 23); "He scarce ever opens his mouth, but that he may bite, nor bites, but that from the *Vesicles* of his Gums he may infuse a venom" (*2RT,* p.

168); he is like a Satyr with "prick-ears, wrinkled horns, and cloven feet" (*2RT*, p. 161). He suffers from pride: he "magnifies himself" (*1RT*, p. 99) and, in telling imagery, is like "Men of a fiery nature that must always be uppermost, and so they may increase their own Splendor, care not though they set all on flame about them" (*1RT*, p. 106). Milton's description of Satan's entrance into Paradise compares him to the "lewd Hirelings [who] climb" into the church and threaten the flock; like him and the churchmen in *Lycidas*, Parker "disdain'd" "due entrance" (*PL*, IV, 193, 180) and "crept into the Church, thorow the Belfry or at the Windows" (*2RT*, p. 163), in a clear echo of Milton's comparison of Satan to "a Thief [who] . . . / In at the window climbs" (IX, 188, 191). The "great Pastors" of Marvell's time "should but exercise the Wisdom of common Shepheards, by parting with one to stop the infection of the whole Flock" (*2RT*, p. 164).

A more striking verbal parallel leads us to see that Parker is most like Satan as a disputant and that, hence, Marvell would judge Satan's rhetoric just as he encourages his reader to judge Parker's. Gabriel's reply to Satan in Book IV closes a disputation of sorts between them:

> To say and straight unsay, pretending first
> Wise to fly pain, professing next the Spy,
> Argues no Leader, but a liar trac't,
> *Satan*, and couldst thou faithful add? (IV, 947–50)

In one of his many characterizations of Parker's rhetoric, Marvell writes: "He has face enough to say or unsay any thing, and 'tis his priviledge, what the School-Divines deny to be even within the power of the Almighty, to make Contradictions true" (*1RT*, p. 63). In both parts of *The Rhetorical Transpros'd*, Marvell consistently makes two important points that surface here: that Parker violates ethos and that he does so behind a false appearance ("face"). Like Satan, who alters his appearance the better to deceive in *Paradise Regained* as well as *Paradise Lost*, Parker also has an exterior appropriate to his deceptive rhetoric:

> In all his Writings he doth so confound terms, he leaps cross, he hath more doubles (nay triples and quadruples) than any Hare, so that he thinks himself secure of the Hunters. . . . I will first, said he in his heart, like a stout Vagrant, beg, and, if that will not do, I will command the Question and as soon as I have got it I will so alter the property and put on another Periwig that I defie them all for discovering me or ever finding it again. (*1RT*, p. 72)

Marvell says that he "cannot resemble [Parker] better" than to a spy who posed "as a *Missionary* amongst the Nonconformists . . . till having got all their Names, he threw off the Vizard, and appear'd in his own Colours, an honest *Informer*" (*1RT*, pp. 42–43). Parker's false rhetoric hides the intention that Marvell discloses; the real object of Parker's attack is not John Owen, "For the truth of it is, the King was the Person concerned from the beginning" (*1RT*, p. 43). To discover as much, Marvell had to dig for what Parker said "in his Heart."

As Marvell, the disputant, must penetrate Parker's rhetoric to bring the real issue to the surface, Marvell, the apologist for satire, excuses his personal attack as a necessary exposure of Parker's true character. He compares analysis of a text to an anatomical dissection, a perfectly apt analogue because if probing into meaning in discourse discovers truth, dissecting the body reveals ethos, the source of what is said in the heart:

> It hath been thus far the odiousest task that ever I undertook, and has look'd to me all the while like the cruelty of a Living Dissection, which, however it may tend to publick instruction, and though I have pick'd out the most noxious Creature to be anatomiz'd, yet doth scarse excuse or recompence the offensiveness of the scent and fouling of my fingers. Therefore I will here break off abruptly, leaving many a vein not laid open, and many a passage not search'd into . . . but leave the Moral to the judicious. (*2RT*, pp. 185–86)

Since Parker was a member of the Royal Society, Marvell's comparison hits at him through the new science, but the idea of probing for meaning appears in an equally serious, nonsatiric context when Marvell urges John Trott to study biblical places and to set an example of proper grieving: "It remains that you be exemplary to others in your own practice. 'Tis true, it is an hard task to learn and teach at the same time. And, where your self are the experiment, it is as if a man should dissect his own body and read the Anatomy Lecture" (Margolionth, II, p. 229). Like the anatomist peeling away layers of flesh, Marvell, the trained disputant, looks for levels of meaning beneath every attractive surface—in argument, the Bible, exempla, single words, sentence rhythms. He grounds interpretation in the postulates of religious Truth; his intellectual precision operates in its service so that he will be ingenious but not theologically adventurous. The techniques of the disputation liberate him within bounds that he is pleased to set for himself; as a reader of *Paradise Lost*, he holds many habits of mind in common with the poem's author.

Imagine respondent Marvell judging Satan's first speech to the fallen angels. He has not only given Parker the satiric name "Bayes," after the blustering Dryden model in *The Rehearsal*, he later mocks him for his true titles: "he improved by degrees to the mysterie of Making *Glass-drops*, and thence in running leaps mounted by these virtues to be Fellow of the Royal Society, Doctor of Divinity, Parson, Prebend, and Arch-

Deacon" (*2RT*, p. 172). He would, then, certainly question the inappropriate titles of Satan's opening line; he would also recognize the false claims in the buried dilemma and the sarcastic tone ("have ye chosen . . . / Or . . . have ye sworn"); he would dismiss the low appeal to fear ("tread us down . . . Transfix us") and would see through the superficially grand conclusion to its negative import: "Awake, arise" undermined by the anticlimactic, negative "fallen":

> Princes, Potentates,
> Warriors, the Flow'r of Heav'n, once yours, now lost,
> If such astonishment as this can seize
> Eternal spirits; or have ye chos'n this place
> After the toil of Battle to repose
> Your wearied virtue, for the ease you find
> To slumber here, as in the Vales of Heav'n?
> Or in this abject posture have ye sworn
> To adore the Conqueror? who now beholds
> Cherub and Seraph rolling in the Flood
> With scatter'd Arms and Ensigns, till anon
> His swift pursuers from Heav'n Gates discern
> Th' advantage, and descending tread us down
> Thus drooping, or with linked Thunderbolts
> Transfix us to the bottom of the Gulf.
> Awake, arise, or be for ever fall'n. (I, 315–30)

Milton's introduction to Satan's first speech before the assembled devils in Book II similarly builds to an anticlimax, one enforced by the repetition of *s* and the final flat *a*, which is all the more reductive after a series of rolling *o* sounds:

> High on a Throne of Royal State, which far
> Outshone the wealth of *Ormus* and of *Ind*,
> Or where the gorgeous East with richest hand
> Show'rs on her Kings *Barbaric* Pearl and Gold,
> Satan exalted sat. (II, 1–5)

In his satires, Marvell frequently uses mixed diction and a pointed style to reduce the object of his attack, as in one long section of *The Rehearsal Transpros'd* where he apologizes for satire, images Parker as evil, and signals his conclusion and values with a heightened style: "wheresoever men shall find the footing of so wanton a Satyr out of his own bounds, the neighbourhood ought, notwithstanding all his pretended capering Divinity, to hunt him throw the woods with hounds and horn home to his harbour" (*1RT*, pp. 164–65). To Marvell, "Satan exalted sat" would be as clear a clue to ethos as any of the explicit statements from the narrator of *Paradise Lost*, for Marvell habitually sees style as projection and embodiment of character. At one point he isolates Parker's fondness for words of like ending as a character flaw. He imagines Parker to have "a *Paroxism* of the *Ism's*" (*1RT*, p. 83) and later to be "sick of many complicated Diseases: or to keep to our rhime, *Sicknesses*. He is troubled not only with the *Ismes* but the *Nesses*" (*1RT*, p. 86).

Marvell's insistence on a bond between stylistic ornament and character makes him a sensitive critic of Milton's style as narrator and of the styles of various speakers. In his multiple talents as respondent and satirist, he can hold levels of diction in mind while evaluating the total effect of expression. Such a reader would find several points of entry for an analysis of Satan's first words to the consultation in hell:

> Powers and Dominions, Deities of Heav'n,
> For since no deep within her gulf can hold
> Immortal vigor, though opprest and fall'n,
> I give not Heav'n for lost. (II, 11–14)

As part of a series of false titles, the plural "Deities" would also be recognized as false theology. "Gulf" and "vigor" carry false insinuations—the first is an error of fact, the level on which Milton questioned Charles's use of "Tumults"; the second, a poor substitute for "spirit" or "soul," terms more proper to "immortal." Marvell, however, might single out "I give not Heav'n for lost" because it unwittingly betrays the speaker's weakness; on the first level of a respondent's analysis, heaven is in fact lost and is not Satan's in any sense to control as a term in a proposition. To Marvell's poetic sensibility a deeper reading is also available: I cannot give heaven to you, the lost. Marvell, who takes delight in multiple levels of meaning, would, I think, be puzzled by Barbara Lewalski's claim that "Satan's initial charge to the Grand Consult (II, 11–44) is manifestly effective as ethical proof."[13] Lewalski's learned study puts *Paradise Lost* in a full literary tradition covering centuries, and she qualifies this statement later in the same paragraph. Nonetheless, to members of Marvell's "communality" of meaning, in Gadamer's term,[14] Satan's ethical deficiency would be immediately manifest and would prejudice all his subsequent attempts at persuasion, including the bravado that some have called heroic.

Marvell's contemporaries would find Moloch's rhetorical strategy laughable for its blunt opening and its inept conclusion. The proposal, calling for more pain, is nakedly set forth when the audience's anticipated hostility calls for indirection ("My sentence is for open War" [II, 50]), and the conclusion, far from being a call to action, embodies a distinction in a relative clause, "Which if not Victory is yet Revenge" (II, 105). The peroration is no place for such a distinction or for negatives; Moloch is clearly a foil to the smoother Belial who, despite his "words cloth'd in reason's garb" (II, 226), concludes with another revealing negative in a conditional clause: "If we procure not to ourselves more woe" (II, 224). John Steadman has discussed deliberative oratory in this hellish council;[15] I would add only that the reader is frequently reminded that a disputation is taking place and that, like the religious controversies that Milton and Marvell censure, it begins in prejudice and ends with a discussion as pointless as those of Parker and Hall. Marvell's account of the dispute over Arianism ends in the reductive Horatian allusion similar in its import to Milton's summary judgment following the debate in hell; the very topics are those of the seventeenth century, and the last word of the sentence is once again a moral tag:

> Others apart sat on a Hill retir'd,
> In thoughts more elevate, and reason'd high
> Of Providence, Foreknowledge, Will, and Fate,
> Fixt Fate, Free will, Foreknowledge absolute,
> And found no end, in wand'ring mazes lost. (II, 557–61)

In his exchange with Gabriel in Book IV, Satan is on the defensive; his belligerent tone would divert attention from his debater's dodges. Gabriel, of course, is not fooled and replies in kind. To the direct question, "Why hast thou, *Satan*, broke the bounds prescrib'd?" (IV, 878), Satan replies by questioning Gabriel's intelligence and by otherwise dodging the question, yet he claims to answer directly: "thus much what was askt" (IV, 899). He interprets his own behavior, the question at issue: "that implies not violence or harm" (IV, 901). In his turn, Gabriel throws the challenge of wisdom back at Satan, uses the language of debate ("judge," "wherefore," "alleg'd," "cause"), and challenges him with a question: "But wherefore thou alone? wherefore with thee / Came not all Hell broke loose?" (IV, 917–18). Satan keeps the exchange on the personal level, "thy words at random, as before, / Argue thy inexperience" (IV, 930–31), before he wills a logic based, as the style suggests, on the self; echoing "wherefore thou alone," he says, "I therefore, I alone first undertook / To wing the desolate Abyss" (935). Gabriel resolves the verbal battle by relating the contradictions in Satan's speech to the hypocrisy in his character; it is an ultimate rejection of an ethical argument: "To say and straight unsay . . . / Argues no Leader, but a liar trac't" (947, 949).

Given his disposition to use the forms of logic and debate in unlikely contexts—the letter to John Trott, "To His Coy Mistress"—Marvell would be struck by the unearned logical connection and the brazen personal assertion in "I therefore, I alone." He might well recall that Satan dictated the terms of the debate in hell and thus perversely earned the "therefore, I": "Thus *Beelzebub* / Pleaded his devilish Counsel, first devis'd / By *Satan*" (II, 378–80). To equate the self with reason is the sort of presumption that a "lewd Hireling" or a Parker would be guilty of in ecclesiastical disputation, and to set human reason above divine truth is akin to the presumption of Satan. Marvell announces the very standard by which he would notice and underscore such revealing usage; he even raises, as Gabriel and Satan do, the topic of wisdom: "having to do with a wise man, as Mr. *Bayes* is, one may often gather more of his mind out of a word that drops casually, than out of his whole watchful and serious discourse" (*1RT*, p. 67). In the rush of Satan's rhetoric, he would surely be struck by the repetition of "I" around a crucial term of logic; the probing disputant would see the association as arrogant and logically false.

In the temptation, Satan crowds questions and assertions together to confuse Eve, who is no trained disputant either as an innocent in Eden or a seventeenth-century woman. The gratuitous insinuations of "thus" with its connotations of logic and clarity are like alarm bells to the naturally skeptical respondent: "Displeas'd that I approach thee thus, and gaze / Insatiate, I thus single, nor have fear'd / Thy awful brow, more awful thus retir'd" (IX, 535–37). Marvell knows that a rhetorician must define central terms, not toss them off parenthetically as in "whatever thing Death be" (IX, 695). He is suspicious of deception, not lulled into acceptance by the logical term in "God therefore cannot hurt thee, and be just" (700), in itself a heretical imposition of human conditions on sacred truth. Most important, in Eve's rationalizing over goodness and wisdom, he would see a person disputing with God and begging the question:

> In plain then, what forbids he but to know,
> Forbids us good, forbids us to be wise?
> Such prohibitions bind not
> . . . .
> For us alone
> Was death invented? (758–60, 766–67)

Unlike Eve, Abdiel meets Satan more as an equal in Book V, and, besides questioning his right to "dispute" with God, Abdiel abstracts Satan's argument, refuses to "grant" (V, 831) a point and reinforms the context for Satan's address to the angels. In Abdiel's usage, the honorific titles become the objects of the Father's action: "the mighty Father . . . to thir Glory nam'd / Thrones, Dominations, Princedoms, Virtues, Powers"

(836, 839–40); like a good respondent, Abdiel turns Satan's own words back upon him. Even angelic heroism relies on the forms of disputation. The point, I trust, need not be further belabored. Disputants were trained to receive argument in a clear sequence. If one could legitimately question the speaker's character, all else that followed was suspect no matter how eloquent it might appear. If the proposition masked the real issue, even in the use of a single term like "Tumults," then no case at all could succeed. If a term was poorly defined or not defined at all, ensuing discourse was beyond indeterminancy; it was pointless.

The disputant who examines discourse for its units of meaning arrives at readings that undermine his opponent's announced position, but close, sympathetic reading can yield positive results. Marvell's reputation, we know, soared when the new criticism examined his lyric poetry in surgical detail, but his focus on single words and other small units of meaning takes in more than the techniques of metaphysical wit, and the topics raised by such usage are often as transcendent as any raised in "The Garden" or "The Definition of Love." The position of "All" in line five of his dedicatory poem to *Paradise Lost* suggests that it is being used in its metaphysical sense: "Heav'n, Hell, Earth, Chaos, All." The last word encloses all being; it is the kind of word he asks Milton about in line forty-five: "Where couldst thou words of such a compass find?" In the opening of Book III, Milton supplies answers to such a question; he begins with a personal hymn to light which, after Genesis, identifies being and light. The first speech of God the Father soon follows; its forty-five lines conclude with the word "shine" (III, 135) and prompt a reply from the Son in which Milton cues the reader: "O Father, gracious was that word which clos'd / Thy sovran sentence, that Man should find grace" (144–45). The "compass" of "shine" has been expanded to enclose heaven and earth because Milton's aristry combines language, light, and spiritual being to recall the promise of redemption. Milton "finds" the word in the tradition aptly summarized by Jaroslav Pelikan in *The Light of the World;*[16] he reinforms it in the context of his hymn to light and the Father's speech.

From Milton's point of view, theologically clear, absolute meanings reside in much of the diction; he will not tamper with those meanings or redefine them so much as he will try to impress on us some measure of their fullness. We can perhaps apprehend, if not fully comprehend, the meaning of divine "light"; like the questions that cannot be raised in dispute, some value terms are beyond our total knowing, just as some abstractions have meanings that put the *res et verba* controversy, for Milton, on the same futile level as the devilish speculations about free will:

Beyond compare the Son of God was seen
Most glorious, in him all his Father shone
Substantially express'd, and in his face
Divine compassion visibly appear'd,
Love without end, and without measure Grace, (III, 138–42)

"Beyond compare," that is, beyond trope; "Substantially express'd," that is, the embodiment of the divine essence. The terms that Parker would call insignificant and, hence, meaningless,[17] can actually be realized, but only in heaven. Milton's poetic challenge is to reach for and lead us to the ineffable; he meets the challenge in ways that Marvell is disposed to appreciate.

Marvell's poetry often compresses absolute meanings, sometimes in sharp juxtapositions; a frequently quoted line in "The Garden" may hold his most striking opposition of being and nothing: "Annihilating all that's made" (47). In the more conventional poem occasioned by Cromwell's death, Marvell tries to control the suggestions of sweeping abstract terms: "More strong affection never reason serv'd" (216); "Valour, religion, friendship, prudence dy'd / At once with him, and all that's good beside" (227–28); "All, all is gone of ours or his delight" (243). The excesses of these lines can be countered by the challenging paradoxes of, among other possible examples, "Magnanimous Despair" and "extended Soul" in "The Definition of Love" (5, 10); but, however distinct the achievements, the poetic concerns are similar. The practicing poet and the engaged disputant encounter meanings in single words and in juxtapositions that operate prior to the force that syntax exerts. Various meanings may complement each other, but when a speaker's style contains unconscious revelations, Marvell would notice them.

The diction and word order of Satan's very first speech create a consistent pattern that undercuts his heroic pose. The opening four lines pose a question; the next line and a half supply the answer. The block of five and a half lines begins with "All" and ends with "me"; it includes, surely not by chance, four units of meaning with insistent, absolute negatives:

All is not lost; the unconquerable Will,
And study of revenge, immortal hate,
And *courage never* to submit or yield:
And what is else *not to be* overcome?
That *Glory never* shall his wrath or might
Extort from me. (I, 106–11, my emphases)

Being, the theological concept that subsumes life, is at issue here, and in three instances is completely negated, with the eternal "Glory" put forever beyond Satan's repossessing. The heroic virtue, courage, is canceled out in a parallel construction. Alert to these patterns in Satan's first speech, a seventeenth-century respondent would see nothing admirable in Satan's vaunting "Evil be thou my good," because it not only reverses the creative formula of Genesis by trying to call forth nonbeing from being, but it also occurs in a context filled with references to the self. Marvell, ever ready to puncture the ego of a satiric target, would also appreciate the ironic loss of "I" in the elliptical "myself am Hell" (IV, 75) and the ambiguity created by placing "to me" after the eternal absolutes in "all Good to me is lost" (IV, 109).

A reader who plays the serious role of respondent will be struck by faulty arguments, false rhetoric, and revealing diction in the first books of *Paradise Lost.* The twentieth-century reader is unlikely to join Marvell in being "afraid . . . that there may be a curse too belong to him who shall knowingly add or diminish in the Scripture" (*1RT*, p. 87), but that reader can acknowledge the primacy of spiritual values in Milton's creation and of an ethos of truth in Marvell's reception. Catherine Belsey generates conflict from the assertion that "God himself is the only guarantee of the truth that he defines," but in the moral hierarchy of Marvell's dedicatory poem such a truth is "sacred."[18] It not only guarantees itself, but its proper treatment renders Milton's ethos pure:

> The Majesty which through thy Work doth Reign
> Draws the Devout, deterring the Profane.
> And things divine thou treat'st of in such state
> As them preserves, and Thee inviolate. (31–34)

Elms College

NOTES

1. "*On Mr.* Milton's *Paradise Lost,*" 1–10, in *The Poems & Letters of Andrew Marvell,* 2nd ed., 2 vols., ed. H. M. Margoliouth (Oxford, 1957), vol. I, p. 131.

2. Among them, Kenneth Gross, " 'Pardon Me, mighty Poet': Versions of the Bard in Marvell's 'On Milton's *Paradise Lost*'," in *Milton Studies* XVI, ed. James D. Simmonds (Pittsburgh, 1982), pp. 77–96; Judith S. Herz, "Milton and Marvell, the Poet as Fit Reader," *MLQ* XXXIX (1978), 239–63; and Joseph A. Wittreich, Jr., "Perplexing the Explanation: Marvell's 'On Mr. Milton's *Paradise Lost*'," in *Approaches to Marvell,* ed. C. A. Patrides (London, 1978), pp. 280–305.

3. Andrew Marvell, *The Rehearsal Transpros'd and The Rehearsal Transpros'd The Second Part,* ed. D.I.B. Smith (Oxford, 1971), p. 76; I have changed "unfound" to "unsound." Page references in the text to *1RT* and *2RT* are to this edition.

4. William T. Costello, S.J., *The Scholastic Curriculum at Early Seventeenth-Century Cambridge* (Cambridge, Mass., 1958), p. 20; Costello provides a full account of the disputation (pp. 14–31).

5. *Complete Prose Works of John Milton,* 8 vols., ed. Don M. Wolfe et al. (New Haven, 1953–82), vol. III, pp. 378, 403. Hereafter cited as YP.

6. *Paradise Lost,* II, 237–41, 313–17, in *John Milton: Complete Poems and Major Prose,* ed. Merritt Y. Hughes (New York, 1957), the edition cited throughout.

7. Thomas Sloane, *Donne, Milton, and the End of Humanist Rhetoric* (Berkeley and Los Angeles, 1985).

8. *Short Historical Essay* appears with *Mr. Smirke; Or, the Divine in Mode,* vol. 4 of *The Complete Works in Verse and Prose of Andrew Marvell,* ed. A. B. Grosart (Blackburn, 1872–75). References in the text are to this edition.

9. Costello, *The Scholastic Curriculum,* p. 20.

10. YP III, p. 383. Traditional rhetorical training led students to ask first whether the issue turned on a question of fact (*An sit?*); see *Rhetorica ad Herennium,* ed. Harry Caplan (Cambridge, Mass., 1954), vol. I, I.xi.18.

11. Stanley Fish, *Surprised by Sin: The Reader in "Paradise Lost"* (New York, 1967), p. 6.

12. Fish, *Surprised by Sin,* pp. 52–53.

13. Barbara Lewalski, *"Paradise Lost" and the Rhetoric of Literary Forms* (Princeton, 1985), p. 88.

14. "The anticipation of meaning that governs our understanding of a text is not an act of subjectivity, but proceeds from the communality that binds us to the tradition" (Hans-Georg Gadamer, *Truth and Method,* trans. ed. Garrett Barden and John Cumming [New York, 1988], p. 261).

15. John Steadman, *Milton's Epic Characters: Image and Idol* (Chapel Hill, N.C., 1968), pt. 5.

16. Jaroslav Pelikan, *The Light of the World: A Basic Image of Early Christian Thought* (New York, 1962); Pelikan specifically locates Milton in the tradition (pp. 13–14, 46).

17. See my "*Res et Verba:* The Reform of Language in Dryden's *All for Love,*" *ELH* LIV (1987), 45–61.

18. Catherine Belsey, *John Milton: Language, Gender, Power* (Oxford, 1988), p. 79.

A Problem of Knowing Paradise in *Paradise Lost*

Ira Clark

EVEN LACKING Adam's unique problem envisioning Michael's presentation of Bible history, readers can find plenty of problems knowing the history of our fallen world, all the more envisioning hell, heaven, and Paradise. But students—Joseph E. Duncan discussing traditions of *Milton's Earthly Paradise*, or Kathleen M. Swaim examining *Before and After the Fall*, or my undergraduates describing passages—often assume that we can know Paradise with considerable accuracy despite persistent signals to a perhaps numerous audience that we are surely unfit to imagine what we cannot know.[1] Our focus on how much we can know rather than on how little hides a lot.

Repeatedly, *Paradise Lost*'s narrators declare their problems of telling caused by problems of knowing. It is not merely that the invoking narrator in Book IX worries that neither his topic nor his bent is heroically martial, that his era is decadent, his years too many, his clime too chill; because of human disobedience and disloyalty all are incalculably alienated from perfection. Nor is it merely in his invocation to Book VII that the audience he resides among is barbarous; all mortals may be deluded. Nor is it merely in his invocations to Books I and III that he is perhaps too impure, physically and maybe spiritually blind; he trespasses on damning presumption for imagining he "may see and tell / Of things invisible to mortal sight" (III, 54–55).[2] Other narrators also recount problems and, except for Sin recalling her family romance for Satan, they count on God's inspiration. Eve remembers for Adam that her first wondering, wandering consciousness had to be corrected and prompted by a voice from above. Adam, recollecting for Raphael his initial consciousness, qualifies that "For Man to tell how human Life began / Is hard" (VIII, 250–51) before he proceeds to narrate his most significant moments (the first self-realization and self-exploration, the first conference with God and introduction to Paradise, and the creation of companionate, reproductive Eve) as dreams. Even for the unfallen, knowing can be awing and unsure. The angel Uriel reminisces for the disguised Satan about what he uncomprehendingly saw of mystery when the Word brought forth cosmos out of chaos. Raphael gets special dispensation to tell of heaven when God orders his mission to forewarn Adam and Eve. But he is troubled by sad memories, and he worries about the lawfulness of disclosing "The secrets of another World" and over the difficulty of "relat[ing] / To human sense th'invisible exploits / Of warring Spirits" (V, 569, 564–66). The mission and special dispensation God grants Michael emphasizes that the problems Raphael faced have been compounded by the fall. So that fallen Adam can begin to know history, the angel has to take him up a mount of vision, remove from his eyes the film of knowledge due to disobedience, purge his sight with medications, and quicken his insight with three drops from the Well of Life; these actions entrance or figuratively kill Adam, whom Michael raises up and whose attention he refocuses. Despite these aids the synoptic vision exhausts Adam's "mortal sight" since "objects divine / Must needs impair and weary human sense" (XII, 9–10); thus, Michael has to tell the rest of history.[3] All the more arduous must be our consideration of hell, heaven, and Paradise.

Signals in the telling of hell, heaven, and Paradise have caused eighteenth-century commentators such as Samuel Johnson to scoff and twentieth-century critics such as Christopher Ricks to recognize "words, actions all infect" (X, 608) or A. Bartlett Giamatti to detect a polysemous "satanic style."[4] Hell and heaven are obviously incomprehensible. First I will survey techniques which point to the impossibility of our comprehending hell and heaven to provide a context for looking at the subtler problem produced because Paradise seems more imaginable in its inconceivability. Next I will discuss a catalog of similar techniques that remind us that while we are hearing about the universe before the Fall, we cannot presume to know it.[5] Recognition of the impossibility of our conception of Paradise, however, is precisely what enables the possibility of presentation. What disallows our thought of it allows us to think we can know it. So these devices lead to questions about the problems and the potential in naming the essentially unnameable, since such namings effectively signify knowing the unknowable. Moreover, epistemology gets irretrievably complicated for being inextricable from moral implication "(Reason also is choice)" (III, 108).

A dominating consensus of those who have coped with this coupling reaffirms Barbara K. Lewalski's thesis: "In *Paradise Lost* the Edenic life is radical growth and process, a mode of life steadily increasing in complexity and challenge and difficulty but at the same time and by that very fact, in perfection."[6] Others, such as Walter R. Davis, detect about Raphael's arrival a change from a "divine" or "epic" language which presents truth in images to a "human" language which offers a "multifaceted analogue of the truth."[7] Both of these prove persuasive and useful. But they avoid issues in Robert Crosman's discussion of multiple points of view of Paradise and even more in Mary Nyquist's description of a "mediated fashion" positing both a "suspended present" in prelapsarian innocence and a temporal causation in our realization of the events' continuity with the outcome.[8] Such insights correlate with concerns about naming in the epic, as in Robert L. Entzminger's analysis of words with Word(s), and particularly with language slippage, as in R. A. Shoaf's criticism.[9] But I will stress more than others that language slippage, with its fallen epistemological as well as moral entailments, is inescapable anywhere any time in *Paradise Lost.*

I will conclude by considering two critical moments in Book IX after the accumulation of problems posed by *Paradise Lost*'s simultaneous denial of the possibility of knowing and its naming of what cannot be known. At one moment Adam and Eve rise to discover and lament their fall into the knowledge of good and evil that they have been hearing named and have been naming from their first appearance. At an earlier moment Eve ponders Satan's temptation to taste the fruit of the Tree of Knowledge of good and evil, under the intense pressure of testimony condensed in the repeated naming of good and evil which cannot be known until after the fruit of that tree has been tasted.

I

As everybody since Isabel Gamble MacCaffrey and Jackson I. Cope realizes, the epic heritage of hastening into the midst of things means, in *Paradise Lost,* descending in sequence, physical locale, and moral status to the base.[10] In hell the narrator seeks from his muse the first cause of the fall. He discovers it through the perspective of an agonized Satan, "throw[ing] his baleful eyes / That witness'd huge affliction and dismay / Mixt with obdurate pride and steadfast hate" (I, 56–58). The modifiers warn that we look through the undoubtedly obscuring, incalculably miserable pain, antagonism, and egoism that attend a fall from God. Only through the blinders of Satan, his cohorts or descendants, and the perhaps inspired narrator, do we perceive hell. Moreover, the narrator marks two further blinders of our own: "At once as far as Angels' ken he views." First, Satan's later "ken" of Uriel and Uriel's watch over earth prove we lack the range and penetration of angelic eyesight. Second, Raphael subsequently testifies that we lack the potent intuition of angelic insight. A set of reminders admonish that we are attempting to know what is impossible for us, things "inutterable, and worse / Than Fables yet have feign'd, or fear conceiv'd" (II, 626–27).

The narrator repeatedly warns that what we can know cannot be identical with what he describes. He naggingly corrects. In case we might cling to stable images of the fallen angels, he explains that "Spirits when they please / Can either Sex assume, or both; so soft / And uncompounded is their Essence pure" (I, 423–25), and he wonders at the miraculous diminution that permits the prodigious to congregate in Pandaemonium. Or he observes the incomparability of hell and its denizens to anything we can experience: "Thus far these beyond / Compare of mortal prowess" (I, 587–88). He reinforces such comments with brief reminders, as when he qualifies that fallen angels also show deep emotion by crying, but with "Tears such as Angels weep" (I, 620). Often he interpolates interpretations, from one-liners such as "O how unlike the place from whence they fell!" (I, 75), to extended homilies such as the one that begins "nor ever thence / Had [the Arch-fiend] ris'n or heav'd his head, but that the will / And high permission of all-ruling Heaven / Left him at large" (I, 210–13). Most often in hell, as Stanley E. Fish and reader response followers have explored, these correct us by reconvicting us of the sinful neglect of the God whose theodicy *Paradise Lost* presents.[11] The most condemnatory of the narrator's admonitions against presuming we can imagine hell or Chaos do more than remind: "Let none admire / That riches grow in Hell." They degrade our achievements in contrast to the fallen angels': "And here let those / Who boast in mortal things . . . Learn how thir greatest Monuments of Fame, / And Strength and Art are easily outdone / By Spirits reprobate" (I, 690–93). "O shame to men" indeed when fallen angels hold concord and we cause chaos (II, 496).

Less obtrusively than the narrator's warnings, a set of devices persistently reminds us that we cannot know what we imagine about hell. Here one of the most conspicuous are oxymora, beginning with "darkness visible" (I, 63) and including "the parching Air / Burns frore, and cold performs th' effect of Fire" (II, 594–95). Physical or polysemous oxymora are matched by those describing fallen, alien mental states, as Belial's projection that fallen angelic psyches "to the place conform'd / In temper and in nature, will receive / Familiar the fierce heat, and void of pain; / This horror will grow mild, this darkness light" (II, 217–20). Often attending such oxymora in hell are pervasive negations, beginning with "flames [which emit] / No light" (I, 62–63) and extending through descriptions of "illimitable" Chaos "Without dimension, where length, breadth, and highth, / And time and place are lost. . . . / Of neither Sea, nor Shore, nor Air, nor Fire" (II, 892–94, 912).[12] Less conspicuous are regular appearances of the subjunctive, which render the substantial tentative, as when Satan escapes the burning lake to "dry Land" "if it were Land that ever burn'd / With solid as the Lake with liquid fire" (I, 227–29). Another prominent device that denies our capacity to know hell is T. S. Eliot's bugaboo. Abstractions pervade the text, from simple descriptions of "sights of woe, / Regions of Sorrow, doleful shades, where peace / And rest can never dwell, hope never comes" (I, 64–66) to complex personifications of the infernal trinity which defy Blake's concrete images. Such is Death, "The other shape, / If shape it might be call'd that shape had none / Distinguishable in member, joint, or limb, / Or substance might be call'd that shadow seem'd, / For each seem'd either" (II, 666–70). As these examples show, devices such as subjunctive mood and negation compound our problems of knowing through conspicuous oxymora. They combine to confound similes. In the comparison of what Satan hears when he launches into Chaos, for instance, "Nor was his ear less peal'd / With noises loud and ruinous (to compare / Great things with small) than when *Bellona* storms . . . or less than if this frame / Of Heav'n were falling, and" (II, 920–27). The narrator's employment of the tradition of extended epic similes is the most obtrusive denial of our capacity to know hell. Here epic similes are heaped highest, their inadequacy emphasized by the multiplication of seemingly endless alternatives, as in the last quotation or at the opening of Book II: "High on a Throne of Royal State, which far / Outshone the wealth of *Ormus* and of *Ind,* / Or." These devices disable our pretensions of knowing what we cannot and lead to such disputes as whether or not a reader gets any direct notion of the length of Satan's spear (I, 292–94).[13]

Intriguing beyond all techniques that focus our incapacity to know hell is the insufficiency of our fallen language. Our problem assigning names gets spotlighted. The narrator intimates our problem when he introduces the talk of "th' Arch-Enemy, / And thence in Heav'n called Satan" to the chief henchman, "Long after known in *Palestine*, and nam'd *Beëlzebub*" (I, 81–82, 80–81). Both are named only after and for characterizing deeds. He lays out the difficulty of the combination of moral and intellectual categories when he introduces the epic catalog of devils:

> Though of thir Names in heav'nly Records now
> Be no memorial, blotted out and ras'd
> By thir Rebellion, from the Books of Life.
> Nor had they yet among the Sons of *Eve*
> Got them new Names, till
> . . . .
> [they seduced man to worship false gods]
> And Devils to adore for Deities:
> Then were they known to men by various Names,
> And various Idols through the Heathen World.
> Say, Muse, thir Names then known (I, 361–76)

The introduction to this encyclopedia of pagan gods is so momentous as to require another brief invocation to the Muse, an act which recalls the narrator's linguistic precariousness. He is posed by naming, poised between two states when Satan's cohorts have names. Known once in heaven before their fall, now they are known, inasmuch as we fallen can know them, by a revelatory record of their guilt, and ours. The no-names' immediate status, in between identifying namings while morally deserving namelessness, is compounded by a set of displacing correspondences. Heaven opposes hell; both differ from Paradise; the three are distanced from our earth; and signifying all, erasure from eternal memory past (a paradox) is supplanted by printing on mortal consciousness to come. These difficulties with having to name (to identify and so to know), and at the same time denying the namings, introduce a general failure of our namings. They reappear with other signals of our insufficiency to know heaven and Paradise. And they constitute a problem-fraught consequence of the Fall.

As we all realize that accommodations surpassing our understanding are necessary for the narrator to present hell's depths and darkness visible, so we all know that his description of heaven's heights and God's skirts "Dark with excessive bright" (III, 380) requires a new invocation of a blindingly illuminating inspiration. Here the narrator is further distanced because he cannot be privy to God's perspective as he was to Satan's. Not even Raphael, a celestial resident and our inspired informant about heaven, can know God's view.

Since our incomprehension has already been established through the rendition of hell, the narrator's reminders of our presumption of the impossible knowledge of the perfection of heaven are less necessary and less numerous. After the invocation he can just suggest the same techniques he has already employed, beginning with the warning that we will read "Of things invisible to mortal sight" (III, 55). Occasionally, as in hell, a statement warrants explanation, as when the Son descends from heaven to judge Adam and Eve: "the speed of Gods / Time counts not" (X, 90–91). More often, comments note the discrepancy between heaven and the fallen world. The "Immortal Amarant, a Flow'r which once / In Paradise, fast by the Tree of Life / Began to bloom, but soon for man's offense / To Heav'n remov'd where first it grew, there grows" (III, 353–56). Striking temporal adverbs and tense markers signal a sequence before the Fall, a consequence of falling into time, and an encompassing timelessness. But typically the text is not so insistent on our lack of comprehension in heaven as it is in hell. For example, the guardian angels who return to heaven after man's lapse express infinite distance by "dim sadness [which] did not spare / That time Celestial visages, yet mixt / With pity, violated not thir bliss" (X, 23–25). Unobtrusive reminders such as "Celestial" modify abstract "Ardors" (V, 249) as well as substantial roses (III, 364). And abstractions are as typical in heaven as in hell. Early on we hear that God is enthroned "above all highth" and radiates "Beatitude past utterance," through his Son who "Beyond compare" makes "Divine compassion" visible (III, 58, 62, 138, 141). Sometimes tentative, as indicated by his use of the subjunctive, the narrator often employs the negative way of describing divinity. Not only is divine "Love without end, and without measure Grace," God is (familiarly) "Omnipotent, / Immutable, Immortal, Infinite, / . . . invisible . . . inaccessible" (III, 142, 372–80). As in many of these quotations, heaven is ever beyond our comprehension as it is beyond our expression through similitude. Janet Adelman has perceived that often the narrator's similes in heaven are self-reflexive, imageless images, as when the angels sing to God in jubilee, "Loud as from numbers without number" (III, 346).[14] In sum, the narrator repeats the same reminders of the impossibility of our knowing heaven that he employed in hell, but he uses them more sparingly and succinctly, and he slants them differently. We may learn more about heaven from Raphael's relation to Adam and Eve than we do from the narrator. Certainly the archangel's devices that disable our sense of knowing are more numerous, more emphatic, and much more complex—more troubling.

Even before Raphael repeatedly emphasizes Adam and Eve's problems of knowing heaven, his arrival introduces their limitations. Adam's question whether or not angels can digest paradisal foods elicits a double discourse about higher orders assimilating lower ones up a graduated and increasingly refined scale of substance. Then he hears the linked, rather contrary discourse about the closeness between mundane and celestial representation, site of the controversy over Platonic mimesis versus typological presentation (V, 574–76).[15] Raphael's speech carries a paramount dual burden: for Adam and Eve's "good / This [warning about free will to disobey] is dispens't"; and "what surmounts the reach / Of human sense, I shall delineate so, / By lik'ning spiritual to corporal forms, / As may express them best" (V, 570–74). Embedded in this declaration of accommodation of God's truth to man's incapacity to understand (a fundamental principle Milton addresses in *De Doctrina Christiana*)[16] is the characteristic hedging use of analogy and of the modal *may.* Raphael reiterates all these hedges when he finishes describing the war in heaven, "measuring things in Heav'n by things on Earth / . . . that thou mayst beware . . . / What might have else to human Race been hid" (VI, 893–96). His rhetorical question at the opening of his account of creation is related: "What words or tongue of Seraph can suffice, / Or heart of man suffice to comprehend?" (VII, 113–14). So is his admonition about the necessity of revelation and of limits on knowing "Things not reveal'd, which th' invisible King, / Only Omniscient, hath suppress in Night, / To none communicable in Earth or Heaven" (VII, 122–24). All such moments reflect heritages of epistemological doubt and of calls to intellectual temperance.[17]

Although Adam and Eve have to recognize their inability to know heaven so as to gain some notion of it, their problems must be less and fewer before the Fall than ours since. The disparity between the two audiences introduces descriptive problems into Raphael's tale, and these focus troublesome discrepancies in our knowledge. Perhaps because the archangel explains to Adam and Eve, perhaps because heaven is further from us than hell is, Raphael's explanations are more numerous and obtrusive than any yet. Many of his explanations deal with time and space, beginning "(For Time, though in Eternity, appli'd / To motion, measures all things durable / By present, past, and future)," and "Wide over all the Plain, and wider far / Than all this globous Earth in Plain outspread, / (Such are the Courts of God)" (V, 580–82, 648–50). The obtrusive parentheses emphasize heaven's incomparability even to Paradise. Likely as much for us as for Adam and Eve, such disconcerting explanations get inserted into speeches to listeners needing no explanation.[18] For example, informing the Son of forthcoming victory on the third day of warfare in heaven, God reminds him that "two days are past, / Two days, as we compute the days of Heav'n" (VI, 684–85). Surely for us these often condemn acts Adam and Eve cannot know in language designating referents which do not yet exist. Thus, in a false subjunctive for their sake, Raphael describes the destructive consequences of cannons: "yet haply of thy Race / In future days, if Malice should abound, / Some one intent on mischief, or inspir'd / With dev'lish machination might devise / Like instrument to plague the Sons of men / For sin, on war and mutual slaughter bent" (VI, 501–06). Raphael's description of the rebel angels fleeing like a "timorous flock" (VI, 857) or his drawn-out explanation about angelic blood as "Nectarous humor" scarcely divisible have been deemed ridiculous from Johnson and Pope through Arnold Stein. Troublingly anachronistic, though all too familiar to us, are Raphael's references to conditions unknown to Adam and Eve in Paradise: "then *Satan* first knew pain" as his "wound" bled (VI, 320–40). And this neglects the question of how much the unfallen couple might know of weapons and armaments, tactics and combat, even anguish and rage, which we shamefully take for granted.

Such problems multiply through devices which disallow our knowledge. These are deployed throughout Raphael's description of heaven. The narrator's techniques describing hell and heaven become complexly compounded problems as Raphael tells us through Adam and Eve about our failures to know the universe of *Paradise Lost.* Raphael's oxymora become superlative credos, as when the angels' dance and the narrator's syntax become circuitous but circular, "yet regular / Then most when most irregular they seem" (V, 523–24). And the negative way, abstraction, and inadequate simile of the angels' "Orbs / Of circuit inexpressible" make way for "Orb within Orb, the Father infinite, / By whom in bliss imbosom'd sat the Son, / Amidst as from a flaming Mount, whose top / Brightness had made invisible" (V, 594–99), replicating ineffability. The subjunctive also becomes more complexly impossible, conjuring consequences for earth (had it existed) of actions in heaven. Because of the celestial war, for example, "all Heav'n / Resounded, and had Earth been then, all Earth / Had to her Centre shook" (VI, 217–19). Moreover, Raphael often supposes consequences that pose dire threats. The war in heaven causes havoc "such as, to set forth / Great things by small, if Nature's concord broke, / Among the Constellations war were sprung, / Two Planets rushing from aspect malign / Of fiercest opposition in mid Sky, / Should combat, and thir jarring Spheres confound" (VI, 310–15).

Other graceless circumlocutions, such as the infamous descriptions of the technical processes of making gunpowder, casting cannons, and firing them (VI, 507–20, 478–91), also threaten malignity. Raphael obtrudes the problem of similes in preparing Adam and Eve and us for the "fight Unspeakable": "who, though with the tongue / Of Angels can relate," can know and then tell the tale? Harder, "to what things / Liken on Earth conspicuous, that may lift / Human imagination to such highth / Of Godlike Power," since "likest Gods they seem'd" (VI, 296–301). The already incomprehensible comparison is doubly hedged by "likest . . . seem'd." Thus, similes like "as if on Earth / Winds under ground or waters forcing way / Sidelong, had pusht a Mountain from his seat" (VI, 195–97) signal concepts impossible for the innocents and menacing to us. Such similes with other devices can also indicate conditions impossible for us to comprehend, though perhaps understandable to Adam and Eve unfallen, or impossible for either them or us to know. Often Raphael associates conceiving by way of multiple similes with naming, which signifies knowing: angels march "high above the ground / . . . as when the total kind / Of Birds in orderly array on wing / Came summon'd over *Eden* to receive / Thir names of thee" (VI, 71–76).

Problems of knowing cannot be segregated from naming. Raphael inserts an ominous implication when telling of the sham "Palace of great *Lucifer*, (so call / That Structure in the Dialect of men / Interpreted)" (V, 760–62). He specifies an intellectual consequence of a moral judgment when warning of the adversary's loss of name and acquisition of the title *Satan*, "so call him now, his former name / Is heard no more in Heav'n" (V, 658–59) and when reporting Michael's challenge to the "Author of evil, unknown till thy revolt, / Unnam'd in Heav'n" (VI, 62–63). Raphael intimates in these the central motif, which he explains when telling of his and Uriel's conquests:

> I might relate of thousands, and thir names
> Eternize here on Earth; but those elect
> Angels contented with thir fame in Heav'n
> Seek not the praise of men; the other sort
> In might though wondrous and in Acts of War,
> Nor of Renown less eager, yet by doom
> Cancell'd from Heav'n and sacred memory,
> Nameless in dark oblivion let them dwell. (VI, 373–80)

Heaven remains exalted above naming in Paradise more than hell is condemned beneath it. Worse, if devils damned go unnamed and unknown to Adam and Eve in Paradise, they are known to us as pagan deities. Thus, when Raphael names Satan through analogy, "Know then, that after *Lucifer* from Heav'n / (So call him, brighter once amidst the Host / Of Angels, than that Star the Stars among) / fell" (VII, 131–34), he recalls unfallen Adam and Eve's incapacities for naming and knowing. But his burden falls the heavier on our moral as well as intellectual inability to understand heaven, hell, and emphatically Paradise before mortality. Simultaneously, however, our fallen naming allows us to talk about what, variously, Adam and Eve and we cannot know. Confessing our incapacity for knowledge permits presentation of what we do not know, licenses our pretense of knowing what we cannot know—Paradise, for instance.

II

Not everybody is so alert to our failures to know Paradise as we all are to our incapacities to understand hell and heaven. No new invocation signals the narrator's need for inspiration. But signals warn. As many have recognized, we first approach (III, 418) and then envision Paradise through Satan's fallen consciousness. Consciousness of our fall has just been raised by descriptions of the amaranth, the Tree of Life, and thornless roses, all of which existed in Paradise before they were removed to heaven (III, 352–64). The first terrain we consider on earth does not yet exist when Satan, plotting predation, alights: "other Creature in this place / Living or lifeless to be found was none, / None yet, but store hereafter from the earth . . . / Both all things vain, and all who in vain things / Built thir fond hopes of Glory" once sin has unmade the world we know (III, 442–49). Having cataloged the presumptuous, superstitious, suicidal, and papist who are to inhabit this "backside of the World," the narrator bars us from Paradise by naming what we recognize all too readily: "since call'd / The Paradise of Fools, to few unknown / Long after, now unpeopl'd, and untrod" (III, 495–97). After projecting with the narrator through Satan and sin what is yet to come, we imagine stairs to heaven's gate now withdrawn. Our progressively exclusionary introduction to Paradise ends with Satan on the potent, alchemical Sun, "The place he found beyond expression bright, / Compar'd with aught on Earth, Metal, or Stone" (III, 590–91). It is described in negatives, subjunctive "ifs," "Imagin'd rather oft than elsewhere seen" (598) by futile seekers of elixirs and the philosophers' stone. Here Satan first inquires about unfallen man from Uriel, who, describing the mystery of creation, introduces another view of Paradise from which we mortals are excluded. Raphael will extend this view in his creation hymn. And of course Eve and Adam produce in commentary and recall yet another view of Paradise with which we may associate but can never know.

With much admonition the narrator proceeds to introduce Paradise and Book IV through Satan's approach. He wails a subjunctive cry of remorse for an invocation which is impossibly late to alarm the parents of mankind:

> O for that warning voice, which he who saw
> Th' *Apocalypse*, heard cry in Heav'n aloud,
> Then when the Dragon, put to second rout,
> Came furious down to be reveng'd on men,
> *Woe to the inhabitants on Earth!* that now,
> While time was, our first Parents had been warn'd
> The coming of thir secret foe, and scap'd
> Haply so scap'd his mortal snare. (IV, 1–8)

But if the narrator cannot warn Adam and Eve, he warns us of our distance from them and Paradise. We have to see through "The Tempter ere th' Accuser of man-kind," whose misery, despair, envy, and hatred seethe through the "Hell within him" in soliloquies throughout Book IV and early in Book IX, when we imagine Paradise the last time anyone could know it.[19] The narrator issues several kinds of warnings about the impossibility of our knowing Paradise, just as he did to introduce hell and heaven. But having offered plenty describing heaven and hell, he makes just one early denial of his capacity to describe Paradise. He assumes his task "to tell how, if Art could tell" (IV, 236) that the waters support indescribable beauties.

If the narrator only once confesses outright the impossibility of telling about Paradise, he often warns of the difference between fallen earth and Paradise. These waters nourish "Flow'rs worthy of Paradise which not nice Art, / In Beds and curious Knots, but Nature boon / Pour'd forth profuse" (IV, 241–43). Limited human craft proffers only an opposed and inadequate realization, as fallen human language is merely a redundant translation to convey Edenic plenitude. Some differences represent simple failure, change, or lack since the Fall. Here gardening is not "toil" but invigoration (IV, 325–31). Around Adam and Eve "frisking play'd / All Beasts of th' Earth, since wild, and of all chase" (IV, 340–41).[20] At night they hear "Celestial voices . . . / With Heav'nly touch of instrumental sounds / In full harmonic number join'd" (IV, 680–88); "There was a place, / Now not, though Sin, not Time, first wrought the change, / Where *Tigris*" (IX, 69–71). Often human fantasies about Paradise fall into this category. Golden fruit in Paradise "Hung amiable, *Hesperian* Fables true, / If true, here only" (IV, 251–52). Human rationales can also produce contradictory, inadequate hypotheses: "whither the prime Orb, / Incredible how swift, had thither rolld / Diurnal, or this less volubil Earth, / By shorter flight to th' East, had left him there . . . / Now came still Ev'ning on" (IV, 592–98).

Most of the postlapsarian differences noted by the narrator, however, blame us, "So little knows / Any, but God alone, to value right / The good before him, but perverts best things / To worst abuse, or to thir meanest use" (IV, 201–04). So, for example, the narrator chastises our vain displays as opposed to the plain perfections of Paradise: "Meanwhile our Primitive great Sire, to meet / His god-like Guest, walks forth, without more train / Accompanied than with his own complete / Perfections; in himself was all his state, / More solemn than the tedious pomp that waits / On Princes, when thir rich Retinue long . . . / Dazzles the crowd, and sets them all agape" (V, 350–57). Most of all, as everyone knows, and as James Grantham Turner has recently emphasized, the narrator affirms forthright sexuality in Paradise against our fallen, lascivious, and sordid lust.[21] His campaign begins with a familiar negation: "Nor those mysterious parts were then conceal'd, / Then was not guilty shame: dishonest shame / Of Nature's works, honor dishonorable, / Sin-bred, how have ye troubl'd all mankind" (IV, 312–15). It achieves a climactic paean in "Hail wedded Love, mysterious Law" and vituperation in "not in the bought smile / Of Harlots, loveless, joyless, unindear'd, / Casual fruition, nor in Court Amours" (IV, 741–75); thereafter, it reinforces intermittently (V, 383–85, 445–50; VIII, 57–63, etc.). A startling form of the narrator's corrections to our presumption of knowing Paradise comes, as in heaven, with inapt explanations. Gabriel, for instance, speculating on Satan's entry into Paradise, interpolates for Uriel: "hard thou know'st it to exclude / Spiritual substance with corporeal bar" (IV, 584–85).

The narrator's stylistic reminders of rifts in our knowledge of Paradise, such as the familiar subjunctives and negatives embedded all along, appear in other ways too. New disillusioning devices include the abrupt syntactic and typographical halt when Satan and we approach the rampant green space segregating Paradise: "Access deni'd" (IV, 137). These devices include a high ratio of superlatives. Adam and Eve, for instance, are "the loveliest pair / That ever since in love's imbraces met, / *Adam* the goodliest man of men since born / His Sons, the fairest of her Daughters *Eve*" (IV, 321–24). Among the most conspicuous are descriptions which use the exalting/bathetic diction of our commercial arts to intimate indescribable paradisal beauties. Thus Eve's blooms "Rear'd high thir flourisht heads between, and *wrought / Mosaic;* underfoot the Violet, / Crocus, and Hyacinth with rich *inlay / Broider'd* the ground, more color'd than with stone / Of *costliest Emblem*" (IV, 699–703; my italics).

As in hell, the lack of words in our dictionary of mortal knowledge compels the most striking examples of our gap in knowing. Both inverted condemning similes and inadequate negating similes convey Paradise's incomprehensible perfection by means of fallen substitutions. One early extended simile condemns insistently. Satan leaps into Paradise like a "prowling Wolf" intent on preying on sheep in a nonexistent shepherds' fenced pen; the "first grand Thief" stealing yet unknown cash from the uninvented walled, bolted, barred, windowed, tiled vault of a merchant; a "Lewd Hireling" undermining an unfounded church (IV, 183–93). Such condemnatory similes, including the Romantics' favored formula for urban congestion and contamination, "long in populous City pent" (IX, 445), reappear all along. The most celebrated sort of simile for Paradise is the negation, particularly the negation of what fallen humanity has mythologized about paradisal perfections. An early one exemplifies:

Not that fair field
Of *Enna*, where *Proserpin* gath'ring flow'rs
Herself a fairer Flow'r by gloomy *Dis*
Was gather'd, which cost *Ceres* all that pain
To seek her through the world; nor that sweet Grove
Of *Daphne* by *Orontes*, and th' inspir'd
Castalian Spring might with this Paradise
Of *Eden* strive; nor that *Nyseian* Isle
Girt with the River *Triton*, where old *Cham*,
Whom Gentiles *Ammon* call and *Lybian Jove*,
Hid *Amalthea* and her Florid Son,
Young *Bacchus*, from his Stepdame *Rhea's* eye;
Nor where *Abassin* Kings thir issue Guard,
Mount *Amara*, though this by some suppos'd
True Paradise under the *Ethiop* Line
By *Nilus* head, enclos'd with shining Rock,
A whole day's journey high, but wide remote
From this *Assyrian* Garden, where the Fiend
Saw undelighted all delight. (IV, 268–86)

Similes which catalogue the inadequacies and negate our heritage of golden-age fantasies deny that our experience, our myths, or our imaginations could provide even partially adequate comparisons to Paradise. Typical series of lesser negated comparisons almost forbid suggestion; certainly they forbid comprehension. For instance, "In shadier Bower / More sacred and sequester'd, though but feign'd, / *Pan* or *Silvanus* never slept, nor Nymph, / Nor *Faunus* haunted" (IV, 705–08). These falsify past conceptions as suppositions and feignings. Moreover, they emphasize that our multiple fallen namings signal futile attempts to verify our equally fallen conceptions. The narrator's similes here and in Book IX, especially those associated with Eve (as in IX, 385–96 or 439–43), reiterate our disability to know Eden. At the same time they enable us to try to know what we cannot. Confession of our inability seems to justify our presumption.

As Raphael's warnings about our incapability of understanding heaven were more pervasive, complex, and problematic than the narrator's, so his warnings about our misperceptions of Paradise are more insistently dissonant. After Adam and Eve have heard of things "So unimaginable as hate in Heav'n / . . . which human knowledge could not reach / . . . Things above Earthly thought, which yet concern'd / Our knowing," they want to know "What may no less perhaps avail us known, / How first began this Heav'n which we behold" (VII, 54–86). He begins his account with a reminder that both his language and their comprehension are inadequate to the mystery to be communicated and understood: "To recount Almighty works / What words or tongue of Seraph can suffice, / Or heart of man suffice to comprehend?" (VII, 112–14). Then he opens his first discussion of the bounds of knowledge and the necessity for temperance in seeking it: "beyond abstain / To ask, nor let thine own inventions hope / Things not reveal'd, which th' invisible King, / Only Omniscient, hath suppress in Night, / To none communicable in Earth or Heaven" (VII, 120–24). This warning before his expansive rendition of the first Genesis creation story is merely preliminary to his later extended discourse, wherein he proceeds to answer and not answer Adam's questions about the perfections of the unfallen universe that not even Adam, much less we, can know (VIII, 66–178).

The peroration recalls how this speech convicts unfallen Adam of insufficiency to understand the universe or heaven: "Live, in what state, condition or degree, / Contented that thus far hath been reveal'd / Not of Earth only but of highest Heav'n" (VIII, 176–78). But the speech's main impetus attacks the presumptuousness of Adam's fallen descendants, who hypothesize about what "the great Architect/Did wisely to conceal." The *confirmatio* ridicules human "conjectures," "disputes," laughable "quaint Opinions wide / Hereafter, when they come to model Heav'n" and contrive silly, contrary calculations (VIII, 71–84). Describing astronomy, Raphael adds confutations to the disclaimers, negations, oxymora, abstractions, and subjunctives that have signaled our incapacity to know: "But this I urge, / Admitting . . . to show / Invalid. . . . / Not that I so affirm, though so it seem / To thee" (VIII, 114–18). He continues proffering multiple contrary hypotheses in a series of "What ifs" and "or ifs." Even before his explanations of what we cannot know, Raphael, when describing creation, has already employed disconcerting language and similes that alert us to our difficulties in knowing. What terrors or harms in Paradise could make the serpent's "brazen Eyes / And hairy Mane terrific, though to thee / Not noxious" (VII, 496–98) meaningful to Adam and Eve? Particularly disconcerting are the recurring surface and submerged metaphors of Mother Earth's teeming, generating, procreating womb, as if Adam and Eve could understand creation as childbirth.

Such signals circle round again to problems of language's indirection, the inseparable necessity and inadequacy of language for knowing. So Raphael explains: "Immediate are the Acts of God, more swift / Than time or motion, but to human ears / Cannot without process of speech be told, / So told as earthly notion can receive" (VII, 176–79). Language itself, as Raphael notes, signifies Adam and Eve's miraculous understanding of the creatures of Paradise: "thou thir Natures know'st, and gav'st them Names" (VII, 493). Besides signifying the upright human dominion of reason and self-knowledge, it signifies human "correspond[ence] with Heav'n," devout heart, eyes, and especially "voice" (VII, 506–16). Yet even Adam and Eve's language, its divine, unified correspondence inexpressibly excelling our failed, mortal, disparate Babel, is inadequate to express the partial notions these grand parents communicate about Paradise.

When Eve recalls for Adam "That day I oft remember, when from sleep / I first awak't . . . / . . . much wond'ring where / And what I was, whence thither brought, and how" (IV, 449–52), she suggests difficulties comprehending Paradise. And her need for a guiding voice to wean her from narcissism and to mate her to Adam warns of limits in her capacity to understand and tell of Paradise. With Adam suggestion and warning become explanation. As soon as Eve leaves, Raphael emphasizes Adam's deficiencies in understanding Paradise. Adam's confession of his need to rein in vain, roving notions of the "perplexing," "remote," "obscure," and "subtle" provides transit into his story, though "For Man to tell how human Life began / Is hard; for who himself beginning knew" (VIII, 250–51). Eve wondered as she woke; Adam explored his body, "who I was, or where, or from what cause, / Knew not." Then he implored Paradise's denizens to "tell, / Tell, if ye saw, how came I thus, how here? . . . / Tell me, how may I know [my "Great Maker"], how adore" (VIII, 270–80). Even more distancing, the voice and vision of Adam's guide to the garden of Paradise came through a trancelike dream he discovered to be true. Finally, he learned of the dominion God granted in his first covenant with humanity, realized his incapacity to understand God, "O by what Name, for thou above all these, / Above mankind, or aught than mankind higher, / Surpassest far my naming" and knowing (VIII, 357–59), debated with God his need for a meet help and so proved his potent though limited rationality and fell exhausted by his exertions into another trance, during which he was granted a glimpse of Eve's creation. Adam's knowledge, immeasurably surpassing our own, has limits. Moreover, that knowledge is specifically signified if not produced by language.[22]

In a not insignificant reminder of the distance between Edenic language and our post-Babel tongues, on exile from Paradise Eve recalls that she gave flowers names (XI, 274–79). Most reminders marvel at the quality of Adam's language, as Raphael does describing the creation or urging Adam to tell his tale, "Nor are thy lips ungraceful, Sire of men, / Nor tongue ineloquent" (VIII, 218–19). Adam is astounded that wondering about origins he "knew not; [yet] to speak I tri'd, and forthwith spake, / My Tongue obey'd and readily could name / Whate'er I saw" (VIII, 271–73) and that "I nam'd [birds and beasts], as they pass'd, and understood / Thir Nature, with such knowledge God endu'd / My sudden apprehension" (VIII, 352–54). And he recounts that God enjoyed proving how much, realizing how little, unfallen man understands: "Thus far to try thee, *Adam*, I was pleas'd, / And find thee knowing not of Beasts alone, / Which thou hast rightly nam'd, but of thyself, / Expressing well the spirit within thee free, / My Image" (VIII, 437–41).

But the real wonder of Adam and Eve's naming and knowing focuses on a problem: they sometimes name more than they can know. For example, the morning after the dream Satan foments in Eve, Adam seems aware of an evil he claims neither can know: "nor can I like / This uncouth dream, of evil sprung I fear; / Yet evil whence? in thee can harbor none, / Created pure" (V, 97–100). Just later "pray'd they innocent," though they have enough knowledge of good by knowledge of ill to ask God to "be bounteous still / To give us only good; and if the night / Have gather'd aught of evil or conceal'd, / Disperse it, as now light dispels the dark" (V, 206–09). For another instance, Adam adds to his tale of Eve's origin and reception a damning forecast of the fall. Although he has no parents other than God, he employs the ritual language of forsaking his parents for his wife: "I now see / Bone of my Bone, Flesh of my Flesh, my Self / Before me; Woman is her Name, of Man / Extracted; for this cause he shall forgo / Father and Mother, and to his Wife adhere" (VIII, 494–98).[23]

III

As everybody realizes and the narrator reiterates, Paradise would be neither so alien nor so unknowable for us had Adam and Eve "know[n] to know no more" (IV, 775). As readers I hope now grant, naming things at least signifies a knowledge of hell and heaven impossible but allowed by denial and foregrounds a knowledge of Paradise wondrously enabled if troublingly disabled. The problem of knowing as signified by naming is an especially important case, mainly because knowing has variously, anachronistically signaled a moral judgment about as well as the intellectual capacity of someone. The fusion makes for a problem, particularly for our understanding of Adam and Eve. The narrator emphatically brings that problem to our attention when Adam and Eve, fallen, rise to "find we know / Both Good and Evil, Good lost, and Evil got, / Bad Fruit of Knowledge, if this be to know" (IX, 1071–73). Obtrusively from here on through *Paradise Lost*, Adam's mistakes prove he is not sure what constitutes knowledge, as, say, he is not sure what death means. Now he quests and questions like the fallen angels "in wand'ring mazes lost." This would indicate that before the fall Adam and Eve knew better—innocently—in contrast to the notions of the narrator, Satan, Sin, the emissary angels (doubtfully), and our own selves, from the epic's opening lines about what knowledge of good and evil signifies. But that clear indication, and often explicit statement, is belied by what much of Adam and Eve's speech implies to us and seems to entail for them. They would seem to have to know enough to say what they do about knowledge, yet what they know gets anachronistically enveloped in naming's implications and entailments. This problem requires our further consideration of how *Paradise Lost* simultaneously disallows and allows, disables and enables, signifies but deceives in seeming to depict a Paradise impossible for us to know.

From his opening declaration of topic through reminders such as "next to [the Tree of] Life, / Our Death the Tree of Knowledge grew fast by, / Knowledge of Good bought dear by knowing ill" (IV, 220–22), the narrator counts on knowledge of evil. Satan proves equally aware. Learning of the Tree of Knowledge, he schemes to stimulate a desire for more knowledge in Adam and Eve so as to motivate his temptation:

> One fatal Tree there stands of Knowledge call'd,
> Forbidden them to taste: Knowledge forbidd'n?
> Suspicious, reasonless
> . . . .
> can it be sin to know,
> Can it be death? and do they only stand
> By Ignorance, is that thir happy state?
> . . . .
> Hence I will excite thir minds
> With more desire to know, and to reject
> Envious commands, invented with design
> To keep them low whom Knowledge might exalt
> Equal with Gods; aspiring to be such,
> They taste and die: what likelier can ensue? (IV, 514–27)

Raphael's knowledge is implicit. In his creation hymn he warns against "the Tree / Which tasted works knowledge of Good and Evil / . . . in the day thou eat'st, thou di'st" (VII, 542–44). So God can report to the angels after the fall, "O Sons, like one of us Man is become / To know both Good and Evil, since his taste / Of that defended Fruit" (XI, 84–86). God's knowledge is assumed, as when Adam remembers God's prohibition on "the Tree whose operation brings / Knowledge of good and ill, which I have set / The Pledge of thy Obedience, and thy Faith / . . . my sole command / Transgrest, inevitably thou shalt die / . . . expell'd from hence into a World / Of woe and sorrow" (VIII, 323–33). Do Adam and Eve know evil before the fall? They do not. And they do, apparently.

How much they know from God's first command is unprovable, since we do not hear their reactions then. Adam suggests they do not know. As Satan eavesdrops, Adam describes uncomprehendingly the sole prohibition

> not to taste that only Tree
> Of Knowledge, planted by the Tree of Life,
> So near grows Death to Life, whate'er Death is,
> Some dreadful thing no doubt; for well thou know'st
> God hath pronounc't it death to taste that Tree. (IV, 423–27)

All they seem to know is a name, not any referent beyond a penalty for disobedience. They do not know what they would if they trespass. This is confirmed by Raphael's and God's causative verb(al)s. "Which tasted works" and "is become . . . since" and "whose operation brings" indicate that unless or until they have tasted, Adam and Eve cannot know what evil is. Yet Adam later seems to say that even before the fall they do know. After Eve's nightmare he takes comfort in the notion that "Evil into the mind of God or Man / May come and go, so unapprov'd, and leave / No spot or blame behind: Which gives me hope / . . . thou never wilt consent" (V, 117–21). Such a naming depends on our knowing. It would also seem to entail Adam and Eve knowing something of evil, at least from the dream and the rendition. Might the same entailments hold at other warnings?

There is a potential escape clause. In *De Doctrina Christiana*, "Of the Special Government of Man Before the Fall," Milton declares that "It was called the tree of knowledge of good and evil from the event; for since Adam tasted it, we not only know evil, but we know good only by means of evil" (Hughes, p. 993). John Carey translates "from the event" more explicitly as "because of what happened afterwards" (YP VI, p. 352). Therefore, the same argument could be made that the narrator and Raphael make for the catalog of fallen angels and Satan: naming the tree *of knowledge of good and evil* appears in warnings to and discussions by Adam and Eve as an accommodation for our fallen understanding; before the fall the tree went nameless. Except for potential interpretations of the couple's puzzlement over knowledge and death, this might hold until Book IX.

But both entailments, that Eve and Adam cannot know until they taste and that they must have some notion, need to be simultaneously operative (at least in our understanding) for Satan's stimulus—desire for knowledge—to so potently affect the temptation scenes. For the climax of the triple temptation (under the rubric devil, vainglory, or godhead in knowledge), in the dream that Satan perpetrates in Eve and in the temptation, depends on Eve and Adam's having a competent sense of knowledge.[24] This mirrors the narrative's dependence for descriptions of Paradise on our sense of knowing perfection by considering the negation of knowing evil and temptation. Slippery entailments, connotations, and implications inseparable from naming *knowledge*, particularly specified as *knowledge of good and evil* by Satan, Eve, and Adam, have created major problems for our discussions of the temptation.[25] For the couple are so presented as to seem to require both an innocent ignorance and a knowing that comes with guilt.

Adam and Eve's "expectation high / Of [more] knowledge" (IX, 789–90) diverges fundamentally from the perspective resulting from the fall. They find "thir Eyes how op'n'd, and thir minds / How dark'n'd; innocence, that as a veil / Had shadow'd them from knowing ill, was gone" and they were "naked left / To guilty shame" (IX, 1053–58). This conspicuously imaged language implicates a gain, a loss, and a fusion. The opening clause fuses clear seeing as implicit knowledge of one kind with diminished illumination as implicit ignorance of a second kind. In the extending clause, "veil" and "shadow'd" connote clouded, darkened, or sheltered from knowledge before the fall, and join with "naked" to connote clear or unobstructed understanding afterwards, thereby reinforcing the first sense; but they simultaneously reverse the flow of the second sense. So the passage seems to posit a loss of knowledge from a loss of the perspective of innocence, simultaneously with a gain of knowledge with guilt from which Adam and Eve had been protected. But the gain of knowledge is all we can know; we cannot know what we lost, except by negation. Adam immediately corroborates all the narrators' views that knowing for Adam and Eve now means knowing "Both Good and Evil, Good lost, and Evil got" (IX, 1072). This seems all the truer for us since the phrasing indicates virtually inextricable loss and gain of knowledge in the loss of good and the gain of evil. To sum up the fusion, or confusion, here, the naming of knowing connotes both epistemological and moral categories so that we cannot segregate them. Furthermore, the inseparability of a loss of knowledge with a loss of virtue has been reinforced throughout *Paradise Lost* before the fall—in techniques that reiterate denial that we can know the Paradise we are trying to imagine.

The fall and its perspective do not create either less or more knowledge. They cause both less and more knowledge of different kinds because knowledge related to the fall, by its very naming—good and evil—provides both a moral and a cognitive sign. Michael Lieb's analysis of God's prohibition on the Tree of Knowledge of good and evil as an arbitrary, suprarational moral test in Milton, especially in *Paradise Lost*, proves to be persuasive theologically. But his substitution of a restrictive definition of knowledge, one that disregards rational cognition, evades the issue that *Paradise Lost*'s readers grapple with in the inescapably common albeit postfall definition of the word.[26] The language of temptation seems to require that Adam, and especially Eve, along with the Satan/serpent and us, know what they cannot.

Sense, then, is made out of Adam and Eve's simultaneously knowing and not knowing, from Eve's wonder at the serpent's ability to name and so to know.[27] Eve's notion of what she is to know and hence her desire to know more is what Satan takes advantage of from his exordium. While his story may be true for the serpent, he lies about his increasing knowledge: "I might perceive / Strange alteration in me, to degree / Of Reason in my inward Powers, and Speech / Wanted not long. . . . / Thenceforth to Speculations high or deep / I turn'd my thoughts, and with capacious mind / Consider'd" (IX, 598–604). Eve's extrapolated knowledge with ignorance continues to be what he takes advantage of in his zealous *confutatio,* seemingly inspired by that "Sacred, Wise, and Wisdom-giving Plant, / Mother of Science": "ye shall not Die: / How should ye? by the Fruit? it gives you Life / To Knowledge. . . . / . . . knowledge of Good and Evil. . . . Why then was this forbid? . . . / Why but to keep ye low and ignorant." And in his *confirmatio:* "in the day / Ye Eat thereof, your Eyes that seem so clear, / Yet are but dim, shall perfetly be then / Op'n'd and clear'd, and ye shall be as Gods, / Knowing both Good and Evil as they know" (IX, 679–709). Both Eve's ignorance and her "infer[ence]" seem confirmed by her meditation *before* tasting the tree's fruit.[28] She considers three integrally related points: The tree "Gave elocution to the mute," endowed speech, the evidence of knowledge. The tree already, conspicuously, has the name "Of Knowledge, knowledge both of good and evil." And good (which she has been said to know as we cannot, positively) seems unknowable because it is uncommunicable, until it is "communicated" by the tree through knowledge of its opposite, negation; "For good unknown, sure is not had, or had / And yet unknown, is as not had at all" (IX, 745–57). For Eve to be able to invent such a scheme, just as for us to be able to understand it, would seem to require her both to know and not to know. The same entailment holds for her conclusion that she would die like the serpent. Since "hee hath eat'n and lives, / And knows, and speaks, and reasons, and discerns, / Irrational till then" (IX, 764–66), so she should fear ignorance, not knowledge of good and evil. In this soliloquy, she is imitating Satan's rationalization, his knowledge, and ours.

One escape from the conclusion that Adam and Eve both know and do not know what they are saying is similar to *De Doctrina*'s explanation and *Paradise Lost*'s ex post facto catalogs: once knowledge is named for us who are fallen, regardless of the status it has for Adam and Eve in Paradise, we cannot escape its connotations, implications, entailments of good by evil, good lost and evil got, negation. Whatever we think we read or know, in *Paradise Lost* this escape perpetually condemns us. Our fall since

Paradise must be taken into our accounts of Paradise. But this escape begs the question. Another escape, the one I have implicitly been following through *Paradise Lost*, is to base knowledge on naming and hence inevitably on the only kind of language we know. This escape forms the base as well of theology's ancient characterization of God or heaven or Paradise by the negative way. I have been aligning these traditional bases in naming as knowing and the negative way with current emphases on definition in language as signs and negations. The naming and the defining by oppositions at the base of any language we know about must also be taken into our accounts of Paradise. But this escape also necessarily begs the question. Essentially, my entailments allow Adam and Eve to both know and not know, suggest that they have to both know and not know. So Milton and his narrators in *Paradise Lost* can, do, perhaps must, have it both ways.

These potential escapes end up resembling paradoxes that are essentially embedded in readers' initial propositions about *Paradise Lost*—from the justly venerable fortunate fall through the currently popular simultaneous prospective and retrospective narration. But whether we see the problem of knowing Paradise in terms of etiology, memorial narration, sin, language, or something else, we must take into account the fact that we cannot know whether the implications and entailments we infer refer only to us and our fallen perception or present a state of Paradise. We must particularly take into account the fact that we cannot know whether Adam and Eve's simultaneous lack-knowledge and knowledge in and of Paradise constitutes a condition of language since Babel, or before Babel, or before the fall. For what is inescapable are the compelling reiterations by a host of techniques in *Paradise Lost* that nag us about the simultaneous fallibility and potential in our naming and knowing. These perpetually disallow and disable our knowledge of Paradise, in Paradise, even whether or not Paradise, at precisely the same time and by precisely the same means that they allow and enable us to produce interpretations which sustain our interest in, or the value of, *Paradise Lost.*

University of Florida

NOTES

1. This is not to say that when Joseph E. Duncan compiled *A Historical Study of Eden* (Minneapolis, 1972) and argued for "Archetypes in Milton's Earthly Paradise," in

Milton Studies XIV, ed. James D. Simmonds (Pittsburgh, 1980), pp. 25–58, or when Kathleen M. Swaim analyzed Raphael's use of analogy and the book of nature in *Contrasting Modes in "Paradise Lost"* (Amherst, 1986), or when others have taught us they failed to recognize extraordinary complications of presentation. Lee A. Jacobus, *Sudden Apprehension: Aspects of Knowledge in "Paradise Lost"* (The Hague, 1976), for example, provides a learned argument on achieving knowledge of Paradise through a tradition of reason. But whereas these imply, sometimes acclaim, that the efforts succeed, *Paradise Lost* explicitly judges that they necessarily fail.

2. I cite and quote *John Milton: Complete Poems and Major Prose*, ed. Merritt Y. Hughes (New York, 1957). A start in examining narrator problems is made by Anne Davidson Ferry, *Milton's Epic Voice: The Narrator in "Paradise Lost"* (Cambridge, Mass., 1963), and William Riggs, *The Christian Poet in "Paradise Lost"* (Berkeley, 1972).

3. An initial sorting appears in Barbara K. Lewalski, "Structure and the Symbolism of Vision in Michael's Prophecy, *Paradise Lost*, Books XI–XII," *PQ* XLII (1963), 25–35.

4. Christopher Ricks, *Milton's Grand Style* (Oxford, 1963), pp. 109–16, and A. Bartlett Giamatti, *The Earthly Paradise and the Renaissance Epic* (Princeton, 1966), pp. 297–347.

5. I do not cite the many commentators over centuries who have noted such techniques, nor do I mention even most of the passages illustrating the techniques; there are far too many of both. Neither do I claim to point out heretofore unrecognized devices. I catalog and register the cumulative weight of these techniques, then bring these to bear on a problem and a potential of knowing Paradise by denying knowledge of it.

6. Barbara K. Lewalski, "Innocence and Experience in Milton's Eden," in *New Essays on "Paradise Lost,"* ed. Thomas Kranidas (Berkeley, 1969), p. 88. Lewalski cites another seminal essay for this notion, Arthur E. Barker's "Structural and Doctrinal Pattern in Milton's Later Poems," in *Essays in English Literature . . . Presented to A.S.P. Woodhouse*, ed. Millar MacLure and F. W. Watt (Toronto, 1964), pp. 169–94, esp. 183–94.

7. Walter R. Davis, "The Languages of Accommodation and the Styles of *Paradise Lost*," in *Milton Studies XVIII*, ed. James D. Simmonds (Pittsburgh, 1983), pp. 103–27; I quote pp. 105, 109.

8. Robert Crosman, *Reading "Paradise Lost"* (Bloomington, 1980), pp. 85–117. I stress the intimation contrary to his next chapter, "Unfallen Narration." Mary Nyquist, "Reading the Fall: Discourse and Drama in *Paradise Lost*," *ELR* XIV (1984), 199–229, particularly pp. 200, 201. I concentrate, perhaps fuse, her modalities.

9. See the culmination of his series of perceptive essays, Robert L. Entzminger, *Divine Word: Milton and the Redemption of Language* (Pittsburgh, 1985), and R. A. Shoaf, *Milton, Poet of Duality: A Study of Semiosis in the Poetry and the Prose* (New Haven, Conn., 1985). Both see complex potential in language, not strictly the evil duplicity opposed to good reflection in Steven Blakemore, "Language and Logos in *Paradise Lost*," *Southern Humanities Review* XX (1986), 325–40. Both focus on the redeeming-redeemable-redeemed potential in language, which can approximate Paradise despite Satan's and the Fall's doublings. In contrast, I focus on failure and fall, especially in descriptions of Paradise. Moreover, I am not so sure about Milton's exploitation of language slippage, but I am not so worried about Milton's intent or complete coherence.

10. Isabel Gamble MacCaffrey, *"Paradise Lost" as "Myth"* (Cambridge, Mass., 1959); Jackson I. Cope, *The Metaphoric Structure of "Paradise Lost"* (Baltimore, 1962).

11. Many contributors have helped refine Stanley E. Fish's seminal *Surprised by Sin: The Reader in "Paradise Lost"* (London, 1967).

12. Regina M. Schwartz's argument for the intimate relationship between hell and

Chaos persuades me to append examples that indicate our incapacity to know Chaos as well as hell. See *Remembering and Repeating; Biblical Creation in "Paradise Lost"* (Cambridge, 1988), pp. 8–39, particularly 11–24.

13. Witness Ralph W. Rader's challenge to Fish, pp. 23–27, in "Fact, Theory, and Literary Explanation," *Critical Inquiry* I (1974), 262–64.

14. Janet Adelman, "Creation and the Place of the Poet in *Paradise Lost*," in *The Author in His work*, ed. Louis L. Martz and Aubrey Williams (New Haven, 1978), p. 66.

15. For a central Platonist argument see Irene Samuel, *Plato and Milton*, (Ithaca, N.Y., 1947). For the prime typologist, see William G. Madsen, *From Shadowy Types to Truth: Studies in Milton's Symbolism* (New Haven, 1968).

16. Many have commented on Milton's definition, found early in I, ii. See Maurice Kelley's edition and excellent annotations, in *The Complete Prose Works of John Milton*, ed. Don M. Wolfe et al., vol. VI (New Haven, 1973), pp. 132–36, hereafter cited as YP.

17. See Howard Schultz, *Milton and Forbidden Knowledge* (New York, 1955).

18. I find Jacobus's double accommodation of the narrator to us and Raphael to Adam and Eve (*Sudden Apprehension*, pp. 89–97) more useful than Crosman's multiple narrative points of view (*Reading "Paradise Lost*," pp. 89–117). But I am intrigued by speculation that multiple points of view in narration as in accommodation are fostered, perhaps necessitated, by the Fall.

19. Arnold Stein, *Answerable Style: Essays on "Paradise Lost"* (Minneapolis, 1953), pp. 52–63, supplies a most suggestive approach to the garden through Satan and negation.

20. Marshall Grossman chooses this passage, which leads into obtrusively fallen connotations of serpent dread, to exemplify a change: the narrator provides a "prelapsarian point of view until he reaches the serpent, which he invests with a significance that it could not have had for Adam and Eve." I agree with Grossman's assessment of a complex dual perspective, but that perspective is present all along, here specified by "since wild" and predatory. See *"Authors to Themselves": Milton and the Revelation of History* (Cambridge, 1987), p. 80.

21. James Grantham Turner, *One Flesh: Paradisal Marriage and Sexual Relations in the Age of Milton* (Oxford, 1987), esp. pp. 230–87.

22. In his essays and book Entzminger emphasizes this point; see *Divine Word*, pp. 21–42. And in *"Such Prompt Eloquence": Language as Agency and Character in Milton's Epics* (Lewisburg, Pa., 1988), Leonard Mustazza, pursuing a different end from mine, invents helpful categories of granted and earned knowledge acquisition and speech function in Paradise; see pp. 71–89, which overlap with interests here.

23. I owe this instance to Anne Kress.

24. On the traditions of the triple temptation, see Elizabeth Marie Pope, *"Paradise Regained": The Tradition and the Poem* (Baltimore, 1947), pp. 51–69.

25. J. M. Evans, *"Paradise Lost" and the Genesis Tradition* (Oxford, 1968), esp. pp. 75–76, 80–81, 88–89, 96–97, 111–12, 243, explicates exegetical traditions that both delineate and complicate some difficulties with knowledge and the Tree of Knowledge in Paradise.

26. Michael Lieb, *Poetics of the Holy: A Reading of "Paradise Lost"* (Chapel Hill, N.C., 1981), pp. 89–99; Lieb adds useful traditions related to Evans's, and helpful analyses.

27. Evans, *The Genesis Tradition*, pp. 275–78, distinguishes important traditions, innovations, and significances in Milton's presentation of Satan speaking through the serpent.

28. Among myriads of discussions of Satan's rhetoric of temptation, I find Jacobus, *Sudden Apprehension*, pp. 119–66, specifically pp. 148–66, especially useful for situating Satan's rationale in the context of Renaissance logic texts; Entzminger, *Divine Word*, pp. 43–71, and Mustazza, *"Such Prompt Eloquence*," pp. 19–68, for tracing the connotations of Satan as persuasive liar through the first nine books of *Paradise Lost;* and Nyquist, "Reading

the Fall," pp. 214–23, for describing Eve as simultaneously implicated by engagement with Satan and yet innocent for suspension from him as he assaults the Word.

My concern with language complements Grossman, "*Authors to Themselves*," pp. 134–46, who focuses on history when he describes a simultaneously prospective and retrospective narration in Eve's deliberation. In this section, which relies mainly on evidence from Eve, I am not unaware of feminine/masculine discrepancies in *Paradise Lost*. Nor am I unaware of the need to rely primarily on evidence from Adam in warnings about the Tree of Knowledge and the limits of human knowledge, or in the wonder and power of naming, knowing, and having dominion over creation. These have momentous critical importance. But here I can effectively pursue only one problem—language, not gender.

ACADEMIC INTERLUDES IN *PARADISE LOST*

Anna K. Nardo

After Mary Powell's return to Milton's household with her entire family, whose Royalist allegiance had been costly, Milton wrote to Carlo Dati, the now eminent Florentine scholar who had befriended and acclaimed him on his Italian trip. When Milton thinks of Dati's earlier letters, which were lost, he feels a "sad longing"; then,

> an even heavier mood creeps over me, a mood in which I am accustomed often to bewail my lot, to lament that those whom perhaps proximity or some unprofitable tie has bound to me, whether by accident or by law, those, commendable in no other way, daily sit beside me, weary me—even exhaust me, in fact—as often as they please; whereas those whom character, temperament, interests had so finely united are now nearly all grudged me by death or most hostile distance and are for the most part so quickly torn from my sight that I am forced to live in almost perpetual solitude. . . . That separation, I may not conceal from you, was also very painful for me; and it fixed those strings in my heart which even now rankle whenever I think that, reluctant and actually torn away, I left so many companions and at the same time such good friends, and such congenial ones in a single city—a city distant indeed but to me most dear. . . . I could think of nothing pleasanter than to recall my dearest memory of you all, of you, Dati, especially. . . . Meanwhile, my Charles, farewell and give my best greeting to Coltellini, Francini, Frescobaldi, Malatesta, Chimentelli the younger, and any other of our group whom you know to be especially fond of me—in short to the whole Gaddian Academy.[1]

Two years earlier when Milton, then separated from his wife, considered God's dictum, "It is not good that the man should be alone; I will make him an help meet for him" (Genesis ii, 18), he argued that the purpose of marriage was not just procreation, but conversation to remedy this loneliness. He specifically rejected Augustine's reasoning that the only help women, surely incapable of friendship, could provide was childbearing. Now, however, so mired in the conflicts of domestic life that he lives "in almost perpetual solitude," Milton longs for the community of learned men he found in the Florentine academies, and his lament echoes the Augustinian position that *Tetrachordon* had rejected: "How much more agreeably could two male friends, rather than a man and woman, enjoy companionship and conversation in a life shared together."[2] The confrontation between his idealization of marriage and his present domestic reality is so painful that he exalts those male friendships fostered in the Italian academies to a treasured memory.

Not just in private correspondence, but in controversial prose, when Milton needs to establish his credentials as a member of an international community of the learned (*RCG*, YP I, pp. 809–10; *2nd Def*, YP IV, pp. 615–17) or to recommend an ideal of the pursuit of knowledge (*RCG*, YP I, p. 819), he praises academies, often specifically mentioning his friendships with prominent Florentines such as Dati, Benedetto Buonmattei, Valerio Chimentelli, and Agostino Coltellini, members of the Accademia della Crusca, the Svogliati, and the Apatisti. Milton's understanding of academic ideals and realities was, however, more complex than his private nostalgia or public self-justifications and exhortations would suggest. As he knew domestic life, what it should be and what it was, he knew academic life. My goal here is to explore how a complex confrontation between academic ideals and realities, and between the academic and the domestic, shaped two interludes in *Paradise Lost:* the devils' activities after Satan's departure and Raphael's visit to Eden. But understanding how academic practices inform the action of these episodes requires a rather detailed description of Italian academies like those Milton frequented on his trip. What were these institutions that fostered the friendship which Milton, wearied by domestic discord, so sorely missed? Why would the defender of the English people adulate a club of Italian wits?

I

The members of these societies—professors of literature and languages, churchmen, nobles, virtuosi, and literati—cite as their origin and model Plato's Academy that met in the groves outside Athens.[3] In a *lezione* praising the leisure necessary for the contemplation and study promoted in the academy that he is addressing, Buonmattei invokes Plato's school, set apart from work-a-day business, "fuggendo mai sempre il commerzio delle città, come troppo dell'ozio nemiche" ("always fleeing the business of cities as quite inimical to leisure"). Dati recommends Plato's Academy and Socratic discourse as the ideal to be upheld by the Accademia della Crusca and the Accademia Fiorentina. And others praise their academies as transcending or retreating from the confusion and dullness of mundane cares.[4] Although their language recalls medieval debates over the *via contemplativa* versus the *via activa,* and Renaissance portraits of the *via otiosa,* nevertheless academicians repeatedly look to the Platonic Academy for their prototype.

In weekly academic meetings, the learned read to one another original poetry, exerpts from plays, *dubbi* or *lezioni* on a broad range of topics, from ethics to archeology, but mostly on matters of literature and language. Between 1550 and 1700 these topics changed very little, although some academies tended to specialize.[5] The Florentine Accademia della Crusca guarded the purity of the Tuscan language in *lezioni* on Petrarch's and Dante's usage and in several editions of a monumental dictionary, which engaged the talents of Dati, Buonmattei, and Chimentelli. The Florentine Svogliati and Apatisti modeled themselves on the older Alterati, a literary society that discussed generic hierarchies and decorum and criticized members' original compositions. The Roman Lincei and the Florentine Accademia del Cimento attended to new scientific theories and discoveries; even Galileo's telescope and its revelations in astronomy were topics for discussion.

Specialization was not, however, an academic goal. These men all seemed to know each other, shared wide intellectual interests, and belonged to several academies, even in distant cities. Dati was a mathematician as well as a professor of Greek and a biographer of painters; Coltellini wrote a treatise on human anatomy as well as sonnets and religious disquisitions; Gaddi, the founder of the Svogliati, belonged to the Venetian Incogniti; and Galileo had followers in the progressive, scientific Roman Lincei, the jocular, literary Apatisti, and the venerable, humanist Accademia Fiorentina. As self-appointed heirs of Plato interpreted by Ficino, these academicians announced as their primary goal to affirm bonds of love and virtue among men of learning, bonds out of which knowledge would arise. The charter of the Oziosi of Naples, founded by Giovanni Manso, describes members as "con si stretto legame di charitatevole amore esser fra noi uniti, che di noi tutti, se ne formi unico, et compite il corpo della nostra nascente Accademia" ("being united with such a close bond of *caritas* among ourselves that from the many of us the body of our emerging academy may be formed single and complete").[6]

To cement their bonds of fellowship the academies frequently sponsored symposia, dinner meetings generally held at the home of a prominent member. Dati regularly hosted such gatherings, where friends enjoyed conversation and debate as well as elegant food and wine. Some academies, like della Crusca, the Apatisti, the Roman Umoristi, and the Accademia delle Cene of Empoli, held regular feasts, even writing statutes to regulate their activities, while others, the Alterati and Svogliati, probably held more modest suppers. Whether formal or informal, these gatherings emulated Plato's *Symposium,* in which the banqueters' easy jocularity and friendship displayed the bonds they praised in their speeches in honor of love.

This homosocial ideal—first articulated in the context of licit Greek homosexuality, the cultural context of the Platonic dialogues—necessitated the exclusion of women. With some notable exceptions, sixteenth- and seventeenth-century academies did not admit women to membership, although some invited wives and daughters to solemn ceremonials or festive occasions.[7] Physically excluded from regular meetings, women were, however, regularly the topic of debate. The hundreds of *dubbi* (or debatable questions) that Anton Maria Salvini read to the Apatisti addressed problems posed by the feminine and by erotic love more often than any other subject: "Che più prevaglia nell'amore, il piacere, o il dolore" ("Whether in love pleasure or sorrow may prevail"), "Se amore sia elezione, o pur destino" ("Whether loving may be a choice or rather destiny"), "Se le buone Leggi dell'amicizia permettano il cedere l'amata all'amico" ("If the good laws of friendship may permit yielding the beloved to one's friend"), and so on. Much academic humor was explicitly antifeminist. One particularly popular genre was the paradoxical praise of the ugly woman: for example, Coltellini's mock-serious explication of a paradoxical blazon by Berni (*PF* 3, I, pp. 47–61) and Alessandro Adimari's fifty sonnets lauding the hunchback, the squint-eyed, the mute, and other female freaks.[8] Buonmattei especially enjoyed antifeminist jokes and specifically blamed women and their domestic business for impeding the study and contemplation necessary to compose academic *lezioni:*

Delle donne io n'ho quattro . . . una padrona, e tre serve; e di queste una sola è giovane. . . . Non fa mai altro, che cantare, e dir mille buffonerie, e studi chi può. L'altre due son tanto vecchie, sconce, e disutili, che'elle non son buone ad altro, che a tossire, a biasciare, e rammaricarsi. . . . La padrona poi, che è peggio di tutte, non può patire di vedermi la penna in mano. Un libro, ch'ella vegga, che non abbia addosso un dito, e mezzo di polvere, i romori fino al cielo. . . . O pensate, s'ella mi lascerebbe comporre una dicería per recitare in questa bugnola? (*PF* 3, I, pp. 77–78)

[I have four women . . . a landlady and three servants; and of these only one is young. . . . She never does anything but sing and chatter idiocies. Who can study? The other two are so old, slatternly, and useless, that they are no good for anything but coughing, mumbling and complaining. . . . The landlady then, who is the worst of all, cannot abide to see me with pen in hand. If she sees a book with a fingerprint or a speck of dust, she screams to the heavens. . . . O do you think [that] she would let me compose a little speech to recite in this rostrum?]

In their Platonic orientation, their exclusion of women, their persistent attention to questions about woman and erotic love, and their traditional antifeminism, these academies functioned, at least in part, like similar all-male groups such as universities: to define masculine identity and align it with the "high," the transcendent, and a privileged space set apart from the feminine, "low," material, and domestic.[9]

These academies also functioned in the specific political context of the counterreformation. Some contemporary and later critics see in their attention to apolitical literary topics, moral clichés, and conventional piety the stifling of independent thought and open debate under the watchful eyes of the Inquisition. Other critics point out that absolutist rulers deliberately diverted the talents of men of considerable erudition away from public affairs toward empty speculations and elaborate election procedures in academies whose charters and rules of censorship rendered them politically impotent. From this perspective the academies' pervasive jocularity and nice refinements of wit, so similar to the contemporary poetic fashion of *concettismo*, seem to be further evidence of cultural decadence.

Academicians did enjoy word games: sonnets in dog Latin; poems with complex rhyme schemes; and exercises in *lingua ionadattica* or *lingua fagiana*, a game, probably invented by a castrato who was valet to a prominent cardinal, in which words with similar first syllables were exchanged. They devoted some meetings solely to amusements. The Apatisti regularly played Sibilla, a game in which a young boy utters a monosyllable in response to a conundrum and two academicians compete in learned discourse to prove that the sibyl had spoken well.[10] Certainly, the Apatisti and other academies debated serious *dubbi*, in the same rhetorical tradition of the *controversia* as Milton's own Prolusions, but many *dubbi* were merely trivial exercises in wit: "Se in volto leggiadro sia più stimabile l'occhio nero, o l'azzurro" ("Whether black or blue eyes are more to be esteemed in a beautiful face"), and "Se il fuoco d'Amore si risvegli più dal vedere il Riso, o il Pianto dell'amata" ("If the fire of love is aroused more by seeing the beloved's smile or tears") (Salvini, *Discorsi*, I, 80; II, 16). Even prominent members of della Crusca like Dati, Chimentelli, and Buonmattei addressed *stravizzi* (banquets, literally debaucheries) with *cicalate* (chats), which were later collected and published, on such subjects as "Chi fosse prima, o la Gall[i]na, o l'Uovo" ("Which came first, the chicken or the egg"), "Delle Lodi dell'Insalata" ("In praise of salad"), and "Sopra la somiglianza tra il popone, e il porco" ("On the similarity of watermelon and pork") (*PF* 3, II, pp. 152–64; 3, II, pp. 83–99; 3, I, pp. 81–104). Academicians often chose cryptic or anagrammatic names for themselves (Dati was Smarrito, or the bewildered, among fellow Cruscans, Agostino Coltellini was Ostilio Contalgeni among the Apatisti); and they adopted witty or ambiguous names for their groups (the Apatisti were either dispassionate or apathetic; the Svogliati were unwilling or listless). In the same vein they held intense and seemingly interminable debates over the symbolism of *imprese* (the Cruscans chose a bran sifter to represent their goal to purify Tuscan). Although this discussion of onomastics and arcana reflects the contemporary fascination with hieroglyphs and emblems, and was conducted with great solemnity, it nevertheless has a certain gamelike air.

To their critics, the theorizing and wit of academicians signaled the exhaustion of Renaissance and humanist culture. This dismissal is, however, a partial judgment. The academies were a significant cultural force, both conservative and progressive, in their social and political contexts. It may seem odd that men so concerned with the purity of their language would enjoy word games that produced nonsense. On the contrary, to get the jokes in the reversals and jumbles of these pastimes, the auditors would have to have mastered the syntactic and semantic rules being trespassed and the learned etymologies being travestied. Paradoxically, the comic reversals confirm the formal linguistic structure; they make the boundaries more evident by violating them.[11] Thus language play in academies fostered their conservative goal: to fix and preserve linguistic meaning and style.

The improvisational skills and wit necessary to play Sibilla, the rhetorical proficiency required to solve the essentially undecideable *dubbi* and to persuade a highly critical audience, and the taste for covert meaning and arcana—all these elements of academic discourse fostered a mindset suited to the political context of absolutist rule in church and state. Academic debates and games gave men of learning a forum to hone their skills in casuistry, ambiguity, and what one academician calls the ethical trinity of patience, *simulazione*, and prudence—skills that allowed intellectual work to continue in a repressive environment. Furthermore, the apparent triviality of many academic activities created a safe and thereby privileged space for theorization and play at self-governance. Slowly, through the seventeenth and eighteenth centuries, a new kind of intellectual evolved—neither a courtier nor a secretary to a prince, but a man whose dignity was founded in his own sphere of study, set apart from direct political interference. And when absolutist regimes began to yield to Enlightenment reforms, the academies had in place the basic structures of governance.

II

On his Italian trip Milton's primary goal was to meet other learned men, not to view ruins or paintings or architecture.[12] He did meet all the academicians so far mentioned, and many others. Minutes in the Biblioteca Nazionale in Florence show he attended Svogliati meetings and read Latin poetry there. He probably gained an introduction to Galileo, blind and under house arrest, through the efforts of academic friends—perhaps Dati, then a young disciple of the venerated, although persecuted, old man. No records confirm our speculations, but scholars have thought it probable that Milton also visited other academies: the Apatisti, known for welcoming foreign visitors and frequented by many of Milton's friends; the Roman Fantastici, one of whose members, Giovanni Salzilli, Milton praised in *Ad Salsillum;* the Umoristi, the most prominent Roman academy whose member, Giovanni Battista Doni, Milton mentions in a letter; the Neapolitan Oziosi, founded by Milton's host Manso; or the Venetian Incogniti, whose membership included several of Milton's friends.

After his return, when he reflected on his academic experience in poetry, published prose, and private correspondence, he always described the academies as an ideal community of learned men: in *Epitaphium Damonis* as graceful, gentle shepherd comrades who serve the muses; in *A Second Defense* as an "institution which deserves great praise not only for promoting humane studies but also for encouraging friendly intercourse" (YP IV, pp. 615–16); and in his letter to Dati, as the longed-for friends whose "character, temperament, interests" he shares. This nostalgic idealization of his experiences notwithstanding, there is much in academic reality antithetical to Milton's beliefs and sensibilities. For one thing, academicians were often aristocratic and always Catholic; of the friends he names in *A Second Defense,* Buonmattei and Chimentelli were priests and Piero Frescobaldi later became a bishop. For another, their discussions were assiduously apolitical; even in their names (Apatisti, Svogliati, Oziosi) they cultivated a stance of learned disinterest. Also, their earthiness and flair for excess clashed with Milton's self-restraint. In *cicalate* for *stravizzi,* Buonmattei, Dati, and Chimentelli joke good-naturedly about their own and their fellows' gluttony and drunkenness; to Buonmattei, drinking is the gentleman's labor (*PF* 3, I, pp. 68–71). Milton, of course, valued temperance highly. In sonnets inviting his friends Lawrence and Skinner to dinner, he recalls the ideal of Greek and Italian symposia in offering a "neat repast . . . light and choice, / Of Attic taste" and "the Lute well toucht, or artful voice / [to] Warble immortal Notes and *Tuscan* Air." But, characteristically, he advises his guests to "judge" their delights, and recommends "mirth, that after no repenting draws" (*Sonnet XX* and *Sonnet XXI*).[13]

Not surprisingly, some ambivalence underlies his open admiration for the academic ideal. He praises his Italian friends, "eminent in rank and learning" (*2nd Def*, YP IV, p. 615), famous for their poetry and studies (*Epitaphium*, 137–38), and elegant in their style (letter to Dati, YP II, pp. 762, 764–65). In his 1645 edition of poetry, he proudly published their encomia heralding him as a new Homer or Virgil—encomia which, in their effusiveness, are quite typical of the poetry academicians addressed to each other. But in *Areopagitica* he reports that these friends bemoaned "the servil condition into which learning amongst them was brought . . . which had dampt the glory of Italian wits," and he has them judge this kind of praise harshly: "nothing had bin there writt'n now these many years but flattery and fustian" (YP II, pp. 537–38).

By the same token, Milton relished his acceptance into academic circles as a kind of initiation into the ranks of international scholars. He attempted to complete a scholarly errand in Florence for the Vatican librarian Lucas Holstensius. In his letter to Dati he envies the retired leisure that allows his friends to pursue scholarship, like Buonmattei's Tuscan grammar, which he had commended in an earlier letter. More significantly, he took their praise as encouragement to his poetic vocation, begun late and still largely unfulfilled at the time of his controversial prose, to "leave something so written to aftertimes, as they should not willingly let it die" (*RCG*, YP I, p. 810). Although his letter to Dati acknowledges the strong appeal of academic leisure for scholarly and poetic pursuits, it also declares his engagement in political and religious controversy. Milton may praise his friend's style, but his own work makes Dati's seem trivial. While Milton publishes a defense of freedom of the press and proposals for reforming basic structures of society, marriage and the church, Dati plans a eulogy for a fellow academic and publishes a description of a royal funeral. Then, in the self-exonerating section of *A Second Defense*, Milton describes his trip through Italy both as a journey to "the lodging-place of *humanitas* and of all the arts of civilization" and as traveling "abroad at my ease for the cultivation of my mind," contrasting his leisure to his "fellow-citizens at home . . . fighting for liberty" and attributing his change of plans to a desire to join them (YP IV, pp. 609, 619). Clearly, Milton was ambivalent about academic self-congratulation and apolitical retreat.

In addition, Italy's reputation for license seems to have caused him some discomfort. Although he refutes the charge that Italy is "a refuge or asylum for criminals," he also asserts his freedom from its potential taint: "in all these places, where so much licence exists, I lived free and untouched by the slightest sin or reproach," (*2nd Def*, YP IV, pp. 609, 620).[14] Even academic wit might stain an aspiring poet who deplored authors "speaking unworthy things of themselves; or unchaste of those names which before they had extoll'd" (*Apology*, YP I, p. 890). Whereas Milton boasts of poetic gifts and tributes from his other Italian friends (*Epitaphium*, 133–35, 181–83; *RCG*, YP I, pp. 809–10), he never mentions the equivocally salacious sonnets about a peasant wench, *La Tina*, so typical of academic antifeminist humor, which Malatesti presented to him, probably as a joke. He also omits Malatesti from the catalog of his friends in published prose. Although not above using bawdry to attack enemies in controversial prose, Milton preferred to ignore the licentious and antifeminist humor enjoyed in the academies. Still, he knew academic reality as well as its ideal.

III

Decades after his journey to Italy, while composing *Paradise Lost*, Milton invented episodes in which characters meet, taking a respite from dramatic action, to discuss topics of ethical, literary, or scientific interest. These interludes—the brief account of the discourse with which some devils "entertain / The irksome hours, till [their] great Chief return[s]" (II, 526–27) and the four-book visit of Raphael to Eden—reflect quite different aspects of Milton's experience in the Italian academies.

Even after Satan masterfully manipulates the fallen angels into renewed obedience to a general who has led them to hell, he faces a precarious political position: his absence might precipitate rebellion. So he leaves his followers with this charge:

> Go therefore mighty Powers.
> Terror of Heav'n, though fall'n; intend at home,
> While here shall be our home, what best may ease
> The present misery, and render Hell
> More tolerable; if there be cure or charm
> To respite or deceive, or slack the pain
> Of this ill Mansion: intermit no watch
> Against a wakeful Foe, while I abroad
> Through all the Coasts of dark destruction seek
> Deliverance for us all. (II, 456–65)

To co-opt their skills into his service and keep them too busy to rebel in his absence, Satan assigns tasks precisely tailored to the inclinations of the three devils who offered rival plans at the great consult. Further, the language with which Milton describes the devils' activities after Satan leaves indicates the appropriate leader for each of the three bands.

Moloch, who had proposed open war, hears in Satan's charge the option of military readiness, and as "the fiercest Spirit / That fought in Heav'n" (II, 44–45) he would appropriately lead one band in war games: "Part on the Plain, or in the Air sublime / Upon the wing, or in swift Race contend, / As at th' *Olympian* Games or *Pythian* fields" (II, 528–30). Mammon, who had counseled making themselves at home in hell by exploiting its resources to "work ease out of pain" (II, 261), now hears the charge to "intend at home / . . . what best may ease / The present misery, and render Hell / More tolerable." Presumably, the devil so curious about "This Desert soil" and "these piercing Fires," which may become the devils' elements (II, 270, 275), leads a second band "On bold adventure to discover wide / That dismal World, if any Clime perhaps / Might yield them easier habitation" (II, 571–73). At the consult, in order to dissuade his fellows from war and advise acquiescence, Belial had painted a vivid picture of the even more horrid torments God might inflict. But if they lie low, he hopes, God might allow the fires to slacken, or the devils' temper might change, rendering "Familiar the fierce heat, and void of pain" (II, 219). Now he hears in Satan's charge an activity suited to his tastes: to seek a "cure or charm / To respite or deceive, or slack the pain / Of this ill Mansion." This "graceful and humane" devil, the masterful rhetorician whose "Tongue / Dropt Manna" but whose true goal was "ignoble ease, and peaceful sloth" (II, 109, 112–13, 227), is a suitable leader for the third "more mild" band. One half "Retreated in a silent valley, sing" epics of their own heroism and laments of their fall (II, 546–51). The other half seeks the "charm" to deceive their pain in eloquent philosophical discussion:

> In discourse more sweet
> (For Eloquence the Soul, Song charms the Sense,)
> Others apart sat on a Hill retir'd,
> In thoughts more elevate, and reason'd high
> Of Providence, Foreknowledge, Will, and Fate,
> Fixt Fate, Free will, Foreknowledge absolute,
> And found no end, in wand'ring mazes lost.
> Of good and evil much they argu'd then,
> Of happiness and final misery,
> Passion and Apathy, and glory and shame,
> Vain wisdom all, and false Philosophie:

Yet with a pleasing sorcery could charm
Pain for a while or anguish, and excite
Fallacious hope, or arm th'obdured breast
With stubborn patience as with triple steel. (II, 555–69)

Whereas the other bands pass the time in martial arts and exploration for conquest, Belial's crew in leisured retirement constitutes an academy.[15]

As astute as any Machiavellian Medici prince, Satan channels the active elements among his ranks into service to his political goals and removes the intellectuals from the sphere of public influence. Many Italian academies met under quasi-government sponsorship which required charters forbidding discussion of affairs of state, and most boasted of a noble "sponsor" who would "protect" their literary and philosophical activities from the troubles of the world.[16] Politically neutralized like Belial's band, academicians regularly praised these sponsors, often tyrants, in effusive prose or verse that rivaled the excesses of Satan's followers as they abase themselves before their protector:

Towards him they bend
With awful reverence prone; and as a God
Extol him equal to the highest in Heav'n:
Nor fail'd they to express how much they prais'd,
That for the general safety he despis'd
His own. (II, 477–82)

This is the kind of "flattery and fustian" bemoaned by Milton's friends, according to *Areopagitica,* but practiced by them nonetheless.

The devils' discussions of "Fixt Fate, Free Will," of "happiness and final misery," of "Passion and Apathy" are finally undecideable, because, like the Stoics whom Christ rejects in *Paradise Regained,* their reason, albeit "high," is "vain" without divine revelation. As well as pagan philosophy, the description of their discourse recalls the academic *dubbi*—disquisitions on doubtful propositions like "Che cosa intendessero per Fortuna gli antichi Filosofi" ("What did the ancient philosophers mean by Fortune"), "Se sia meglio la Servitù con molti comodi, o la Libertà con molte miserie" ("Whether servitude with many comforts or liberty with much misery is better"), "Supposto che si dia nel mondo felicità, in che cosa si deva questa ritrovare" ("Supposing one may have happiness in this world, in what should one discover it"), "Qual sia la passione dell'animo, che più travagli l'uomo" ("What passion of the soul most vexes man"), "Se nella umane operazioni abbia maggior forza, o la speranza del premio, o il timore della pena" ("Whether hope of reward or fear of punishment has the greater force in human affairs") (Salvini, *Discorsi* II, disc. 15, 57; I, disc. 41, 12). Whereas the devils' goal fulfills Satan's charge—"with a pleasing sorcery [to] charm / Pain for a while"—the academicians' stated purpose in discussing *dubbi,* so "capace d'infinite, erudite, e dotte riflessioni" ("capable of infinite, erudite, and learned reflections"), was to provide "campo amplissimo, e giocondissimo, per lo quale i virtuosi, e spiritosi ingegni possano tuttora spaziare, e esercitarsi" ("a most ample and pleasant field in which virtuosi and lively wits may ever range and exercise themselves") (Salvini, *Discorsi* II, disc. 96, p. 516). Neither among devils nor academicians, however, does their discourse decide matters of public import, and in both cases it produces "wand'ring mazes"—the "false Philosophie" of lost angels and the ingenious arguments of academic debate.

To portray this hellish academy, Milton drew on his own experience, concentrating and exaggerating the debased and decadent aspects of the Italian academies: their political impotence, acquiescence to tyranny, flattery of the powerful, and trivialization of philosophy into a pastime. In suggesting that the philosopher devils, who discuss "Will" and "Apathy" but draw no conclusions and take no actions, are followers of the slothful Belial, Milton may even allude to the specific academies attended by his friends: the Svogliati (the unwilling or listless), the Apatisti (the dispassionate or apathetic), and the Oziosi (the leisured or idlers).[17]

IV

In keeping with his pattern of first presenting in hell debased versions of ideals to be realized in heaven or Eden, Milton devotes Books V through VIII to an idyllic academic symposium, Raphael's visit to Eden. Previous studies have analyzed the diverse materials Milton used in creating this episode. Raphael's flight, arrival in Eden like "*Maia's* son" (V, 285), and hospitable reception recall the many descents from heaven in classical poetry. Adam's sight of the angel's approach while sitting at his bower's door and his instructing Eve to hasten to prepare fit hospitality recall the angelic visit to Abraham and Ṣarah in Genesis, chapter xviii. And Raphael's characterization as "the sociable Spirit, that deign'd / To travel with *Tobias,* and secur'd / His marriage with the seven-times-wedded Maid" (V, 221–23) recalls the Book of Tobit. There Raphael, whose name signifies medicine of God, converses freely with Tobias, as Milton's angel does with Adam; helps Tobias heal his father's blindness, as Milton's Raphael heals any remaining perturbation from Eve's satanic dream; and helps Tobias win his bride from the devil Asmodeus, as Milton's Raphael, who defeated Asmadai in the war in heaven (VI, 362–68), advises Adam on marital matters.[18] Attending more to the structure of the entire conversation than to angelic visits, Northrop Frye and Barbara Lewalski have classified the four-book dialogue as a Platonic symposium, and Kathleen Swaim has emphasized its Hellenic quality in contrast to the Hebraic tone of Michael's instruction.[19]

God's charge to Raphael establishes the ideal for symposia, a meal and discourse shared by male friends:

> Go therefore, half this day as friend with friend
> Converse with *Adam,* in what Bow'r or shade
> Thou find'st him from the heat of Noon retir'd,
> To respite his day-labor with repast,
> Or with repose. (V, 229–33)

During their dialogue, both Adam and Raphael repeatedly rejoice in their friendship and conversation (VII, 98–108; VIII, 5–10, 204–28, 648–51), and they hope for future meetings (V, 496–500; compare VII, 569–73). The remainder of God's charge (V, 233–45), however, to "advise . . . warn . . . tell him withal / His danger," does not frame the ensuing discourse as leisured speculation of "Happiness" and "free Will" without political consequences. What will follow is essential advice on how to preserve "his happy state"—the prelapsarian *polis,* two newlyweds in a garden. This charge presents God's point of view, an awareness of the couple's tragic failure to heed the advice. Still, when Raphael arrives in Eden, he does not immediately sound "that warning voice" the narrator calls for when Satan swoops down to earth (IV, 1–8). Instead, the angel graciously accepts Adam's invitation to food and rest as a welcome recreation:

> *Adam,* I therefore came, nor art thou such
> Created, or such place hast here to dwell,
> As may not oft invite, though Spirits of Heav'n
> To visit thee; lead on then where thy Bow'r
> O'ershades; for these mid-hours, till Ev'ning rise
> I have at will. (V, 372–77)

In the unfallen garden, acquiring knowledge crucial for salvation is, like work, part of Adam and Eve's blissful *otium,* one more opportunity for pleasure. God makes the pursuit of knowledge a joy of leisure, but unlike Satan he does not remove it from decisions about action.

Milton undoubtedly drew on the Platonic dialogues, especially the *Symposium,* as a model for Adam's and Raphael's friendship, in which a superior instructs a willing listener through dialogue, for their leisured meal and discourse, and for their final discussion of love. Although he had read the dialogues, he actually attended Italian academies. The specific issues Adam and Raphael raise were common topics for academic debate between 1500 and 1700, particularly among the Florentines. This academic prose was not a direct source for the details of Raphael's disquisitions. Milton had more authoritative sources in biblical and classical texts, some of which academicians also cited in their *lezioni.* Some topics discussed by the angel and the first man were commonplace, and Milton had considered many before his trip to Italy. Furthermore, while Adam poses academic questions, Raphael's answers sometimes differ from academic positions in content and presentation; the angel is chiefly a storyteller. Nevertheless, Milton's familiarity with the structure and common topics of academic discourse helped him frame the angelic visit as an academic symposium more like the modern Italian than the ancient Greek ideal. In this interlude, he dramatizes a discussion appropriate for academic meetings.

In response to Adam's questions about angelic eating, Raphael explains "the scale of Nature set / From centre to circumference," how all things in God's orderly universe are "in thir several active Spheres assign'd, / Till body up to spirit work, in bounds / Proportion'd to each kind" (V, 509–10, 477–79). Divine order was, of course, a commonplace in the Renaissance, discussed in academies as in sermons and political treatises. In one sixteenth-century example, Pier Francesco Giambullari delivered a *lezione* to the Accademia Fiorentina, "Dell'Ordine dell'Universo" ("Of the Order of the Universe"), in which, while analyzing two *terzine* from the *Purgatorio,* he explains the scale of nature, ranging from pure potency, or primal matter, to pure act, or spirit. In between, "i gradi, per salire dal più basso fino al supremo, hanno chiamati lo essere, la vita, il senso, la ragione, e lo intelletto. E lo essere hanno detto, che è quello della pietra: il vivere, quello delle piante: il sentire, degli animali: la ragione, dell'uomo: e lo intelletto, dell'Angelo" ("[the philosophers] have called the degrees, rising from the lowest to the highest, being, life, sensation, reason, and intellect. They have called being that which is of rocks: living, that of plants: feeling, of animals: reason, of man: and intellect, of angels") (*PF* 2, II, pp. 41–42). Whereas Giambullari offers a philosophical explanation, Raphael presents his lesson on universal order in the poetic image of a tree; whereas the Neoplatonic academician predictably emphasizes the imperfection of matter, Milton's angel asserts the essential oneness and perfection of the entire cycle of creation. Still, both address the relation between matter and angels in an academic setting. Indeed, Adam's questions about angelic eating and sexuality would have been appropriate material for *dubbi.* Although many academies forbade discussion of theology, Coltellini allowed the Apatisti to consider *dubbi* on the nature of angels.[20]

When Adam asks how angels could fail to love their maker, Raphael launches into his long narration of the war in heaven, which raises several issues addressed in academies. First, he hesitates, wondering,

> how shall I relate
> To human sense th'invisible exploits
> Of warring Spirits
> . . . .
> how last unfold
> The secrets of another World, perhaps
> Not lawful to reveal? (V, 66, 568–70)

As the teller of a story that includes divinity, Raphael, like Milton and his Italian and classical predecessors, must "[liken] spiritual to corporal forms, / As may express them best" (V, 573–74). Academic exercises in literary criticism explored this problem of accommodation. Benedetto Averani delivered an apposite *lezione* to the Apatisti, entitled "Se i Poeti abbiano contro al poetico decoro peccato, quando attribuirono agli Dei passioni indegne della divinità" ("If poets may have sinned against poetic decorum when they attributed to the gods passions unworthy of divinity") (*PF* 2, I, pp. 232–42).[21] To both academician and angel, the issue extends beyond literary communication to sin; Averani asks whether poets "empiamente insieme delle natura degli Dei favellano" ("likewise fable impiously about the nature of the gods") (p. 232). In defense of poetry, Averani denies that these representations are allegories; poets, he decides, must accommodate their readers' vulgar conceptions. Again, Raphael's view differs: "what if," the angel asks, "Earth / Be but the shadow of Heav'n, and things therein / Each to other like, more than on Earth is thought?" (V, 574–76).[22] Still, his question about accommodation is a subject of academic literary criticism.

Raphael's story itself broaches other problems of literary representation. His tale of heroic deeds—such as Abdiel's lonely rejection of Satan, Michael's and his own martial feats, and the Son's triumphant rescue—naturally takes epic form. But the outcome of the war is never in doubt, and the fighting only serves to illustrate the truth of God's original proclamation of the Son's rule. So Raphael must tell a story of might that demonstrates the limitations of might. His solution to this narrative problem—to interpose such comic moments as the cannon's rout of the loyal angels encumbered by arms—raises questions about epic decorum. To what extent may epic include comedy? Can epic form express Christian values? Questions of decorum were a staple for discussion among the Florentine Alterati, the model for the Apatisti and Svogliati. They debated the usefulness of comedy for producing moral effects, the limitations of epic, whether *The Divine Comedy* was properly a comedy or an epic, and whether the mixed form of Ariosto's epic romance was inferior or preferable to Tasso's more unified epic. In the Accademia Fiorentina and the Accademia della Crusca as well, what elements properly constitute epic form was matter for frequent quarrels.[23] In these debates, Raphael's story of Christian heroism and of might rendered laughable takes its stand with the supporters of Dante and Ariosto.

V

Perhaps the most important subject of academic discussion was language, particularly but not exclusively among the Cruscans, who set out to purify Tuscan by the best Trecento models, laboring for years over their dictionary to fix linguistic meaning. In a letter to Buonmattei, Milton wholeheartedly applauds their values:

> Whoever in a state knows how to form the manners of men wisely, to rule them at home and at war with excellent precepts, him before others do I think especially worthy of all honor. Next to him, however, is the one who tries to fix by precepts and rules the order and pattern of writing and speaking received from a good age of the nation, and in a sense to enclose it within a wall; indeed, in order that no onc may overstep it, it ought to be secured by a law all but Romulean. For if we wish to compare the usefulness of the two men, the one alone is able to effect an upright and holy society of Citizens; the other alone can make it truly noble, and splendid, and brilliant, which is the next thing to be wished. The one provides, I believe, a noble ferocity and intrepid strategy against an enemy invading the boundaries; the other, with a learned censorship of ears and a light-armed guard of good Authors, undertakes to overcome and drive out Barbarism, that filthy civil enemy of character which attacks the spirits of men. Nor is it to be thought unimportant what speech people have, whether pure or corrupted, or how correct their daily use of it, a matter which more than once involved the welfare of Athens. (YP I, p. 329)

God's charge to Raphael combines both these tasks; the angel must warn Adam of

> His danger, and from whom, what enemy
> Late fall'n himself from Heaven, is plotting now
> The fall of others from like state of bliss;
> By violence, no, for that shall be withstood,
> But by deceit and lies. (V, 239–43)

Like the angelic guard of Eden's bounds, Raphael is to protect the "upright and holy society" of Eden "against an enemy invading the boundaries," but he can do so only by teaching the unfallen citizens about what they cannot yet know, "deceit and lies"—that is "speech . . . pure or corrupted."[24]

Since their danger will come from "Ambiguous words" (V, 703), Raphael, like the academic lexicographers, alerts his auditors to the complexities of determining linguistic meaning. He teaches Adam and Eve about equivocation, for example, in Satan's abuse of the word *equal.* In the speech rousing his cohort to resentment against the Son and to preference for his own leadership, Satan faces a problem. His justification for rebellion rests on angelic equality to the Son, but in order to sustain his leadership he must acknowledge that all are "not *equal.*" If some are "in power and splendor less," he reasons, still all are "In freedom *equal*"; so, he concludes, "Who can in reason then or right assume / Monarchy over such as live by right / His *equals?*" (V, 791–97, emphasis mine). Abdiel immediately grasps Satan's equivocation, the slide from equally free to equal, and asks,

> But to grant it thee unjust,
> That *equal* over *equals* Monarch Reign:
> Thyself though great and glorious dost thou count,
> Or all Angelic Nature join'd in one,
> *Equal* to him begotten Son, by whom
> As by his Word the mighty Father made
> All things, ev'n thee? (V, 831–37, emphasis mine)

The first day's battle shows the rebels, now "liable to fear . . . flight . . . pain," unequal even to the loyal angels, "Unwearied, unobnoxious to be pain'd / By wound" (VI, 391–405). Further, Satan's own words while concocting his offensive strategy for the second day's battle give the lie to his earlier equivocal boast of equality:

> perhaps more valid Arms,
> Weapons more violent, when next we meet,
> May serve to better us, and worse our foes,
> Or *equal* what between us made the odds,
> In Nature none. (VI, 438–42, emphasis mine)

Now Satan needs more elaborate weaponry to *equal* the mere followers of the superior Son to whom Satan had earlier claimed equality. As if catching himself in his own contradiction, he parenthetically (and nonsensically after the day's rout) reasserts the natural equality of rebel and loyal angels.

Through such examples of the corruption and proper use of language, Raphael fulfills a key academic goal, as Milton perceived it in his letter to Buonmattei. Ideally, attending to shades of linguistic meaning in such activities as compiling dictionaries and grammars was not a scholarly pursuit removed from ethical and political action. In showing Adam and Eve how Satan manipulates the meaning of "equal," Raphael gives them a defense against Satan's lethal weapon, "deceit and lies."[25]

Raphael's story includes another, more benign form of linguistic deception—jesting. Symposia were appropriate settings for jocularity, and Raphael's miniature epic is contained within the larger dialogue, a comic genre as described by Lewalski.[26] Like his exposition of equivocation, Raphael's accounts of verbal play further the educative goals of the symposium. When Satan gathers his legions for a ludicrous armed rebellion against omnipotence, God sets the standard for jesting. "Smiling," the God who elsewhere speaks the tautologies of bare truth here addresses his Son with words that signify the opposite of what he means:

> Nearly it now concerns us to be sure
> Of our Omnipotence.
> . . . .
> Let us advise, and to this hazard draw
> With speed what force is left, and all imploy
> In our defense, lest unawares we lose
> This our high place, our Sanctuary, our Hill.
> (V, 721–22, 729–32)

Like the war itself, God's irony gives the Son an opportunity to manifest his nature by his response:

> Mighty Father, thou thy foes
> Justly hast in derision, and secure
> Laugh'st at thir vain designs and tumults vain,
> Matter to mee of Glory, whom thir hate
> Illustrates. (V, 735–39)

In reading the complete meaning of God's words within their context, the Son shows himself to be the Logos, the namer whose words will bring things into being. Here, as when "with a smile" (VIII, 368) God allows Adam to complete his unspoken plan by arguing for a mate, God withdraws his omniscience from his language and speaks in jest what he does not finally intend in order to bring the Son into the fullness of his knowledge. By smilingly saying what he does not mean, God gives others room to learn, affirm, and complete his meaning.

Satan's and Belial's "scoffing in ambiguous words" (VI, 568) as they fire their "devilish Enginry" (553) are a parodic debasement of God's jest. Their puns have struck most critics as bad jokes. They are bad, but not simply because they are heavy-handed. Whereas God's irony calls the Son to complete his meaning, the rebels' puns yield no insight, misleading their hearers instead. "Commanding loud" so that both sides may hear his order to open the flanks that hide the cannons, Satan enjoys puzzling the loyal angels with his offer of an "open breast" and an "overture" to "Peace," and his intent to "discharge" and "touch / What we propound" (VI, 557–67). To his fellow rebels, who catch his meaning, he gives only an opportunity to jeer at their supposed victims—an opportunity "*Belial* in like gamesome mood" seizes:

> Leader, the terms we sent were terms of weight,
> Of hard contents, and full of force urg'd home,
> Such as we might perceive amus'd them all,
> And stumbl'd many; who receives them right,
> Had need from head to foot well understand;
> Not understood, this gift they have besides,
> They show us when our foes walk not upright. (620–27)

Unlike the Son's response to God's jest, Belial's reading of the intended meaning beneath Satan's ironic puns does not manifest the truth of the situation. His own double entendres confound the language of debate ("terms of weight . . . hard contents . . . full of force"), which among the unfallen refines and clarifies meaning, with the language of material force, which would compel assent but only ends in chaos.[27] These jests voice the rebels' pride, "highth'n'd in thir thoughts beyond / All doubt of Victory" (629–30), but immediately the falsity of their position is evident when they are buried under mountains. The resulting "horrid confusion heapt / Upon confusion" (668–69) mirrors the linguistic confusion unleashed by Satan's rejection of the Logos.

As hearers of Raphael's story, Adam and Eve must discriminate the levels of meaning that Satan and Belial would confound: an overture to peace that escalates the war, an offer of dialogue that describes cannon shot. On the other hand, they hear in Raphael's apposite punning multiple meanings that expand understanding. When Satan exposes his cannons, "Pillars most they seem'd," from the loyal angels' perspective, "Or hollow'd bodies made of Oak or Fir / . . . thir mouths / With hideous orifice gap't on us wide, / Portending hollow truce" (VI, 573–74, 576–78). The pillars are hollow, but so is Satan's "overture" to peace. Whereas Satan's and Belial's puns reduce dialogue to corrupted matter, Raphael reads in matter an apt emblem of Satan's use of language. By punning on "hollow," he both asserts that Satan has hollowed out language, emptying it of meaning, and illustrates how linguistic complexity can reveal, not obscure, truth.

In these examples of play with language, Raphael promotes in Adam and Eve a quite sophisticated linguistic understanding. To get the point of God's irony, the rebels' taunts, and the angel's pun, Adam and Eve must be able to distinguish the levels of meaning that verbal humor reverses and conflates. The apparently trivial wordgames enjoyed in academic meetings and recreative symposia had a similar function. Men devoted to an ideal of linguistic purity relished nonsense poetry, playful etymologies, and equivocal wit that deliberately violated the rules of semantic and syntactic meaning that they were so busy codifying. But a jesting violation makes the boundaries of the code more apparent and thus confirms its structure. Similarly, in the context of a leisured symposium, Raphael's story includes verbal play that confirms his auditors' understanding of linguistic meaning. Their attention to the complex ways in which language can make sense and nonsense is not, however, removed from the sphere of political action; their blissful state depends on it.[28]

VI

Although the knowledge pursued in the academies prior to the eighteenth century was primarily linguistic and literary, science and technology attracted increasing attention. There were early scientific societies like the Roman Accademia dei Lincei and the Florentine Accademia del Cimento whose members included Galileo, Torricelli, and their followers. Even among the literati who composed the majority of the academies, many, like Milton's friends Dati and Coltellini, had scientific interests. It is not surprising then that the scientific and technological topics raised in the Edenic symposium—Raphael's prophetic lament over Satan's invention of firearms (VI, 501–06) and Adam's question about the apparent rotation of heavenly bodies (VIII, 13–38)—broach issues of academic interest. Salvini asked the Apatisti to consider "Se l'invenzione dell'Arme da fuoco sia degna di lode, o di biasimo" ("Whether the invention of firearms should merit praise or blame") (*Discorsi* II, disc. 52). Against Ariosto's attribution of firearms to the devil, Salvini argues that human weakness makes such weapons necessary to defend the good and just. Also, as we have seen, Galileo's astronomical discoveries, despite his forced recantation, prompted discussion among the Apatisti and in the more solemn Accademia Fiorentina. Slowly, during the seventeenth century, attention to scientific and technological advances began to grow as interest in literary theory waned.

Adam's and Raphael's symposium, however, teaches knowledge suited to life in an unfallen garden, far from the cities of Enlightenment academicians. In Eden, God's revelation is knowledge sufficient for happiness, and there is no lack that technology could fill. Raphael's descent, his story of the war, and the discussion of astronomy point out the limitations of technology and advocate a more literary form of knowledge than science. Before his flight to Eden, the angel surveys earth with perfect sight despite the vast distance: "As when by night the Glass / Of *Galileo*, less assur'd, observes / Imagin'd Lands and Regions in the Moon" (V, 261–63). Milton's allusion to the telescope of Galileo, whom Dati calls "nostro Accademico" ("our academician") (*PF* 2, V, pp. 305–06), frames the symposium with a pointed contrast between angelic vision and fallen human sight aided by technology. The startling reference to the only contemporary mentioned in *Paradise Lost* alerts the fit though fallen reader that the knowledge to be shared at this simple meal will far surpass that of even the most illustrious modern scientist and inventor. Raphael's story of the war further questions the efficacy of technology in his descriptions of the equipage of battle. Satan admits to needing artillery to supply a lack in his now fallen forces, and if the loyal angels had been "unarm'd" they "might / Have easily as Spirits evaded swift" the "Iron Globes" of cannon shot (VI, 595–96, 590). To the unfallen such inventions are at best superfluous, at worst, detrimental.[29]

Raphael states categorically that the information sought by Galileo is useless in Eden. Like many academicians, the angel argues that knowledge should have limits: "Knowledge is as food, and needs no less / Her Temperance over Appetite" (VII, 126–27). In deciding "Se la curiosità sia vizio, o pur virtù" ("Whether curiosity may be a vice or virtue"), Salvini shares with Raphael (and Seneca) this commonplace: "Vengo alla curiosità dell'intelletto, la quale quando passa una certa giusta misura, è viziosa; dandosi anche negli studi, come ben disse Seneca, l'intemperanza. . . . Le quistioni troppo curiose, come non necessarie al ben dell'animo, sono da'filosofi dilleggiate" ("I come to intellectual curiosity which, when it exceeds a certain just measure, is vicious; yielding itself even in studies, as Seneca well said, to intemperance. . . . Over-curious questions are mocked by philosophers as unnecessary to the good of the mind") (*Discorsi* I, disc. 9, p. 32).[30] After Galileo's quarrel with the Inquisitors, academicians most often discussed restraints to intellectual curiosity in the counterreformation context of preserving endangered orthodoxy. Raphael, however, does not describe astronomy as dangerous. Rather, he redirects Adam's attention away from factual knowledge toward an approach to knowledge more suited to human life, toward what "best may serve / To glorify the Maker, and infer / Thee also happier" (VII, 115–17)—in short, toward the arts of interpretation.

When Adam wonders why the nobler celestial bodies speed through vast distances around the earth, which could move around them more efficiently, Raphael, whom Adam had earlier addressed as "Divine Interpreter" (VII, 72), draws Adam's attention to his premises. Whereas Adam finds the principle of nature's frugality and proportion violated by heavenly motion (VIII, 26–27), Raphael reminds him of the first premise in interpreting any divine act: it will manifest God's power and love. On this assumption, Raphael teaches Adam how to reinterpret the data in a way that glorifies God and delights Adam in God's love and care for him:

> consider first, that Great
> Or Bright infers not Excellence: the Earth
> Though, in comparison of Heav'n, so small,
> Nor glistering, may of solid good contain
> More plenty than the Sun that barren shines,
> Whose virtue on itself works no effect,
> But in the fruitful Earth; there first receiv'd
> His beams, unactive else, thir vigor find.
> Yet not to Earth are those bright Luminaries
> Officious, but to thee Earth's habitant.
> And for the Heav'n's wide Circuit, let it speak
> The Maker's high magnificence.
> . . . .
> The swiftness of those Circles áttribute,
> Though numberless, to his Omnipotence.
>
> (VIII, 90–101, 107–108)

Interpreted thus, the appearance of the heavens exalts mankind as the center of loving attention and bespeaks God's glory. Raphael's instruction in interpretation bordering on hymnic praise redirects Adam to appropriate human knowledge, to reading: "for Heav'n / Is as the Book of God before thee set, / Wherein to read his wond'rous Works" (VIII, 66–68). Reading texts and interpreting stories was, of course, the primary knowledge pursued in seventeenth-century academies, not the observation, measurement, and experimentation that gradually replaced literary exercises.

So Raphael teaches Adam a quintessentially humanistic and academic skill, but also warns about the excesses potential in the academic pursuit of knowledge. Beyond those high "Things not reveal'd" to creatures, such as the movement of celestial bodies, he assures Adam, "Anough is left besides to search and know" (VII, 122, 125). Still, within these bounds of permitted knowledge, not everything is worth knowing; a surfeit of knowledge oppresses the mind and "soon turns / Wisdom to Folly, as Nourishment to Wind" (VII, 129–30). Adam learns this lesson, abjuring "things remote / From use, obscure and subtle" and preferring "That which before us lies in daily life" (VIII, 191–92, 193). In these rejections of useless, obscure, and overly subtle, although permitted, knowledge as "fume, / Or emptiness, or fond impertinence" (VIII, 194–95), the Edenic symposium sets itself apart from such less than ideal academic practices as interminable debates over *imprese*, learned expositions of trivial *dubbi*, and witty *cicalate*. Milton affirms the academic ideal, not its sometimes debased reality.

VII

The academic ideal was, however, male, and Eve attends this symposium. Like their Platonic model, Italian academies excluded women—only to discuss them regularly in disquisitions on erotic love, beauty, Petrarch's *Canzoniere*, and so on. At these gatherings, woman was the absent presence necessary to define male identity, and academic humor in particular relegated her to the physical, mundane, domestic world that by contrast exalted the abstract, transcendent, contemplative sphere of male academic thought. But Milton's paradisal symposium differs from its models in calling attention to Eve's presence, to her leave-taking before the discussion of astronomy, and to her absence during the dialogue on love. In its attention to Eve, present and absent, the narrative suggests some limitations in academic discourse for teaching truth.

With carefully chosen details, Milton locates the symposium in a domestic, even feminine setting. Adam first sees the angel approach

> as in the door he sat
> Of his cool Bow'r, while now the mounted Sun
> Shot down direct his fervid Rays, to warm
> Earth's inmost womb . . .
> And *Eve* within, due at her hour prepar'd
> For dinner savoury fruits. (V, 299–304)

The suggestion of sexuality in this description makes the bower an emblem of the marriage whose preservation is Raphael's goal.[31] Adam "walks forth" from the bower to meet his guest, but not to leave the private, domestic world so often associated with women for the public world of men. Rather, he goes to bring the spirit into this domestic world, and

Milton contrasts Adam's simplicity to public display, "the tedious pomp that waits / On Princes" and "Dazzles the crowd, and sets them all agape" (V, 354–55, 357). Nor are the food for the feast and its elegant presentation trivialities to be passed over to get to the matter for discourse. The lavish poetic detail of the description dignifies Eve's domestic arts of "frugal storing," choosing fruits "for delicacy best," arranging dishes to "bring / Taste after taste upheld with kindliest change," concocting "inoffensive must, and meaths," tempering "dulcet creams," providing "fit vessels," and strewing "the ground / With Rose and Odors from the shrub unfum'd" (V, 321–49).[32] Food and its female preparer are of interest; indeed, the first topic of conversation is eating.

Academicians at the *stravizzi* of the Accademia della Crusca also discussed food, but in a quite different vein. After-dinner speakers punctuated their *cicalate* with references to the sumptuous meal and the members' gluttony or drunkenness and frequently discoursed learnedly on food. In addition to the disquisitions on salad, chickens and eggs, pork and watermelon mentioned earlier, Dati held forth "Sopra Le Fave" ("On beans"), and Buonmattei "Sopra il proverbio: Molti a tavola, e pochi in coro" ("On the proverb: many at table, and few in the choir") (*PF* 3, II, pp. 165–76; 3, I, pp. 62–80). Their comic strategy is generally to use their finely tuned powers of argumentation on the most mundane subjects, thereby mocking on festive occasions the academic skills they practiced and refined at their regular meetings. In carnivalesque style, the base topics expose and puncture the pomposity of their exposition. Such ludic juxtapositions of high and low, however, tend to confirm the structure they travesty, and are not meant to reform.[33] Milton's strategy is quite different in his emphasis on the domesticity of the symposium in Eden, his careful attention to Eve's culinary arts, and the seriousness with which he has Raphael turn an explanation of angelic digestion into ontology. In Eden the domestic and physical are not the opposites that exalt the academic and transcendent; they are, as their root and base, one with intellect and spirit.[34] Food becomes thought, even prayer, and the only knowledge angels bring is that which could preserve a homey couple's marital joy.

Eve is present, although silent, to hear the knowledge sufficient to protect her home: Raphael's disquisition on universal order, his epic of the war in heaven, and his hymn to creation. In her silence, she enacts the Pauline advice, "Let the woman learn in silence with all subjection. But I suffer not a woman to teach, nor to usurp authority over the man, but to be in silence" (1 Tim. ii, 11–12); "Let your women keep silence in the churches. . . . And if they will learn any thing, let them ask their husbands at home" (1 Cor. xiv, 34–35).[35] Albeit from a subordinate position,

Eve receives instruction, must choose to act on it, and is responsible for her actions. In Eden, knowledge is not the sole preserve of men in groups.[36]

When Adam broaches his question on astronomy, Eve perceives it as "studious thoughts abstruse" and goes "forth among her Fruits and Flow'rs, / To visit how they prosper'd, bud and bloom, / Her Nursery" (VIII, 40, 44–46). Her present errand is singularly domestic and points toward her future care for children. Several critics have read Eve's timely withdrawal as anticipating and dramatizing Raphael's lesson to the over-curious Adam:

> Solicit not thy thoughts with matters hid,
> . . . .
> joy thou
> In what [God] gives to thee, this Paradise
> And thy fair *Eve:* . . .
> . . . be lowly wise:
> Think only what concerns thee and thy being.
> (VIII, 167, 170–72, 173–74)[37]

The structure of the narrative, Eve's leaving followed by Raphael's admonition that validates her choice, offers her useful domestic labor as an alternative to leisured speculation among males, with its potential for excess.

Against this academic, and thus male, model for the pursuit of knowledge, the narrator juxtaposes a description, from Eve's perspective, of the companionate marriage:

> Yet went she not, as not with such discourse
> Delighted, or not capable her ear
> Of what was high: such pleasure she reserv'd,
> *Adam* relating, she sole Auditress;
> Her Husband the Relater she preferr'd
> Before the Angel, and of him to ask
> Chose rather: hee, she knew, would intermix
> Grateful digressions, and solve high dispute
> With conjugal Caresses, from his Lip
> Not Words alone pleas'd her. (VIII, 48–57)

Here is the blend of intellect, sociability, recreative eroticism, and gender hierarchy that the divorce treatises propose as the "apt and cheerfull conversation" of Milton's marital ideal. *Tetrachordon* considers what God intended to be perfection in prelapsarian society and rejects Augustine's position that "manly friendship . . . had bin a more becomming solace for

Adam, then to spend so many secret years in an empty world with one woman" (YP II, p. 596). After the fall, Milton argues, the "solace" that female companionship offers in marriage is a recreative retreat from the "contemplative, or pragmaticall" male world "abroad," and it yields "delightfull intermissions" from "severe schooling" (*Tetra.*, YP II, p. 597).[38] But Eden suffers as yet no division of the public world of action or thought from the private world of the home, and thus no segregation of gender that relegates woman to the domestic sphere, where she provides "hollidaies to joy and harmles pastime" for the man. Eve is present at all of the symposium necessary for "pragmaticall" action, her departure to tend the garden silently rebukes the excesses of "contemplative" speculation, and her preference for discourse mixed with kisses portrays the idyllic unity of mind and body possible in marriage. The "grave friendship" that both man and angel value so highly cannot match this "amiable and attractive society of conjugal love" (*Colas.*, YP II, pp. 739–40). Furthermore, the purpose of the friendship is to serve and protect the marriage.

Raphael, who will later help Tobias wed his bedeviled bride, tries to fulfill this purpose in part by offering Adam marital advice. With Eve absent, the stage is set for the discussion that most concerns her. As in academic debate, she is now the absent presence by which males define maleness and the proper place of women.[39] Earlier in the symposium Milton had suggested how the academic ideal might become debased, but the dialogue on love conducted in Eve's absence reveals not a debasement, but a flaw in the very structure of academic discourse that limits its ability to teach the only knowledge worth knowing, knowledge for life.

Adam's question about his feelings for Eve raises three related problems: why does sexual passion cause such "Commotion strange" that he feels weakened by desire; how can an "inferior" so move him; and why does feminine beauty seem to subsume wisdom, virtue, authority, and reason? Raphael responds by reasserting the rightness of male supremacy and by devaluing "the sense of touch" as common "To Cattle and each Beast" in favor of "What higher in her society" leads to "the scale / By which to heav'nly Love thou may'st ascend" (VIII, 521–94). The commonplace topics and Neoplatonic conclusions of this dialogue match those in such academic *lezioni* as Averani's "Perchè l'animo umano sia dominato dalle passioni, e onde si debba a quelle apportar rimedio" ("Why the human mind may be dominated by passions, and from where one should summon remedy from them") and "Se nelle Donne si trovi l'Eroica Virtù" ("If heroic virtue may be found in women") (*PF* 2, IV, pp. 315–20; 2, I, pp. 260–68), or in such *dubbi* as Salvini's "Quale abbia più forza sugli affetti umani, la bellezza, o la virtù" ("Which may have more power over human affections, beauty or virtue") and "In chi spicchi più la Virtù, nell'uomo, o nella donna" ("In whom does virtue more show forth, in man or woman") (*Discorsi* I, disc. 91; II, disc. 9). In the absence of women, these academicians debate sexual passion, the relative merits of feminine beauty and masculine virtue, and the extent of woman's capacity for virtue at all. Although some grant that women are disadvantaged by restricted education, not by nature, academicians nevertheless assume the subordination of women. Salvini concludes one lecture with a representative statement of academic opinion:

se la Bellezza esercitasse maggiore possanza su i nostri affetti, di quello che si faccia la Virtù; già le femmine, che sortita hanno, come proprio pregio, la Bellezza, comanderebbero, e regnerebbero; gli uomini, ai quali è toccata, come in patrimonio, la Virtù, a quelle servirebbero. Ma la bisogna va al contrario. Il sesso più bello, il quale anche Aristotile spoglia della Virtù Eroica, è servo; ed il men bello, ma più valoroso, comanda. (*Discorsi* I, disc. 91, p. 397)

[If beauty wielded greater power over our affections than virtue; then women, who have been allotted beauty as their proper merit, would command and rule; men, who hold virtue as a patrimony, would serve them. But it needs must be otherwise. The more beautiful sex, to whom Aristotle even denies heroic virtue, is the servant; and the less beautiful, but more valorous, commands.]

Thus Raphael's disdain for sexual passion and emphasis on male supremacy are academically correct.

In context, however, they are questionable, as several critics have recently argued.[40] First, Adam's reply (VIII, 595–611) qualifies the harshness of the angel's suggestion that he, as yet unfallen, may become "sunk in carnal pleasure" (VIII, 593). Adam holds "the genial Bed" in "mysterious reverence," and describes "those graceful acts, / Those thousand decencies," that "Union of Mind" which make his marriage a companionship. This reply echoes the narrator's earlier description of unfallen sexuality as "the Rites / Mysterious of connubial Love" (IV, 742–43) and his portrait, from Eve's perspective as she leaves the symposium, of their marriage as a union of body and mind. In the context of the narrator's confirmation of Adam's position, the reader may wonder how much an angel can know about human sexuality and marriage. We have seen that good angels are not infallible when Satan dupes Uriel and eludes Eden's angelic guard. Then, when Adam asks point-blank about angelic love, Raphael's description of airy embraces without "restrain'd conveyance . . . / As Flesh to mix with Flesh, or Soul with Soul" (VIII, 628, 629) only increases our doubts that the angel could comprehend the man's experience of "Transported touch" with "Union of Mind . . . one Soul" (VIII, 530, 604).

Second, Raphael's earlier description of cosmic hierarchy in gendered language conflicts with Adam's certainty of his superiority and with Raphael's present insistence that Adam be the "Head" to which Eve's "shows," made for his "delight," should yield. In answering Adam's query about noble heavenly bodies that seem to serve the lesser earth, Raphael had described the masculine Sun as "barren" in contrast to "the fruitful Earth" that the Sun serves (VIII, 90–97). By this point in the epic, the reader has already seen and will see again crucial incidents illustrating this Christian reversal of hierarchy. In Christ's volunteering to save humankind and in fallen Eve's pleading for Adam's forgiveness, the meekness and love Milton associates with the feminine, not masculine strength or intellect, bring salvation.

So Milton leaves the Edenic dialogue on love inconclusive. Debate between males about how to understand a relationship with the woman absent from the debate finally resolves nothing. This irresolution in the climactic dialogue of the symposium, the one that most concerns daily life in Eden, manifests a serious limitation in the structure of academic discourse.[41] Adam must discover how to conduct a relationship with his wife in the process of that relationship, and Milton shows us this complex process in the very next episode, the couple's debate about separate work. Only in the crucible of domestic life, not in academic debate among males, can Adam learn how to be a husband.

From that crucible, in a patched-up marriage, Milton wrote the letter to Dati with which we began. Lamenting domestic life as a wearisome trial and longing for his male friends of the Gaddian Academy, so congenial in "character, temperament, interests," he vividly describes the split unknown in Eden. When he came to write *Paradise Lost*, he knew fallen marriage from experience, but had envisioned in the divorce tracts an ideal of married life; he remembered his visits to Italian academies with nostalgic idealization, but had acknowledged in *Areopagitica* their tendency to "flattery and fustian." Out of this mixed experience he fashioned a hellish debasement of the academic ideal and an idyllic symposium in Eden. The topics Adam and Raphael discuss are those often debated in Italian academies, and both angel and man highly value their dialogue and friendship. Finally, however, male friendship and the knowledge it promotes cannot, in the absence of woman, teach how to be married to one. Like Milton, Adam must leave the academy and try to learn that with his wife.

Louisiana State University

NOTES

1. *Complete Prose Works of John Milton*, ed. Don M. Wolfe et al., 8 vols. (New Haven, 1953–82), vol. II, pp. 762–65, hereafter cited in the text as YP with volume and page number.

2. *St. Augustine: The Literal Meaning of Genesis*, trans. John Hammond Taylor, 2 vols. (New York, 1982), vol. II, p. 75. See *Tetrachordon*, YP II, pp. 596–97. For a discussion of the Augustinian position, see James Grantham Turner, *One Flesh: Paradisal Marriage and Sexual Relations in the Age of Milton* (Oxford, 1987), pp. 98–101.

3. This survey relies on the following studies: Ernest Hatch Wilkins, *A History of Italian Literature*, rev. ed., ed. Thomas G. Bergin (Cambridge, Mass., 1974); *Dictionary of Italian Literature*, ed. Peter Bondanella and Julia Conaway Bondanella (Westport, Conn., 1979); J. H. Whitfield, *A Short History of Italian Literature* (Manchester, 1980); Gaetano Imbert, *La Vita Fiorentina nel Seicento Secondo Memorie Sincrone: 1644–70* (Firenze, 1906); Lacy Collison-Morley, *Italy after the Renaissance: Decadence and Display in the Seventeenth Century* (London, 1930); Lucien Marcheix, *Un Parisien à Rome et à Naples* (Paris, n.d.); Michele Maylender, *Storia delle Accademie d'Italia*, 5 vols. (Bologna, 1926–30); Eric W. Cochrane, *Tradition and Enlightenment in the Tuscan Academies: 1690–1800* (Chicago, 1961), and *Florence in the Forgotten Centuries: 1527–1800* (Chicago, 1973); Edoardo Benvenuti, *Agostino Coltellini e L'Accademia degli Apatisti a Firenze nel Secolo XVII* (Pistoia, 1910); Allessandro Lazzeri, *Intellettuali e consenso nella Toscana del Seicento: L'Accademia degli Apatisti* (Milan, 1983), and "Recenti Studi Sulle Accademie," *Ricerche Storiche* X (1980), 433–41; Bernard Weinberg, "The Accademia degli Alterati and Literary Taste from 1570 to 1600," *Italica* XXXI (1954), 207–14.

4. Benedetto Buonmattei, "Sopra l'Ozio," in *Prose Fiorentine Raccolte dallo Smarrito Accademico della Crusca*, ed. Carlo Roberto Dati, 4 parts, 17 vols. (Firenze, 1716–45), pt. 2, vol. IV, p. 276. Dati, "Chi fosse prima, o la Gall[i]na, o l'Uovo," *PF* pt. 3, vol. II, pp. 152–53; "Sopra le Zazzere," *PF*, pt. 2, vol. V, p. 273. Subsequent references to *Prose Fiorentine* will be cited in the text as *PF* with part, volume, and page when appropriate. All translations from Italian are mine; I would like to thank Robert McMahon for his assistance.

5. Since topics changed so little, I will be citing some late seventeenth-century *lezioni* and *dubbi* as representative examples of the kinds of topics discussed, even though they were delivered after Milton's trip.

6. Quoted in John Arthos, *Milton and the Italian Cities* (New York, 1968), p. 107.

7. For one exemplary exception, see *Beyond Their Sex: Learned Women of the European Past*, ed. Patricia H. Labalme (New York, 1980), pp. 140–43. The Venetian *Incogniti*, whose members attended meetings in masks, did admit women, and later in the eighteenth century the Arcadian academies often admitted women.

8. *Discorsi Accademici di Anton Maria Salvini . . . Sopra Alcuni Dubbi Proposti nell' Accademia degli Apatisti*, 2 vols. (Firenze, 1695, 1712), vol. I, disc. 16, 75; vol. II, disc. 63. Subsequent references will be cited in the text by volume, discourse, and page when appropriate. Salvini was a leader of the last generation of literary and philosophical academicians before the academies began in the eighteenth century to pursue projects for scientific and social improvement. Alessandro Adimari, *La Tersicore overo Scherzi, e Paradossi Poetici sopra la Beltà delle Donne Fra'difetti ancora ammirabili, e vaghe* (Firenze, 1637). Milton heard Adimari read a moral sonnet while attending a *Svogliati* meeting: *Atti dell'Accademia degli Svogliati*, Biblioteca Nazionale, Firenze, MSS. Magliabecchiana, cl. IX, cod. 60, fol. 52v.

9. See Walter J. Ong, *Fighting for Life: Contest, Sexuality, and Consciousness* (Ithaca, 1981).

10. *Sibilla* became popular in the 1650s, after Milton's trip to Italy.

11. *The Reversible World: Symbolic Inversion in Art and Society*, ed. Barbara Babcock (Ithaca, 1978), p. 29.

12. The following survey of Milton's academic experience relies on these studies: David Masson, *The Life of John Milton: Volume I, 1608–39* (1881; rev. ed. Gloucester, Mass., 1965); *The Life Records of John Milton*, 5 vols., ed. J. Milton French (New Brunswick, N.J., 1949); William Riley Parker, *Milton: A Biography*, 2 vols. (Oxford, 1968); A. N. Wilson, *The Life of John Milton* (Oxford, 1983); James Holly Hanford, "Milton in Italy," *Annuale Mediaevale* V (1964), 49–63; John Arthos, *Milton and the Italian Cities* (New York, 1968); Edward Rosen, "A Friend of John Milton: Valerio Chimentelli," *Bulletin of the New York Public Library*, LVII (1953), 159–74; Roland Mushat Frye, "Milton's Florentine Friend, Bishop Frescobaldi: A Biographical Note and Portrait," *MQ* VII (1973), 74–76; Donald Sears, "*La Tina:* The Country Sonnets of Antonio Malatesti as Dedicated to Mr. John Milton, English Gentleman," in *Milton Studies* XIII, ed. James D. Simmonds (Pittsburgh, 1979), pp. 275–317; Louise Schleiner, "Milton, G.B. Doni, and the Dating of Doni's Works," *MQ* XVI (1982), 36–42; James A. Freeman, "Milton's Roman Connection: Giovanni Salzilli," in *Milton Studies* XIX, ed. James D. Simmonds (Pittsburgh, 1984), pp. 87–104.

13. All references to Milton's poetry will be cited in the text. The edition used is *John Milton: Complete Poems and Major Prose*, ed. Merritt Y. Hughes (New York, 1957).

14. On his way home, Milton wrote in an album in Geneva the last two lines of *Comus*—"Or if Virtue feeble were, / Heav'n itself would stoop to her"—and a verse from Horace, which French, *Life Records* I, p. 419, translates "I change the sky but not my mind when I cross the sea." Despite his contact with Italian vice and Catholicism, he asserts he has maintained his virtue and religious convictions.

15. Freeman, "Milton's Roman Connection," p. 91, has anticipated my point here. He also suggests that Satan's consult resembles academic debate. Although the devils' debate has no final effect on public policy, they believe themselves advisors to a prince on a matter of great moment. The consult portrays political manipulation in the corridors of power, not the leisured speculations of apolitical academic discussion.

16. The charter of Manso's academy, the Oziosi of Naples, forbade "che non si debba leggere alcuna Materia di Teologia e della Sacra Scrittura, delle quali per riverenza dobbiamo astenerci: è medesimamente niuna delle cose appartenenti al publico governo, i quali si deve lasciare alla cura de Principi che ne reggono" ("that any material concerning theology or holy scripture be read, from which we ought to abstain out of reverence: and likewise nothing pertaining to public government, which ought to be left to the care of princes who govern these matters"). Quoted in Maylender, *Storia* IV, p. 184. This co-opting of the intelligentsia by political power is even more pronounced in France, where from its beginning the academic movement centered on the court. See Frances A. Yates, *The French Academies of the Sixteenth Century* (London, 1947).

17. In alluding to the grim story of "the Sons / of *Belial*" in the catalogue of demons (I, 500–05; compare Judges xix, 22–25), Milton associates Belial with homosexuality. The Platonic Academy flourished in a specifically homosexual context, and the homosocial Italian academies were accused of homosexuality. Responding to *A First Defense*, Claudius Salmasius says that the Italians used Milton as a female, praised him as a pretty youth, and probably debauched him. See French, *Life Records* I, p. 417.

18. Thomas Greene, *The Descent from Heaven: A Study in Epic Continuity* (New

Haven, 1963), pp. 374–78; Charles Martindale, "Paradise Metamorphosed: Ovid in Milton," *CL* XXXVII (1985), 325–28; John E. Parish, "Milton and the Well-Fed Angel," *English Miscellany* XVIII (1967), 87–109; Jack Goldman, "Perspectives of Raphael's Meal in *Paradise Lost,* Book V," *MQ* XI (1977), 31–37; Beverly Sherry, "Not by Bread Alone: The Communication of Adam and Raphael," *MQ* XIII (1979), 111–14, and "Milton's Raphael and the Legend of Tobias," JEGP LXXVIII (1979), 227–41; Virginia R. Mollenkott, "The Pervasive Influence of the Apocrypha in Milton's Thought and Art," in *Milton and the Art of Sacred Song,* ed. J. Max Patrick and Roger H. Sundell (Madison, Wis., 1979), pp. 23–43; Mark Wollaeger, "Apocryphal Narration: Milton, Raphael, and The Book of Tobit," in *Milton Studies* XXI, ed. James D. Simmonds (Pittsburgh, 1985), pp. 137–56; Jason P. Rosenblatt, "Celestial Entertainment in Eden: Book V of *Paradise Lost,*" *Harvard Theological Review* LXII (1969), 411–27.

19. Northrop Frye, *The Return of Eden: Five Essays on Milton's Epics* (Toronto, 1965), p. 12; Barbara Kiefer Lewalski, *"Paradise Lost" and the Rhetoric of Literary Forms* (Princeton, 1985), pp. 144, 151, 175, 196–219, sees within the frame of the Platonic symposium a variety of genres in an ascending scale of complexity: a moral interlude, an entertainment such as a host might present to a royal guest on a progress, and a Neoplatonic dialogue on love; Kathleen M. Swaim, *Before and After the Fall: Contrasting Modes in "Paradise Lost"* (Amherst, Mass., 1986); Anthony Low, "Angels and Food in *Paradise Lost,*" in *Milton Studies* I, ed. James D. Simmonds (Pittsburgh, 1969), pp. 135–45, sees Adam's and Raphael's communion as a forerunner of the communion of the saints in heaven.

20. Giambullari was a sixteenth-century academician with scientific interests. He used a *lezione* on the location of Dante's purgatory as a means to discuss contemporary cosmography and geography. See Cochrane, *Tradition,* p. 31. For *dubbi* on angels, see Lazzeri, *Apatisti,* p. 50.

21. Averani followed in the footsteps of Adimari, Doni, and Dati, becoming a celebrated teacher of Greek. In the early eighteenth century, he delivered many lectures on Petrarch's use of Tuscan in his sonnets. See Cochrane, *Tradition,* pp. 2, 11–13, 80–81.

22. For the debate over whether this shadowing is Platonic or typological, see William G. Madsen, *From Shadowy Types to Truth: Studies in Milton's Symbolism* (New Haven, 1968).

23. Bernard Weinberg, *A History of Literary Criticism in the Italian Renaissance* (Chicago, 1961), vol. II, pp. 819–911, 954–1073.

24. Robert L. Entzminger, *Divine Word: Milton and the Redemption of Language* (Pittsburgh, 1985), p. 44.

25. Later in the symposium, Raphael enacts, in contrast to Satan's equivocations, an unfallen understanding of what it means to be equal before God. The angel accepts Adam's praise of his discourse, in return praising the man, beneath him in "the scale of Nature," but in another sense equal:

> Nor less think wee in Heav'n of thee on Earth
> Than of our fellow servant, and inquire
> Gladly into the ways of God with Man:
> For God we see hath honor'd thee, and set
> On Man his *Equal* Love. (VIII, 224–28, emphasis mine)

These distinctions—between equality in freedom, equality in love and service, and equality to one's source—are crucial to Milton's hierarchical universe. Fallen Eve, however, forgets them when she considers keeping the forbidden fruit to herself,

so to add what wants
In Female Sex, the more to draw his Love,
And render me more *equal*, and perhaps,
A thing not undesirable, sometime
Superior: for inferior who is free? (IX, 821–25, emphasis mine)

Her consciousness now transformed by her fall, Eve conflates equality to Adam with greater love and freedom. This conflation of meaning is what Raphael's *lezione* was to prevent.

26. Lewalski, *Rhetoric of Literary Forms*, p. 199.

27. Entzminger, *Divine Word*, pp. 52–53; Arnold Stein, *Answerable Style: Essays on "Paradise Lost"* (Seattle, 1953), pp. 31–32. On Satan's and Belial's scoffing, see also Lewalski, *Rhetoric of Literary Forms*, pp. 83, 125; Stella Purce Revard, *The War in Heaven: "Paradise Lost" and the Tradition of Satan's Rebellion* (Ithaca, N.Y., 1980), pp. 103–06.

28. For example, Eve might have remembered God's wit when Satan, to tempt her, suggests that God was jesting when he forbade eating the fruit. "Will God incense his ire," he asks, "For such a petty Trespass, and not praise / Rather your dauntless virtue" (IX, 692–94)—as if God had really wanted his creatures to do what he told them not to do. Remembering what she had learned about divine irony, Eve might have replied, "God didn't smile when he commanded, 'Ye shall not eat thereof.' "

29. In an earlier reference (I, 284–91), Milton connects satanic and Galilean technology, comparing Satan's armor to the moon as seen through Galileo's telescope. For Galileo, see Frye, *Return of Eden*, pp. 57–58. For technology, see Joan Malory Webber, "The Politics of Poetry: Feminism and *Paradise Lost*," in *Milton Studies* XIV, ed. James D. Simmonds (Pittsburgh, 1980), pp. 3–24; Revard, *War in Heaven*, p. 190.

30. Salvini, however, ends by praising Galileo as one of the "Toscani ingegni" (Tuscan wits) whose "bella, e buona curiosità" ("fine and good curiosity") brought knowledge to light after centuries of darkness (pp. 33–34).

31. Turner, *One Flesh*, p. 270.

32. Diane Kelsey McColley, *Milton's Eve* (Urbana, Ill., 1983), pp. 110–39, and "Eve and the Arts of Eden," in *Milton and the Idea of Woman*, ed. Julia M. Walker (Urbana, Ill., 1988), pp. 100–19.

33. See Mikhail Bakhtin, *Rabelais and his World*, trans. Helene Iswolsky (Cambridge, Mass., 1968), and the critique of Bakhtin in Peter Stallybrass and Allon White, *The Politics and Poetics of Transgression* (London, 1986), pp. 1–26.

34. Janet E. Halley, "Female Autonomy in Milton's Sexual Poetics," in *Milton and the Idea of Woman*, pp. 230–53, discusses how in the early poems Milton seeks transcendence as a way to evade dangers posed by the feminine sphere, but in *Paradise Lost* he subordinates the feminine to the control of phallocentric meaning.

35. Maureen Quilligan, *Milton's Spenser: The Politics of Reading* (Ithaca, N.Y., 1983), p. 223; Joseph Wittreich, *Feminist Milton* (Ithaca, N.Y., 1987), p. 106.

36. Webber, "Feminism and *Paradise Lost*," p. 15.

37. To Jon S. Lawry, *The Shadow of Heaven: Matter and Stance in Milton's Poetry* (Ithaca, N.Y., 1968), p. 222, and David Aers and Bob Hodge, " 'Rational Burning': Milton on Sex and Marriage," in *Milton Studies* XIII, ed. James D. Simmonds (Pittsburgh, 1979), p. 19, Eve's withdrawal signifies a fateful tendency to wandering, or a lesser intelligence. Eve's choice is defended by McColley, *Milton's Eve*, p. 114; Quilligan, *Milton's Spenser*, p. 232; F. Peczenik, "Fit Help: The Egalitarian Marriage in *Paradise Lost*," *Mosaic* XVII (1984), 36; Entzminger, *Divine Word*, pp. 39–40; Stevie Davies, *The Idea of Woman in Renaissance*

Literature: The Feminine Reclaimed (Brighton, Eng., 1986), pp. 242–43; and Wittreich, *Feminist Milton*, pp. 10, 92.

38. See Quilligan, *Milton's Spenser*, p. 177; Mary Nyquist, "The Genesis of Gendered Subjectivity in the Divorce Tracts and in *Paradise Lost*," in *Re-membering Milton: Essays on the Texts and Traditions*, ed. Mary Nyquist and Margaret W. Ferguson (New York, 1987), pp. 99–127; Turner, *One Flesh*, pp. 38–123, 188–229.

39. Although we are told that spirits can assume either sex, and although Isis and Astarte appear in the catalogue of demons (I, 419–46, 476–78), all the angels we see seem male. The narrator uses the masculine pronoun to refer to Raphael.

40. Aers and Hodge, "'Rational Burning,'" pp. 23–27; McColley, *Milton's Eve*, p. 88; Peczenik, "Fit Help," p. 31; Lewalski, *Rhetoric*, pp. 216–18; Davies, *Idea of Woman*, p. 228–29; Turner, *One Flesh*, pp. 273–81.

41. For Milton's break "with the entire Platonic system of transcending earthly love and certainly with the homosexual matrix from which it sprang," see Jean H. Hagstrum, *Sex and Sensibility: Ideal and Erotic Love from Milton to Mozart* (Chicago, 1980), pp. 29–32. Swaim in *Before and After the Fall*, argues that the Hebraism Michael teaches for a fallen world qualifies Raphael's unfallen Hellenism. I am arguing, however, that the Hellenic academic ideal is qualified even before the fall.

THE SON'S PRESUMED CONTEMPT FOR LEARNING IN *PARADISE REGAINED*: A BIBLICAL AND PATRISTIC RESOLUTION

Donald Swanson and John Mulryan

THE ATTITUDE toward learning that Milton conveys through the Son's responses to Satan in *Paradise Regained* is surprisingly at odds with everything else Milton had previously written on the subject. After Satan has composed what is perhaps the most magnificent verbal portrait of Greco-Roman civilization in world literature, the Son responds with surprising ambiguity and sophistry:

> Think not but that I know these things; or think
> I know them not; not therefore am I short
> Of knowing what I ought; he who receives
> Light from above, from the fountain of light,
> No other doctrine needs, though granted true;
> But these are false, or little else but dreams,
> Conjectures, fancies, built on nothing firm. (IV, 286–92)[1]

After recounting the supposed deficiencies of Greek and Roman learning, the Son, alluding to the myth of the centaurs, summarizes his position: "Who therefore seeks in these / True wisdom, finds her not, or by delusion / Far worse, her false resemblance only meets, / An empty cloud" (318–21).[2] The Son's diatribe against the intellectual pretensions of pagan writers sets the stage for a comparison of Hebrew and pagan learning that is most unflattering to the latter:

> Or if I would delight my private hours
> With Music or with Poem, where so soon
> As in our native Language can I find
> That solace? All our Law and Story strew'd
> With Hymns, our Psalms with artful terms inscrib'd
> Our Hebrew Songs and Harps in *Babylon*,
> That pleas'd so well our Victors' ear, declare
> That rather *Greece* from us these Arts deriv'd;
> Ill imitated, while they loudest sing
> The vices of thir Deities, and thir own

In Fable, Hymn, or Song, so personating
Thir Gods ridiculous, and themselves past shame.
Remove their swelling Epithets thick laid
As varnish on a Harlot's cheek, the rest,
Thin sown with aught of profit or delight,

. . . .

Thir Orators thou then extoll'st, as those
The top of Eloquence, Statists indeed,
And lovers of thir Country, as may seem;
But herein to our Prophets far beneath,
As men divinely taught, and better teaching
The solid rules of Civil Government
In thir majestic unaffected style
Than all the Oratory of *Greece* and *Rome*.
In them is plainest taught, and easiest learnt,
What makes a Nation happy, and keeps it so,
What ruins Kingdoms, and lays Cities flat;
These only, with our Law, best form a King. (IV, 331–45, 353–64)

The problem exemplified by these passages can be briefly stated: why did Milton, who had a lifelong devotion to learning, and Greco-Roman learning in particular, so contemptuously reject, in the person of the Son, Satan's temptation to learning? And why, almost as an afterthought, did he have the Son present an *appreciation* of Hebrew learning through a disdainful *depreciation* of Greco-Roman learning?

Miltonists have not been loathe to respond to these questions, but in some ways their proposed solutions to the learning crux are as sophistical as the Son's retort to Satan. Many, for example, take the position that the Son rejects learning not for its own sake, but because Satan presents it as an end in itself and uses it as a method of displacing the Son's higher responsibility to God the Father. Stanley Fish regards this false hierarchy of values as true of all the temptations in *Paradise Regained:* "In each of the plots Satan constructs, one or more of these things has been put forward as the highest possible value; and therefore to resist the appeal to act in its name is to resist the temptation to substitute that value for the value of obedience to God."[3] Or, as James R. McAdams put it: "Moreover, in the case of Athens, Satan follows the procedure he has used in all of the attempted seductions: he urges Christ to choose a lesser over a greater good—in effect, to distrust God's scale of values and claim a right to judgment he has not yet won in his current trial."[4] Similarly, Douglas Bush views the temptation to learning as a violation of the Son's (and Milton's) hierarchy of values: "It is only in comparison with the divine light of humble Christian faith and virtue that Greek philosophy, like science, appears as the product and instrument of arrogant human pride. In itself, as far as it goes, it is good. . . . His condemnation is relative rather than absolute."[5] Elaine B. Safer sees the Son as a latter-day Socrates rebuking Satan for presenting "codified wisdom," simple answers to profound questions, and thinks that Milton is rebuking the reader "for not realizing that the offer [of Greek learning] itself, without comparison to higher truths, is valueless."[6]

Lawrence A. Sasek argues that the poet elevates Hebrew culture at the expense of Greek on the principle "that Hebrew literature is superior to Greek in artistry because of its priority in time."[7] Sasek quotes Tertullian's axiom, "Verum quod primum, quod posterius adulterum est," and translates it as "that is true whatsoever is first, and that is adulterate which is not the first." Thus, "Christ as a dramatic figure must look upon the original Hebrew poetry as far superior to imitations, which, however skillful, are adulterations," and "The reader [of *Paradise Regained*] can only recognize the fact that if his taste were perfect, he would find Hebrew poetry aesthetically far superior" (pp. 162, 165). Against Sasek, however, it seems unlikely that Milton's subtle mind would allow him to embrace an axiom which, taken to its logical conclusion, implies the superiority of Judaism to his own faith, Christianity.

Another favored explanation for the Son's disparagement of pagan learning is the distinction he supposedly makes between real and worldly wisdom. Gary D. Hamilton suggests that Milton "could best display Christ's true wisdom in a setting in which worldly notions of wisdom were portrayed," and that he "could more dramatically call attention to that spiritual dimension which transcends all kinds of earthly pursuits."[8] And Barbara Lewalski (who admits that Christ's position may not be completely justified or explained) provides an impressive list of precedents for the Son's contemptuous analysis of pagan learning, both the sentiments and the language itself. She also asserts that Christ is, in fact, distinguishing between two different kinds of wisdom: "In assuming a radical distinction between knowledge (*scientia*), which derives from the study of things of the world, and wisdom (*sapientia*), which comes only from above, Milton's Christ is defending a Christian commonplace prevalent from Augustine's time through the seventeenth century."[9]

Nevertheless, and despite these scholarly protestations, the Son goes much further than merely putting classical literature and learning in its place; he approaches it, as Ralph W. Condee has observed, with "laconic brusqueness" and treats it as markedly inferior to Hebrew literature.[10]

Jesus might simply have reminded the devil that "No one . . . can form correct ideas about God, guided by nature and reason alone, without the word or message of God" (*Christian Doctrine*, YP VI, p. 132) and that "True Religion is the true Worship and Service of God, learnt and believed from the Word of God [Scripture] only" (*Of True Religion, Haeresie, Schism, Toleration*, YP VIII, p. 419).[11] Yet in *Paradise Regained* the Son even goes beyond a trivialization of pagan learning as not worth knowing: he also insists that there is no aesthetic pleasure in reading its "swelling Epithets thick laid / As varnish on a Harlot's cheek" (IV, 343–44), in comparison to the "majestic unaffected style" (IV, 359) of Hebrew prose and the "artful terms" (IV, 335) of Hebrew poetry.

The question of the extent of the Son's role as Milton's persona lurks in the background of the problem of the Son's presumed contempt for learning. Does Milton really believe that Jesus, the son of a carpenter, became a classicist and Hebraist? Milton's Christ is hardly omniscient; he even needs to be "educated" (*educari*) at Nazareth.[12] The Christ child studies and reads the law of Moses (*PR* I, 202–03, 207), feels a need to expand his knowledge (I, 213), and yet needs divinely imparted knowledge to clear up his own confusion about his mission (I, 292–93). The Son credits his knowledge of decadent Roman culture to hearsay and perhaps to personal reading: "(For I have also heard, perhaps have read)" (IV, 116). His ensuing diatribe against Greco-Roman poetry, philosophy, and mythology suggests the same two sources for his knowledge of these subjects as well. Without probing the details of Jesus' educational history, Malcolm Kelsall emphasizes Milton's awareness that the problem of Christ's own learning must be faced in reading the poem:

> Milton places in Christ's mouth the odd and ambiguous claim: "Think not but that I know these things, or think / I know them not; nor therefore am I short / Of knowing what I ought" (IV, 286–88). These lines imply that the absence of classical references in the Gospels does not necessarily indicate Christ's ignorance of such matters: but even if he were ignorant, the views attributed to him in the poem are those he would have been most likely to present had he been so informed. It may be an odd piece of reasoning, but Milton felt the necessity of raising the interpretive issue to justify the literal fact. As far as the poem is concerned, Christ manifestly is tolerably well informed about the classical world. There is no historical reason why he should not have been. Milton lets his imagination have free rein, but he does not cheat.[13]

Indeed, sufficient evidence is available to warrant the conjecture that Milton imagines Jesus conversing without an interpreter with Greek-speaking Palestinian natives.[14] The Son articulates the need to exorcise the Roman emperor with an allusion to Jesus' initial response to the Syrophoenician woman's request for an exorcism (*PR* IV, 131; compare Matt. xv, 24). In Mark vii, 26, this solicitous woman is identified as a Greek, a fact attributed by Milton's contemporary, John Diodati, to the decision of "Alexander and his successors" to transplant to Palestine "reliques of the ancient Canaanites, who in those days used the Greek tongue and religion."[15] Since Milton's allusion to Jesus' encounter with the Gentile swineherdsmen remains (after *PR* IV, 131) the poem's only succeeding allusion to an exorcism story, Milton may likewise imagine that Jesus' conversation with these Gentiles is conducted in Greek (IV, 629–32; compare Matt. viii, 28–34).

The subject of Christ's knowledge of classical learning and by implication his competency in the Greek language is implicitly broached in Milton's *Commonplace Book:* "Whether it is permissible to give attention to profane writers. Socrates says that it is: Book 3, c[hapter] 16, using not only *other sound reasons,* but also the example of the Apostle Paul and the most venerable Church Fathers" (YP I, pp. 376–77; emphasis ours). The Christian Socrates's "other sound reasons" presuppose Jesus' familiarity with and mixed assessment of classical learning:

> Greek literature certainly was never recognized either by Christ or his Apostles as divinely inspired, nor on the other hand was it wholly rejected as pernicious. And this they did, I conceive, not inconsiderately. For there are many philosophers among the Greeks who were not far from the knowledge of God; and in fact these being disciplined by logical science, strenuously opposed the Epicureans and other contentious Sophists who denied divine Providence.[16]

There is admittedly ample Miltonic precedent to suggest that he would endorse the negative assessment of the Epicureans and Sophists implicitly ascribed to Christ by the Christian Socrates. But beyond the *Commonplace Book* and apart from *Paradise Regained,* Milton's other writings certainly create the impression that throughout his career he would applaud the positive estimation of "many philosophers" that is ostensibly imputed to Christ by Socrates. Milton often expresses his high regard for pagan philosophers such as Socrates, Plato, and Aristotle,[17] and in *Pro Se Defensio* passionately defends himself against the charge that he holds Greek learning in low esteem: "Since I am not unlearned in Greek, and since, if anyone does, I value it highly, you were able to fabricate nothing less to the point, than that I despise Greek letters" (YP IV, pp. 822–23).

Other Miltonic "sound reasons" for studying "profane writers" find expression in Socrates' comparison of the relative value of classical and biblical learning:

> The divinely inspired Scriptures . . . tend to produce piety and integrity of life. . . . But they do not instruct us in the art of reasoning, by means of which we may be enabled successfully to resist those who oppose the truth. Besides, adversaries are most easily foiled when we can use their own weapons against them. . . . Moreover, both Christ and his Apostle enjoin us . . . to "beware lest anyone should spoil us through philosophy or vain deceit" [Col. ii, 8]. But this we cannot do unless we possess ourselves of the weapons of our adversaries. (III, p. 16)

This text could easily have served as a mandate for Milton's construction of a contest of "persuasive Rhetoric" in which the Son continually "foils" or beats Satan at his own duplicitous game (*PR* IV, 4, 13).

Clearly, then, the reader of *Paradise Regained* must somehow resolve the tension between the poet's vaunted reverence for Greco-Roman thought and his divine persona's generic disparagement of that same tradition. The authors of this paper seek the resolution of this tension in the dense network of biblical allusions in the poem, allusions either imperfectly understood or completely missed by Satan, and in the Son's use of deceptive rhetorical ploys to deflect and degrade his great adversary. This biblical and rhetorical nexus embraces all of the temptations in the poem and moves (in relation to the temptation to learning) through four successive phases: (1) Satan's bafflement over the nature of the Son's mission; (2) the Son's refusal to dispel Satan's ignorance; (3) The Son's rhetorical deception of Satan; and (4) Jesus' deliberate distortion of his (and hence Milton's) perspective on Greco-Roman thought.

These phases are thoroughly informed by a particular patristic tradition shaped especially by Justin Martyr, Irenaeus, John Chrysostom, Hippolytus, Augustine, Ambrose, and Gregory of Nyssa, a tradition that Milton has apparently assimilated directly from the church fathers rather than indirectly from contemporary Protestant exegetes such as Martin Luther, John Calvin, Theodore Beza, and John Diodati. Luther, for example, insists that satanic temptation and destruction serve as the instrument of the divine will despite the opposite purposes that motivate their ostensibly cooperative ventures.[18] But neither Luther nor the other Protestant commentators familiar to Milton construe the overlap in divine and satanic activity as evidence that a puzzled Satan is himself the victim of divine duplicity.

In the first phase, the demons are perplexed by the ambiguity of the acclamation "my Son belov'd" (equals the Son of God) bestowed by the heavenly voice on the newly baptized Jesus (*PR* I, 82–85, 384–85). The title "Son of God, which bears no single sense" (IV, 517), is sufficiently multivalent to encompass "All men" (IV, 520; compare 501). Satan is well aware that his own security depends on his ability to fathom the mystery of Jesus' identity (IV, 204–05).

Milton has mined a pattern of satanic uncertainty and rhetorical intrigue from a rich patristic quarry. Irenaeus, too, imagines that the heavenly voice perplexes Satan as to whether the baptized Jesus is merely human or the divine Son of God (*Adversus haereses* V, xxi, 2 [Migne, PG VII, p. 1180]). John Chrysostom concurs and imagines that Satan's confusion prompts him to match rhetorical wits with Jesus in an effort to discern his true identity (*Homiliae in Matthaeum* xiii, 3–4 [Migne, PG LVI, pp. 707–08]). Hippolytus sharpens the concealment of Jesus' divinity with a string of adjectives depicting the unbaptized Jesus as blandly unmemorable: "the devil is dumfounded by such a testimony from John; indeed, the Lord appears plain (*litos*), solitary (*monos*), destitute (or barely clad: *gymnos*), without escort (*aprostateutos*), wearing the body of a man like a garment, and concealing the dignity of the divinity in order to elude the Dragon's snares" (*Sermo in sancta theophania* iv [Migne, PG x.p. 856]). This series of adjectives may well have inspired a comparable series in Milton's portrait of the Son at the beginning of his ministry: "Thou art unknown, unfriended, low of birth / . . . Bred up in poverty" (*PR* II, 413, 415; compare I, 24–25; II, 81–82). If so, then Milton might easily have taken his cue from Hippolytus in appealing to the sheer banality of the Son's debut in order to flesh out the camouflage of his divinity. Augustine insists that it is precisely because of Christ's decision "to make . . . signs [of his divinity] somewhat less obvious and to keep Himself more hidden" that Satan "was left in doubt and tempted Him to find out whether or not He were Christ."[19]

In his quest to discover Jesus' identity, Milton's Satan is impaled on the horns of a dilemma by his astrological analysis of Jesus' life. On the one hand, the stars consign Jesus to "Violence and stripes, and lastly cruel death" (IV, 388). Unlike Satan, the Son recognizes that "the promis'd Kingdom" (I, 265) and "Redemption for mankind" (I, 266) somehow depend on his path of suffering and death. Satan tries to flush out Jesus' true plans with the argument that, without his infernal help, there "Will be for thee no sitting, or not long / On David's Throne, be prophesi'd what will" (IV, 107–08). Milton no doubt has in mind Satan's prompting of Judas to betray Christ (Luke, xxii, 3; John xiii, 2, 27). On the other hand, Satan realizes that "A Kingdom they [the stars] portend thee, but what Kingdom, / Real or Allegoric I discern not" (IV, 389–90). Satan's confusion about this issue is later expressed in terms reminiscent of synoptic sayings and parables of Jesus about the kingdom of God:

> thy way
> Of gaining *David's* Throne no man knows when,
> For both the when and how is nowhere told. (*PR* IV, 470–72)

And when he was demanded of the Pharisees, when the kingdom of God should come, he answered them and said, "The kingdom of God cometh not with observation: Neither shall they say, Lo here! or lo there! (Luke xvii, 20–21a)[20]

So is the kingdom of God, as if a man should cast seed into the ground,
And should sleep, and rise night and day, and seed should spring and grow up, he knoweth not how. (Mark iv, 26–27)

Milton recognizes that the quest for "the when and how" entails a search in the Old Testament for eschatological signs that help locate the promised kingdom in time and space. But the poet, following Luke xvii, 20–21a, envisages a spiritual kingdom that is neither accompanied by eschatological signs nor located in space. The interiority of the kingdom in Book IV of *Paradise Regained* is implicit in Jesus' rebuttal to the devil:

> I shall, thou say'st, expel
> A brutish monster [the emperor]; what if I withal
> Expel a Devil who first made him such? (127–29)

> What wise and valiant man would seek to free
> These thus degenerate, by themselves enslav'd,
> Or could of inward slaves make outward free? (143–45)

The inner or spiritual nature of the kingdom might easily have been inferred from the parable of the seed growing secretly or from Luke xvii, 21b: "for, behold, the kingdom of God is within you."

Right after hinting at the interiority of the kingdom, Milton's Son discourages the devil's quest for signs ("means"):

> Know therefore when my season comes to sit
> On *David's* Throne, it shall be like a tree
> Spreading and overshadowing all the Earth. (*PR* IV, 146–48)

> Means there shall be to this, but what the means,
> Is not for thee to know, nor me to tell. (IV, 152–53)

The Son's insistence that "the means" is "not for . . . me to tell" reflects Milton's belief that Jesus "oftener obscures his mind in short, and vehement, and compact sentences, to blind and puzzle them the more who could not understand" (*DDD*, YP II, p. 301) and that Jesus spoke in parables in order to deprive those who have rejected divine grace of whatever spiritual insight they may currently possess (*CD*, YP VI, p. 200). The defiant response from Milton's Son in *Paradise Regained* (IV, 151–53) suggests that "our Saviour" has indeed "answer'd with disdain" (170). The Son in effect challenges the devil to penetrate the parabolic tree symbolism.[21] In Milton's mind this challenge apparently implies Jesus' willingness to use deception in his rhetorical skirmish with the devil.

In *Paradise Regained* a clear indication of the Son's willingness to deceive can be gleaned from the portrayal of the devil as "a man who had been matchless held / In cunning, over-reach't where least he thought" (IV, 10–11). The words "matchless" and "over-reach't" react to the description of the Son as the devil's "over-match" (IV, 7). The phrase "In cunning, over-reach't where least he thought" therefore means that the devil has been over-matched in rhetorical cunning, the very skill in which Satan never expected to meet his match. In this sense, then, both the Son and Satan seem to be locked in a contest of "persuasive Rhetoric" (IV, 4) in which both contestants are allowed to score debating points without necessarily committing themselves to their respective positions. The Son's rhetorical strategy for this contest is governed by the definition of veracity that is explicitly rendered and justified in *Christian Doctrine:*

> Veracity makes us tell the truth to anyone to whom it should rightly be told. . . . Who but a madman would deny that we are absolutely justified in concluding that some people ought to be deceived?
>
> What about . . . people who are . . . hostile, or themselves deceitful. . . . if giving an answer which is intended to deceive . . . must always be accounted falsehood, then nothing was more common for the saints and prophets than to tell falsehoods. (YP VI, pp. 759–60)

In *Paradise Regained* the Son's rhetorical silencing of Satan (IV, 22) echoes Jesus' act of silencing a demon, an act which, in the opinion of puzzled onlookers, must covertly symbolize an unknown "new doctrine" (Mark i, 25, 27). From the standpoint of Milton's Son, this temporarily hidden "new doctrine" concerns the defeat of Satan engineered by the cross and resurrection (*PR* I, 57–61, 404–05; III, 198–202). Satan's anticipation of personal defeat makes him obsessed with the question of the Son's timetable. Jesus reacts to this obsession with one of his several veiled allusions to the cross and resurrection:

But what concerns it thee when I begin
My everlasting Kingdom? Why art thou
Solicitous? What moves thy inquisition?
Know'st thou not that my rising is thy fall,
And my promotion will be thy destruction? (III, 198–202)

Milton's devil is highly suspicious of the evasive Jesus' willingness to resort to duplicity. The devil even argues that the Son's addiction to "profound dispute" once prompted him to use stealth in "slipping from thy Mother's eye" to engage the temple authorities in debate (IV, 214–16); by contrast, Luke ii, 43, reads, more neutrally, "tarried behind." Milton's Son informs Satan that "God hath justly giv'n the Nations up / To thy Delusions" (I, 442–43). This concession is based on Paul's claim that God envelops those who succumb to Satan's wiles in "a strong delusion, that they should believe a lie" (2 Thess. ii, 11).

An inability to penetrate the Son's various cryptic allusions to his redemptive plan places Satan and his minions in jeopardy of being "to torment sent before thir time" (*PR* IV, 632; compare 635–36). This phrase echoes the terrified uncertainty expressed in the demons' question: "What have you to do with us, O Son of God? Have you come to torment us before the time?" (Matt. viii, 29). The version of this question in Mark i, 24, is adduced by Augustine in support of his contention that Jesus limits the extent of his self-disclosure to the minimum necessary to terrify demons (*De civitate Dei* IX, xxi [Migne, PL XLI, pp. 273–74]). Satan's fear of divine retribution exacted by "the Seed of Eve" is a prominent theme in *Paradise Regained* (for example, I, 53–54, 58–59, 66, 69, 110, 451; IV, 204–05, 626–32). Augustine's influence might explain why Milton's Satan is teased by a few veiled hints about the relevance of the Son's death to his own demise.[22]

The theory of Christ's deception of Satan evolves as a patristic response to the New Testament portrayal of Christ's death as a ransom payment (for example, Mark x, 45; Matt. xx, 28; 1 Tim. ii, 6). The question of the recipient of the ransom payment is left unanswered in the New Testament. The recipient is designated as the devil by Ambrose (*Epistolae* xli, 7 [Migne, PL XVI, p. 1162]), Gregory of Nyssa (*Oratio catechetica* xxiii–xxiv [Migne, PL XLV, pp. 61–65]), and Augustine (*Enarrationes Psalmos* XCV, 5 [Migne, PL XXXVI, pp. 1230–31]); *De trinitate* IV, xiii [Migne, PL xlii, pp. 898–901]), who alternatively identifies the recipient as Death in *De natura et gratia contra Pelagium* XXIV [Migne, PL XLIV, p. 260]). Operating within the same patristic tradition, Milton often incorporates ransom soteriology into *Paradise Lost* (for example, III, 220–21,

297; X, 61; XII, 424). The immediate recipient of the ransom payment is Death (*PL* XII, 424; compare XI, 255–58). However, since Death is identified as Satan's son or arm (II, 804; XII, 431), the ultimate recipient is Satan himself.

The ransom soteriology of Ambrose, Gregory of Nyssa, and Augustine raises the question of how Satan's pride and hatred of the divine could induce him to accept Christ's death as payment for human sin. Ambrose replies graphically that the devil is "deceived so as to wound himself with his own bite" (*De poenitentia* I, xiii [Migne, PL XVI, p. 506—translation ours]). Augustine and Gregory label Jesus' body on the cross as "bait" to lure a fishy Satan to his demise (Augustine, *Sermones* CCLXIII, i; CXXXIV, v [Migne, PL XXXVIII, pp. 745–46, 1209–10]); Gregory, *Oratio catechetica* xxiv). Because Satan gulped down "the hook of the Deity" like a "ravenous fish," "the deceiver was in his turn deceived" (*Oratio catechetica* xxiv and xxvi [Migne, PG XLV, pp. 64–65, 68–69]). The rhetorical deception of Satan by Milton's Son becomes quite intelligible once it is realized that the poet stands in the same patristic tradition.

In *Paradise Regained* (IV, 127–32), the Son's phrase, "For him I was not sent," appropriately adapts Jesus' language in Matthew, xv, 24, to create the misleading impression that his mission in no sense involves the liberation of the Roman people:

> I shall, thou say'st, expel
> A brutish monster [the emperor]: what if I withal
> Expel a Devil who first made him such?
> Let his tormentor Conscience find him out;
> For him I was not sent, nor yet to free
> That people victor once, now vile and base.

The concluding disclaimer contradicts both the great commission to make disciples of all nations (Matt. xxviii, 19–20) and the hint in the quoted passage that the Son would rather exorcise and sensitize the emperor than effect his political demise. The disclaimer seems to be a ruse designed, first, to blind the devil to the Son's love for all humanity, whether Jewish or Greco-Roman (see *CD*, YP VI, pp. 171–75, 444; *PL* III, 401–05), and, second, to deflect Satan away from the universal scope of the redemption inherent in Christ's crucifixion and resurrection (see *PR* I, 3; IV, 635; compare *CD*, YP VI, pp. 444–48).

In his advocacy of the need to exorcise the Roman emperor, Milton's Jesus takes up Jesus' initial words in Matthew's exorcism story: "I was not sent but to the lost sheep of the house of Israel" (xv, 24 [RSV]; compare *PR* IV, 131). In the Matthew story, a Syro-Phoenician woman implores Jesus to exorcise her young daughter. Jesus initially ignores her request and the disciples urge him to send her away. Then Jesus addresses her in the words just quoted and thereby informs her that his mission does not encompass Gentiles like herself. Undaunted, the woman presses her request for help. The dialogue then continues:

> But he answered and said, It is not meet to take the children's bread, and to cast it to dogs. And she said, Truth, Lord: yet the dogs eat of the crumbs which fall from their masters' table. Then Jesus answered . . . her, O woman, great is thy faith: be it unto thee even as thou wilt. And her daughter was made whole from that very hour. (Matt. xv, 26–28)

Jesus is gladly bested in his rhetorical skirmish with this woman because his deceptive comments are merely intended to test and expose her faith. Contrary to initial impressions, it is precisely for the Gentiles that Jesus' message is ultimately intended (Matt. xxviii, 19–20). So the story of the Syro-Phoenician woman seems an ideal source of inspiration for the tongue-in-cheek denigration of Greek philosophy in *Paradise Regained* (IV, 291–364). Likewise, the allusion to Matthew xv, 24 in Book IV, line 131, suggests rhetorical duplicity in Jesus' statement: "I was not sent . . . to free / That people victor once, now vile and base" (*PR* IV, 131–32).

As in Book IV, line 131, the allusion to a saying of Jesus in Book III, lines 396–97, seems similarly motivated by a desire to draw from gospel texts that depict an occasionally deceptive Jesus. Milton's Son quotes Jesus' duplicitous response in John vii, 6, to the veiled antagonism of his skeptical brothers: "Means I must use thou say'st, prediction else / Will unpredict and fail me of the Throne: / *My time* I told thee (and that time for thee / Were better farthest off) *is not yet come*" (III, 394–97; our emphasis).

Having just treated the likelihood of his own martyrdom as tantalizingly uncertain ("What if?" [III, 188–97]), the Son concludes this speech with an allusion to his resurrection so equivocal that it eludes Satan's understanding: "Know'st thou not that my rising is thy fall, / And my promotion will be thy destruction?" (III, 201–02; compare IV, 388–90)[23] The Son's citation of John vii, 6 in *Paradise Regained* (III, 196–97) is duplicitous because it downplays the interrelated imminence of both Satan's defeat and the Son's enthronement in "Heaven's Kingdom" implied by Book I, lines 57–59 and 20, respectively (compare I, 240–41; III, 152–53).

In John vii, 2–10, Jesus' brothers urge him to accompany them to Jerusalem for the feast of Tabernacles. They explain that such a trip would enable them to gain more public recognition for his miracles. But this suggestion is merely a ruse to mask their own skepticism (John vii, 5).

Discerning their unbelief, Jesus deliberately creates the false impression that he will remain behind in Galilee (vii, 8–10). This false impression elicits Augustine's prolonged rationalization of the apparent duplicity:

For those who think that He lied speak thus, "He said that He should not go up to the feast day, and He went up." . . . That they might not anticipate Him, then, and announce that He was coming, and plots be prepared, He said, "I go not up." . . . Something He expressed, something He suppressed . . . He gave His weak disciples . . . an example of being on their guard against the snares of enemies.[24]

Similarly, a biblical commentator from Milton's era feels constrained to argue against both Grotius's claim that *eti* ("yet") is a later addition to "I go not up [yet] to this feast" (John vii, 8) and Jerome's claim that *eti* is inserted here "because Porphyry accuses Christ of Inconstancy."[25] In *Christian Doctrine* Milton's comments about an analogous passage in Numbers, chapter xxii, suggest that the duplicitous inconsistency in John vii, 6–10, would pose no problem for him: "when God himself has been tried more than once by some insistent questioner, he has sometimes given conflicting replies, (as he did to Balaam for instance, Num. xxii. 12, 20: 'do not go with them . . . Get up, go with them')" (YP VI, p. 690). The Satan of *Paradise Regained* certainly qualifies as "some insistent questioner": "So Satan . . . / . . . gives not o'er though desperate of success, / And his vain importunity pursues" (IV, 21, 23–24).

The question now arises as to whether Milton's Son also masks his true attitude toward Greco-Roman philosophy and culture. Jesus plays down his own familiarity with Greek philosophy by claiming that all essential knowledge and doctrine are directly available to him through divine revelation (IV, 285–90). He then disparages Greek philosophy in general and Socrates in particular: "But these are false, or little else but dreams, / Conjectures, fancies, built on nothing firm. / The first and wisest of them all profess'd / To know this only, that he nothing knew" (IV, 291–94). Here Socrates's profession of ignorance is deprecated as an illustration of the false and lamentably conjectural nature of Greek philosophy. But this disrespectful attitude toward Socrates in the fourth book of *Paradise Regained* is strikingly contradicted by Christ's view of the pagan philosopher in the third book. There Jesus extols him by placing him in the same category as "patient *Job*" and by acknowledging that Socrates died unjustly "for truth's sake" (III, 95–99). The disparagement of Socrates in the fourth book seems to be nothing more than a tongue-in-cheek debating ploy to beat the devil at his own dissembling game. In fact, uncharacteristically for this poem, the Son briefly lifts the veil from his rhetorical ruse in Book IV and implies that even virtuous Greco-Roman writers can be divinely inspired (IV, 350–52)! Nowhere in this poem are Greco-Roman writers ever explicitly denied salvation.

Why, then, is a polemic against Greco-Roman philosophy a part of Jesus' ruse against Satan in the first place? The rationale for this polemic is supplied by the programmatic role of 1 Corinthians, chapters i–ii, as a source of basic premises for Milton's poem. Prior to the contest with Satan in the wilderness, a heavenly chorus lauds Jesus for "ent'ring his great duel, not of arms, / But to vanquish by wisdom hellish wiles" (I, 174–75). Even Satan recognizes that Jesus is destined to "Be famous then / By wisdom" (IV, 221–22). But it is Greco-Roman wisdom that the devil tempts Jesus to spread throughout the world (IV, 223–84). Milton feels constrained to come to terms with Paul's assertion that, although "the Greeks seek wisdom," the gospel of "Christ crucified" remains "folly to Gentiles" and can be caricatured as "the weakness of God," which "is stronger than men" (1 Cor. i, 22–25). A sarcastic affront to Greco-Roman wisdom, this caricature serves as the basis for the divine mandate that God issued to Milton's Son: "I send him forth / To conquer Sin and Death the two grand foes, / By Humiliation and strong Sufferance: / His weakness shall o'ercome Satanic strength" (*PR* I, 158–61). Paul administers the concepts "the foolishness of God" and "the weakness of God" (1 Cor. i, 25) as a palliative to compensate for any intellectual insecurity on the part of Corinthian Christians: "For consider your call, brethren; not many of you were wise according to worldly standards" (i, 26). Milton's Son, ever on the offensive, transforms Paul's admission into an aristocratic indictment of

> A miscellaneous rabble, who extol
> Things vulgar, and well weigh'd, scarce worth the praise?
> They praise and they admire they know not what;
> And know not whom, but as one leads the other
> . . . .
> Th' intelligent among them and the wise
> Are few, and glory scarce of few is rais'd. (III, 50–53, 58–59)

The rabble's ignorance is merely reinforced by the alleged Greco-Roman penchant for "swelling Epithets" (IV, 343), a phrase no doubt inspired by Paul's disdain for "lofty words of wisdom" (1 Cor. ii, 1). And so Milton's Jesus takes up the Pauline debating challenge directed to the Gentile intelligentsia in 1 Corinthians i, 19–20: "For it is written, 'I [God] will destroy the wisdom of the wise and the cleverness of the clever I will thwart' [compare *PR* IV, 13]. . . . Where is the debater of this age?"

At this point, Milton finds himself confronted with an inconsistency in Pauline soteriology. On the one hand, the Gentiles are castigated for forfeiting the salvation available through "the secret and hidden wisdom" of Christ crucified (1 Cor. ii, 7a; compare i, 18); and in the *Christian Doctrine* Milton seems at first sight to champion the Pauline view that the Gospel "contains a promise of eternal life to all . . . who believe in the revealed Christ and a threat of eternal death to unbelievers" (YP VI, p. 521). On the other hand, Milton's Son feels the need to downplay Paul's insistence that virtuous pagans, too, are recipients of divine revelation: "Such [saints] are from God inspir'd, not such [learned pagans] from thee; / Unless where moral virtue is express'd / By light of Nature, not in all quite lost" (*PR* IV, 350–52; compare Rom. ii, 14–15).

In *Christian Doctrine*, what Milton really thinks about this Pauline inconsistency is that pagans can attain salvation without believing in Christ by various other means such as following the dictates of their inner light (YP VI, p. 623) or believing in their God (YP VI, p. 455). But in *Paradise Regained* Milton comes to terms with the Pauline inconsistency by recasting Paul's invective against Greco-Roman wisdom (1 Cor., i–ii) as part of Jesus' ruse against Satan.

The Pauline warrant for this ruse is provided by 1 Corinthians ii, 7–8: "But we impart a secret and hidden wisdom of God, which God decreed before the ages for our glorification. None of the rulers of this age [for example, Satan's cohorts] understood this; for if they had, they would not have crucified the Lord of glory" (compare *PR* IV, 151–53, 471–72). Justin Martyr, an early apologist who seems to have influenced Milton's outlook in Book IV of *Paradise Regained*, correctly construes this Pauline text to mean that "a secret power of God attaches to the crucified Christ" and destroys Satan's power.[26] Elsewhere Justin insists that "though they [the demons] heard the words of the prophets [about the coming of Christ] they did not understand them accurately" (*Apologia I pro christianis* liv [Migne, PG VI, p. 409]—translation ours). A similar interpretation of 1 Corinthians ii, 7–8 is inherent in a patristic resolution of the apparent contradiction between Satan's inducement of Judas's betrayal of Christ (Luke xxii, 3; John xiii, 2, 27) and the regret of Satan's minions ("the princes of this world") over failing to anticipate the threat posed for them by "the hidden wisdom" of the cross (1 Cor. ii, 6–8). The contradiction is dissolved by the development of a patristic theory that Satan is victimized by Christ's deception.[27]

In summary, Milton's reading of Socrates's *Historia ecclesiastica* III, xvi had apparently helped to convince him of the historical Jesus' familiarity with classical learning. Socrates claims here that pagan philosophy, unlike Scripture, can teach rhetorical skills that can help the Christian foil the "philosophy or vain deceit" (Col. ii, 8) of his adversaries. This claim might have served as a catalyst for Milton's composition of a contest of "persuasive Rhetoric" in which the Son continually beats Satan at his own duplicitous game. Milton has woven various strands of a rich patristic tradition (Irenaeus, John Chrysostom, Augustine, and Hippolytus) into a pattern of satanic perplexity over Jesus' true identity. The confusion of Milton's Satan about the nature and timetable of the Son's kingdom is expressed in terms reminiscent of a saying of Jesus that denies the existence of such a timetable (Luke xvii, 20–21) and a parable that insists that no one understands the germination of the kingdom's "seed" (Mark iv, 26–29). The Son's covert use of tree symbolism is ostensibly based on a patristic depiction (Hippolytus, Origen) of the cross as a tree which, to use a favorite Miltonic image, crushes the serpent's head (*PR* I, 52–55, 59–61; compare I, 404; IV, 620–23).

The Son's strategy of rhetorical deception is consistent with a Miltonic explication of veracity in *Christian Doctrine* that cites the common practice of biblical "saints and prophets" of lying to "people who are . . . hostile, or themselves deceitful" (YP VI, pp. 759–60). The theory of Christ's deception of Satan is a corollary of a patristic soteriology (Augustine, Ambrose, and Gregory of Nyssa) that treats Christ's death as a ransom payment to Satan. Milton incorporates allusions (Matt. xv, 24; John vii, 6) to explicit biblical precedents for the Son's use of duplicity in *Paradise Regained.*

The Son's concealment in Book IV of his true respect for classical learning is illustrated by the inconsistency of his positive (III, 95–98) and negative (III, 291–94) verdicts on Socrates. This inconsistent attitude reflects the mixed signals sent by Paul as to the possibility of Gentile salvation apart from formal profession of faith in Christ (contrast Rom. ii, 14–15 with 1 Cor. i, 18). In *Christian Doctrine* (YP VI, pp. 455, 623), Milton detects in these mixed signals a loophole for the possibility of pagan salvation on other grounds, such as heeding one's inner light. Even in *Paradise Regained* the Son concedes the possibility of divine revelation for virtuous pagans. But in the interests of rhetorical duplicity the Son plays down this possibility for pagans in general (IV, 350–52; compare Rom. ii, 14–15) and focuses on the contention in 1 Corinthians i, 18–25, that the Greek quest for wisdom disparages the gospel as both "folly" and proof of the "weakness" of the Christian God. Through the rhetorical duplicity of Milton's Son, Satan's demise is vouchsafed by his failure to perceive the Pauline irony that it is precisely the Son's "weakness" that thwarts "Satan's strength" (i, 22–25). The rationale for the Son's polemic against classical learning is supplied by the programmatic role of 1 Corinthians i, 18–ii, 8, particularly as interpreted by a patristic tradition which detects in chapter ii, verses 6–8 Satan's regret for having induced Judas to betray Christ.

In short, the Son's contemptuous dismissal of the temptation to learning and positive hostility to ancient Greek and Roman learning are acts of duplicity supported by biblical, patristic, and Miltonic authority. A rich tapestry of biblical texts provides ample documentation of Satan's ignorance of the Son's mission, the Son's ability and willingness to deceive his great adversary and even others in pursuit of his mission, and Paul's ironic awareness of the misjudgments inherent in the pagan (and demonic) approach to learning. These phenomena receive additional support from the patristic tradition. Milton's own acceptance of these traditions of a learned Jesus, satanic bewilderment, withholding of truth, and rhetorical duplicity is established by extensive references in his prose works, particularly *Christian Doctrine*. Thus, in attempting to resolve such cruxes, Milton scholars should follow their poet's example and look first to the Scriptures and then to the ancient patristic authorities. In *Paradise Regained* Milton mined these authorities to supply the Son with a rationale that confirmed his choice of Jerusalem over Athens and confounded his demonic adversary.

Saint Bonaventure University

NOTES

1. All citations of Milton's poetry are taken from *John Milton: Complete Poems and Major Prose*, ed. Merritt Y. Hughes (New York, 1957).

2. Compare Natale Conti's account in *Mythologiae* VI, 16 (Frankfurt, 1581):

> In return for Jupiter's kindness and generosity toward himself, Ixion tried to seduce Juno. When Juno had disclosed this to Jupiter, he found it difficult to believe her, since the misfortunes of Hippolytus and Bellerophon were common knowledge. He wanted to see the seduction with his own eyes. It is said, therefore, that he made a cloud in Juno's shape, and presented it to Ixion. Ixion lay with the vision and produced the Centaurs.

Translated by John Mulryan and Steven Brown, from their translation of the *Mythologiae* (Ithaca, N. Y., forthcoming).

3. Stanley Fish, "Things and Actions Indifferent: The Temptation of Plot in *Paradise*

Regained," in *Milton Studies* XVII, ed. Richard S. Ide and Joseph Wittreich (Pittsburgh, 1983), p. 167.

4. James R. McAdams, "The Pattern of Temptation in *Paradise Regained,"* in *Milton Studies* IV, ed. James D. Simmonds (Pittsburgh, 1972), p. 184.

5. Douglas Bush, *English Literature in the Earlier Seventeenth Century 1600–1660*, 2nd ed. (Oxford, 1962), p. 398.

6. Elaine B. Safer, "The Socratic Dialogue in *Paradise Regained,"* in *Milton Studies* VI, ed. James D. Simmonds (Pittsburgh, 1974), p. 221.

7. Lawrence A. Sasek, "Milton's Criticism of Greek Literature in *Paradise Regained,"* in *Essays in Honor of Esmond Linworth Marilla*, ed. T. A. Kirby and W. J. Olive (Baton Rouge, 1970), p. 162.

8. Gary D. Hamilton, "Creating the Garden Anew: The Dynamics of *Paradise Regained,"* *PQ* L (1970), 579.

9. Barbara Lewalski, *Milton's Brief Epic: The Genre, Meaning, and Art of "Paradise Regained,"* (Providence, 1966), p. 291. See also John Shawcross, *"Paradise Regain'd": "Worthy T'Have Not Remain'd So Long Unsung"* (Pittsburgh, 1988), pp. 112–14.

10. Ralph W. Condee, "Milton's Dialogue with the Epic: *Paradise Regained* and the Tradition," *Yale Review* LIX (1970), 358.

11. All quotations from Milton's prose are taken from *Complete Prose Works of John Milton*, ed. Don M. Wolfe, et al., 8 vols. (New Haven, 1953–82), hereafter cited as YP.

12. *Christian Doctrine* (YP VI, p. 428). In this work Milton often draws the reader's attention to the limitations in Christ's knowledge (see pp. 227, 265–66, 270, 292).

13. Malcolm Kelsall, "The Historicity of *Paradise Regained,"* in *Milton Studies* XII, ed. James D. Simmonds (Pittsburgh, 1977), p. 240.

14. For an overview of this problem, see Donald Swanson, "Milton's Scholarly Jesus in *Paradise Regained,"* *Cithara* XXVII, no. 2 (May 1988), pp. 3–10.

15. John Diodati, *Pious and Learned Annotations Upon the Holy Bible.* trans. R. G. [?], 2nd ed. (London, 1648), p. 23.

16. *Historia ecclesiastica* III, xvi (PG LXVII, pp. 418–23), quoted from *The Ecclesiastical History of Socrates Scholasticus*, trans. A. C. Zenos, in *Nicene and Post-Nicene Fathers of the Christian Church.* 2nd series, ed. Philip Schaff and Henry Wace (New York, 1890), vol. II, p. 87. Socrates would agree with Celsus that "Jesus . . . had read Plato" (Origen, *Contra Celsum* VI, xvi [Migne, PG XI, p. 1314]). All patristic citations, translations, and allusions have their source in Jacques Paul Migne's edition, *Patrologiae cursus completus . . . omnium SS. patrum, doctorum scriptorumque ecclesiasticorum*, "Series Graeca" (Paris, 1857–99) and "Series Latina" (Paris, 1878–90), hereafter abbreviated as PG and PL [*not* to be confused with *Paradise Lost*] respectively, and preceded by "Migne."

17. See the entries in *A Milton Encyclopedia*, 9 vols., ed. William B. Hunter Jr. (Lewisburg, Pa., 1978–83) on "Aristotle," "Plato," and "Philosophy, Milton's."

18. For a succinct documentation and discussion of Luther's perspective on Satan see Paul Althaus, *The Theology of Martin Luther* trans. Robert C. Schultz (Philadelphia, 1966), pp. 161–68.

19. *De civitate* IX, xxi [Migne, PL XLI, pp. 273–74], quoted from *Saint Augustine: The City of God* VIII–XVI, ed. J. Deferrari, trans. G. G. Walsh and G. Monahan, *The Fathers of the Church* (New York, 1952), vol. XIV, pp. 108–09.

20. Unless otherwise specified, the King James Version is the Bible translation employed in the present study. Luke's Jesus is immediately contradicted by the lengthy discussion of signs of the coming of the Son of Man (xvii, 22–37). Modern critical New Testament

scholarship often challenges the authenticity of these verses. One wonders whether Satan's confusion about "the when and the how" (*PR* IV, 472) might not be shared by Milton himself.

21. The relevance of such tree symbolism to Satan's demise is clarified by early patristic thought. For example, prior to the crucifixion, Satan "had not yet been conquered by the tree" (Origen, *Commentaria in Mattheaum* XII, xl [Migne, PG XIII, p. 1073], quoted from Jean Danielou, *Gospel Message and Hellenistic Culture* [Philadelphia, 1973], p. 189. For analogous patristic examples see Danielou, p. 187.

22. Some critics have argued that the banquet of unclean food (II, 319–404) "inartistically repeats the first temptation in other terms" (*A Variorum Commentary on the Poems of John Milton*, ed. Walter MacKellar (New York, 1975), vol. IV, pp. 127–28). However, the banquet really performs a totally different function: it serves as a Miltonic tease of Satan inspired by Augustine. Oddly, the Son admits that he would taste the banquet if he approved of the giver (*PR* II, 320–21). This concession apparently stems from Augustine's insinuation that, were it not for the infernal source of the suggestion, Jesus actually might have changed the stones into bread (*Sermones* lxxii, 2 [Migne, PL XXXVIII, pp. 467–68]). But there is an ironic twist to the offer tendered by Milton's Satan in response to a hungry Jesus' "dream, / Of meats and drinks" (II, 264–65)—the offer is ultimately inspired by a hungry Peter's vision in Acts x, 10–16, where the banquet of unclean food symbolizes the initial offer to "unclean" Gentiles of a salvation made possible by Christ's death and resurrection (Acts x, 28–29, 39–42; *PR* II, 319–404).

23. In Book III Satan imagines that to sit on David's throne the Son must usurp soveriegnty from the dominant earthly kingdoms (III, 351–62, 383–85; IV, 100–08). Several verbal jousts with Jesus leave the devil confused as to whether the Son's portended kingdom is "Real or Allegoric" (IV, 388–90). As a result, a thoroughly duped Satan launches a counterproductive crusade to intimidate Jesus with the threat of suffering and death (IV, 374–79, 478–83).

24. *Sermones* lxxxiii, 2 and 7 [Migne, PL XXXVIII, pp. 513, 518–19], quoted from *Sermons on Selected Lessons of the New Testament*, tr. R. G. MacMullen, in *Nicene and Post-Nicene Fathers of the Christian Church*, ed. Philip Schaff (New York, 1888), vol. VI, pp. 506–09.

25. Daniel Whitby, *A Paraphrase and Commentary upon the New Testament*, 5th ed. (London, 1727), vol. I, pp. 534–35.

26. Justin Martyr, *Dialogus cum Tryphone Judaeo* xlix [translation ours]; cf. xxx; xli [texts in Migne, PG VI, pp. 585, 540, 564]. Justin may have influenced Book IV of *Paradise Regained* in this respect and in other ways as well. Like Milton, Justin seems to have had an ambivalent attitude towards Socrates. On the one hand, pagan martyrs like Socrates were Christians in the sense that they were disciples of the Logos (*Apologia I pro christianis* xlvi [Migne, PG VI, p. 397]; cf. *Apologia II pro christianis* xiii [Migne, PG VI, p. 465]. On the other hand, Greek philosophy is based on a severely limited "discovery and contemplation of some part of the Logos," highly conducive to internal philosophical contradictions (*Apologia II pro christianis* x [Migne, PG VI, pp. 460–61—translation ours]).

27. For example, see the treatment of this contradiction in Irenaeus, *Adversus haereses* I, xxiv, 4 [Migne, PG VII, pp. 676–78]; Origen, *Commentaria in Matthaeum* XIII, viii; XVI, viii [Migne, PG XIII, pp. 1112–16, 1588–99]; *De principiis* III, ii, 1 [Migne, PG XI, pp. 303–05].

A LONG DAY'S DYING: TRAGIC AMBIGUITY IN *SAMSON AGONISTES*

Henry McDonald

> Since this days Death denounc't, if ought I see,
> Will prove no sudden, but a slow-pac't evill,
> A long day's dying to augment our pain
> And to our Seed (O hapless Seed!) deriv'd.
>
> —*Paradise Lost* (X, 962–65)

For much of this century, critics of *Samson Agonistes* have insisted that there is a basic difference between Milton's Samson and the Samson of the Book of Judges, on which Milton based his dramatic poem. As William Riley Parker wrote in 1937, "the character of Samson [in *Samson Agonistes*] has been altered to suit the tone . . . the prankish, rather fantastic fellow of the Biblical story never once puts in his appearance. Whatever his past may have been, Milton's protagonist is now terribly in earnest. . . . [Milton] has taken a primitive tale and made it a challenge to modern minds."[1] Such contrast between the two Samsons has served a crucial purpose; it has allowed critics to argue that the Miltonic Samson is a heroic, regenerate figure who manages to overcome his own inner weaknesses.[2]

In this essay, by contrast, I will argue that the two Samsons are fundamentally similar—that the biblical Samson is quite as much "in earnest" as the Miltonic one and that both are possessed of elements of "the fantastic." What makes the Samson of both accounts "in earnest" is the calling each receives from God to free his people. What makes him "fantastic" or at least puzzling is the way such a mission of divine deliverance is at various points derailed, shifting the focus of the story to Samson's unheroic, eccentric behavior. These dual tendencies give Samson's acts and deeds an ambiguous character; he seems to be pulled in opposite directions by divine commission and betrayal of that commission.

Such ambiguity is, of course, conveyed by very different means in the two accounts of Samson. As Robert Alter has argued about biblical narrative in general, the Judges account is a succession of scenes oriented around a central narrative consciousness that is selectively withheld and rendered problematic by the manipulation of type-scenes and key words and phrases.[3] Meaning is made problematic by narratively treating Samson as an external agent about whose inner motivations little is said and much, often of a contradictory nature, implied. *Samson Agonistes,* by contrast, is a narrative of scenes, a succession of dramatized narratives whose ambiguity unfolds psychologically from within the consciousness of Samson and the other characters. We are provided not with a dearth but with an excess of personal motivation.

Recognition of the paradox that lies at the heart of Samson's character should help to put into perspective—and sharply qualify—regenerationist views of *Samson Agonistes.* What is at issue is not a wholesale rejection of such views. Rather, the possibility of Samson's regeneration is vital to our reading of *Samson Agonistes,* but it is a possibility that is progressivly displaced into the future as the drama unfolds—until, at the very end, it is displaced offstage into the consciousness of the reader, still unrealized and unresolved. Such irresolution is characteristic, I think, of a certain kind of tragedy, one which I will call "ambiguous" to distinguish it from another type of tragedy in which a greater degree of resolution is achieved. Before discussing the Judges account of Samson and *Samson Agonistes,* then, I will provide a context for such discussion by defining the differences between these two types of tragedy.

I

Heracles, a drama by Euripides, Milton's favorite Greek tragedian, consists largely of two discrete, almost autonomous actions between which, as William Arrowsmith says, "there is neither causal necessity nor even probability"[4]—actions which lack, in other words, what Samuel Johnson accused *Samson Agonistes* of lacking, a "middle."[5] The first action, which is presented in a melodramatic, conventional manner, casts Heracles as a nearly unblemished hero who returns home to save his wife and children from being killed by a cruel tyrant. In the second action, which follows immediately upon the first, Heracles is possessed by Madness (sent by Hera) and viciously slaughters the wife and children he has just saved. These two actions are jammed tightly against one another with no attempt to mitigate the violence of their contradiction.

Heracles's words at the end of the play are not adequate to resolve the contradiction. Referring to the disreputable deeds recounted of the gods (among which we may include the one Hera has just committed), Heracles says: "If god is truly god, he is perfect, lacking nothing. These [that is, the gods' disreputable deeds] are poets' wretched lies" (1346). Heracles's words seem merely to deny the murders he has just committed; certainly he has not taken the horror of what he has done into himself and learned in some fashion to understand it. On the contrary, as Adrian Poole says, "Nothing can erase the horror of the rift in Heracles' life. It has turned a hero into a murderous maniac."[6] The result is two radically incongruent images of Heracles that fracture his being and render him a highly paradoxical, ambiguous figure. Heracles does not, in the Aeschylean formulation, "suffer into truth";[7] the senselessness or unmeaning that invades his self is not encompassed and contained by newly gained powers of wisdom. Rather, it is allowed to dwarf and overwhelm Heracles's character and consciousness.

The case is different with many of the protagonists of Sophocles such as Oedipus or the Heracles of *The Women of Trachis.* Although both Sophocles's and Euripides's protagonists are made subject to radically destructive forces that negate system, order, and providence, in Sophocles's heroes there is a movement toward cohesion and coherence of character. This movement is propelled in at least two ways. First, Sophocles's protagonists are from the very beginning flawed heroes; Oedipus is arrogant and boastful, Heracles (of *The Women of Trachis*) a philanderer. The tragic fate that befalls them is therefore (to a greater extent than in the case of Euripides's Heracles) prepared for and made continuous with our initial view of them. Secondly, the horror that invades these heroes does not finally overwhelm them but becomes the vehicle of an enlargement of consciousness. That is why the Oedipus of *Oedipus at Colonus* is so articulate, so successful at fashioning a harmony between words and deeds or words and emotions; he is able to give voice self-consciously to tragic despair and thereby stem or contain its destructiveness. Of course, this is exactly what Oedipus in *Oedipus the King* is unable to do; there he is subjected to a dramatic irony in which his words are deprived of the meaning that he intends. But in *Oedipus at Colonus,* the Oedipus who was marked by the gods has become somewhat godlike; he has been invested with such powers of understanding, has gained such a comprehensive vantage point from which to observe human existence, that what he knows becomes crucial to the future of Athens. Just as Athene, near the end of the Aeschylus's *Oresteia,* warns the people of Athens "not to cast fear [in the form of the Furies] utterly from your city" (698), so too Oedipus passes on to Theseus the terrible but life-constituting knowledge he has gained in the course of his sufferings.

The point here is not that Sophoclean tragedy is affirmative, Euripidean tragedy pessimistic. Rather, there are positive and negative elements in both types of tragedy. Indeed, as Nietzsche, especially in his later work, stressed, the affirmativeness of tragedy is founded on its negativity. To grasp this, it is necessary to distinguish between tragedy as representational (in a modern, non-Aristotelian sense) and tragedy as constructive (of a certain form of reality).

Very briefly, the modern representational view of tragedy rests on a distinction between tragedy as work of art and the tragic as extraartistic reality. This distinction assumes a conception of the tragic as a fixed, universal condition that all people are subject to—that is, the condition of being placed in a world where we must die and suffer the extinction of individuality and consciousness. The representational view leads logically to a pessimistic interpretation of tragedy since it dictates that the function of tragedy is to mirror or reflect the tragic condition.

By contrast, the "constructive" view of tragedy sees the chief function of tragedy not as representation but as enactment. Tragedy creates the categories by which the tragic is conceptually delimited and encompassed. Prior to this delimitation, the tragic subsists only as a dimension of meaninglessness and irrationality that cannot be represented or even named because it cannot be juxtaposed against a contrary dimension of reason, freedom, or divine providence. Disorder constantly spills into and subsumes any form of order, including the order implicit in art. It is only when the unnameable—or what Sophocles's *Oedipus at Colonus* describes as "something awful, / Fearful and unendurable to see"[8]—can be incorporated within a signifying process, encompassed within an artistic structure, that tragedy's crucial function, the negation of system, order, and providence, can be served. Unlike the epic poet, who acts as a mouthpiece of the gods, the tragic poet is a mouthpiece of unmeaning.

Such negation, however, implies an affirmation. Although tragedy enacts the tragic, this very enactment provides the conditions for the latter's overcoming. At the same time tragedy unfolds unmeaning, it creates a space of discourse within which tragic knowledge can be concealed and made bearable. The silences enunciated by tragic heroes like Prometheus, Oedipus, and Hamlet give form to such concealment; they act as containers of unmeaning, not so much justifying injustice as allowing us to enclose it within the category of the tragic and thereby give it reference.

This containment is necessarily ideological; it affirms moral and political meaning and gives support to, or even helps to create in a revolutionary sense, a form of life. That is why Greek tragedy flourished during a period when the belief in reason, the foundation of the city-state, was at its height; and it is also why Renaissance tragedy achieved its greatest triumphs at a time when a new concept of human freedom and individuality was on the rise. Tragedy in general gives vision to blind fate. It creates a horizon of possibility, a canopy of consciousness, under which meaning can emerge.

Yet tragedy serves this function in very different ways. In Sophoclean tragedy, as we have seen, the affirmation formed by the unfolding and concealment of the tragic is a feature of the protagonist's character; the unmeaning that invades his being does not finally overwhelm that being but is rather incorporated within it as he undergoes the process of "suffering into truth." The silence that serves as a container of unmeaning is indicated self-consciously by the protagonist. In Euripidean tragedy, by contrast, the integrity of that self-consciousness is itself interrogated and made the vehicle of ambiguity and paradox. Such ambiguity can only be resolved outside the parameters of the play itself—within the consciousness of the audience and the historical situation in which that consciousness exists. When Euripides has Heracles say, "If god is truly god, he is perfect, lacking nothing. These are poets' wretched lies," he points at once to the fractured nature of Heracles's character and consciousness and to the possibility of healing that fracture outside the context of Heracles's actions as presented—that is, in a radical debunking of the myths upon which the play is founded.

It is precisely the inadequacy of the protagonist's consciousness, combined with an appeal to a context that transcends such consciousness, that the two Samson stories embody. As I will try to show, the Judges account of Samson, far from being a "primitive tale," as Parker would have it, takes a highly critical view of the folk materials on which it is based. To a greater extent than in Sophoclean tragedy, the character and consciousness of the protagonist in the Samson accounts is what is at issue. The blind Oedipus, for example, remains to the end an awesome figure who needs no guidance in his final walk to death. The blind Samson, by contrast, is a human, all-too-human man who needs in the final scene to be guided to the pillars he brings down.[9]

Samson's last destructive act, in both Judges and *Samson Agonistes*, is radically ambiguous. Moreover, such ambiguity is prepared for from the beginning of the stories, being fueled by a narrative silence which at once gives form to and contains unmeaning. Such containment makes possible the incorporation of a tragic dimension of life within a larger context of meaning. Thus, Judges' Samson, whose judgment (to say the least) is rendered questionable, affirms the potential for a stronger and truer judge and looks forward to the Hebrew classical age of great kings. Similarly, the

Samson of *Samson Agonistes*, who enacts the failure of the Puritan revolution, points by his example to the possibility of a successful, more spiritually enlightened revolution.

II

The Samson narrative in Judges begins almost at once on a note of ambiguity, as Robert Alter has observed (*Biblical Narrative*, p. 101). When the angel of the Lord first appears to Manoah's wife, he says that the son who will be born to her "shall be a Nazirite to God from birth and he shall begin to deliver Israel from the hand of the Philistines" (xiii, 5). The somewhat disturbing implication of this prophecy, that Samson will not necessarily complete the deliverance of Israel, is greatly magnified by the words Manoah's wife uses to report the angel's prophecy to her husband: "he said to me . . . the boy shall be a Nazirite to God from birth to the day of his death" (xiii, 7).

As Alter points out, it is a common practice of biblical narrative to juxtapose two accounts of the same event that follow a prescribed formula, except that one of them omits or adds certain information; in this way, attention is drawn to such information. That the second account of the prophecy makes no mention of Israel's deliverance, and instead adds a reference to Samson's death, has the effect of subverting or problematizing the first account.

Some may object that the words spoken by Manoah's wife turn out to be incorrect, since Samson desecrated his status before dying by letting Delilah cut his hair (it was a duty of the Nazirites to keep their heads unshaven).[10] But in fact, as rabbinical commentators have argued, "her words were fulfilled since Samson's hair began to grow back before he died (16:22)" (Fishelis, p. 110c). That the account given by a mere mortal, Manoah's wife, is in one respect more complete than that given by an angel of the Lord provides yet another reason for attributing significance to the disparity between (and consequent ambiguity of) the two accounts.

But the authority of Manoah's wife is important for other reasons as well. Rabbinical commentary "suggests that Samson's seemingly paradoxical qualities (reflected in the varied comments of the Sages) may have been implanted by his parents" (Fishelis, p. 109). The idea is that Samson's mother, who is traditionally said to be from the great tribe of Judah, and to whom the angel first appears, imbued Samson with the potential to be a respected leader and Nazirite. Manoah, by contrast, was from the lowly tribe of Dan ("notorious for their idolatry" [Fishelis, p. 109]), who by themselves were incapable of producing a judge. The rabbinical commentator Abravanel "suggests that she possessed greater wisdom than Manoah, as seen by her reasoning in verse 23" (Fishelis, p. 109). This view is reiterated elsewhere: "she was more prepared for the Divine revelation than he" (Fishelis, p. 111). Indeed, Manoah's inferior status is suggested by the fact that on the occasion of the angel's second appearance, the latter approached Manoah's wife, not Manoah, even though it was he who prayed to God for such appearance. It is also suggested by the obtuseness of Manoah's questions to the angel—questions that had already been answered—and by Manoah's failure to realize that "the man of God" was really an angel (xiii, 16).

Whether or not the ambiguity of Samson's character was imbued by his parents, rabbinical commentary strongly implies that Samson was possessed of a split personality. It will be recalled that when Manoah and his wife objected to Samson's choice of the Timnite woman as a wife, asking why he could not have chosen from among the daughters of Israel, he replied only (to translate his words literally): "Take her for me, because she is pleasing in my eyes" (xiv, 3). Commentary consequently states: "Since Samson would go after his eyes, the Holy One made him a Nazirite since wine [Nazirites are forbidden wine] leads to lewdness. (Likewise, *Ralbag* adds that the Lord sanctified him from birth to help curb his desires)" (Fishelis, p. 110b). Abravanel even reasons that "Samson's abstention from wine would prevent him from being labeled a drunkard when behaving strangely" (Fishelis, p. 110b).

That Samson "behaves strangely" and that such behavior runs counter to the divine mission with which he has been invested is well recognized by the rabbis. Even Samson's marriage to the Timnite woman, sanctioned in the text by the Lord (xiv, 4)—his relations with Delilah receive no such sanction—is treated by some commentators as "strange behavior" on Samson's part. Thus, explaining the swarm of bees and honey found in the body of the lion Samson had killed, Kli Yakar notes that "the honey was designed as a warning to Samson to refrain from marrying the Timnite. The 'sweetness' that he could derive from this woman who was pleasing in his eyes would certainly be offset by her heathen 'sting' " (Fishelis, p. 117). That Samson disregarded or was unaware of such a warning is shown by the fact that he immediately ate the honey on discovering it. It is also significant, as Robert Alter has noted, that in the account of Samson's betrothal to the Timnite woman, "there is no well, no ritual of hospitality" customary in such betrothals in the Bible. On the contrary, "the impetuous rush of Samson's career is already communicated in his impatient movement from seeing a woman to taking her without the ceremonious mediation of a betrothal type-scene, and we all know what calamities the marriage itself will engender" (p. 61–62).

A still more important indication of the "split" in Samson's character is his remark to the Timnite men after they had coerced Samson's wife, the Timnite woman, to tell them the answer to Samson's riddle about the lion and the honey: "Had you not plowed with my heifer, you would not have found out my riddle" (xiv, 18). Rabbinical commentary, noting the term "plowed," states: "This expression is appropriate because through Samson's wife, they delved and uncovered his innermost thoughts" (Fishelis, p. 120). Samson's "wisdom" lies buried within him and as such stands in marked contrast to his external, highly impetuous behavior. Unlike other Israelite leaders, who freely offer the fruits of their wisdom to others, Samson can only preserve his knowledge—indeed, his better self, as in the case of Delilah cutting his hair—by hiding it. His strength, in a spiritual sense, is weak; once exposed, it dissolves. His real weakness, however, consists not in the inadequacy of his defenses, but in the fact that he must be so defensive in the first place—an aspect of his character that Milton, as we shall see, was to make much of. Samson's defensiveness leaves him with only one recourse: to strike out violently at those who would expose him. But in doing this he only perpetuates the split between inner and outer self that caused him to be defensive initially. Thus his actions, from the killing of thirty men at Askelon, to the "great slaughter" of Philistines after they had burnt the Timnite woman and her father, to the slaying of one thousand men with the jawbone of a donkey, to the final cataclysm enveloping three thousand people, grow progressively more violent, bloody, and vengeful as the narrative proceeds.

It is no accident, in this regard, that fire plays such a prominent role in the Samson narrative (xiv, 15; xv 4–5, 6, 15). As Alter comments, "By the time we get to the captive Samson bringing down the temple of Dagon on himself and several thousand of his enemies, though there is no actual fire in this climactic scene, fire has become a metonymic image of Samson himself: a blind, uncontrolled force, leaving a terrible swath of destruction behind it, finally consuming itself together with whatever stands in its way" (p. 95). A related, though more peaceful image of Samson is suggested by chapter xvi, verse 4, where it is said that Samson "loved a woman by the brook of Sorek, and her name was Delilah." The Hebrew for "Sorek" is pronounced similarly to (though spelled differently from) another word meaning "fruitless tree," and the rabbis comment as follows: "The name suggests that his involvement in this sin caused him to be without purpose, as a fruitless tree" (Fishelis, p. 128). Like a fire or a fruitless tree, Samson's acts of vengeance are "without purpose," unguided by the divine commission that has been bestowed on him. Both the image of the fruitless tree and of fire suggest that Samson leaves nothing behind him after his final act of self-destruction. (The fate of the Danites, Manoah's people, gives substance to these images. The Danites continued reprobate throughout the Book of Judges and were omitted from the lists of twelve tribes in the Book of Revelation. Further, Dan is described as a "serpent in the way" in Jacob's prophecy of the twelve tribes at the end of Genesis [xlix, 17]).

But Samson, as the embodiment of the image of fire, does not merely cause the death of others; he also desires it for himself. This fact is highlighted by the numerous and complex ways death is referred to in the text. For example, if we compare the accounts of the manner in which the woman from Timnah and Delilah extract Samson's secrets from him, we see that in both cases the Hebrew formulation, which is translated, "she pressed him hard," is provided as the reason Samson finally yields his secret. But in the second account, involving Delilah, there is a crucial addition: "his soul was vexed to death" (xvi, 16; a more literal translation is, "his soul was shortened to die"). The association of death with Delilah and not with the woman from Timnah is significant because Samson's relations with the latter, and possibly also his marriage to her, were sanctioned by God, while his relations with Delilah received no such sanction. Further, the mention of death in the Delilah temptation scene looks backward to the second Annunciation account of Manoah's wife, as well as foward to Samson's last words, "Let me die with the Philistines" (xvi, 30), which might be rendered more literally as "Let my soul die with the Philistines."

These words may seem at first heroic and sacrificial—less so in the more literal translation—but in fact the notion of Samson giving himself over to the Philistines is treated in two earlier scenes that evoke not Samson's deliverance of Israel but his betrayal of her. The first scene occurs after the Philistines, in retaliation for Samson's trick of setting the foxes' tails on fire, have burned the woman from Timnah and her father and Samson avenges himself on them, declaring, "I swear I will be avenged upon you, and after that I will quit" (xv, 7).

What is important is not just that Samson twice violates this promise but that his vengeance is a private, not a public act, which pointedly ignores the plight of his people. Thus, after the Philistines have in turn avenged Samson's attack by staging a raid on the men of Judah, three thousand of the latter approach Samson and say: "Do you not know that the Philistines are rulers over us? What then is this that you have done to us?" (xv, 11). The Hebrew word for "know" here is the same one used for knowledge of good and evil in Genesis. Its use in this case is consistent with the view that Samson lacks such knowledge. Further, three thousand is the same number of people "on the roof" (xvi, 27) whom Samson destroys at the end. An equation is thus set up between the Israelites whom Samson endangers and the Philistines whom he kills.

The second scene alluded to in Samson's closing words, "Let me die with the Philistines," is the one that occurs after Samson has slain one thousand men with the jawbone of an ass, became thirsty, and called on the Lord: "Thou has granted this great deliverance by the hand of thy servant; and shall I now die of thirst and fall into the hands of the uncircumcised?" (xv, 18). The Hebrew word for deliverance here is the same one used in the first account of the Annunciation in the opening. These are, I believe, the only times the word is employed in the Judges narrative of Samson. As such, its use has an ironic overtone, for the first occurrence referred to the communal deliverance of Israel, the second to the personal deliverance of Samson from thirst and then bloodshed. The incident, in which Samson is saved by divine intervention, is a clear transgression of the usual miracle story, in which the miracle is performed to advance a public good.

Also important in this passage is the verb phrase "called on," used in Samson's address to God, "he called on the Lord" (xvi, 18). This is the same Hebrew word translated as "pray" at the end when Samson says: "O Lord God, remember me, I pray thee, and strengthen me, I pray thee, only this once, O God, that I may be avenged upon the Philistines for one of my two eyes" (xvi, 28). The Hebrew word here is extremely common and is used about a dozen times in the Judges narrative of Samson alone. It is most commonly translated "called," as in passages of Genesis like "God called the dry land Earth" (i, 10), or in passages of Judges like the one where the Philistines "called Samson from his prison" (xvi, 25). Brown, Driver, and Brigg's (lexicon, a standard, acclaimed tool of Hebrew scholars, devotes more than two pages to the various forms of this Hebrew root, yet fails to translate even one of them as "pray."[11] Moreover, when Manoah prays to or entreats the Lord early in the narrative (xiii, 8), a different word is used.

Nonetheless, the issue here is debatable because the Hebrew for words like "call" and "say" have in certain contexts an internalized dimension lacking in English, and "pray" is admittedly a possible translation. The choice of "pray" in this case would seem to depend on an interpretation of Samson's character as having undergone a spiritual conversion, since before this he has not once, for certain, actually "prayed." The question then presents itself: Did Samson undergo a final spiritual conversion?

This question, I think, cannot be answered definitively, but it is at least instructive to note that the narrator is silent on the issue of whether Samson's call or prayer, if it is a prayer, is heard and answered. (Such silence stands in sharp contrast to the earlier account in Judges vi, 36–40, of Gideon "testing God" to ensure that his prayers really have been answered.) One might also note the way several earlier scenes provide a backdrop to this silence. For example, early in the narrative, we are unambiguously told that Samson's pursuit of the woman from Timnah "was from the Lord" (xiv, 4). Such narrative authority is rendered problematic by the fact that the marriage turns out disastrously. Simiarly, the formulaic expression, "the spirit of the Lord came mightily upon" Samson is in two places followed by actions that are violent and impulsive (xiv, 6; xv, 14). One might conclude from these passages that Samson is obtuse and misguided, a conclusion that is certainly consistent with the narrative remark, made after Samson's locks have been shorn, that "he did not know that the Lord had left him" (xvi, 20). But then the complicating statement is added that "the hair of his head began to grow again after it had been shaved" (xvi, 22). This statement is followed not too long afterward by Samson's final, monumental display of strength. Not only can we not be sure that Samson has undergone a spiritual conversion; we cannot be sure that he *hasn't* undergone one.

Robert Alter notes that "one of the most probing general perceptions of the biblical writers is that there is often a tension, sometimes perhaps even an absolute contradiction, between election and moral character" (p. 117). In Judges, there is indeed an "absolute contradiction" between Samson's divine mission and the moral tenor of his actual deeds. This contradiction is comparable to the conflicting images we receive of Heracles in Euripides's play. In both cases, one detects an intentional lack of a "middle" that would connect the two images. Thus, the first we hear about Samson after learning of his divine election is his peremptory demand to marry the Timnite woman—a marriage which, even if it is authorized by God, emphasizes the private and petty, rather than the public and divine, side of Samson. The shift from Samson as savior of his people to a man intent on gratifying his personal desires is not, admittedly, as shockingly violent as in the case of Euripides's Heracles. But the two accounts nonetheless appear more similar than dissimilar when compared to the continuously developed transformation of character that Sophocles sets forth in his portraits of Oedipus and the Heracles of *The Women of Trachis*. In the latter cases, not only is our initial view of the hero anything but rosy, but we become witness to a process in which a flawed man gradually sheds certain (not, of course, all) elements of his private self in the acquisition of an encompassing and tragic view of human existence. In the cases of Samson and the Euripidean Heracles, by contrast, the private self of the hero undergoes a progressive series of accretions that seem to have little relation to his higher, more heroic calling. The Judges Samson, at least in the general sense that Aristotle contrasted Sophocles and Euripides, is a Euripidean hero: "Sophocles . . . said that he drew men as they ought to be, and Euripides as they are."[12] But if Samson is a figure closer to reality than the typical Aeschylean and Sophoclean hero, the very persistence of the image of him in the story as a divinely appointed savior keeps alive, if unrealized, the possibility that such a human, all-too-human side may, in Nietzsche's formulation, be "overcome."

The Judges narrative, in sum, suggests a providential role for Samson in the deliverance of Israel, then emphatically undercuts that role. It does not rehearse the cycle of petition, intervention, and deliverance recounted in many biblical stories, but breaks that cycle to reveal a world from which God has departed, suggesting at the same time that it is a world to which he may return. Assignment of either a clearly positive or clearly negative meaning to the story, or to Samson's character, is thus frustrated. Rather, a dimension of unmeaning, a narrative silence, unfolds within the text that can only be resolved in a broader context.

III

Samson Agonistes encloses a similar silence within its text. Like the Judges narrator, Milton, as we will see, gives only highly ambiguous answers to the all-important questions of whether Samson was really praying at the end and whether those prayers were answered by God. It cannot be known with certainty, of course, whether Milton subjected the Samson story in Judges to the sort of analysis I have performed above, which has drawn from a compilation of Rashi, the Talmud, and other rabbinic sources. What can be known with probability, nonetheless, is that he was fully capable of doing so (and that he would not have needed the aids in English that I have relied on). As Jason Rosenblatt maintains,

> Milton's competence in Biblical Hebrew would have enabled him to read Rashi's *Commentary*, which appeared in more editions of the Hebrew Bible than any other. . . . Yet of course Rashi's *Commentary*, despite its likely influence on *Para-*

dise Lost, cannot account for other rabbinic presences in Milton's prose and poetry, such as the Talmud, Midrash, and Maimonides.[13]

However much or little Milton drew on rabbinic sources in his exegesis of Judges, *Samson Agonistes*, I will maintain in what follows, captures the fundamental spirit of the biblical story. Naturally, there are many important differences between the two accounts. Milton has transposed a chronological narrative to a poetic drama that continually turns back on itself, stressing through repetition certain events in the original chronology and excising and adding others. The new form is directed not by a central narrative voice, as in Judges, but is filtered through the viewpoints of several characters, principally Samson's. As I said in the introduction, these changes give *Samson Agonistes* an internalized, psychological dimension lacking in Judges. What the Judges narrator accomplishes through selective silences Milton intensifies through psychological dramatization. Such dramatization is overlaid by an implied narrative silence that derives from Milton's assumption that the reader would be well acquainted with the original account in Judges.

Consider, for example, the passage where Milton almost directly transmutes into Samson's mouth the Judges' narrative assertion that Samson's pursuit of the woman from Timnah "was from the Lord" (219). Samson's parents, he says, "knew not / That what I motion'd was of God; I knew / From intimate impulse, and therefore urg'd / The Marriage on; that by occasion hence / I might begin Israel's Deliverance, / The work to which I was divinely call'd" (221–26).[14] Samson's subjective certainty of his divine commission provides a psychologically dramatic counterpart to the narrative authority exerted in the Judges account. Yet, precisely because the terms are dramatic and psychological, recollected by a character rather than reported by an omniscient narrator, the sense of certainty and authoritativeness can be far more radically and speedily undermined than in Judges. What was "from the Lord" in Judges is now what Samson thinks (or "knew") was "from the Lord." Samson's unreliability can thus be conveyed much more directly, in a psychological sense, than was the case in Judges, which had to rely on techniques of narrative manipulation that treated Samson as an external agent. Thus, the effect achieved by a lengthy recital in Judges of the disastrous consequences of the marriage with the woman from Timnah is conveyed in Milton's work by a three-word phrase immediately following the passage quoted above: "She proving false." This phrase is used by Samson as a transition to the expression of certain feelings and comments about Dalila and himself. As such, it does not merely conceal a part of Samson's story, but reveals a great deal about his inner state of mind. It must therefore be distinguished from the kind of narrational silence used in Judges. To clarify this point, I'll examine the rest of the passage in full:

> The first I saw at *Timna*, and she pleas'd
> Mee, not my Parents, that I sought to wed,
> The daughter of an Infidel: they knew not
> That what I motion'd was of God; I knew
> From intimate impulse, and therefore urg'd
> The Marriage on; that by occasion hence
> I might begin *Israel's* Deliverance,
> The work to which I was divinely call'd;
> She proving false, the next I took to Wife
> (O that I never had! fond wish too late)
> Was in the vale of Sorec, *Dalila*
> That specious Monster, my accomplisht snare,
> I thought it lawful from my former act,
> And the same end; still watching to oppress
> *Israel's* oppressours: of what now I suffer
> She was not the prime cause, but I my self,
> Who vanquisht with a peal of words (O weakness)
> Gave up my fort of silence to a Woman. (219–36)

Samson implicitly justifies his quick transition from "She proving false" to "the next I took to Wife . . . *Dalila*" by reasoning that since God's plan had not worked out with one infidel woman, he would try another. Or, to put this in another way, he clings to his subjective certainty that it is part of God's plan for him to marry infidel women, even when the first marriage turns out to be a mistake. Once having married Dalila, however—a marriage, significantly, that does not occur in the Judges narrative, as I will discuss later—and finding that it too was a mistake, he tries to justify the second mistake with reference to the first: "I thought it [that is, the marriage with Dalila] lawful from my former act."

When Samson terms Dalila, then, a "specious Monster," this characterization is in part ironic, for it is Samson's reasoning itself that has been shown to be specious. (Also, it is entirely possible that Milton was using the reference to the "vale of Sorec" in a manner similar to that indicated by rabbinical commentary—that is, as a means of pointing up "the fruitlessness" of Samson's actions.) That Samson mirrors Dalila is elaborated at length later in the drama, where it is shown that both attempt the deliverance of their respective peoples, the Israelites and the Philistines, through wrongful means, which include in Samson's case not just the marrying of unconverted, infidel women, but personally motivated acts of destruction and vengeance very much akin to those of the Philistines. Samson himself points up the contradiction in relation to Dalila's cutting of his hair:

> But zeal mov'd thee;
> To please thy gods thou didst it; gods unable
> To acquit themselves and prosecute their foes
> But by ungodly deeds, the contradiction
> Of their own deity, Gods cannot be:
> Less therefore to be pleas'd, obey'd, or fear'd;
> These false pretexts and varnish'd colours failing,
> Bare in thy guilt how foul must thou appear! (895–902)

Later, Samson will argue for Gods being just such a "contradiction / Of their deity" when he says that God "may dispense with me or thee / Present in Temples at Idolatrous Rites / For some important cause, thou needst not doubt" (1377–79). Moreover, Samson, in the passage beginning on line 219, has defended the use of wrongful means in carrying out his divine commission—the line "I knew from intimate impulse" being perhaps an ironic reference to the Judges account where what Samson is said to know from intimate impulse is only his own desire for the woman from Timnah. Similarly, Samson thinks it was right for him to try to "oppress Israel's oppressours" (232–33) and doesn't grasp that such an attempt has made him similar to what he accuses the Philistines of being: "an impious crew / Of men, conspiring to uphold thir state / By worse then hostile means" (891–93). This is likely an allusion to the "fruitless tree" which the Puritan revolution engendered.

Nor does Samson's propensity to blame himself, as in "of what now I suffer / She [Dalila] was not the prime cause, but I my self" (233–34), show a real recognition of fault. What Samson is doing here is portraying himself as having shown weakness in trying to carry out a noble and divinely inspired enterprise; he does not see that the enterprise itself, its use of wrongful means, is the problem. The weakness that Samson admits to is, like the one Dalila admits to, a venial one motivated by love; it consists of giving up "my fort of silence to a Woman" (236).

The irony is that Samson, in this passage, *has*, albeit unconsciously and self-deceptively, maintained silence, a silence or ambiguity that is really twofold. In the first place, Samson's silence is the silence embedded in his "She proving false" (227), the silence consisting of his omitted narration about the woman from Timnah. Samson is performing here in a way that is technically comparable to the performance of the Judges narrator in that his silence is a silence about the occurrence of external events. Yet Samson is not, of course, like the Judges narrator, omniscient; his silence points not just outward, toward the presence of missing events, but inward, toward Samson's subjective certainty that he is divinely inspired. In this way, Milton does not merely intensify the narrative ambiguity of the Judges account; he creates a second silence or ambiguity (suggested only in a very oblique way in Judges) that focuses on Samson's internal state. Milton, or at any rate the implied narrator, uses Samson's absurdly brief summary of his relations with the woman from Timnah as a means of pointing up the fact that Samson is hiding something from himself. His subjective certainty is, in fact, uncertain. Such uncertainty is conveyed by the implied narrator, not by Samson himself. Indeed, Samson can only *display* his confusion, self-doubt, and split personality; he does not have narrative control over them.

Such lack of control is evident in the way Samson responds to and uses language. When the Chorus first approaches him, for example, they say: "This, this is he; softly a while, / Let us not break in upon him" (115–16). As Anne Davidson Ferry points out, the words "break in" evoke the image of penetration by some external force[15]—very much as we saw that the Judges Samson was "plowed" by the words of his "heifer," Delilah. (Compare such images to Theseus's characterization of Heracles in Euripides's play as womanly.) In both cases, words are being imaged as alien, hostile objects or things that threaten some inner, vulnerable part of Samson. "Ay me, another inward grief awak't" says Samson when he hears Manoa coming, "With mention of that name renews th' assault" (330–31). Manoa's name is here an "assault" on Samson's being, just as Dalila's words broke down the secret of his strength: "She was not the prime cause, but I my self, / Who vanquisht with a peal of words (O weakness!) / Gave up my fort of silence to a woman" (234–36). But by the time the drama begins, Samson has learned to strengthen his fort of silence: "So much of Adders wisdom I have learn't / To fence my ear against thy [Dalila's] sorceries" (936–37). Words are treated now with contempt—as mere "talk": "I learn / Now of my own experience, not by talk / How counterfeit a coin they are" (187–89; compare 652–66).

Language is thus treated in *Samson Agonistes*—by Samson, if not by Milton—in a manner almost exactly opposite to that of *Paradise Lost*, in which, as Ferry says, "the fallen state is loss of eloquence, redemption is recovery of the creative powers of language" (p. 127). This view of language is, as we have seen, similar to that reflected in the plays of Sophocles. For Samson, by contrast, language, or what he calls "the popular noise" (16), is something to make oneself deaf to, just as visual images have disappeared as a result of his blindness:

The Sun to me is dark
And silent as the Moon,
When she deserts the night,
Hid in her vacant interlunar cave. (86–89)

However, it is not just sounds and sights, language and color, that Samson is alienated from, but his own thoughts:

Retiring from the popular noise, I seek
This unfrequented place to find some ease;
Ease to the body some, none to the mind
From restless thoughts, that like a deadly swarm
Of Hornets arm'd, no sooner found alone,
But rush upon me thronging, and present
Times past, what once I was, and what am now. (16–22)

Those who would interpret Samson's flight from the outside world, his attempt to enclose himself in a "prison" (6) where no sounds or sights can penetrate, as the pursuit of a higher order of being lying in individual experience, forget that such pursuit is, and must be, futile. Samson sees such escape as his only salvation, but the reader is meant to see it as something quite different: self-delusion. For even Samson's thoughts are colored by the external world—by "Times past, what once I was, and what am now" (22)—and thoughts, like the Furies, cannot be escaped; they can only be transformed into more friendly presences (like the Eumenides). Samson is like one who, fleeing from the world, finds his own self to be part of that world. His flight is therefore a flight from himself, a 'self" that grows progressively more impotent as it attempts to repel the external world. To put this another way, the more Samson shuns external influences, the more he makes himself vulnerable to them and puts himself under their control. His problem is very much like that which we observed in the case of the Judges Samson; his defensiveness is the product of an inner weakness which the continued building of defenses only exacerbates. His vulnerability increases with his defensiveness. As Stanley Fish says, "Self-deprived of an inward integrity that would repel alien significances, he takes on the significances projected onto him by those who behold. He becomes quite literally a 'gaze,' an extension of whatever glance happens to fall on him, a continually mounted spectacle, a commodified object of appropriation, always in the power of others and never in his own."[16]

I said above that Samson's effort to flee the force of language and his own thoughts is futile, but this is not quite true, for there is an "unfrequented place" where he may "find some ease" from the "deadly swarm" of his own thoughts (17–19). That place is death. Death will grant Samson the obliteration of self that he seeks, and it is toward death that he is progressively driven—much in the manner of the Judges Samson, only with the obsession rendered now explicitly in psychological terms—over the course of the dramatic poem. "Consume me," says Samson in response to the chastisement of the Chorus, "and oft-invocated death / Hast'n the welcom end of all my pains" (575–76). Or, replying to the warnings of Manoa, Samson invokes the balm of the ultimate forgetfulness: "Sleep hath forsook and giv'n me o're / To deaths benumming opium as my only cure" (629–30). Like the Judges Samson, who feels his "soul vexed unto death," Samson cries: "This one prayer yet remains, might I be heard, / No long petition, speedy death, / The close of all my miseries, and the balm" (649–51).

Samson desires death because it would realise for him his quest for silence, for a state of rest and inertness freed from moral responsibility—for a state of self, as Ferry puts it, "which has become like an unconscious object or force of nature" (p. 177). In this sense, Samson (once again, in the manner of the Judges protagonist) is like a fire that seeks to burn itself out, to reduce itself to a pile of ashes. Samson's blustering in the presence of Harapha and the Officer are the leap of flames that presage the final conflagration that will bring about his transformation to ashes. It is significant that Samson's greatest act of destruction is preceded by silence: "And eyes fast fixt he stood, as one who pray'd / Or some great matter in his mind revolv'd" (1637–38). For peace, inner peace, is the motive of Samson's desperate act; to gain rest within, he will reduce the world around him to inertness. Such peacefulness is the opposite of the subdued moods of Oedipus, Prometheus, and Hamlet at the end of their dramas. For the latter proceed from an inner wisdom and restfulness gained through long confrontation with the tragic nature of existence; it is the blessing of this wisdom, and the substratum of terrible knowledge on which it rests, that they seek to confer on their fellow man. Samson, by contrast, has only his mighty act of destruction to confer; he does not convey a life-nourishing silence that is the fruit of his suffering so much as make silent, in a tremendous act of vengeance, those whom he blames for his suffering.

But this is not, of course, the whole story. For as much as Samson gives in to his private feelings of vengeance and dissatisfaction with self—to his insatiable lust for death, both his own and others'—he also keeps alive in himself a sense of his divine mission of public redemption. This sense is exhibited in many ways, not the least of which is his successful resistance to the entreaties of Dalila and Manoa to take only his private interests into account. "I was no private," says Samson to Harapha, "but a person rais'd / With strength sufficient and command from Heav'n / To free my Countrey" (1211–13). It is crucial, however, to read this assertion in the context of Samson's contention, made only a few lines before, that he is merely "a private person, whom my Countrey / As a league-breaker gave up bound" (1208–09). Such double-talk expresses the essence of Samson's being, which is not to know who he is. One may note, for example, that at the same time Milton's Samson seems to despair of his divine commission, blaming his failures on his people or on Dalila, he also aggrandizes that commission: "Promise was that I / Should Israel from Philistian yoke deliver" (38–39). The most that is said in Judges is that Samson "shall *begin* to deliver Israel from the hand of the Philistines" (emphasis mine).

But it is not just Samson who doesn't know who he is; it is the reader as well. Milton induces this uncertainty in at least three ways. First, he entangles Samson in such a net of self-contradiction that the reader is left with no definitive grounds upon which to adjudicate Samson's conflicting pronouncements. Secondly, he casts the report of Samson's actions at the end in a series of secondhand accounts that make whatever kernel of certainty is in them almost impossible to dig out. Not only is what Samson does reported at second hand by the Messenger; not only is part of this secondhand report itself second hand: says the Messenger, "he his guide / (For so from such as nearer stood we heard)" (1630–31); but also the reports of these two witnesses are fraught with so much ambiguity that it is impossible to say, as in the Judges' account, whether Samson was really praying when, with "eyes fast fixt he stood, as one who pray'd, / Or some great matter in his mind revolv'd" (1637–38). As for the words of the Chorus and Manoa, these also present difficult interpretive problems, for, as Joseph Wittreich points out,

> The Chorus had never previously vested its confidence in Samson's interpretation of events, and we may find it difficult now to vest much confidence in its interpretations. Indeed, to the very end, Manoa and the Chorus are found contradicting Samson and, in the end, contradict Samson into a heroism he is perhaps not meant to enjoy.[17]

Until the final scene, Milton relies heavily on Samson's own confusions and fractured psychology to complicate and make our view of the situation ambiguous. With Samson removed from the scene, he must resort to other means to achieve the same purpose.

Finally, Milton induces uncertainty in the reader by the implicit connection he draws between Samson's marriages and his final act of destruction. As I have already mentioned, Milton alters the Judges account in many ways, but perhaps the single most important change is that he portrays Samson as married to Dalila (no mention of such marriage is made in Judges) and gives little attention to Samson's marriage to the Timnite woman. In Judges, Samson's relations with the Timnite woman, and probably also his marriage to her, were sanctioned by God, while his relations with Delilah received no such sanction. By focusing on Samson's relationship with Dalila, at the expense of his divinely sanctioned relations with the Timnite woman, Milton brings to the forefront the issue of Samson's moral integrity. But that is not all. Jewish tradition holds that Samson not only married Delilah but converted both his wives before marrying them. Rashi, apparently dissenting from tradition, believed that "The woman from Timnath he [Samson] married, whereas he lived with this woman [Delilah] out of wedlock" (Fishelis, p. 133). Other rabbinical commentary sets forth the opinion that "although Samson converted his wives before marrying them, nevertheless, he did not adhere to the principle of accepting converts only when there is no ulterior motive [that is, the motive of seeking an occasion against the Philistines]" (Fishelis, p. 133).

One senses in both these opinions a tremendous uneasiness among the rabbis, notwithstanding tradition, concerning the Halachic legitimacy of Samson's actions. Milton picks up on this uneasiness and makes it the centerpiece of his dramatic poem. In consorting with and marrying Dalila, was Samson acting out of love in conformity with God's laws, or was he giving vent to his own willful and lustful nature? *Samson Agonistes* gives no certain answer to this question, but nonetheless accents the sharp contrast between Samson's private motives and his public mission of deliverance. In so accenting this theme, Milton sets the stage for the ambiguity of Samson's final act. For, as Christopher Hill says, once the rightness of Samson's marriage to Dalila is questioned, "how certain [is it] that the destruction of the Philistines at the end of the play was really inspired by God?"[18] A man motivated by his private passions concerning the most consequential issue of his life is not likely to suddenly subordinate his desires to divine intention. Or is he?

Like Euripides's *Heracles,* like the Judges account of Samson, *Samson Agonistes* is a work that inscribes within it a conventionalized interpretation of its protagonist and his story, then radically subverts without completely destroying that interpretation. As Frank Kermode says in another context, it "contrives to bring into question the validity of the assumptions on which it was written."[19]

University of Oklahoma, Norman

NOTES

1. William Riley Parker, *Milton's Debt to Greek Tragedy in "Samson Agonistes"* (Baltimore, 1937), pp. 200, 83–84.

2. See Anthony Low, *The Blaze of Noon: A Reading of "Samson Agonistes"* (New York, 1974). For an opposing view, see Irene Samuel, "*Samson Agonistes* as Tragedy," in *Calm of Mind: Tercentenary Essays on "Paradise Regained" and "Samson Agonistes,"* ed. Joseph A. Wittreich (Cleveland, 1971), pp. 237–57.

3. Robert Alter, *The Art of Biblical Narrative* (New York, 1981).

4. In the introduction to his translation of the play, in *Euripides II: The Cyclops, Heracles, Iphigenia in Tauris, Helen*, eds. David Grene and Richmond Lattimore (Chicago, 1969), p. 46. All quotations of the play are from this edition.

5. Samuel Johnson, *The Rambler*, (no. 2, 16 July 1751).

6. Adrian Poole, *Tragedy: Shakespeare and the Greek Example* (Oxford, 1987), p. 69.

7. Aeschylus, *The Eumenides*, trans. Richmond Lattimore, in *Greek Tragedies*, vol. 3, eds. David Grene, and Richmond Lattimore (Chicago, 1953), p. 23, lines 1651–52.

8. Sophocles, *Oedipus at Colonus*, trans. Robert Fitzgerald, in *Greek Tragedies*, vol. 3, eds. Grene and Lattimore, p. 182, lines 1651–52.

9. Samson's words in Judges, "Let me feel the pillars" (xvi, 26) are interpreted by Radak as "draw me near to the pillars." Avrohom Fishelis and Shmuel Fishelis, *The Book of Judges: A New English Translation of the Text, Rashi, and A Commentary Digest*, ed. A. J. Rosenberg, (New York, 1987), p. 135, cited hereafter in the text as Fishelis. All quotations from the Book of Judges follow this translation.

10. Note that the name is "Dalila" in Milton's version, with the emphasis when pronounced placed on the *first* syllable, but "Delilah" in the Hebrew version of Judges, with the emphasis when pronounced on the *second* syllable. The transliteration, "Delilah," is in accordance with probable Hebrew pronunciation during classical times.

11. Francis Brown et al., *A Hebrew and English Lexicon of the Old Testament* (Oxford, 1951), pp. 89–96.

12. Aristotle. *The Basic Works of Aristotle: De Poetica*, chap. 25, II, 35, ed. Richard McKeon (New York, 1941), p. 1484.

13. Jason P. Rosenblatt, "Milton's Chief Rabbi," in *Milton Studies XXIV*, ed. James D. Simmonds (Pittsburgh, 1989), p. 46.

14. *Samson Agonistes* is quoted from *The Complete Poetry of John Milton*, ed. John T. Shawcross (Garden City, N.Y., 1963), with line references in the text.

15. Anne Davidson Ferry, *Milton and the Miltonic Dryden* (Cambridge, Mass., 1968), p. 144.

16. Stanley Fish, "Spectacle and Evidence in *Samson Agonistes*," *Critical Inquiry XV* (Spring 1989), 582.

17. Joseph Wittreich, *Intrepreting "Samson Agonistes"* (Princeton, N.J., 1985), pp. 120–21.

18. Christopher Hill, *Milton and the English Revolution* (New York, 1977), p. 433.

19. Frank Kermode, *The Art of Telling* (Cambridge, Mass., 1983), p. 74.